The War in the Air
Volume 1

The War in the Air
Volume 1
A History of the RFC, RAF & RNAS during the First World War 1914-18

Walter Raleigh

The War in the Air
Volume 1
A History of the RFC, RAF & RNAS during the First World War 1914-18
by Walter Raleigh

First published under the title
The War in the Air Volume 1

Leonaur is an imprint of Oakpast Ltd
Copyright in this form © 2017 Oakpast Ltd

ISBN: 978-1-78282-688-0 (hardcover)
ISBN: 978-1-78282-689-7 (softcover)

http://www.leonaur.com

Publisher's Notes

The views expressed in this book are not necessarily those of the publisher.

Contents

Preface	7
Introduction	9
The Conquest of the Air	20
The Aeroplane and the Airship	60
Flight in England	92
The Beginnings of the Air Force	119
The Royal Flying Corps	159
The War: The Royal Flying Corps from Mons to Ypres	217
The Royal Naval Air Service in 1914	284
The Expansion of the Air Force	326

Preface

The History of which this is the first volume is, in the main, the history of the part played in the war by British air forces. It is based chiefly on the records of the Air Ministry collected and preserved at the Historical Section. The staff of the Section have spared no trouble to collect an immense amount of material and arrange it for use, to consult living witnesses, to verify facts down to the minutest details, and to correct any errors that may have crept into the narrative. Their main purpose has been to secure that any statement of fact made in this book shall be true and demonstrable. If in any particular instances they have failed in this purpose, it has not been for lack of pains and care.

Official records do not in themselves make history. They are colourless and bare. In the business of interpreting and supplementing them we have been much helped by the kindness of many military and naval officers and of many civilian experts. Their help, most of which is acknowledged in the text, has supplied us with the liveliest things in this book. We could wish that we had more of it. Naval and military officers do not advertise, and are reluctant to speak publicly of the part that they played in the war. They are silent on all that may seem to tell to their own credit or to the discredit of others, and this silence easily develops into a fixed habit of reticence. We are the more grateful to those who have helped us to a true account by telling of what they saw. The best part of the book is yet to come; if the theme is to be worthily treated, it must be by the help of those who remember and of those who know.

The writer of this history has endeavoured to make his narrative intelligible to those who, like himself, are outsiders, and, with that end in view, he has avoided, as far as possible, the masonic dialect of the services. For the few and cautious opinions that he has expressed he alone is responsible. In controverted questions, though he has not always been careful to conceal his own opinion, he has always tried so to state the grounds for other opinions that those who hold these other opinions may think his statement not unfair. If his own opinion is wrong, the corrective will usually be found near at hand. The position of an outsider has grave disabilities; if a measure of compensation for these disabilities is anywhere to be found, it must be sought in freedom from the heat of partisan zeal and from the narrowness of corporate loyalty.

Some of the men who early took thought for their country's need, and quietly laboured to prepare her against the day of trial, are here celebrated, and their names, we hope, rescued from neglect. The men who flew over the fire of enemy guns were so many that comparatively few of their names, and these chosen almost by accident, can here be mentioned. There were thousands of others just as good. The heroes of this story, let it be said once and for all, are only samples.

Some apology perhaps is necessary for the variety which has been found inevitable in naming particular men. A man's Christian name and surname are his own, but change and promotion were rapid during the war, so that the prefixes to these names varied from year to year. Where we are describing a particular deed, we give the actors the rank that they held at the time. Where we speak more generally, we give them the rank that they held when this history was written.

Walter Raleigh.

Introduction

When Great Britain declared war upon Germany in August 1914, she staked her very existence as a free nation upon an incalculable adventure. Two new means and modes of warfare, both of recent invention, enormously increased the difficulties of forecast and seemed to make precedents useless. Former wars had been waged on the land and on the sea; the development of submarines and aircraft opened up secret ways of travel for armed vessels under the sea and promised almost unlimited possibilities of observation and offence from the heights of the air.

Of these two new weapons the submarine was brought earlier to a state of war efficiency, and because it seemed to threaten the security of our island and the power of our navy, it excited the greater apprehension. But the navigation of the air, whether by airship or aeroplane, is now recognised for the more formidable novelty. The progress of the war has proved that within the narrow seas the submarine can be countered, and that the extension of its capabilities on the high seas is beset with difficulties. For aircraft the possibilities are immense. It is not extravagant to say that the 17th of December 1903, when the Wright brothers made the first free flight through the air in a power-driven machine, marks the beginning of a new era in the history of the world.

The differences to be looked for in this new era were both over-estimated and under-estimated, according to the temper of those who considered them.

Imaginative people, and sentimental people, looked for the speedy fulfilment of Tennyson's vision:

> *For I dipt into the future, far as human eye could see,*
> *Saw the Vision of the world, and all the wonder that would be;*
> *Saw the heavens fill with commerce, argosies of magic sails,*

Pilots of the purple twilight, dropping down with costly bales;
Heard the heavens fill with shouting, and there rain'd a ghastly dew
From the nations' airy navies grappling in the central blue;
Far along the world-wide whisper of the south-wind rushing warm,
With the standards of the peoples plunging thro' the thunder-storm;
Till the war-drum throbb'd no longer, and the battleflags were furl'd
In the Parliament of man, the Federation of the World.

The Germans, who as a people fall easy victims to agreeable sentiment, indulged extravagant hopes from war in the air, and expected great achievements from their Zeppelins. On the other hand, the English, who are less excitable, were comparatively slow as a nation to appreciate the importance of the new invention. Conservative and humorous minds are always conscious chiefly of the immutable and stable elements in human life, and do not readily pay respect to novelty. Those who were responsible for the naval and military defences of the country preserved great coolness, and refused to let judgement outrun experience. They knew well that the addition to man's resources of yet another mode of travel or transport does not alter the enduring principles of strategy. They regarded the experiment benevolently, and, after a time, were willing to encourage it, but an official report says:

> Up to the end of the year 1911, the policy of the Government with regard to all branches of aerial navigation was based on a desire to keep in touch with the movement rather than to hasten its development. It was felt that we stood to gain nothing by forcing a means of warfare which tended to reduce the value of our insular position and the protection of our sea-power.

When the Wright brothers offered to sell their invention to the British Admiralty, the offer was refused.

It is natural enough that believers in the new art, who devoted years of disinterested thought and labour to getting it recognised, and who truly foresaw its enormous importance, should be impatient of so cautious an attitude. But the attitude itself was also natural and excusable. The British navy is a great trust, responsible not so much for the progress of the nation as for its very existence. Untried courses, new investments, brilliant chances, do not commend themselves to trustees. By adherence to a tried policy and to accustomed weapons the navy had ridden out many a storm that threatened national wreckage; what it had done so often it believed that it could do again; and it was slow to grasp at new weapons before their value was proved.

So, the progress of aerial science followed what, in this country, is the normal course. We have had many great poets and many great inventors. We sometimes starve our poets, but we make classics of their works. We sometimes leave our inventors to struggle unaided with difficulties, but when they succeed we adopt their inventions as part of the national inheritance, and pay to their names a respect greater than bounty-fed dependence can ever command or deserve. Their failures are their own, their successes belong to their country; and if success brings them no other reward, they can at least claim a part in the honour universally paid to soldiers and sailors, whose profession is sacrifice.

As soon as it became clear that no nation could without extreme peril to itself neglect the new weapon, the Government took up the problem in earnest. Private enterprise might, no doubt, have been trusted to improve and develop aircraft for the various uses of peace, but the question was a question of war. The purposes and ambitions of the German Empire had again and again been freely expressed, in no moderate language, and the German menace lay like a long vague shadow across the peace of Europe. Peaceful citizens, with many other things to think of, might fail to see it, but no such blindness was possible for those who had charge of the defences of the country. The Committee of Imperial Defence, in the few years before the war, took expert advice.

The government, acting on this advice, furnished us with the nucleus of an air force. They made their own flying school, and established their own factory for the output of aircraft. They organised an air service with naval and military wings. They formed advisory and consultative committees to grapple with the difficulties of organisation and construction. They investigated the comparative merits and drawbacks of airships and aeroplanes. The airships, because they seemed fitter for reconnaissance over the sea, were eventually assigned wholly to the Naval Wing. No very swift progress was made with these in the years before the war. The expenses of adequate experiment were enormous, and the long tale of mishaps to Zeppelins seemed to show that the risks were great.

The experts who were consulted pointed out that the only way to test the value of the larger type of airship was to build such airships ourselves, that Germany had patiently persevered in her airship policy in the face of disaster and loss, and that if we were to succeed with airships it would be necessary to warn the public that heavy losses, in the initial stage, were unavoidable. Opinion in this island, it is right to remember, was strong against the airship, or gasbag, and Germany's enthusiastic championship of the Zeppelin made the aeroplane more popular in England.

So, our airship policy was tentative and experimental; a few small airships were in use, but none of the large size and wide range required for effective naval reconnaissance. Good and rapid progress, on the other hand, was made with aeroplanes and seaplanes, and when war broke out we had a small but healthy service, both naval and military, ready to take the air. Four squadrons of the Military Wing, or Royal Flying Corps, that is to say, forty-eight machines, with a few additional machines in reserve, bore a part in the retreat from Mons. A detachment of the Naval Wing, or Royal Naval Air Service, was sent to Belgium, and after bearing a part in the defence of Antwerp, established itself at Dunkirk, which remained throughout the war a centre for aerial operations. These were the beginnings; in the four years and three months of the war the air service grew and multiplied a hundredfold.

At the date of the armistice, the 11th of November 1918, there were operating in France and Belgium ninety-nine squadrons of the Royal Air Force. In August 1914 there had been less than two hundred and fifty officers in the service, all told; in November 1918 there were over thirty thousand. In August 1914 the total of machines, available for immediate war service, was about a hundred and fifty; in November 1918 there were more than twenty-two thousand in use, almost all of them enormously more powerful and efficient than the best machines of the earlier date.

In the course of the war our air forces accounted for more than eight thousand enemy machines; dropped more than eight thousand tons of bombs on enemy objectives; fired more than twelve million rounds of ammunition at targets on the ground; took more than half a million photographs; brought down nearly three hundred enemy balloons; and suffered a total of casualties not far short of eighteen thousand. Not less important in its influence on the fortunes of the war than any of these achievements, perhaps more important than all of them, was the work done by aircraft in detecting movements of the enemy and in directing the fire of our gunners upon hostile batteries. This work cannot be exactly assessed or tabulated, but the German gunner knew where to look for the enemy he most dreaded.

A rapid summary of this kind shows that the history of the war in

the air is inseparable from the history of the development of the art of flying. Of those who were competent to handle a machine in the air during the years before the war by far the greater number served with the colours. With the outbreak of war civilian flying, except for training purposes, abruptly ceased. The necessities of war compelled and quickened invention. When a nation is fighting for its life, money and energy are expended without check, and it may be doubted whether in the whole history of mankind any art in its infant stage has been so magnificently supported and advanced by war as the art of flying was supported and advanced by the greatest war of all.

No history can be expected to furnish a full record of all the acts of prowess that were performed in the air during the long course of the war. Many of the best of them can never be known; the Victoria Cross has surely been earned, over and over again, by pilots and observers who went east, and lie in unvisited graves. The public dearly loves a hero; but the men who have been both heroic and lucky must share their honours, as they are the first to insist, with others whose courage was not less, though their luck failed them. There is a quaint system, in use in the air service, of reckoning the activities of the service in terms of hours flown, taking as the unit for addition every single hour flown by each individual machine. By this method of calculation, the hours flown by the air service, on all fronts, during the war can be shown to be much over a million.

The work of an ant-hill, reckoned on the same basis, would present a stupendous total. If the heroism of the air service, that is to say, their deeds of surpassing courage and devotion, could be thus computed, the figure would run into thousands; and this would be the fairest, though not the most dramatic, statement of the case. The officers in command have always been unwilling to pay regard to 'star turns'; what they have coveted for the service is not a low range of achievement rising now and again into sharp fantastic peaks, but a high tableland of duty and efficiency. They obtained their desire, in a result more surprising than any single exploit can ever be. They made courage and devotion the rule, not the exception.

The work of the air service on a war front consists of often repeated short periods of intense strain. One pilot described it well by saying that it is like going to the dentist every day. To exact the highest standard of conduct under this strain, not as an ideal to be aimed at, but as a working rule, might well seem to be winding up human nature to a point where it must break. The commanders of the air service did not hesitate to take the risk. They trusted human nature, and were amply rewarded. The experiences of the war revealed, to a generation that had almost forgotten them, the ancient and majestic powers of man, the power of his mind over his body, the power of his duty over his mind. When the builders have been praised for their faith and for their skill, the last word of wonder and reverence must be kept for the splendid grain of the stuff that was given them to use in the architecture of their success.

Those matters are fittest for history which exhibit a process of growth. The great periods of human history are not the long periods; they are those times of change and crisis when the movements of humanity are quickened and made visible, when the stationary habits and conservative traditions of mankind are broken up, and one phase of civilization gives place to another, as the bud, long and slowly matured, suddenly bursts into flower. The story of the war in the air is a perfect example of this quickening process, whereby developments long secretly prepared, and delayed until hope is saddened, are mysteriously touched with life, and exhibit the tendencies of ages condensed in the events of a few crowded years. The flying machine, which at the end of the nineteenth century was a toy, ten years later was added to the most valuable resources of man, and ten years later again bid fair to alter the conditions of his life on the surface of the earth.

The war, though it did not cause this great change, accelerated it enormously. War is exacting, and it is difficult to think of any peaceful uses of aircraft which do not find their counterpart in naval and military operations. When General Townshend was besieged in Kut, there came to him by aeroplane not only food (in quantities sadly insufficient for his needs), but salt, saccharine, opium, drugs and surgical dressings, mails, spare parts for wireless plant, money, and a millstone weighing seventy pounds, which was dropped by means of a parachute. In the actual operations of the war the uses of aircraft, and especially of the aeroplane, were very rapidly extended and multiplied. The earliest and most obvious use was reconnaissance. To the commander-in-chief a detailed knowledge of the enemy's dispositions and movements is worth more than an additional army corps; aeroplanes and balloons furnished him with eyes in the air.

As observation was the first purpose of aircraft, so it remains the most important. During the war it was developed in many directions. The corps machines operating on the western front devoted themselves among other things to detecting enemy batteries and to directing the fire of our own artillery. As soon as a wireless installation for aeroplanes came into use, and the observer was thus brought into close touch with his own gunners, this kind of observation became deadly in its efficiency, and was the chief agent in defeating the German scheme of victory by gun-power. When once a hostile battery was located, and our guns, by the aid of observation from the air, were ranged upon it, the fire of that battery was quickly silenced.

Other branches of observation, developed during the war, were photography from the air and contact patrol. Complete photographic maps of Hun-land, as the territory lying immediately behind the enemy lines was everywhere called, were made from a mosaic of photographs, and were continually renewed. No changes, however slight, in the surface of the soil could escape the record of the camera when read by the aid of a magnifying glass. Contact patrol, or reports by low-flying aeroplanes on the exact position of the advancing infantry, came later, and supplemented the use of the telephone, which was liable to be destroyed by shell-fire. Our contact patrols saved us from a world of those most distressing of casualties, the losses inflicted on troops by their own guns.

Serious battle in the air, which was engaged on no large scale until the second year of the war, was, in its essence, an attempt to put out the eyes of the other side. In the early days officers often took a revolver, a carbine, or a rifle, into the air with them, but machines designed expressly for fighting, and armed with Lewis or Vickers guns, did not appear in force until it became necessary to counter the attacks made by the Fokker on our observation machines. Then began that long series of dramatic combats, splendid in many of its episodes, which fascinated the attention of the public, and almost excluded from notice the humbler, but not less essential, and not less dangerous, duties of those whose main business it was to observe.

Lastly, the offensive powers of aircraft have been so rapidly developed, especially during the latest period of the war, that it was only the coming of the armistice that saved mankind from a hurricane of slaughter. In 1914 a few small bombs were carried by officers into the air, and were gingerly dropped over the side of the machine. Accuracy of aim was impossible. In the large modern bombing machine, the heavier bombs weigh almost three-quarters of a ton; they are mechanically released from the rack on which they are hung, and when the machine is flying level, at a known pace and height, good practice can be made, by the aid of an adjustable instrument, on any target.

Even more desolating in its effect is the work done by low-flying aeroplanes, armed with machine-guns, against enemy troops on the march. Raids on the enemy communications, for the destruction of supplies and the cutting off of reinforcements, played a great part in the later phases of the war; and long-distance raids over enemy centres served to bring the civil population into sympathy with the sufferings of the army.

All these activities belong to war on the land, and the aeroplanes of the Royal Naval Air Service bore a part in them. Members of the naval squadrons at Antwerp carried out the earliest bombing raids into Germany. The kite balloons, which rose like a palisade behind our lines and kept the enemy under observation, were, in the early time of the war, supplied by the navy. Moreover, the navy had work of its own to do in the air. The business of coast defence and patrol, the convoy of vessels—in short, all the office-work that would fall to an Inspector-General of the Seven Seas had to be done by the navy.

The seaplane and the flying boat can come to rest on the surface of the sea, but it is no secret that they are not always comfortable there, and there were attached to the Naval Air Service certain special vessels, constructed or adapted to be seaplane-carriers. The credit of defeating Germany's submarine campaign belongs, in part at least, to the air service, working in co-operation with the destroyers and a swarm of smaller craft. In favourable weather submarines below the surface of the water can sometimes be seen from the air, and the depth-charge, another invention of the war, dropped by surface craft, is the means of their destruction.

An occasional duty of aircraft may fitly be mentioned here. It is sometimes desirable that a missionary should be deposited at a quiet spot behind the enemy lines, and when he wishes to communicate with those who sent him out it sometimes becomes necessary to supply him with a basket of pigeons. When communication is interrupted on the troubled surface of the earth, it can often be renewed in the air.

As the uses of aircraft multiplied, so did their designs, and where many various tasks were performed, in the beginning of the war, by a single type of machine, good in its day, there are now many types of machine, each with special fitness for its own purpose. How far these developments may yet go, no man can tell, and prophecy is idle; what is certain is that many operations of war and peace which have never yet been performed are within the reach of the aircraft that are now at our disposal. A beleaguered city could be victualled. A force of a thousand men, with rations and ammunition, could be landed, in a few hours, to operate in the rear of an invading army. But the world is tired of war, and the advances of the immediate future will rather be made in the direction of peaceful traffic and peaceful communication.

The history of the war in the air is the history of the rapid progress of an art and the great achievements of a service. In the nature of things, the progress of the art must claim a share in the record. If the Battle of Trafalgar had been fought only some ten short years after the first adventurer trusted himself to the sea on a crazy raft, the ships, rather than the men, would be the heroes of that battle, and Nelson himself would be overshadowed by the *Victory*. The men who fought the war in the air have overcome more than their enemies; they, and those who worked for them on the ground, have successfully grappled with problem after problem in the perfecting of the art of flight.

A whole world of scientific devices, from the Pitot tube, which indicates the speed of the machine through the air, to the Dreyer automatic oxygen apparatus, which enables the pilot to breathe in the rarefied upper reaches of the atmosphere and to travel far above the summit of high mountain ranges, has become a part of daily usage. A machine is the embodiment of human thought, and if it sometimes seems to be almost alive, that is because it springs of live parents.

The men of science, who worked for humanity, must have an honour only less than the honour paid to the men of action, who died for their country. These last, the pilots and observers who are dead and gone, would not ask to be exalted above other branches of the fighting services. Their pride was to serve the army on the land and the navy on the sea. The men who march often admire and extol the courage of the men who fly, and they are right; but the men who fly, unless they are very thoughtless, know that the heaviest burden of war, its squalor and its tediousness, is borne on the devoted shoulders of the infantryman.

All other arms, even ships of war themselves, in many of their uses, are subservient to the infantry. Man must live, and walk, and sleep on the surface of the earth, and there, in the few feet of soil that have been fertilized by contact with the air, he must grow his food. These are the permanent conditions, and they give the infantry its supremacy in war. A country that is conquered must be controlled and administered; a city that surrenders must be occupied. Battles can be won in the air or on the sea, and the mark of victory is this, that the patient infantry, military and civil, can then advance, to organise peace. An immense sympathy for the sufferings of the infantry, an immense admiration for their dogged perseverance in their never-ending task, is felt by all those whose business it is to assist them from the air. It would be an ill service to the men of the air force, and a foolish ambition, to try to raise them in consideration above the heads of the men whose servants and helpers they are.

There is one glory of the sun, and another glory of the moon. The air service has its own advantages, its own trials, and its own marks of distinction. Life in the service was lived at high pressure, and was commonly short. Throughout the war our machines were continually at work over enemy territory, but the pilots of the beginning of the war were not crossing the lines at its close. A few were acting in administrative posts; some had returned, disabled, to civil life; the rest have passed, and their work has been carried on by generation after generation of their successors. The air service still flourishes; its health depends on a secret elixir of immortality, which enables a body to repair its severest losses.

The name of this elixir is tradition, and the greatest of all the achievements of the air service is that in a very few years, under the hammer of war, it has fashioned and welded its tradition, and has made it sure. Critics who speak of what they have not felt and do not know have sometimes blamed the air service because, being young, it has not the decorum of age. The Latin poet said that it is decorous to die for one's country; in that decorum the service is perfectly instructed. But those who meet the members of a squadron in their hours of ease, among gramophones and pictorial works of art suggestive of luxury, forget that an actor in a tragedy, though he play his part nobly on the stage, is not commonly tragic in the green-room. If they desire intensity and gravity, let them follow the pilot out on to the aerodrome, and watch his face in its hood, when the chocks are pulled away, and he opens the throttle of the engine.

No Greek sculpture is finer in its rendering of life and purpose. To see him at his best they would have to accompany him, through the storm of the anti-aircraft guns, into those fields of air where every moment brings some new trial of the quickness of his brain and the steadiness of his nerve. He is now in the workshop where tradition is made, to be handed down as an heirloom to the coming generations. It will not fail to reach them. The Royal Air Force is strong in the kind of virtue that propagates itself and attains to a life beyond a life. The tradition is safe.

CHAPTER 1

The Conquest of the Air

We know next to nothing of man's greatest achievements. His written history is the history of yesterday, and leaves him very much the same being as it finds him, with the same habits, the same prejudices, and only slightly enhanced powers. The greatest and most significant advances were prehistoric. What invention, of which any record remains, can compare in importance with the invention of speech; and what day in the world's history is more worthy of celebration than that day, the birthday of thought and truth, when a sound, uttered by the breath, from being the expression of a feeling became the mark of a thing? The man who first embarked on the sea has been praised for the triple armour of his courage; but he must be content with praise; his biography will never be written.

The North American Indians are reckoned a primitive people, but when first they come under the notice of history they bring with them one of the most perfect of human inventions—the birch-bark canoe. What centuries of dreams and struggles and rash adventures went to the inventing and perfecting of that frail boat? What forgotten names deserve honour for the invention of the paddle and the sail? The whole story is beyond recovery in the rapidly closing backward perspective of time. Man's eyes are set in his head so that he may go forward, and while he is healthy and alert he does not trouble to look behind him.

If the beginnings of European civilization are rightly traced to certain tribes of amphibious dwellers on the coast of the Mediterranean, who reared the piles of their houses in the water, and so escaped the greater perils of the land, then some sort of rudimentary navigation was the first condition of human progress, and sea-power, which defies the devastators of continents, had earlier prophets than Admiral

Mahan. But the memory of these thousands of years has passed like a watch in the night. The conquest of the sea can never be recorded in history; even the conquest of the air, which was achieved within the lifetime of all but the very youngest of those who are now alive, admits of no sure or perfect record. The men who bore a part in it, and still survive, are preoccupied with the future, and are most of them impatient of their own past. Where knowledge begins, there begin also conflicting testimonies and competing claims. It is no part of the business of this history of the war in the air to compare these testimonies or to resolve these claims.

To narrate how man learned to fly would demand a whole treatise, and the part of the history which ends in December 1903 is the most difficult and uncertain part of all. Yet the broad outlines of the process can be sketched and determined. It is a long story of legends and dreams, theories and fancies, all suddenly transformed into facts; a tale of the hopes of madmen suddenly recognised as reasonable ambitions. When in the light of the present we look back on the past our eyes are opened, and we see many things that were invisible to contemporaries. We are able, for the first time, to pay homage to the pioneers, who saw the promised kingdom, but did not enter it. No place has hitherto been found for their names in serious history.

The Dictionary of National Biography, with its supplement, includes the lives of all the famous men of this nation who died before King George the Fifth was king. Yet it contains no mention of Sir George Cayley, the Father of British Aeronautics; nor of John Stringfellow, who, in 1848, constructed the first engine-driven aeroplane that ever flew through the air; nor of Francis Herbert Wenham, whose classic treatise on Aerial Locomotion, read at the first meeting of the Aeronautical Society, in 1866, expounds almost every principle on which modern aviation is founded; nor of James Glaisher, who, in 1862, made the highest recorded balloon ascent; nor of Percy Sinclair Pilcher, who lost his life in experimenting with one of his own gliders in 1899. These men attracted little enough notice in their own day, and were regarded as amiable eccentrics; but they all thought long and hard on aerial navigation, and step by step, at their own costs, they brought it nearer to accomplishment.

Now that the thing has been done, it seems strange that it was not done earlier. At no time was it possible for man to forget his disabilities; the birds were always above him, in easy possession. If he attributed their special powers wholly to the lightness of their structure and the strength of their muscles, the variety of flying creatures might have taught him better. The fact is that there is no unique design for flight; given the power and its right use, almost anything can fly. If the sea-gull can fly, so can the duck, with a much heavier body and a much less proportion of wing. The moth can fly; but so, can the beetle. The flying-fish can fly, or rather, can leap into the air and glide for a distance of many yards. With the requisite engine-power a portmanteau or a tea-tray could support itself in the air. The muscular power of man, it is now generally accepted, is not sufficient to support his weight in level flight on still air, but if the principles of flight had been understood, there was no need to wait for the invention of the powerful internal-combustion engine; a steam-engine in a well-designed aeroplane might have performed very useful nights. It was knowledge that lingered.

Newton, when he saw an apple fall in his garden at Woolsthorpe, 'began to think of gravity extending to the orb of the moon'. If he had been in the habit of skimming flat stones on calm water, he might have bent his mind to the problem of flight, and might even have anticipated some of the discoveries in aerodynamics which were reserved for the last century—in particular, the relations of speed and angle of incidence to the reactions of air resistance on a moving plane. The fact which is the basis of all aeroplane flight is that a perfectly horizontal plane, free to fall through the air, has its time of falling much retarded if it is in rapid horizontal motion. This is what makes gliding possible.

Now let the plane which is being propelled in a horizontal direction be slightly tilted up, so that its front, or leading edge, is higher than its back, or trailing edge. The reaction of the air can then be resolved into two components, technically called 'lift' and 'drag'; lift, which tends to raise the plane, and drag, which retards it in its forward motion. When the angle of incidence of the plane is small, that is, when it is only slightly tilted from its direction of motion, the greater part of the air reaction is converted into lift. This is what makes flying possible. A moderate speed through the air will enable the plane to lift much more than its own weight.

This is not a technical treatise, but some further facts of signal importance in the theory and practice of flight are better explained at once, in so far as the beautiful exactitude of mathematical demonstration can be expressed in the crudities of popular speech. The lift produced by the reaction of the air acts on the whole plane, but not equally on all parts of it. At a flying angle, that is, when the angle of incidence of the plane is small, the upward force is greatest on those parts of the plane which are immediately behind the leading edge. The wings of any soaring bird are long and narrow, and thus are perfectly designed for their work. A square-winged bird would be a poor soarer; a bird the breadth of whose wings should be greater than their length could hardly fly at all.

The wings of a flying machine are called planes, or aerofoils; the length of the wing is called the span of the plane; the breadth of the wing is called the chord of the plane. The proportion of the span to the chord, that is, the proportion of the length of the wing to its breadth, is called the 'aspect ratio' of the plane; and a plane, or wing, that is long and narrow is said to have a high aspect ratio. A higher aspect ratio than is found in any bird or any flying machine would theoretically improve its powers of flight, but the practicable span of the plane, or length of the wing, is limited by the need for rigidity and strength. The albatross, nevertheless, the king of soaring birds, has enormously long and narrow wings; and the planes of some flying machines have an aspect ratio almost as high as the slats of a Venetian blind.

The wings of a flying machine, it has been said, are called planes, but they are not true planes. Like the wings of a bird, they are 'cambered', that is to say, they curve upward from the leading edge and downward again to the trailing edge. Some of the most valuable work contributed by the laboratory to the science of flight has had for its object the determination of the best form of camber, or curve of the plane. In the result, that form of camber has been found to be best which attains its maximum depth a little way only behind the leading edge, and gradually becomes shallower towards the trailing edge. Such a form of curve produces a comparatively smooth and untroubled partial vacuum above the plane, just behind its leading edge, and this vacuum is the factor of chief importance in the lift of the plane.

The above is a brief and rough statement of some principles of aviation which have been ascertained by long experiment and the labour of many minds. It is by experiment that flight has been achieved. The Newton who shall reduce all the observed phenomena to a few broad and simple laws is yet to come. A bird is simpler than an aeroplane in that its wings both support it and drive it forward, whereas all aerial machines, both those that are heavier than air and those that are lighter than air, are at present driven forward by the thrust of an airscrew, revolving at the rate of some twenty to thirty times a second.

There are only two kinds of flying machine, the lighter than air and the heavier than air, of which two kinds the simplest types are the soap-bubble and the arrow. These two kinds have often been in competition with each other; and their rivalry, which has sometimes delayed progress, still continues. The chief practical objection to machines lighter than air is that they are buoyed up by vulnerable receptacles containing hydrogen or some other highly inflammable gas. As soon as helium, which is a light non-inflammable gas, shall be produced in quantity at a reasonable expense, this objection will be lessened. The advantage of the lighter-than-air, or floating, machine over the heavier-than-air, or soaring, machine is that it can remain stationary in the air without loss of height, and that its great size and lifting power enable it to supply comfortable quarters for its staff, who not only travel in it, but, if need be, can inhabit it for days. The airship has a promising future, but it can never wholly supersede the soaring machine, which is heavier than air, and flies as birds fly.

A fascinating story, part legend, part fiction, might be told of the earliest reputed inventors. The fable of Daedalus perhaps grew up round the memory of a man of mechanical genius, for Daedalus was the author of many inventions before he flew from Crete to Italy. Aulus Gellius, in his entertaining book of anecdotes called the *Attic Nights*, tells how the philosopher Archytas of Tarentum invented a mechanical pigeon, which was filled with some kind of light air, and flew. The two schools of aeronautics were here reconciled. Other mechanists were Roger Bacon, who is reported to have designed a flying chariot; and Regiomontanus, astronomer and mathematician, who made a mechanical eagle which flew to meet the Emperor Charles the Fifth, on his solemn entry into the city of Nuremberg.

It is not necessary to inquire whether these stories are true or false; what is certain is that the inventors did not leave their inventions as a legacy to their fellows. For a like reason Leonardo da Vinci, who busied himself with a mechanism which should enable man to operate wings with his legs, and who left a short treatise on the art of flight, has no place in the history. His mechanism is merely a drawing; his treatise remained in manuscript. The adventurers who risked their lives on wings of their own making are truer ancestors of the flying man. In 1507 John Damian, who was held in esteem as an alchemist and physician at the court of King James IV of Scotland:

> Took in hand to fly with wings, and to that effect he caused make a pair of wings of feathers, which being fastened upon

him, he flew off the castle wall of Stirling, but shortly he fell to the ground and brake his thigh-bone.' From the *History of Scotland*, by John Lesley, Bishop of Ross, written about 1570.

The poet Dunbar attacked him in a satirical poem, and the reputation of a charlatan has stuck to him, but he deserves credit for his courageous attempt. So, does the Marquis de Bacqueville, who, in 1742, attached to his arms and legs planes of his own design, and launched himself from an upper storey of his house in Paris, in the attempt to fly across the River Seine to the Tuileries, about two hundred yards away. He glided some distance, and then fell on a washerwoman's barge in the stream, breaking his leg in the fall. These and other disastrous attempts might be defended in the words of Wilbur Wright, written in 1901, while he was experimenting with his own gliders.

There are two ways of learning how to ride a fractious horse: one is to get on him and learn by actual practice how each motion and trick may be best met; the other is to sit on a fence and watch the beast awhile, and then retire to the house and at leisure figure out the best way of overcoming his jumps and kicks. The latter system is the safest; but the former, on the whole, turns out the larger proportion of good riders. It is very much the same in learning to ride a flying machine; if you are looking for perfect safety you will do well to sit on a fence and watch the birds; but if you really wish to learn you must mount a machine and become acquainted with its tricks by actual trial.—*Journal of the Western Society of Engineers*, vol. vi, No. 6, December 1901.

This pronouncement, by the highest authority, may serve as an apology for some of those whose attempts were reckoned madness or quackery, and whose misfortunes, during many long centuries, are the only material available for the history of human flight.

Two periods of modern European history are notable for a quickening of human interest in the problem of aerial navigation. They are the age of Louis XIV of France, and the age of the French Revolution. Both were times of great progress in science, and of illimitable hopes; but the earlier period, which in England witnessed the foundation of the Royal Society, was notable chiefly for advance in the physical and mathematical sciences; while the later period was more addicted to chemistry, and was the age of Lavoisier, Priestley, Cavendish, and Black. The former age, though it attained to nothing practical, made some progress in the theory of flight; the latter age invented the balloon.

The Royal Society took its origin in the meetings in London, during the troublous times of the Civil War, of 'divers worthy persons inquisitive into natural philosophy'. One of these worthy persons was John Wilkins, mathematician, philosopher, and divine, who, being parliamentarian in his sympathies, was, on the expulsion of the Royalists from Oxford, made Warden of Wadham College in that University. At Wadham, in the Warden's lodgings, the 'Experimental philosophical Club', as Aubrey calls it, renewed its meetings.

Sprat, the early historian of the Royal Society, explains that religion and politics were forbidden topics.

> To have been always tossing about some theological question would have been to make that their private diversion of which they had had more than enough in public; to have been musing on the Civil Wars would have made them melancholy; therefore, Nature alone could entertain them.

After the Restoration a meeting was held at Gresham College in London, and a committee was appointed, with Wilkins as chairman, to draw up a scheme for the Royal Society.

The king approved of the scheme submitted to him, and the society received its charter in 1662.

Wilkins was a famous man in his day; he married a sister of Oliver Cromwell, and in his later years was Bishop of Chester. But his great work was the founding of the Royal Society; and his philosophical (or, as they would now be called, scientific) writings, which belong to his earlier years in London, show very clearly with what high expectations the society started on its labours. The first of these writings, published in 1638, is a discourse to prove that there may be another habitable World in the Moon. The second considers the possibility of a passage thither. The third maintains that it is probable that our Earth is one of the planets. The fourth, which is entitled *Mercury; or, the Secret Messenger*, discusses how thoughts may be communicated from a distance. The fifth and last, published in 1648, is called *Mathematical Magic*, and is divided into two books, under the titles *Archimedes; or, Mechanical Powers*, and *Daedalus; or, Mechanical Motions*.

In this latter book Wilkins treats of mills, clocks, and the contrivance of motion by rarefied air; of the construction of an ark for submarine navigation, and of its uses in war; of a sailing chariot, to be driven on the land as ships are on the sea; of the possibility of perpetual motion; and, in chapters vii and viii, of the art of flying. There are four ways, according to Wilkins, whereby flying in the air may be attempted. The first is by spirits or angels; but this branch of the subject does not belong to natural philosophy. The next is by the help of fowls, which the learned Francis Bacon thought deserving of further experiment. Two ways remain of flying by our own strength; we may use wings fastened immediately to the body, or we may devise a flying chariot. If we are to use wings, he says, we must be brought up in the constant practice of them from youth:

> First running on the ground, as an ostrich or tame goose will do ... and so by degrees learn to rise higher. ... I have heard it from credible testimony, that one of our own nation hath proceeded so far in this experiment, that he was able by the help of wings, in such a running pace, to step constantly ten yards at a time.'

The arms of a man extended are weak, and easily wearied, so he thinks it would be worth the inquiry whether the wings might not be worked by the legs being thrust out and drawn in again one after the other, so as each leg should move both wings. But the best way of flying would be by a flying chariot, big enough to carry several persons, who might take turns to work it. Wilkins is quite honest in recognising the difficulties of this scheme. He deals fully with the chief of them—whether so large and heavy a machine can be supported by so thin and light a body as the air; and whether the strength of the persons in it can be sufficient for the motion of it.

In his attempt to show that these objections are not insuperable, he makes some true remarks. He had watched soaring birds, and had seen how they could swim up and down in the air without any sensible motion of the wings. When the right proportions of the machine are found out, and men by long practice have attained to skill and experience, we may perhaps, he thinks, be able to imitate the birds. If, after all, it be found that some greater motive power is required, we must not despair of the invention of such a power. The main difficulty will be not so much in maintaining the machine in flight as in raising it from the ground.

> When once it is aloft in the air, the motion of it will be easy, as it is in the flight of all kind of birds, which being at any great

distance from the earth, are able to continue their motion for a long time and way, with little labour and weariness.

The right proportion of the wings, both for length and breadth; the special contrivances necessary for ascent, descent, or a turning motion—these and many more such questions can only be resolved, he maintains, by particular experiments. The sails of ships have been perfected by degrees, and the attempt to fly must meet with many difficulties and inconveniences for which only long experience and frequent trial can suggest a remedy.

So far Wilkins went; and he went no farther. His speculations, however, made a deep impression on his own age, gave a bias to the researches of his fellows, and, incidentally, aroused a storm of ridicule. When Joseph Glanvill, in his vigorous little treatise called *Scepsis Scientifica* (1665), wrote a forecast of the possible achievements of the Royal Society, he borrowed his hopes from Wilkins, he says:

> Should these heroes go on as they have happily begun, they will fill the world with wonders, and posterity will find many things that are now but rumours, verified into practical realities. It may be, some ages hence, a voyage to the southern unknown tracts, yea, possibly the Moon, will not be more strange than one to America. To them that come after us it may be as ordinary to buy a pair of wings to fly into remotest regions, as now a pair of boots to ride a journey. And to confer at the distance of the Indies, by sympathetic conveyances, may be as usual to future times, as to us in a literary correspondence. The restoration of grey hairs to juvenility, and renewing the exhausted marrow, may at length be effected without a miracle; and the turning the now comparative desert world into a paradise, may not improbably be expected from late agriculture.

Again, when Sir William Temple, some thirty years later, cast contempt upon the Moderns in his *Essay of Ancient and Modern Learning*, it was the speculations of Wilkins that provoked his keenest satire.

> I have indeed heard of wondrous pretensions and visions of men, possess'd with notions of the strange advancement of learning and sciences, on foot in this age, and the progress they are like to make in the next; as, the universal medicine, which will certainly cure all that have it; the philosopher's stone, which will be found out by men that care not for riches: the

transfusion of young blood into old men's veins, which will make them as gamesome as the lambs, from which 'tis to be derived; an universal language, which may serve all men's turn, when they have forgot their own: the knowledge of one another's thoughts, without the grievous trouble of speaking: the art of flying, till a man happens to fall down and break his neck: double-bottom'd ships, whereof none can ever be cast away, besides the first that was made: the admirable virtues of that noble and necessary juice called spittle, which will come to be sold, and very cheap, in the apothecaries' shops: discoveries of new worlds in the planets, and voyages between this and that in the moon, to be made as frequently as between York and London: which such poor mortals as I am think as wild as those of Ariosto, but without half so much wit, or so much instruction; for there, these modern sages may know where they may hope in time to find their lost senses, preserved in vials, with those of Orlando.

Both Sir William Temple and Joseph Glanvill were men of acute intelligence and complete sanity; the one an aged statesman deeply versed in the deceits and follies of men; the other a young cleric, educated in the Oxford of the Commonwealth, and stirred to enthusiasm by what he had there heard of the progress of natural philosophy. In this perennial debate the man of the world commonly triumphs; he plays for the stakes that are on the table, and does not put faith in deferred gains. For something like two hundred years Sir William Temple's triumph was almost complete. Now things have changed, and Glanvill's rhapsody comes nearer to the truth. Wireless telegraphy, radium, the discoveries of bacteriology, and not least the conquest of the air, have taken the edge off the sallies of the wit, and have verified the dreams of the prophet.

What most delayed the science and art of flight, which made no progress during the whole of the eighteenth century, was an imperfect understanding of the flight of birds. The right way to achieve flight, as events were to prove, was by the study and practice of gliding. But birds were believed to support, as well as to raise, themselves in the air chiefly by what in the jargon of science is called orthogonal flight, that is, by direct downward flapping of the wings. This view received authoritative support from a famous treatise written in the seventeenth century by Giovanni Alfonso Borelli, an Italian professor of mathematical and natural philosophy.

Borelli, who held professorships at the Universities of Florence and Pisa, and corresponded with many members of the Royal Society, was an older man than Wilkins, but his book on the movements of animals (*De Motu Animalium*), which included a section on the flight of birds (*De Volatu*), was not published till 1680, when both he and Wilkins were dead. It was long held in high esteem for its anatomical exposition of the action of flying, and some of its main contentions cast a damp upon the hopes of man. The bones of a bird, says Borelli, are thin tubes of exceeding hardness, much lighter, and at the same time stronger, than the bones of a man. The pectoral muscles, which move the wings, are massive and strong—more than four times stronger, in proportion to the weight they have to move, than the legs of a man.

And he states his conclusion roundly—it is impossible that man should ever achieve artificial flight by his own strength. This view, dogmatically stated by one who was a good mathematician and a good anatomist, became the orthodox view, and had an enduring influence. All imitation of the birds by man, and further, all schemes of navigating the air in a machine dynamically supported, seemed, by Borelli's argument, to have been thrust back into the limbo of vanities.

There remained only the hope that some means might be found of buoying man up in the air, thereby leaving him free to apply his muscular and mechanical powers to the business of driving himself forward. Another celebrated treatise of the seventeenth century pointed the way to such a means. Francesco Lana, a member of the Society of Jesus in Rome, spent the greater part of his life in scientific research. He planned a large encyclopaedia, embodying all existing science, in so far as it was based on experiment and proof. Of this work only two volumes appeared during his lifetime; he died at Brescia in the year 1687.

But long before he died, he had produced, in 1670, a preliminary sketch of his great work; and it is this earlier and shorter treatise which contains the two famous chapters on the Aerial Ship. The aerial ship is to be buoyed up in the air by being suspended from four globes, made of thin copper sheeting, each of them about twenty-five feet in diameter. From these globes the air is to be exhausted, so that each of them, being lighter than air, will support the weight of two or three men. The ship being thus floated can be propelled by oars and sails.

Any modern reader, without asking for further specifications, can pronounce this design absurd. Lana was prevented by his vow of poverty from spending any money on experiment, so that he had to meet only argumentative objections, not those much more formidable obstacles, the ordeal of the inventor, which present themselves when a machine is theoretically perfect and will not work. The difficulties which he foresaw are real enough. The process of exhausting the air from the globes might, he thought, prove troublesome. The pressure of the atmosphere on the outer surface, it might be held, would crush or break the globes, to which he replied that that pressure would be equal on all sides, and would therefore rather strengthen the globes than break them.

The ship, some might object, could not be propelled by oars; Lana thinks it could, but suggests, to comfort the objectors, that oars will rarely be necessary, for there will always be a wind. The weight of the machine and of the persons in it will fortunately prevent it from rising to heights where breathing becomes impossible. Lana says:

> I do not foresee any other difficulties that could prevail against this invention, save one only, which to me seems the greatest of them all, and that is that God would never surely allow such a machine to be successful, since it would create many disturbances in the civil and political governments of mankind. Where is the man who can fail to see that no city would be proof against surprise, when the ship could at any time be steered over its squares, or even over the courtyards of dwelling-houses, and brought to earth for the landing of its crew? . . . Iron weights could be hurled to wreck ships at sea, or they could be set on fire by fireballs and bombs; nor ships alone, but houses, fortresses, and cities could be thus destroyed, with the certainty that the airship could come to no harm as the missiles could be hurled from a vast height.

The extravagance of Lana's design must not be allowed to rob him of the credit of being, in some sense, the inventor of the balloon. A balloon filled with gas, and lighter than air, was in his day inconceivable; the composition of the atmosphere was unknown, and the chemistry of gases was not understood. But he had followed the physical investigations of the seventeenth century, and was well acquainted with Torricelli's demonstration of the weight of the atmosphere. The only practical way for him to make a vessel lighter than air was to empty it of the air within it, and Torricelli's invention of the barometer seemed to bring such a device within reach. The common pump begat the barometer; the barometer begat the balloon.

But the enormous pressure of the atmosphere on a vessel encasing a vacuum, though Lana had triumphed over it in argument, could not be so easily dealt with in practice. The success of the balloon was delayed until, by the discovery and production of a gas lighter than air, a frail and thin envelope could be supported against the pressure from without by an equal pressure from within.

For ballooning what was chiefly necessary was a thorough knowledge of gases and of the means of producing them. The older chemistry, or alchemy, devoted all its attention, for centuries, to the precious metals, and knew nothing of gas. Medical chemistry, which succeeded it, was concerned chiefly with the curative properties of various chemical preparations. When Robert Boyle, and the investigators who came after him, put aside this age-long preoccupation with wealth and healing, and set themselves to determine, by observation and experiment, the nature of common substances, and the possibility of resolving them into simpler elements, modern chemistry began. Four states of matter, namely, earth, air, fire, and water, were recognised by the older chemists, and were by them called elements; it was the work of the eighteenth century to investigate these, and especially to separate the constituents of air and of water.

In 1774 Joseph Priestley discovered oxygen. In 1782 Henry Cavendish showed that hydrogen, when burnt, produces water. At a much earlier date hydrogen had been produced by the action of acid on metals, and had been found to be many times lighter than air. Dr. Joseph Black, professor of chemistry in the University of Edinburgh, was the first to suggest, in 1767, that a balloon inflated with hydrogen would rise in the air; and the experiment was successfully tried with soap-bubbles by Tiberius Cavallo, in the year 1782.

Nevertheless, the famous first balloon, which ascended in 1783, was not filled with hydrogen, and was invented by what may be called a happy accident. The brothers Joseph and Jacques Montgolfier were the sons of a wealthy paper-maker at Annonay, not very far from Lyons. The suggestion of their balloon came to them from observing that thick opaque clouds float high in the air. Linen material was readily accessible to them at the factory, and they resolved to try whether a large balloon, some thirty-three feet in diameter, filled with smoke vapours, would rise in the air. Their experiment was successful.

On the 5th of June 1783 they filled their balloon with smoke (and therefore with hot air) over a fire of chips and shavings; it rose easily, and travelled to a distance of about a mile and a half before it cooled and sank. The fame of this experiment quickly reached Paris, the centre of science and fashion, and awakened rivalry. Under the direction of Professor Charles, a well-known physicist, two brothers whose surname was Robert made from varnished silk a balloon of about thirteen feet in diameter; it was filled with hydrogen, and on the 27th of August 1783, in the presence of a large and excited assembly, it rose from the Champ de Mars and travelled some fifteen miles into the country, where it fell, and produced a panic among the peasantry.

On the 19th of September Joseph Montgolfier was brought to Versailles to give a demonstration of his new invention in the presence of the king and queen. On this occasion his balloon rose 1,500 feet into the air, carrying with it a sheep, a cock, and a duck, the first living passengers, whom it deposited unhurt when it came to ground again after a short flight. Thereafter society went balloon-mad. Pilâtre de Rozier, a young native of Metz, determined to attempt an aerial voyage. During the month of October, he experimented with a captive balloon of the Montgolfier type, from which he suspended a brazier, so that by a continued supply of heated air the balloon should maintain its buoyancy.

On the 21st of November 1783, accompanied by the Marquis d'Arlandes, he rose in a free balloon from the Bois de Boulogne, and made a successful voyage of twenty minutes, during which time he travelled over Paris for a distance of about five miles. Ten days later, on behalf of the savants, M. Charles retorted with a voyage of twenty-seven miles, in a hydrogen balloon, from Paris to Nesle; he was accompanied by one of the brothers Robert, and when Robert left the car at Nesle the balloon, lightened of a part of its burden, rose rapidly with M. Charles to a height of two miles in the air. Most of the fittings of the modern hydrogen balloon, the hoop and netting, for instance, from which the car is suspended, and the valve at the top of the balloon for the release of the gas, were devised by Charles.

The unfortunate Pilâtre de Rozier met his death on the 15th of June 1785, in an attempt to cross from Boulogne to England. In order to avoid a constant wastage of hydrogen in controlling the height of the balloon, he devised a double balloon; the larger one, above, was filled with hydrogen, the smaller one, below, was worked with hot air from a brazier, on the Montgolfier principle. At a height of some three thousand feet, while it was still over French territory, the double balloon caught fire and fell flaming to the earth.

The earliest balloon ascents in England followed close upon the

French experiments. On the 25th of November 1783 Count Francesco Zambeccari sent up an oil-silk hydrogen balloon, ten feet in diameter, from the Artillery Ground in Moorfields; it travelled forty-eight miles, and fell at Petworth in Sussex. On the 22nd of February 1784 a balloon of five feet in diameter, liberated at Sandwich in Kent, travelled seventy-five miles, and after crossing the Channel, fell at Warneton in Flanders. To inflate a bag with gas and let it take its chance in the air is no great achievement, but these were flights of good promise.

The first person in Great Britain to navigate the air was James Tytler, a Scot, who on the 27th of August 1784 ascended in a fire-balloon, that is, a balloon filled with hot air, from Comely Gardens, Edinburgh, and travelled about half a mile. Tytler had been employed by the booksellers to edit the second edition of the *Encyclopaedia Britannica*, of which he wrote the greater part, at a salary of seventeen shillings a week; he passed his life in poverty, and his balloon adventure attracted little attention.

The public mania for ballooning as a spectacle began with the ascents of Vincenzo Lunardi, secretary to the Neapolitan ambassador in England. Lunardi's first ascent, which was well advertised, was made from the Artillery Ground in Moorfields on the 15th of September 1784, in the presence of nearly two hundred thousand spectators. His hydrogen balloon, of about thirty-two feet in diameter, sailed high over London, and descended near Ware in Hertfordshire. His record of his sensations, written in imperfect English, and published in 1784 under the title of *An Account of the First Aerial Voyage in England*, deserves quotation:

> At five minutes after two, the last gun was fired, the cords divided, and the balloon rose, the company returning my signals of *adieu* with the most unfeigned acclamations and applauses. The effect was that of a miracle on the multitudes which surrounded the place; and they passed from incredulity and menace into the most extravagant expressions of approbation and joy. At the height of twenty yards, the balloon was a little depressed by the wind, which had a fine effect; it held me over the ground for a few seconds, and seemed to pause majestically before its departure.
> On discharging a part of the ballast, it ascended to the height of two hundred yards. As a multitude lay before me of a hundred

and fifty thousand people, who had not seen my ascent from the ground, I had recourse to every stratagem to let them know I was in the gallery, and they literally rent the air with their acclamations and applause. In these stratagems I devoted my flag, and worked with my oars, one of which was immediately broken and fell from me. A pigeon too escaped, which, with a dog, and cat, were the only companions of my excursion.

When the thermometer had fallen from 68° to 61° I perceived a great difference in the temperature of the air. I became very cold, and found it necessary to take a few glasses of wine. I likewise eat the leg of a chicken, but my bread and other provisions had been rendered useless by being mixed with the sand which I carried as ballast.

When the thermometer was at fifty, the effect of the atmosphere, and the combination of circumstances around, produced a calm delight, which is inexpressible, and which no situation on earth could give. The stillness, extent, and magnificence of the scene rendered it highly awful. My horizon seemed a perfect circle; the terminating line several hundred miles in circumference. This I conjectured from the view of London; the extreme points of which, formed an angle of only a few degrees. It was so reduced on the great scale before me, that I can find no simile to convey an idea of it.

I could distinguish Saint Paul's and other churches, from the houses. I saw the streets as lines, all animated with beings, whom I knew to be men and women, but which I should otherwise have had a difficulty in describing. It was an enormous beehive, but the industry of it was suspended.

All the moving mass seemed to have no object but myself, and the transition from the suspicion, and perhaps contempt, of the preceding hour, to the affectionate transport, admiration and glory of the present moment, was not without its effect on my mind. I recollected the puns on my name, (in some of the papers, witticisms appeared on the affinity of Lunatic and Lunardi), and was glad to find myself calm. I had soared from the apprehensions and anxieties of the Artillery Ground, and felt as if I had left behind me all the cares and passions that molest mankind.

Indeed, the whole scene before me filled the mind with a sublime pleasure, of which I never had a conception. The critics imagine, for they seldom speak from experience, that terror is an ingredient in every sublime sensation. It was not possible for me to be on earth in a situation so free from apprehension. I had not the slightest sense of motion from the machine, I knew not whether it went swiftly or slowly, whether it ascended or descended, whether it was agitated or tranquil, but by the appearance or disappearance of objects on the earth.

I moved to different parts of the gallery, I adjusted the furniture, and apparatus, I uncorked my bottle, eat, drank, and wrote, just as in my study. The height had not the effect, which a much lesser degree of it has near the earth, that of producing giddiness. The broomsticks of the witches, Ariosto's flying-horse, and even Milton's sunbeam, conveying the angel to the earth, have all an idea of effort, difficulty, and restraint, which do not affect a voyage in the balloon.

Thus tranquil, and thus situated, how shall I describe to you a view, such as the ancients supposed Jupiter to have of the earth, and to copy which there are no terms in any language. The gradual diminution of objects, and the masses of light and shade are intelligible in oblique and common prospects. But here everything wore a new appearance, and had a new effect. The face of the country had a mild and permanent verdure, to which Italy is a stranger.

The variety of cultivation, and the accuracy with which property is divided, give the idea ever present to a stranger in England, of good civil laws and an equitable administration; the rivers meandering; the sea glist'ning with the rays of the sun; the immense district beneath me spotted with cities, towns, villages, houses, pouring out their inhabitants to hail my appearance: you will allow me some merit at not having been exceedingly intoxicated with my situation.

The interest which the spectators took in my voyage was so great, that the things I threw down were divided and preserved as our people would relicks of the most celebrated saints. And a gentlewoman, mistaking the oar for my person, was so affected with my supposed destruction, that she died in a few days.

For many months after this the Flying Man was the chief topic of conversation in the town. Even in the previous year reports of the French ascents had produced a fever of excitement in London. Horace

Walpole, writing in December 1783, said:

> Balloons, occupy senators, philosophers, ladies, everybody.

All other interests yielded precedence. Miss Burney's *Cecilia* was the novel of the season, but it had to give way. Mrs. Barbauld, in a letter written in January 1784, said:

> Next to the balloon, Miss Burney is the object of public curiosity.'

A few weeks earlier, Dr. Johnson passed the day with three friends, and boasted to Mrs. Thrale that no mention had been made by any of them of the air balloon, 'which has taken full possession, with a very good claim, of every philosophical mind and mouth'. Some days after Lunardi's first ascent Johnson wrote to a friend:

> I had this day in three letters three histories of the flying man in the great ballon. I am glad that we do as well as our neighbours.

Three letters were enough, and on the same day Johnson wrote to Sir Joshua Reynolds:

> Do not write about the balloon, whatever else you may think proper to say.

On the 29th of September 1784 Lunardi's balloon caught fire by accident, and was burnt on the ground. Johnson's quiet and sensible comment is conveyed in a letter to his friend Dr. Brocklesby, on the 6th of October:

> The fate of the balloon I do not much lament: to make new balloons is to repeat the jest again. We now know a method of mounting into the air, and, I think, are not likely to know more. The vehicles can serve no use till we can guide them; and they can gratify no curiosity till we mount with them to greater heights than we can reach without; till we rise above the tops of the highest mountains, which we have yet not done. We know the state of the air in all its regions, to the top of Teneriffe, and therefore, learn nothing from those who navigate a balloon below the clouds. The first experiment, however, was bold, and deserved applause and reward.

Johnson died in December of that same year; the balloon had made its appearance just in time for his comments. Another critic, Horace Walpole, was in two minds about balloons. Sometimes they seemed to him 'philosophic playthings'. He was growing old, and did not care to spend his time in divining with what airy vehicles the atmosphere will be peopled hereafter, or how much more expeditiously the east, west, or south will be ravaged and butchered, than they have been by the old clumsy method of navigation '. Yet in spite of his elegant indifference, he could not help being interested; and some of his divinations come very near to the truth. He pictures Salisbury Plain, Newmarket Heath, and all downs, arising into dockyards for aerial vessels; and he professes himself willing to go to Paris by air, 'if there is no air sickness'. The best defence of the new invention was spoken by Benjamin Franklin, who when he was asked in Paris, 'What is the use of balloons?' replied by another question—'What is the use of a new-born infant?'

The infancy of the balloon lasted long; indeed, if lack of self-control be the mark of infancy, the balloon was an infant during the whole of the nineteenth century. In the early days, new achievements, in distance or height, kept public expectation alive. Jean Pierre Blanchard, a French aeronaut, and rival of Lunardi, succeeded, on the 7th of January 1785, in crossing the English Channel from Dover. Thereafter ascents became so numerous that it is impossible to keep count of them. Glaisher, writing about 1870, says that the most remarkable ascent of the century was that fitted out by Robert Hollond, Esq., M.P. The balloonist was Charles Green, and they were accompanied by Mr. Monck Mason, who published an account of the voyage.

In Mr. Green's balloon, afterwards called the Great Nassau, they left Vauxhall Gardens on the afternoon of Monday, the 7th of November 1836, with provisions to last a fortnight. They were soon lost in the clouds, and after crossing the sea, had no very clear idea of what country they were over. After eighteen hours' journey, fearing that they had reached Poland or Russia, they came to earth, and found that they had travelled five hundred miles, to the neighbourhood of the town of Weilburg, in the duchy of Nassau.

Charles Green was the most experienced aeronaut of his time; he was the first to use coal-gas in place of hydrogen, and he was the inventor of the guide-rope, which is dropped from a balloon to allow her to be secured by a landing party, or is trailed on the ground to reduce her speed and to assist in maintaining a steady height.

The dangers of the balloon were diminished by the labours of scientific men, but its disabilities remained. No one who travelled in a balloon could choose his destination. The view of the earth, and of the clouds, obtainable from a height, was beautiful and unfamiliar, but in the absence of any specific utility the thing became a popular toy. In public gardens a balloon could be counted on to attract a crowd, and the showman soon gave it its place, as a miracle of nature, by the side of the giant and the dwarf, the living skeleton, and the fat woman. A horse is not seen to advantage in the car of a balloon, but it is a marvel that a horse should be seen there at all, and equestrian ascents became one of the attractions of the Cremorne Gardens in 1821.

It was not until 1859 that an organised attempt was made to reclaim the balloon for the purposes of science. In that year a committee, appointed by the British Association to make observations on the higher strata of the atmosphere, met at Wolverhampton. Volunteers were lacking until, in 1862, James Glaisher, one of the members of the committee, declared his willingness to prepare the apparatus and to make the observations from a balloon. Glaisher had spent many years on meteorological observation, in Ireland, at Cambridge University, and at the Royal Observatory, Greenwich. He proposed to investigate the effect of different elevations on the temperature of the dew-point; on the composition and electrical condition of the atmosphere, and on the rate and direction of the wind currents in it; on the earth's magnetism, and the solar spectrum; on sound, and on solar radiation.

From 1862 to 1866 he made twenty-eight ascents, with Henry Coxwell as his balloonist. The most famous of these was from Wolverhampton on the 5th of September 1862, when Glaisher claimed to have reached a height of fully seven miles. After recording a height of 29,000 feet Glaisher swooned; Coxwell lost the use of his limbs, but succeeded in pulling the cord of the valve with his teeth. When Glaisher swooned the balloon was ascending rapidly; when he came to, thirteen minutes later, it was descending rapidly, and the height that he claimed was an inference, supported by the reading of a minimum thermometer.

Critics have pointed out that his calculations made no allowance for the slackening of the upward pace of the balloon as it neared its limit, nor for the time it would take, with the valve feebly pulled, to change its direction and acquire speed in its descent. They are inclined to allow him a height of about six miles, which is a sufficiently remarkable achievement.

All these ascents, though they proved that the balloon had a certain utility for the exploration of the upper reaches of the atmosphere, did little or nothing for aerial navigation. The great vogue of the balloon distracted attention from the real problem of flight. That problem was not abandoned; a number of men, working independently, without any sort of public recognition, made steady advance during the whole course of the nineteenth century. By the end of the century, three years before flight was achieved, those who were most deeply concerned in the attempt knew that success was near. The great difficulty of scientific research lies in choosing the right questions to ask of nature. Every lawyer knows that it is easy to put a question so full of false assumptions that no true answer to it is possible; and many a laborious man of science has spent his life in framing such questions, and in looking for an answer to them. The contribution of the nineteenth century to the science of flight was that it got hold of the right questions, and formulated them more or less exactly, so that the answers, when once they were supplied by continued observation and experiment, were things of value.

The earliest of these pioneers was Sir George Cayley, a country gentleman with estates in Yorkshire and Lincolnshire, who devoted his life to scientific pursuits. He was born in 1773, and the balloons which excited the world during his boyhood directed his mind to the subject of aerial navigation. He invented many mechanical contrivances, and he laid great and just stress on the importance of motive power for successful flight. In 1809 he published, in *Nicholson's Journal*, a paper on Aerial Navigation, which has since become a classic, for although it stops short of a complete exposition, it is true so far as it goes, and contains no nonsense and no fantasy. He endeavoured, in the first year of Queen Victoria's reign, to establish an aeronautical society, but the ill repute of the balloon and the bad company it kept deprived him of influential support. He did his duty by his county, as a Whig magnate, and amused his leisure with science, till his death in 1857.

Cayley's work is difficult to assess. He had all the right ideas, though the means of putting them into practice did not lie ready to his hand. If he had been a poor man, he might have gone farther. He designed, so to say, both an airship and an aeroplane; there was no one to execute his designs, and the scheme fell through. He more than once anticipated later inventions, but he put nothing on the market. His mind was fertile in mechanical devices, so that if one proved troublesome, he could always turn his attention to another. He is content to enunciate a truth, and to call it probable, he says:

Probably, in discussing engines of small weight and high power, a much cheaper engine of this sort might be produced by a gas-light apparatus and by firing the inflammable air generated with a due portion of common air under a piston.

This is an exact forecast of the engine used today in all flying machines. He has some good remarks on the shape that offers least resistance to the air in passing through it, that is, on the doctrine of the streamline. He knew that the shape of the hinder part of a solid body which travels through the air is of as much importance as the shape of the fore-part in diminishing resistance. He does not seem to have known that it is of more importance. He knew that the resistance of the air acting on concave wings, or planes, at a small angle of incidence was resolved chiefly into lift, and he suspected that the amount of the lift was greater than the mathematical theory of his day allowed. Above all, his treatise is stimulating, and suggests further inquiry and experiment along lines which have since proved to be the right lines.

Cayley's ideas were developed in practice by John Stringfellow, a manufacturer of lace machinery at Chard, in Somersetshire, and by his friend W. S. Henson, a young engineer. They constructed a light steam-engine, and designed an aeroplane, of which they entertained such high hopes that they took out a patent, and applied to Parliament for an Act to incorporate an Aerial Steam Transit Company. The reaction of public opinion on their proposals took the form of drag rather than lift, and they were thrown back on their own resources. In 1847 they made a model aeroplane, twenty feet in span, driven by two four-bladed airscrews, three feet in diameter, and they experimented with it on Bala Down, near Chard.

It did not fly. Henson, completely discouraged, married and went to America; Stringfellow persisted, and in 1848 made a smaller model, ten feet in span, with airscrews sixteen inches in diameter. This machine, which had wings slightly cambered, with a rigid leading edge and a flexible trailing edge, made several successful flights, first in a long covered room at Chard, and later, before a number of witnesses, at Cremorne Gardens. After this success Stringfellow did no more for many years, until the foundation of the Aeronautical Society of Great Britain in 1866 roused him again to activity. At the society's exhibition of 1868, held in the Crystal Palace, he produced a model triplane, which ran along suspended from a wire, and, when its engine was in action, lifted itself as it ran.

The foundation of the Aeronautical Society, with the Duke of Argyll as president and with a council of men of science, attracted fresh minds to the study of flight, and gave the subject a respectable standing. Mr. Wenham's paper, read to the society on the 27th of June 1866, proved that the effective sustaining area of a wing is limited to a narrow portion behind the leading edge; that, in order to increase this area, the planes of a flying machine might advantageously be placed one above another—an idea which was borrowed and put into practice by Mr. Stringfellow in his triplane—and that a heavy body, supported on planes, requires less power to drive it through the air at a high speed than to maintain it in flight at a low speed.

For some years the society flourished; then its energies declined, and it fell into a state of suspended animation. At its second exhibition, in 1885, there were only sixteen exhibits as against seventy-eight at the exhibition of 1868. The prospects of practical success seemed remoter than ever. At last, thirty years after its foundation, it sprang into renewed activity, and, with Major B. F. S. Baden-Powell as secretary, did an immense work, from 1897 onwards, in directing and furthering the study of aviation. The *Aeronautical Journal*, which was published quarterly by the revived society, is a record of the years of progress and triumph.

The cause of this sudden revival is to be sought in the extraordinary fermentation which had been going on under the surface, both in Europe and America. The public was careless and sceptical; inventors who were seeking practical success were shy of premature publicity; papers read to learned societies were more concerned with theory than with practice; but there was hope in the air, and hundreds of minds were independently at work on the problem of flight. Some idea of the variety of suggestions and devices may be gathered from Mr. Octave Chanute's *Progress in Flying Machines*, a reprint of a series of articles by him, which appeared, from 1891 onwards, in *The Railroad and Engineering Journal* of New York City.

It was said in the ancient world that there is nothing so absurd but some philosopher has believed it; there is no imaginable way of flight that has not engaged the time and effort of some inventor. Yet among the multitude of attempts it is not difficult to trace the ancestry of the modern flying machine. Wing-flapping machines left no issue. Machines supported in the air by helicopters, that is, by horizontal revolving blades, can be made to rise from the ground, but cannot easily be made to travel. The way to success was by imitation of soaring birds; and it is worthy of note that some of the best minds were, from the first, fascinated by this method of flight, and were never tired of observing it.

Cayley remarks that the swift, though it is a powerful flyer, is not able to elevate itself from level ground. Wenham records how an eagle, sitting in solitary state in the midst of the Egyptian plain, was fired at with a shotgun, and had to run full twenty yards, digging its talons into the soil, before it could raise itself into the air. M. Mouillard, of Cairo, spent more than thirty years in watching the flight of soaring birds, and devoted the whole of his book, *L'Empire de l'Air* (1881), to the investigation of soaring flight. The pelican, the turkey-buzzard, the vulture, the condor, have all had their students and disciples.

M. Mouillard, indeed, maintains that if there be a moderate wind, a bird can remain a whole day soaring in the air, with no expenditure of power whatever. To those who have watched sea-gulls this may perhaps seem credible; but air is invisible, and soaring birds are skilful to choose a place, in the wake of a ship or in the neighbourhood of a cliff, where there is an up-current of air, so that when they glide by their own weight, though they are losing height in relation to the air, they are losing none in relation to the surface of the earth.

The parents of the modern flying machine were the gliders, that is, the men who launched themselves into the air on wings or planes of their own devising. The scientific investigators, who experimented with machines embodying the same principle, did much to assist the gliders, but in justice they must take a second place. The men who staked their lives were the men who, after many losses, were rewarded with the conquest of the air. There are stories of a certain Captain Lebris, how in 1854, near Douarnenez in Brittany, he constructed an artificial albatross, and tying it by a slip rope to a cart which was driven against the wind, mounted in it to a height of three hundred feet.

But the first glider of whom we have any full knowledge is Otto Lilienthal of Berlin. He devoted his whole life to the study of aviation at a time when in Germany people looked upon such a pursuit as little better than lunacy. The principal professor of mathematics at the Berlin Gewerbe Academie, on hearing that Lilienthal was experimenting with aeronautics, advised him to spend no money on such things—a piece of advice which, Lilienthal remarks, was unhappily quite superfluous. In 1889 he completed, with the help of his brother, a series of experiments on the carrying capacity of arched, or cambered, wings, and published the results in a book entitled *Bird Flight as the Basis of Aviation*. In his youth every crow that flew by presented him with a problem to solve in its slowly moving wings. Prolonged study led him to the conclusion that the slight fore-and-aft curvature of the wing was the secret of flying.

But he knew too much to suppose that this conclusion solved the problem. A dozen other difficulties, including the difficulty of balance, remained to be mastered. When German societies for the advancement of aerial navigation began to be formed, he at first held aloof from them, for the balloon, which he regarded as the chief obstacle to the development of flight, monopolized their entire attention. His insistence on the cambered wing did not convince others, who went on experimenting with flat planes. German and Austrian aviators, it is true, were induced by his book to put aside flat surfaces and introduce arched wings, he remarks:

> However, as this was done mainly on paper, in projects, and in aeronautical papers and discussions, I felt impelled myself to carry out my theory in practice.

So, in the summer of 1891, on a pair of bird-like wings, with eighty-six square feet of supporting surface, stabilised by a horizontal tail and a vertical fin aft, he began his gliding experiments. His whole apparatus, made of peeled willow sticks, covered with cotton shirting, weighed less than forty pounds. He was supported in it wholly on his forearms, which passed through padded tubes, while his hands grasped a cross-bar. He guided the machine and preserved its balance by shifting his weight, backwards or forwards or sideways. In this apparatus, altered and improved from time to time, Lilienthal, during the next five years, made more than two thousand successful glides.

At first, he used to jump off a spring-board; then he practised on some hills in the suburbs of Berlin; then, in the spring of 1894, he built a conical hill at Gross-Lichterfelde to serve him as a starting-ground. Later on, he moved to the Rhinow hills. His best glides were made against a light breeze at a gradient of about 1 in 10; and he could easily travel a hundred yards through the air, he says:

> Regulating the centre of gravity, becomes a second nature, like balancing on a bicycle; it is entirely a matter of practice and experience.

His most alarming experiences were from gusts of wind which would suddenly raise him many metres in the air and suspend him in a stationary position. But his skill was so great that he always succeeded in resuming his flight and alighting safely. He continued to improve and develop his machine. He made a double-surface glider, on the biplane principle, and flew on it. He experimented with engines, intended to flap the extremities of the wings—first a steam-engine of two horse-power, weighing forty-four pounds, then a simpler and lighter type, worked by compressed carbonic acid gas. But he explains that these can be safely introduced only if they do not impair the gliding efficiency of the machine, and he does not seem to have made much progress with them.

His last improvement was a movable horizontal tail, or elevator, worked by a line attached to his head, to control the fore-and-aft balance of the machine. This fresh complexity was perhaps the cause of his death. On the 9th of August 1896 he started on a long glide from a hill about a hundred feet high; a sudden gust of wind caught him, and it is supposed that the involuntary movements of his head in the effort to regain his balance made matters worse; the machine plunged to the ground, and he was fatally injured.

Lilienthal was a good mathematician, a careful recorder of the results of his experiments, and a disinterested student of nature. Complete success was denied to him, but his work informed and stimulated others. The Wright brothers, when they first took up the problem of flight, had the advantage of acquaintance with Professor S. P. Langley's aeronautical researches, but their gliding experiments were shaped and inspired by what they had read of Lilienthal's achievements.

The other pioneer, who has earned a place beside Lilienthal, is Percy Pilcher. In 1893, at the age of twenty-seven, he became assistant lecturer in naval architecture and marine engineering at Glasgow University. He devoted all his spare time to aeronautics, and in 1895 built his first glider, which he named 'The Bat'. The machine was built, with the help of his sister, in the sitting-room of their lodging in Kersland Street, Glasgow, and was tested on the banks of the Clyde, near Cardross. Some defects were revealed by the tests; when these were remedied, and the glider was towed by a rope, Pilcher rose to a height of twenty feet, and remained in the air for nearly one minute.

Thereafter he built, in rapid succession, three new gliders, all of different design, which he called 'The Beetle', 'The Gull', and 'The Hawk'. The professor of naval architecture at Glasgow, Sir John Biles, says of him:

He was one of the few men I have met who had no sense of

fear. . . . I was deterred from helping him as much as I ought to have done by a fear of the risks that he ran. He at one time talked to Lord Kelvin about helping him: Lord Kelvin spoke to me about it, and said that on no account would he help him, nor should I, as he would certainly break his neck. This was unfortunately too true a prophecy.'

The Hawk was the best of his gliders; at Eynsford in Kent, on the 19th of June 1897, he made a perfectly balanced glide of 250 yards across a deep valley, towed only by a thin fishing line, 'which one could break with one's hands'. After this, Pilcher began to make plans for fitting an engine to his glider. Since the first appearance of the Otto engine in 1876, and of the Daimler engine eight years later, the oil-engine had steadily developed in lightness and power, but no engine exactly suitable for his purpose was on the market, so he resolved to build one. An engine of four horse-power, weighing forty pounds, with a wooden airscrew five feet in diameter, was, by his calculations, amply sufficient to maintain his glider in horizontal flight.

The light engine has now been so enormously improved, that it comes near to developing one horse-power for every pound of weight. The violent have taken the kingdom of the air by force: in Pilcher's day the problem was more delicate. He worked at his engine in his leisure time, and, leaving the firm of Maxim & Nordenfeldt, by whom he had been employed from 1896 onwards, made, in 1898, his own firm of Wilson & Pilcher.

In the spring of 1899 he was much impressed by Mr. Laurence Hargrave's soaring kites, exhibited by the inventor at a meeting of the Aeronautical Society, and it seems that he embodied some of Mr. Hargrave's ideas in his latest built machine, a triplane. He intended to fly this machine at Stanford Hall, Market Harborough, where he was staying with Lord Braye, but on the day appointed, the 30th of September 1899, the weather proved too wet.

Nevertheless, Pilcher consented to give some demonstrations on The Hawk, towed by a light line; during the second of these, while he was soaring at a height of thirty feet, one of the guy-wires of the tail broke, and the machine turned over and crashed. Pilcher never recovered consciousness, and died two days later. His name will always be remembered in the history of flight. If he had survived his risks for a year or two more, it seems not unlikely that he would have been the first man to navigate the air on a power-driven machine. He left behind him his gallant example, and some advances in design, for he improved the balance of the machine by raising its centre of gravity, and he provided it with wheels, fitted on shock-absorbers, for taking off and alighting.

Lilienthal and Pilcher are pre-eminent among the early gliders, for their efforts were scientific, continuous, and progressive. But there were others; and it is difficult, if not impossible, to determine the comparative value of experiments carried on, many of them in private, by inventors of all countries. Professor J. J. Montgomery, of California, carried out some successful glides, on machines of his own devising, as early as 1884; and Mr. Octave Chanute, the best historian of all these early efforts, having secured the services of Mr, A. M. Herring, a much younger man who had already learned to use a Lilienthal machine, made a series of experiments, with gliders of old and new types, on the shores of Lake Michigan, during the summer of 1896.

About the same time some power-driven machines, attached to prepared tracks, were successfully flown. In 1893 Horatio Phillips flew a model, with many planes arranged one above another like a Venetian blind, on a circular track at Harrow; and in the same year Sir Hiram Maxim's large machine, with four thousand feet of supporting surface, was built at Baldwin's Park in Kent, and, when it was tested, developed so great a lift that it broke the guide rails placed to restrain it. Clement Ader, a French electrical engineer, worked at the problem of flight for many years, and, having obtained the support of the French Government, constructed a large bat-like machine, driven by a steam-engine of forty horse-power.

In 1897 this machine was secretly tried, at the military camp of Satory, near Paris, and was reported on by a government commission; all that was known thereafter was that the government had refused to advance further funds, and that Ader had abandoned his attempts. When the Wrights had made their successful flights, a legend of earlier flights by Ader grew up in France; a heated controversy ensued, and the friends of M. Santos Dumont, who claimed that he was the first to fly over French soil, at length induced the French Government to publish the report on the trial of Ader's machine. The report proved that the machine had not left the ground.

It is not in mortals to command success; but those who study the record of the ingenious, persevering, and helpful work done for a quarter of a century by Mr. Laurence Hargrave, of Sydney, New South Wales, will agree with Mr. Chanute that this man deserved success. His earliest important paper was read to the Royal Society of New South Wales in 1884. In the course of the next ten years he made with his own hands eighteen different flying machines, of increasing size, all of which flew. His earlier machines were not much larger than toys, and were supplied with power by the pull of stretched india-rubber. On this scale he was successful with a machine driven by an airscrew and with a machine driven by the flapping of wings.

As his machines grew in size he turned his attention to engines. He was successful with compressed air; he made many experiments with explosion motors; and he succeeded in producing a steam-engine which weighed seven pounds and developed almost two-thirds of one horse-power. In 1893 he invented the box-kite, which is a true biplane, with the vertical sides of the kite doing the work of a stabilizing fin. This kite had a marked influence on the design of some early flying machines. He also invented the soaring kite. His hope that man would fly was more than hope; he refused to argue the question with objectors, for 'I know, he said, 'that success is dead sure to come'.

Moreover, he put all his researches at the disposal of others. He refused to take out any patents. He did all he could to induce workers to follow his example and communicate their ideas freely, so that progress might be quickened. His own ideas, his own inventions, and his own carefully recorded experiments were a solid step in that staircase of knowledge from which at last man launched himself into the air, and flew.

In America the pioneer who did most to further the science of human flight was Professor Samuel Pierpont Langley, of the Smithsonian Institute, in Washington. He was well known as an astronomer before ever he took up with aeronautics. From 1866 to 1887 he was professor of astronomy at the Western University of Pennsylvania, at Pittsburg. During his later years there he built a laboratory for aerial investigations, and carried out his famous experiments. His whirling table, with an arm about thirty feet long, which could be moved at all speeds up to seventy miles an hour, was devised to measure the lifting power of air resistance on brass plates suspended to the arm.

In 1891 he published his *Experiments in Aerodynamics*, which embodied the definite mathematical results obtained by years of careful research. It would be difficult to exaggerate the importance of this work. The law which governs the reaction of the air on planes travelling at various speeds and various angles of incidence had been guessed at, or seen in glimpses, by earlier investigators; but here were ascertained numerical values offered to students and inventors. The main result is best stated in Professor Langley's own words:

> When the arm was put in motion I found that the faster it went the less weight the plates registered on the scales, until at great speed they almost floated in the air.... I found that only one-twentieth of the force before supposed to be required to support bodies under such conditions was needed, and what before had seemed impossible began to look possible.... Some mathematicians, reasoning from false data, had concluded that if it took a certain amount of power to keep a thing from falling, it would take much additional power to make it advance. My experiment showed just the reverse ... that the faster the speed the less the force required to sustain the planes, and that it would cost less to transport such planes through the air at a high rate of speed than at a low one. I found further that one horse-power could carry brass plates weighing two hundred pounds at the rate of more than forty miles an hour in horizontal flight.

When these researches were known and understood, their effect upon the practical handling of the problem of flight was immediate and decisive. The aeroplane, or gliding machine, had many rivals; they were all killed by Professor Langley's researches, which showed that the cheapest and best way to raise a plane in the air is to drive it forward at a small upward inclination; and that its weight can be best countered not by applying power to raise it vertically, but by driving it fast. In the statistical tables that he prepared he called the upward pressure of the air *Lift*; the pressure which retards horizontal motion he called *Drift*. The words make a happy pair, but the word Drift is badly needed to describe the leeway of an aeroplane in a cross-wind, so that in England another pair of words, *Lift* and *Drag*, has been authoritatively substituted.

From this time onward Langley devoted himself to those other problems, especially the problems of balance, of mechanical power, and of safety in taking off and alighting, which had to be solved if he was to make a machine that should fly. He was much influenced, he says, by a mechanical toy, produced as early as 1871 by an ingenious Frenchman called Penaud, and named by its inventor the 'planophore'. This toy, which weighed only a little over half an ounce, was supported on wings, and was driven forward by an airscrew made of two feathers. The motive power was supplied by twisted strands of rubber which, as they untwisted, turned the airscrew.

The wings were set at a dihedral angle, that is, they were bent upwards at the tips; and fore-and-aft stability was secured by a smaller pair of wings just in front of the airscrew. Professor Langley says:

> Simple as this toy looked, it was the father of a future flying machine, and France ought to have the credit of it.

His own steam-driven flying machine was produced and successfully flown in 1896. It had two wings and a tail, with a supporting surface in all of seventy square feet; its total weight was seventy-two pounds; the engine, constructed by himself, weighed only seven pounds and developed one horse-power, which served to drive two airscrews, revolving in opposite directions. The best flight of this machine was more than three-quarters of a mile, and was made over the Potomac River. When, on its first flight, it had flown for a minute, Professor Langley says:

> I felt that something had been accomplished at last, for never in any part of the world or in any period had any machine of man's construction sustained itself in the air before for even half of this briefs time.

His flying machines were called by Langley 'aerodromes', and the word 'aeroplane' was used by him, as it is used in the *New English Dictionary* of 1888, only in the sense of a single plane surface used for aerial experiments. But no usage, however authoritative, can withstand the tide of popular fashion; the machine is now an aeroplane, while aerodrome is the name given to the flying-ground from which it starts.

The success of his machine became widely known, and in 1898 the War Department of the United States, having ascertained that Langley was willing to devote all his spare time to the work, allotted fifty thousand dollars for the development, construction, and test of a large 'aerodrome', big enough to carry a man. The construction was long delayed by the difficulty of finding a suitable engine. This difficulty hampered all early attempts at flight. The internal-combustion engine was by this time pretty well understood, and, with the will to do it, might have been made light enough for the purpose. But it was almost an axiom with engineering firms that a very light engine could not wear well and was untrustworthy in other ways. One horse-power to the hundredweight was what they regarded as the standard of solid merit.

Further, they were prejudiced against that extremely rapid movement of the parts which is necessary if the crank-shaft is to revolve more than a thousand times a minute. They were asked to depart from all their cherished canons and to risk failure and breakdown in order that man should achieve what many of them regarded as an impossibility. It was with Langley as it was with Pilcher and the Wrights; he had to make his own engine. By 1901 he had completed with the aid of his assistants an engine of fifty-two horse-power, weighing, with all its appurtenances, less than five pounds to the horse-power.

A year and a half more was spent in adapting and co-ordinating the frame and appliances, and in carrying out the shop tests. At last, on the 7th of October 1903, from a house-boat moored in the Potomac River, about forty miles below Washington, the first trial was made. The machine caught in the launching mechanism, and fell into the river, where it broke. It was repaired, and a second trial was made on the 8th of December 1903. Again, the machine failed to clear the launching car, and plunged headlong into the river, where the frame was broken by zealous efforts to salve it in the dark. Nine days after this final failure the Wrights made their first successful power-driven flight, at Kitty Hawk, on the coast of North Carolina.

Langley was almost seventy years old when his last and most ambitious machine failed. He lived for two years more. If his contributions to the science of flight, which are his chief title to fame, were ruled out of the account, he would still be remembered as something more than a good astronomer—a man of many sciences, who cared little for his own advancement, and much for the advancement of knowledge.

From what has been said it is now possible to conceive how things stood when the brothers, Wilbur and Orville Wright, first attacked the problem of flying in the air. Men had flown, or rather had glided through the air, without engines to support and drive them. Machines had flown, without men to control and guide them. If the two achievements could be combined in one, the problem was solved; but the combination, besides bringing together both sets of difficulties and dangers, added new dangers and difficulties, greater than either. Plainly, there were two ways, and only two, of going about the business.

Professor Langley held that in order to learn to fly, you must have a flying machine to begin with. Wilbur Wright, whose views on the point never varied from first to last, held that you must have a man to begin with. The brothers were impatient of:

> The wasteful extravagance of mounting delicate and costly machinery on wings which no one knew how to manage.

When they began their experiments, they had already reached the conclusion that the problem of constructing wings to carry the machine, and the problem of constructing a motor to drive it, presented no serious difficulty; but that the problem of equilibrium had been the real stumbling-block, and that this problem of equilibrium was the problem of flight itself. Wilbur Wright says:

> It seemed to us that the main reason why the problem had remained so long unsolved was that no one had been able to obtain any adequate practice. We figured that Lilienthal in five years of time had spent only about five hours in actual gliding through the air. The wonder was not that he had done so little, but that he had accomplished so much. It would not be considered at all safe for a bicycle rider to attempt to ride through a crowded city street after only five hours' practice, spread out in bits of ten seconds each over a period of five years; yet Lilienthal with this brief practice was remarkably successful in meeting the fluctuations and eddies of wind gusts. We thought that if some method could be found by which it would be possible to practise by the hour instead of by the second there would be hope of advancing the solution of a very difficult problem.

When this was written, in 1901, it was a forecast; it is now the history of a triumph. By prolonged scientific practice, undertaken with every possible regard to safety, on soaring and gliding machines, the Wrights became master pilots and conquerors of the air. Their success had in it no element of luck; it was earned, as an acrobat earns his skill. So confident did they become that to the end their machines were all machines of an unstable equilibrium, dependent for their safety on the skill and quickness of the pilot. Their triumph was a triumph of mind and character. Other men had more than their advantages, and failed, where these men succeeded. Great things have sometimes been done by a happy chance; it was not so with the Wrights. They planned great things, and measured themselves against them, and were equal to them.

Wilbur and Orville Wright were the sons of Milton Wright, of Dayton, Ohio. They came of New England stock. One of their ancestors emigrated from Essex in 1636, and settled at Springfield, Massachusetts; a later ancestor moved west, to Dayton. Wilbur was born in 1867, and Orville in 1871. They had two elder brothers and one younger sister; but Wilbur and Orville were so closely united in their lives and in their thoughts, that it is not easy to speak of them apart. Mr. Griffith Brewer, who knew them both, was often asked which of the two was the originator, and would reply, 'I think it was mostly Wilbur'; but would add, 'The thing could not have been done without Orville'.

Wilbur, being four years the elder, no doubt took the lead; but all their ideas and experiments were shared, so that their very thought became a duet. Wilbur, who died in 1912, was a man of a steady mind and of a dominant character, hard-knit, quiet, intense. He has left some writings which reflect his nature; they have a certain grim humour, and they mean business; they push aside all irrelevance, and go straight to the point.

After adventures in printing and journalism the two brothers set up at Dayton as cycle manufacturers. The death of Lilienthal, reported in the newspapers in 1896, first called their attention to flight, and they began to read all available books on the subject. They found that an immense amount of time and money had been spent on the problem of human flight—all to no effect. Makers of machines had abandoned their efforts. As for gliders, after the death of Lilienthal, Mr. Chanute had discontinued his experiments, and, a little later, Mr. Pilcher fell and was killed. When knowledge of these things came to the brothers, it appealed to them like a challenge.

From 1899 onwards, they turned all their thoughts to the problem. They watched the flight of birds to see if they could surprise the secret of balance. They studied gliding machines, and resolved to construct a machine of their own, more or less on the model of Mr. Chanute's most successful glider, which was a biplane, or 'double-decker'. When their machine was partly built, they wrote to the weather bureau at Washington, and learned that the strongest and most constant winds were to be found on the coast of North Carolina. They then wrote to the postmaster of Kitty Hawk, who testified that the sand-hills of that place were round and soft, well fitted for boys playing with flying machines. They took the parts of their machine to Kitty Hawk, assembled and completed it in a tent, and forthwith began their long years of continuous and progressive experiment. Their chief helper was Mr. Chanute, they said:

In the summer of 1901, we became personally acquainted with Mr. Chanute. When he learned that we were interested in flying as a sport and not with any expectation of recovering the money we were expending on it, he gave us much encouragement. At our invitation he spent several weeks with us at our camp at Kill Devil Hill, four miles south of Kitty Hawk, during our experiments of that and the two succeeding years.

The first two summers, 1900 and 1901, brought them some familiarity in the handling of their first two gliders, which they navigated lying face downward on the lower plane. In all their gliding experiments they studied safety first. They knew that the business they had embarked on was of necessity a long and dangerous one; that they were bound to encounter many dangers, and that each of them had only one life. They took no avoidable risks. Gliding seemed to them, at first, to have been discredited by the deaths of Lilienthal and Pilcher, so they planned to try their machine by tethering it with a rope and letting it float a few feet from the ground, while they practised manipulation.

The wind proved to be not strong enough to sustain the weighted machine, and they were compelled to take to gliding. All their early glides were made as near the ground as possible. The machine had no vertical rudder, but they fitted it, in front, with what they called a horizontal rudder, that is, an elevator. By the use of this they could bring it to the ground at once when the wind was tricky and their balance was threatened. The lateral balance they attempted to control by warping the wings, but with no satisfactory results. They made glides longer than any on record, but while the problem of stability was still unsolved, there could be no real progress. At the end of 1901, Wilbur Wright made the prediction that men would some time fly, but that it would not be in their lifetime.

They returned to Dayton, and spent the winter in experiment and research. They had taken up aeronautics partly as a sport; they were now drawn deeper and deeper into the scientific study of it. They made a wind-tunnel, sixteen inches square and about six feet long, and tested in it the lift and drag of model wings, made in various sizes and with various aspect ratios. The tables which they compiled from these experiments were continually used by them thereafter, and superseded the tables of Lilienthal and Langley, which took no account of the aspect ratio.

When they returned to Kitty Hawk, in the autumn of 1902, they took with them a greatly improved glider. The aspect ratio of the planes was six to one, instead of about three to one, as in their second glider. Further, while preserving the horizontal vane, or elevator, at the front of the machine, they added a vertical vane, or rudder, at the rear. It was their failure to control the lateral balance in the experiments of 1901 that suggested this device to them. From the first they had discarded the method, practised by Lilienthal and Pilcher, of adjusting the lateral balance by shifting the weight of the operator's body. This method seemed to them:

> Incapable of expansion to meet large conditions, because the weight to be moved and the distance of possible motion were limited, while the disturbing forces steadily increased, both with wing area and with wing velocity.

Accordingly, they invented a method of warping the wings, to present them to the wind at different angles on the right and left sides. Thus, the force of the wind was used to restore the balance which the wind itself had disturbed. But in their early gliders this warping process acted in an unexpected way. The wing which, in order to raise that side of the machine, was presented to the wind at the greater angle of incidence often proved to be the wing which lagged and sank. The decrease in speed, due to the extra drag, more than counterbalanced the effect of the larger angle. When they attempted to remedy this by introducing a fixed vertical vane in the rear, 'it increased the trouble and made the machine absolutely dangerous'. Any side-slip became irrecoverable by causing the vertical fixed vane to strike the wind on the side toward the low wing, instead of on the side toward the high wing, as it should have done to correct the balance, the brothers remark:

> It was some time before a remedy was discovered. This consisted of movable rudders working in conjunction with the twisting of the wings.'

So that now three different parts of the machine had to be controlled by wires, worked swiftly and correctly by the operator, to preserve the balance. There were the wing tips which had to be warped. There was the horizontal vane in front which had to be adjusted, to keep the machine in level flight or to bring it to the ground. There was the vertical vane behind which had to be moved this way and that to secure the desired effect from the warping of the wings. Wilbur Wright says:

> For the sake of simplicity, we decided to attach the wires controlling the vertical tail to the wires warping the wings, so that the operator, instead of having to control three things at once, would have to attend to only the forward horizontal rudder and the wing warping mechanism; and only the latter would be needed for controlling lateral balance.

The thing was done. They had built an aeroplane that could fly; and the later introduction of an engine was as simple a matter as the harnessing of a horse to a carriage. Wilbur Wright, speaking of the glider of 1902 says:

> With this apparatus, we made nearly seven hundred glides in the two or three weeks following. We flew it in calms and we flew it in winds as high as thirty-five miles an hour. We steered it to right and left, and performed all the evolutions necessary for flight. This was the first time in the history of the world that a movable vertical tail had been used in controlling the direction or the balance of a flying machine. It was also the first time that a movable vertical tail had been used, in combination with wings adjustable to different angles of incidence, in controlling the balance and direction of an aeroplane. We were the first to functionally employ a movable vertical tail in a flying aeroplane. We were the first to employ wings adjustable to respectively different angles of incidence in a flying aeroplane. We were the first to use the two in combination in a flying aeroplane.

It is a large claim, and every word of it is true. New inventions are commonly the work of many minds, and it would be easy to name at least half a dozen men to whose work the Wrights were indebted. But these were tributaries; the main achievement belongs wholly to the Wrights. Their quiet perseverance, through long years, in the face of every kind of difficulty, is only a part of their distinction; the alertness and humility of mind which refused all traffic with fixed ideas, and made dangers and disappointments the material of education, is what stamps them with greatness. They put themselves to school to the winds. They knew that there is no cheap or easy way to master nature, and that only the human spirit, at its best and highest, can win through in that long struggle. Their patience never failed. Wilbur Wright says:

Skill comes by the constant repetition of familiar feats rather than by a few over-bold attempts at feats for which the performer is yet hardly prepared. (Man must learn to fly as he learns to walk.) Before trying to rise to any dangerous height a man ought to know that in an emergency his mind and muscles will work by instinct rather than by conscious effort. There is no time to think.

The machine of 1902, which might be called the victory machine, deserves a full description. It was a double-decked machine, with two planes fixed by struts one above the other about five feet apart. The planes were thirty-two feet in span, and five feet in chord. The total area of their supporting surfaces was about three hundred and five square feet. The operator lay on his face in the middle of the lower plane. The horizontal rudder in front had a supporting surface of fifteen square feet. The vertical tail, as they called it, which was the true rudder, was reduced after trial to six square feet. The machine was supported on the ground by skids, and was very strongly built. It weighed a hundred and sixteen and a half pounds, to which must be added about a hundred and forty pounds for the weight of the operator. It performed about a thousand glides, with only one injury, though it made many hard landings at full speed on uneven ground. The longest glide was 622½ feet, traversed in twenty-six seconds. The glides were made from the Kill Devil sand-hills, near Kitty Hawk—mounds of sand heaped up by the wind, the biggest having a height of a hundred feet.

The time had now come to invite an engine to bear a part in the proceedings. In the autumn of 1903 the brothers returned to Kitty Hawk for their fourth season of experiment. They had built in the winter a machine weighing six hundred pounds, including the operator and an eight horse-power motor. Finding that the motor gave more power than had been estimated, they added a hundred and fifty pounds of weight in strengthening the wings and other parts. The airscrews, built from their own calculations, gave in useful work two-thirds of the power expended. Before trying this machine, however, they continued their practice with the old glider, and made a number of flights in which they remained in the air for over a minute, often soaring for a considerable time in one spot, without any descent at all.

It was late in the season, the 17th of December 1903, when they first tried the power machine. A general invitation to be present at the trial had been given to the people living within five or six miles, but:

> Not many were willing to face the rigours of a cold December wind in order to see, as they no doubt thought, another flying machine *not* fly.

Five persons besides the brothers were present. Mr. Orville Wright's narrative, written for the Aeronautical Society of Great Britain, must be given in his own words:

> On the morning of December 17th, between the hours of 10.30 o'clock and noon, four flights were made, two by Mr. Orville Wright, and two by Mr. Wilbur Wright. The starts were all made from a point on the levels, and about 200 feet west of our camp, which is located about a quarter of a mile north of the Kill Devil Sand Hill, in Dare County, North Carolina.
>
> The wind at the time of the flights had a velocity of twenty-seven miles an hour at 10 o'clock, and 24 miles an hour at noon, as recorded by the anemometer at the Kitty Hawk weather bureau station. This anemometer is 30 feet from the ground. Our own measurements, made with a hand-anemometer at a height of four feet from the ground, showed a velocity of about 22 miles when the first flight was made, and 20½ miles at the time of the last one. The flights were directly against the wind. Each time the machine started from the level ground by its own power alone, with no assistance from gravity or any other sources whatever.
>
> After a run of about 40 feet along a mono-rail track, which held the machine eight inches from the ground, it rose from the track and, under the direction of the operator, climbed upward on an inclined course till a height of 8 or 10 feet from the ground was reached, after which the course was kept as near horizontal as the wind gusts and the limited skill of the operator would permit. Into the teeth of a December gale the Flyer made its way forward with a speed of 10 miles an hour over the ground, and 30 to 35 miles an hour through the air.
>
> It had previously been decided that, for reasons of personal safety, these first trials should be made as close to the ground as possible. The height chosen was scarcely sufficient for manoeuvring in so gusty a wind and with no previous acquaintance with the conduct of the machine and its controlling mechanisms. Consequently, the first flight was short. The succeeding

flights rapidly increased in length and at the fourth trial a flight of 59 seconds was made, in which time the machine flew a little more than a half-mile through the air and a distance of 852 feet over the ground. The landing was due to a slight error of judgement on the part of the operator.

After passing over a little hummock of sand, in attempting to bring the machine down to the desired height the operator turned the rudder too far, and the machine turned downward more quickly than had been expected. The reverse movement of the rudder was a fraction of a second too late to prevent the machine from touching the ground and thus ending the flight. The whole occurrence occupied little, if any, more than one second of time.

Only those who are acquainted with practical aeronautics can appreciate the difficulties of attempting the first trials of a flying machine in a 25-mile gale. As winter was already well set in, we should have postponed our trials to a more favourable season, but for the fact that we were determined, before returning home, to know whether the machine possessed sufficient power to fly, sufficient strength to withstand the shock of landings, and sufficient capacity of control to make flight safe in boisterous winds, as well as in calm air.

When these points had been definitely established, we at once packed our goods and returned home, knowing that the age of the flying machine had come at last.

CHAPTER 2

The Aeroplane and the Airship

The age of the flying machine had come at last. A power-driven aeroplane had been built, and had been flown under the control of its pilot. What remained to do was to practise with it and test it; to improve it, and perfect it, and put it on the market. The time allowed for all this was not long; in less than eleven years, if only the world had known it, the world would be at war, and would be calling for aeroplanes by the thousand.

Romance, for all that it is inspired by real events, is never quite like real life. It makes much of prominent dates and crises, and passes lightly and carelessly over the intervening shallows and flats. Yet these shallows and flats are the place where human endurance and purpose are most severely tested. The problem of flight had been solved; the people of the world, it might be expected, springing to attention, would salute the new invention, and welcome the new era. Nothing of the kind happened. America, which is more famous for journalistic activity than any other country on earth, remained profoundly inattentive. The Wrights returned to their home at Dayton, and there continued their experiments.

A legend has grown up that these experiments were conducted under a close-drawn veil of secrecy. On the contrary, the proceedings of the brothers were singularly public—indeed, for the preservation of their title to their own invention, almost dangerously public. Wilbur Wright says:

> In the spring of 1904, through the kindness of Mr. Torrence Huffman, of Dayton, Ohio, we were permitted to erect a shed, and to continue experiments, on what is known as the Huffman Prairie, at Simms Station, eight miles east of Dayton. The

new machine was heavier and stronger, but similar to the one flown at Kill Devil Hill. When it was ready for its first trial every newspaper in Dayton was notified, and about a dozen representatives of the Press were present. Our only request was that no pictures be taken, and that the reports be unsensational, so as not to attract crowds to our experiment grounds. There were probably fifty persons altogether on the ground. When preparations had been completed a wind of only three or four miles was blowing—insufficient for starting on so short a track—but since many had come a long way to see the machine in action, an attempt was made.

To add to the other difficulty, the engine refused to work properly. The machine, after running the length of the track, slid off the end without rising into the air at all. Several of the newspaper men returned again the next day, but were again disappointed. The engine performed badly, and after a glide of only sixty feet the machine came to the ground. Further trial was postponed till the motor could be put in better running condition. The reporters had now, no doubt, lost confidence in the machine, though their reports, in kindness, concealed it. Later, when they heard that we were making flights of several minutes' duration, knowing that longer flights had been made with airships, and not knowing any essential difference between airships and flying machines, they were but little interested.

The indifference and scepticism of the public and the press provided a very effective veil of secrecy, and the brothers prosecuted their researches undisturbed. In 1904 they made more than a hundred flights, practising turning movements and complete circles, and learning how to handle the machine so as to prevent it from 'stalling', that is, from losing flying speed and falling to earth out of control when the air resistance caused by its manoeuvring reduced its speed. In 1905 they built another machine and resumed their experiments in the same field. They did not want to attract a crowd. The cars on the electric line adjoining the field ran every thirty minutes, and they timed their flights between the runs.

The farmers living nearby saw the flying, but their business was with the earth, not the air, and after looking on for two years they lost what little interest they had. On the 5th of October 1905 one of them, from a neighbouring field, saw the great white form rushing round on its circular course in the air. 'Well,' he remarked, 'the boys are at it again'; and he kept on cutting corn.

The season's work is summarised by Mr. Orville Wright in a letter dated the 17th of November 1905, and communicated to the Aeronautical Society of Great Britain:

> Up to September 6 we had the machine on but eight different days, testing a number of changes which we had made since 1904. . . . During the month of September we gradually improved in our practice, and on the 26th made a flight of a little over eleven miles. On the 30th we increased this to twelve and one-fifth miles, on October 3 to fifteen and one-third miles, on October 4 to twenty and three-fourth miles, and on the 5th to twenty-four and one-fourth miles.
>
> All of these flights were made at about thirty-eight miles an hour, the flight of the 5th occupying thirty minutes three seconds. . . . We had intended to place the record above the hour, but the attention these flights were beginning to attract compelled us suddenly to discontinue our experiments in order to prevent the construction of the machine from becoming public. The machine passed through all of these flights without the slightest damage. In each of these flights we returned frequently to the starting-point, passing high over the heads of the spectators.

A young druggist called Foust, a friend of the Wrights, was present at the flight of the 5th of October. He was told not to divulge what he had seen, but his enthusiasm would not be restrained, and he talked to such effect that next day the field was crowded with sightseers and the fences were lined with photographers. Very reluctantly the brothers ended their work for the year. They took apart their flyer, and brought it back to the city.

From this time on, for a period of almost three years, the brothers disappear from view. The secrets which it had cost them so much time and effort to discover might, by a single photograph, be made into public property. They were bound to do what they could to assert their claim to their own invention. Their first task was to secure patent rights in their machine; and, after that, to negotiate with the American, French, and British Governments for its purchase. The bringer of so great a gift as flight is worthy of his reward; but the attitude of the brothers to their hard-won possession was not selfish or commercial.

They thought more of their responsibilities than of their profits; and in attempting to dispose of their machine they handled the matter as if it were a public trust.

These years were full of disappointment, much unlike the earlier years of progress and open-air holiday and happiness. No one, except a few intimates and disciples, believed in the Wrights' achievements. The American Government would not touch their invention. When it was thrice offered to the British Government, between the years 1906 and 1908, it was thrice refused, twice by the War Office and once by the Admiralty. At an earlier period, the French Government, more active than the other two, sent Captain Ferber, who had made many gliding experiments of his own, to report after viewing the machine at Dayton. The Wrights refused to show it to him, but their account of what they had done impressed him by its truthfulness, and he reported in their favour, though he told them that there was not a man in all France who believed that they had done what they claimed.

The French Government would not buy; and things were at a standstill, until Mr. Hart O. Berg, a good man of business who had helped the Wrights to secure their patents, urged on them the necessity of putting in an appearance in Europe and showing what they could do. By this time, they had made various improvements, especially in their engine, and had supplied themselves with two machines. With one of these, in the summer of 1908, Wilbur Wright came to France; with the other Orville Wright was to attempt to secure the contract in America for an army aeroplane.

A French syndicate had agreed to buy the Wright patents and a certain number of machines on condition that two flights of not less than fifty kilometres each should be made in a single week, the machines to carry a passenger or an equivalent weight, and the flights to be made in a wind of not less than eleven metres a second, that is, about twenty-five miles an hour. The conditions for the American army contract were no less severe. The machine was to remain in continuous flight for at least an hour; it was to be steered in all directions; and was to land, without damage, at its starting-point.

The place chosen for the French tests was the Hunaudières racecourse, near Le Mans. There Wilbur Wright set up his shed, and, from the 8th of August onward, made many little flights, showing his complete control of his machine by the elaborate manoeuvres which he performed in the air.

On the 9th of September there came the news that Orville Wright had flown for over an hour at Fort Myer in America. This liberated Wilbur Wright, who had been holding back in order to give America the precedence, and on the 21st of September he flew for more than an hour and a half, covering a distance of over sixty miles. About three weeks later he fulfilled the conditions of his test by successive passenger-carrying flights. Encouraged by his example, two distinguished French pioneers, Henri Farman and Léon Delagrange, soon began to make long flights on French machines, and from this time onwards the progress of flying was rapid and immense.

A great industry came into being, and, after a short time, ceased to pay any tribute whatever to the inventors. Merely to secure recognition of their priority, it became necessary for the Wrights to bring actions at law against the infringers of their patents. The tedious and distasteful business of these law-suits troubled and shortened the days of Wilbur Wright, who died at Dayton on the 30th of May 1912. In 1913, by arrangement between the parties, a test action was begun against the British Government. When the war broke out, and the trial of this action was still pending, the supporters of the Wrights hastily met, and offered to forgo all their claims for fifteen thousand pounds, a sum substantial enough to establish the Wrights' priority, yet merely nominal as a payment for the benefits conferred.

So, the matter was settled. The last thoughts of Wilbur Wright were given, not to financial profits, but to further developments of the art of flight. He was constantly meditating on the possibility of soaring flight, which should take advantage of the wind currents, and maintain the machine in the air with but little expenditure of power. In a letter written not many days before he died, and addressed to a German aviator at the Johannisthal flying camp, he says:

> There must be a method whereby human beings can remain in the air once they really find themselves aloft. . . . The birds can do it. Why shouldn't men?

The coming of the war, with its peremptory demand for power and yet more power, did much to develop strong flight, but postponed experiment on this delicate and fascinating problem.

The name of the Wrights is so much the greatest name in the history of flying that it is only fair to give their achievements a separate place. In 1905 they were in possession of a practical flying machine. In 1908 they proved their powers and established their claims in the sight of the world. During these three years events had not stood still; European inventors were busy with experiments. There were rumours of the American success, but the rumours were disbelieved, and the problem was attacked again from the beginning. Long after the Wrights had circled in the air, at their own free will, over the Huffman Prairie, European inventors were establishing records, as they believed, by hopping off the ground for a few yards in machines of their own construction.

The earliest of these European pioneers was Mr. I. C. H. Ellehammer, a Danish engineer, who had built motorcycles and light cars. In 1904 he built a flying machine, and having prepared a ground in the small Danish island of Lindholm, suspended the machine by a wire attached to a central mast, and tested its lifting power. In the course of his experiments he increased his engine-power, and added to the first birdlike pair of wings a second pair placed above them. With this improved machine he claims to have made, on the 12th of September 1906, the first free flight in Europe, travelling in the air for forty-two metres at a height of a metre and a half.

With later machines he had some successes, but the rapid progress of French aviation left him behind, and his latest invention was an application to the aeroplane of a helicopter, to raise it vertically in the air. The helicopter idea continues to fascinate some inventors, and it would be rash to condemn it, but the most it seems to promise is a flight like that of the lark—an almost vertical ascent and a glide to earth again. A machine of this kind might conceivably, at some future time, become a substitute, in war, for the kite balloon; it is not likely to supersede the aeroplane.

Of all European countries France was the most intelligent and the most alert in taking up the problem of flight. The enduring rivalry between the airship and the flying machine is well illustrated in the history of French effort. Long before the first true flying machine was built and flown balloons of a fish-like shape had been driven through the air by mechanical airscrews. A bird is much heavier than the air it displaces; a fish is about the same weight as the water it displaces; and the question which of the two examples is better for aircraft, whether flying or swimming is the better mode, remained an open question, dividing opinion and distracting effort.

The debate is not yet concluded. It is now not very hazardous to say that both methods are good, and that the partisans of the one side and the other were right in their faith and wrong in their heresy-hunting. National rivalry certainly quickened the competition between the two modes; the early progress of aviation in France gave a great impulse to the. development of the Zeppelin in Germany. But the two modes are so entirely distinct that they are better treated separately. None of the chief nations of the world has dared wholly to neglect either; from the very beginning the two have grown up side by side, and interest has been concentrated now on the one and now on the other.

When, in 1912, Great Britain took in hand the creation of an air force, military and naval, France was already furnished with a very large number of aeroplanes, organised for service with the army, and Germany was provided with airships of unprecedented power and range. France also had some airships, and Germany, alarmed by the progress of French aviation, had begun to turn her attention to aeroplanes, but the pride of Germany was in her airships, and the pride of France was in her aeroplanes. These were the conditions with which Great Britain had to reckon; they had grown up rapidly in the course of a few years; and it will be convenient to speak first of the airship, which, invented by France, was adopted and improved by Germany; and then of the aeroplane, which was made by France into so formidable a military engine that Germany had no choice but to imitate again.

Meantime Great Britain, during the earlier years of these developments, entrusted her aerial fortunes to a few balloons, which were operated by the Royal Engineers and were not very favourably regarded by the chiefs of the army. The unpreparedness of Great Britain in all national crises is a time-honoured theme. The Englishman, if he does not wholly distrust science, at least distrusts theory. Facts excite him, and rouse him to exertion. In an address delivered in 1910, Mr. R. B. Haldane, who consistently did all that he could to promote and encourage science, uttered a prophecy which deserves record.

> When a new invention, like the submarine or the motor, comes to light, the Englishman is usually behind. Give him a few years and he has not only taken care of himself in the meantime, but is generally leading. As it was with these inventions, so I suspect it will prove to be with aircraft.

The airship, like the balloon, was a French invention. When the balloon first came into vogue many attempts were made to deflect or guide its course by the use of oars. Those who made these attempts were almost unanimous in declaring that the use of oars enabled them to alter the course of a balloon by several points of the compass. Another method of steering employed sails, held up to the wind by the drag of a guide-rope on the ground. The control to be obtained by means like these was pathetically small, and the real problem was soon seen to be the problem of a motor. The spherical balloon is obviously unsuited for power-navigation; in 1784, only a year after the invention of the balloon, General Meusnier, of the French Army, made designs for an egg-shaped power-balloon to be driven by three airscrews, supported on the rigging between the car and the balloon.

To keep the balloon fully inflated and stiff, in order to drive it against the wind, he planned a double envelope, the inner space to contain hydrogen, the outer space to be pumped full of air. He may thus be said to have invented the ballonet, or air-chamber of the balloon, and to be the father of later successful airships. His designs were mere descriptions; they could not be carried out; there was at that time no light engine in existence, and his own suggestion that the airscrews should be worked by manual labour may be called a design for an engine that weighs something over half a ton for every horsepower of energy exerted.

In 1798 the French author Beaumarchais recommended the construction of airships in the long shape of a fish. As the years passed, models were made on this plan. In 1834 Mr. Monck Mason exhibited at the Lowther Arcade in London a model airship, thirteen and a half feet long, and six and a half feet in diameter; its airscrew was operated by a spring; it was fitted with horizontal planes for setting its course; and in its very short flights it attained a speed of something over five miles an hour.

A larger model, with two airscrews driven by clockwork, was exhibited in 1850 by M. Jullien, a clockmaker of Paris, and flew successfully against a slight breeze. The first successful man-carrying airship was built in 1852 by Henry Giffard, the French engineer, and was flown at Paris on the 24th of September in that year. It was spindle-shaped, with a capacity of 87,000 cubic feet, and a length of 144 feet. The airscrew, ten feet in diameter, was driven by a steam-engine of three horsepower, and the speed attained was about six miles an hour. It would take long to record all the unsuccessful or partially successful experiments in the history of the airship—the elaborately constructed ships which never rose from the ground, the carefully thought out devices which did not work.

Progress was very slow and gradual, a mere residue in a history of failures. The first use of the gas-engine was in an Austrian dirigible, which made a single captive ascent at Brunn in 1872, and developed a speed of three miles an hour. After 1870 the reconstituted French Government showed itself willing to encourage aeronautics, and in 1872, at the cost of the State, a large dirigible was built by Dupuy de Lôme, the inventor of the ironclad. This ship, with an airscrew driven by manpower, attained a speed of five and a half miles an hour.

The first really successful power-driven airship, that is, the first airship to return to its starting-point at the end of a successful voyage, was built in 1884 for the French Army by Captain Krebs and Captain Charles Renard, who subsequently became director of the French department of military aeronautics, This dirigible, named *La France*, was fish-shaped; its length was a hundred and sixty-five feet; its greatest diameter, near the bows, was twenty-seven and a half feet, or one-sixth of its length; it was fitted with an electric motor of eight and a half horsepower which operated an airscrew of twenty-three feet in diameter, situated in front of the car; it was steered by vertical and horizontal rudders, and made several ascents in the neighbourhood of Mcudon. It was the progenitor and type of all later non-rigid dirigibles.

The success of *La France* brought Germany into the field. Towards the close of the century a German engineer called Wölfert constructed a dirigible rather smaller than the French airship, with a slightly more powerful engine, and two airscrews of twelve feet in diameter. This was in one respect a forerunner of the most famous of the German airships, for the car, instead of hanging loose, was rigidly connected to the envelope by means of struts. The trials took place in 1896 at Tempelhof, near Berlin; the airship was held captive by ropes; it answered well to its rudders, and attained a speed of about nine miles an hour. Encouraged by this experiment, Dr. Wölfert in the following year built a second smaller dirigible, fitted with a Daimler benzine motor, and made a free ascent in it on the 14th of June 1897, near Berlin.

As soon as it was well in the air, the ship caught fire and fell flaming to the ground, killing Dr. Wölfert and his assistant. Later in the same year the first completely rigid dirigible was built by a German called David Schwarz; it was made of thin aluminium sheeting, infernally braced by steel wires, and was driven by a twelve horse-power Daimler motor which worked twin airscrews, one on either side. It took the air near Berlin on the 3rd of November 1897, but something went wrong with the airscrew belts, and it was seriously damaged in its hasty descent. Thereupon the crowd of people who had assembled to applaud it fell upon it, and wrecked it. The behaviour of the crowd deserves a passing mention in any history of flight; it was not the least of the ordeals of the early aeronaut.

The aeroplane or airship pilot who disappointed the expectations of his public found no better treatment than Christian and Faithful met with in Bunyan's *Vanity Fair*. There is here no question of national weaknesses; in France and Germany, in England and America, the thing has happened again and again. If an ascent was announced, and was put off because the weather was bad, the crowd jeered, and hooted, and threw stones. On more than one occasion a pilot has been driven by the taunts of the crowd to attempt an impossible ascent; and has met his death. If a damaged machine fell to earth, the crowd often wreaked their vengeance on it, as deer fall upon a wounded comrade.

The men who made up the crowd were most of them kind and trustworthy in their private relations, and in matters that they understood were not unreasonable or inconsiderate. But aerial navigation was a new thing, and their attitude to it was wholly spectacular. They came to see it because they craved excitement, and under the influence of that cruel passion they were capable of the worst excesses of the Roman populace at a gladiatorial show.

In the years that joined the centuries, that is, from 1898 to 1903, aviation seemed a forlorn hope, but there was great activity in the construction of airships, and something like a race for supremacy between France and Germany.

In 1898 the Brazilian, Alberto Santos Dumont, made his first gallant appearance in an airship of his own construction. Born in 1873, the son of a prosperous coffee-planter of San Paulo in Brazil, Santos Dumont was a young and wealthy amateur, gifted with mechanical genius, and insensible to danger. The accidents and perils that he survived in his many aerial adventures would have killed a cat. One of his airships collapsed and fell with him on to the roofs of Paris. Another collapsed and fell with him into the Mediterranean. A third caught fire in the air, and he beat out the flames with his Panama hat.

He survived these and other mishaps, unhurt, and after making more than a hundred ascents in airships, turned his attention to aeroplanes, and was the first man to rise from French soil in a flying machine. From his boyhood mechanisms had attracted him; he was well acquainted with all the machines on his father's plantation, and he records an observation that he made there—the only bad machine on the plantation, he says, was an agitating sieve; the good machines all worked on the rotary principle. He became a champion of the wheel, and of the rotary principle. There was something of the fierceness of theological dispute in the controversies of these early days. The wheel, it was pointed out, is not in nature; it is a pedantic invention of man. Birds do not employ it to fly with, nor fish to swim with. The naturalist school of aeronauts declared against it.

In 1892 M. A. le Compagnon made experiments, not very successfully, in Paris, with a captive dirigible balloon driven by a pair of oscillating wings. As late as 1904 Mr. Thomas Moy, in a paper read to the Aeronautical Society of Great Britain, maintained that the greatest hindrances to the solution of the problem of mechanical flight have always been the balloon and the airscrew. Mr. William Cochrane, in a paper read a few months earlier, laid it down that the airscrew must give place to a more efficient form of propulsion.

Utterances like these help to explain the fervour with which Santos Dumont, in the book called *My Airships* (1904), defends the rotary principle, which is the life of machines. Like the Wrights, he believed in practice, and was a skilled and experienced balloonist before he attempted to navigate an airship. His first airship was almost absurdly small; it had little more than six thousand feet of cubic capacity, was cigar-shaped, and was driven by a three and a half horse-power petrol motor. The others followed in rapid succession.

M. Deutsch de la Meurthe had offered a prize of a hundred thousand *francs* for the first airship that should rise from the Aero Club ground at St. Cloud and voyage round the Eiffel Tower, returning within half an hour to its starting-point. On the 19th of October 1901 the prize was won by Santos Dumont in the sixth of his airships. The ship had over twenty-two thousand feet of cubic capacity; its length was more than five times its diameter; and it was driven by a twelve horse-power petrol motor. It travelled six and three-quarter miles within the half-hour, part of the journey being accomplished against a wind of about twelve miles an hour.

This achievement quickened interest in airships and gained a European fame for Santos Dumont. His later airships were modelled on the egg rather than the cigar; the smallest of these was so perfectly under control that he was able, he says, to navigate it by night through the streets of Paris.

The development of the airship continued for many years to pay toll in wreckage and loss of life. In 1902 three notable airships were built and flown in France; two of these were destroyed in the air above Paris, within a few minutes of their first ascent. Senhor Augusto Severo, a Brazilian, made a spindle-shaped airship, ninety-eight feet long, driven by two airscrews, placed one at each end of a framework which formed the longitudinal axis of the airship. It ascended on the 12th of May, and when it had reached a height of thirteen hundred feet, exploded in flames. Senhor Severo and his assistant perished in it.

The other ship was designed by Baron Bradsky, secretary to the German Embassy in Paris; its total weight was made exactly equivalent to the weight of the air that it displaced, and it was to be raised by the operation of an airscrew rotating horizontally under the car. By the action of this screw the car itself began to rotate, and to drag the ship round with it; the resistance of the air on the body of the ship put too great a strain on the steel wires by which the car was suspended; they broke, and from a height of many hundred feet Baron Bradsky and his engineer, M. Morin, fell to earth with the car, and were killed. This second disaster happened on the 13th of October 1902, at Stains, near Paris.

Twelve days later, on the 25th of October, a much more fortunate airship, the dirigible built for the brothers Lebaudy, made its first ascent at Moisson. This vessel was more successful than any of its predecessors, and became the model for airships of the semi-rigid type. It was fish-shaped, with a capacity of more than eighty thousand cubic feet, and was driven by a forty horse-power Daimler petrol motor, which worked two airscrews, eight feet in diameter, at a rate exceeding a thousand revolutions a minute. The lower part of the envelope was flat, and secured to a rigid metal framework; six steel tubes, attached to this framework, supported the car below, and, besides distributing the load, conveyed the thrust of the airscrew to the ship above. In the course of a year the ship made twenty-eight return journeys, covering distances up to twenty-two miles.

In November 1903 it broke all records, first by making the longest voyage that had ever been made by a navigable balloon, that is, from Moisson to Paris, a distance of about forty miles, and next, a week later, by successfully combating a wind of more than twenty miles an hour. Colonel Renard, who witnessed this trial, said:

Aerial navigation is no longer a Utopia.'

After a time, the ship was taken over by the French Army, and its immediate Lebaudy successors, *La Patrie* of 1906 and *La République* of 1908, also became military airships. Both were wrecked after a short career, but the military airship had made good its promise, and three new airship-building firms were established in France. In 1902 the Astra Company, in 1909 and 1910 the Zodiac Company and the Clement-Bayard Company, began to build airships, some for the French Army and some for foreign powers.

Meanwhile, at the time when Santos Dumont was gaining credit for the smallest airship ever known, the largest known airship had been designed and launched in Germany. On the 2nd of July 1900 the first Zeppelin made its trial trip from the floating shed at Manzell, near Friedrichshafen, on Lake Constance. When the Great War shall be only a faded memory, when the sufferings of millions of men and women shall be condensed into matter for handbooks, and their sacrifices shall be expressed only in arithmetical figures, certain incidents and names, because they caught the popular imagination, will still be narrated and repeated.

The names that will live are the names that symbolise the causes for which they stood. Edith Cavell will never be forgotten; when she persevered in her work of mercy, and calmly faced the ultimate cruelties of a monstrous system, all that was best in the war seemed to find expression in that lonely passion. She was brought home to England in a warship, and was carried to her grave on a gun-carriage, under the Union Jack, because her cause was her country's cause, and England claimed a title in her sacrifice. (*Nurse Edith Cavell*, containing *The Martyrdom of Nurse Cavell* by William Thomson Hill, and *With Edith Cavell in Belgium* by Jacqueline Van Til is also published by Leonaur.)

It is a far cry from Edith Cavell to the old soldier who gave Germany the giant airship, but the Zeppelin will also be remembered, because the popular imagination, which is often both just and fanciful, found a symbol of Germany's cause in this engine of terror, so carefully and admirably planned down to the minutest detail, so impressive by its bulk, so indiscriminate in its destructive action, and so frail. Its inventor was Count Ferdinand von Zeppelin, a lieutenant-general in the German Army. His first balloon ascent had been made during the American Civil War, in one of the military balloons of the Federal Army.

Later on, in the Franco-Prussian War, he distinguished himself by his daring cavalry reconnaissances in Alsace. At about that time there was in Alsace a Frenchman named Spiess, who had drawn a design for a rigid airship not unlike the later Zeppelin, and had endeavoured, without success, to patent it. The suggestion has been made, but with no proof, that Count Zeppelin may have seen Spiess's plans, and borrowed from them. If so, the borrowed idea took long in maturing. It was not until 1898 that the count went to work on a large scale, and formed a company with a capital of a million marks. It was not until 1908, after ten years of struggle and disaster, that the German Government made him a grant for the continuance of his experiments, and the German people, impressed by his pertinacity and courage in misfortune, raised for him a subscription of three hundred thousand pounds, to enable him to build the great airship works at Friedrichshafen.

From this time the Zeppelin was a national ship. Sheds to harbour airships were built at strategic points on the western and eastern fronts, and plans were set on foot to house naval Zeppelins at Heligoland, Emden, and Kiel. With characteristic German thoroughness a network of weather stations on German soil, and, it is believed, of secret weather reports from other countries, was provided for the guidance of airship pilots. All this was a monument to the perseverance, which might almost be called obstinacy, of the indomitable count. He built enormous and costly airships, one after another; one after another they were wrecked or burnt, and then he built more. The German people watched him as King Robert the Bruce watched the spider, with a scepticism that was gradually turned into wonder, till, in the end, when disaster after disaster found him willing patiently to begin again, they resolved to make him their teacher and to take a lesson from him.

Count Zeppelin was about sixty years old when he began to make airships; he had been long studying the problem and preparing his plans; so that his many airships do not much differ among themselves in general design, and a description of the first gives a fair enough idea of its successors. It was a pencil-shaped rigid structure, about four hundred and twenty feet long, with a diameter almost exactly one-eleventh part of its length. The framework, built of aluminium, consisted of sixteen hoops, connected by longitudinal pieces, and kept rigid by diagonal wire stays. Before it was covered it resembled a vast bird-cage, and looked as frail as a cobweb, but was stronger and stirrer than it looked. It was divided by aluminium bulkheads into seventeen compartments; of these all but the two end compartments contained separate balloons or gas-bags. Two or three of these might collapse without completely destroying the buoyancy of the ship.

The whole structure was covered with a fabric of rubberized cotton. A triangular latticed aluminium keel ran along below, to give strength to the ship, and to furnish a passage-way from end to end. At points about a third of the way from either end of the ship spaces in the keel were made for the two cars, in each of which was a sixteen horse-power Daimler motor driving two small high velocity airscrews, one on each side of the ship. The lateral steering was done by a large vertical rudder, placed aft. The longitudinal balance was controlled in several ways.

In the first ship a heavy sliding weight in the keel was moved at will, fore and aft. This was supplemented or superseded in later ships by four sets of elevating planes, two sets in the fore-part and two sets aft. An advantage of the rigid ship is that she can tilt herself without danger from the pressure of the gas on the higher end. Moreover, she can be driven at a very high speed, and the gas-bags, being housed in the compartments and protected from the outer air, are less liable to sudden contraction and expansion caused by variations of temperature.

The great disadvantage of the rigid type has hitherto been that in bad weather the airship cannot land. A non-rigid airship in a nasty wind can land and deflate itself at once by ripping the panel in the envelope, at no greater price than the loss of its gas, and probably some damage to its car. To land in a rigid ship is at best a ticklish business; indeed, the rigid airship is in exactly the same case as a large seagoing vessel; its chief dangers are from the land, which it cannot touch with impunity. Its troubles have been greatly diminished, since the war, by the development of the mooring-mast, which does away with the necessity of housing the ship after every flight.

The prevailing type of weather in this country is unsettled, and the changes in the force and direction of the wind are rapid and numerous. The landing and housing of an airship demands hundreds of men for its performance, and is not safely to be undertaken in a wind that blows more than eighteen miles an hour. A staff of from eight to ten men is sufficient to anchor a large airship to a mooring-mast, where it has been proved by experiment that she can safely ride out a wind that blows fifty miles an hour.

At Pulham, our largest airship station, which was taken over from the Royal Air Force by the Controller-General of Civil Aviation in December 1920, a number of valuable experiments have since been carried out with an improvised mooring-mast, and it has been shown that with a properly designed and constructed mast, fitted with adequate receiving gear and hauling apparatus, there will be no difficulty in landing the largest rigid airships in a wind of from thirty-five to forty miles an hour. This spells an immense advance. Sheds will still be necessary for overhauls and repairs, as a dry dock is necessary for sea-going vessels. But an airship on service may be moored to the mast, as a sea-going vessel is moored to a quay, and can take on board or discharge cargo, passengers, and fuel.

The trial trip of the first Zeppelin was short, because of accidents to the steering-gear, but on the whole, was not unsuccessful. The ship was perfectly stable, and in its voyage of three and a half miles proved that it could make headway against a wind of sixteen miles an hour. A second ascent, lasting for an hour and twenty minutes, was made on the 17th of October 1900. These trials were of value in discovering the faults of the ship; in the following year it was broken up, and Count Zeppelin went to work again. In his second ship of 1905 the power of each engine was increased to eighty-five horse-power, and other improvements were made. This ship suffered many minor mishaps. At last, in January 1906, it ascended over Lake Constance to a height of 1,800 feet; then the motors failed, the helm jammed; when the ship attempted to descend the ground was frozen and the anchors would not hold, it was driven against some trees, and a high wind arising in the night made it a total wreck.

The following list shows the number of Zeppelin airships built up to the outbreak of the war, and the fate of each of them:

Zeppelin No.	Year of Completion	Name.	Remarks.
1	1900	L.Z. I	Broken up after experiments spring 1901.
2	1905	L.Z. II	Wrecked January 1906.
3	1906	Z. I	Taken over by the army. Broken up February 1913.
4	1908	L.Z. IV	Burnt August 1908.
5	1909	Z. II	Taken over by the army. Wrecked April 1910.
6	1909	L.Z. VI	Burnt September 1910.
7	1910	Deutschland	Wrecked June 1910.
8	1911	Ersatz Deutschland	Wrecked May 1911.
9	1911	Ersatz Z. II	Taken over by the army. Broken up summer 1914.
10	1911	Schwaben	Wrecked June 1912.
11	1912	Viktoria Luise	Wrecked June 1915.
12	1912	Z. III	Taken over by the army. Broken up summer 1914.

13	1912	*Hansa*	Broken up summer 1916.
14	1912	L. 1	Taken over by the navy. Wrecked September 1913.
15	1913	Ersatz Z. I	Taken over by the army. Wrecked March 1913.
16	1913	Z. IV	Taken over by the army. Broken up spring 1916.
17	1913	*Sachsen*	Broken up spring 1916.
18	1913	L. 2	Taken over by the navy. Burnt October 1913.
19	1913	Ersatz E.Z. I	Taken over by the army. Wrecked June 1914.
20	1913	Z. V	Taken over by the army. Crashed after damage by gunfire in Poland, August 1914.
21	1913	Z. VI	Taken over by the army. Crashed at Cologne after damage by gunfire over Liége, 6th August 1914.
22	1914	Z. VII	Taken over by the army. Crashed in the Argonne after damage by gunfire, August 1914.
23	1914	Z. VIII	Taken over by the army. Brought down by gunfire at Badonvillers, 23rd August 1914.
24	1914	L. 3	Taken over by the navy. Wrecked off Fanö, 17th February 1915.
25	1914	Z. IX	Taken over by the army. Dismantled August 1914.

The list is full of wreckage; what it does not show is the immense progress made in a few years. As early as 1907 Count Zeppelin made a voyage of eight hours in his third airship, covering 211 miles. In 1909 he voyaged, in stages, from Friedrichshafen to Berlin, landing at Tegel in the presence of the emperor on the 29th of August, and returning safely to Friedrichshafen by the 2nd of September. But the growing efficiency of the Zeppelin and the growing confidence of the German public are best seen in the records of passenger-carrying flights. The Zeppelin Company, being founded and supported by national enterprise, did not sell any ships to foreign powers. For passenger-carrying purposes it supplied ships to the subsidiary company usually called the Delag (that is, the Deutsche Luftschiffahrt Aktien-Gesellschaft), which had its headquarters at Frankfort-on-the-Main.

The Delag acquired six Zeppelin airships, which, unlike the military and naval ships, bore names. A record of the voyages made by the *Viktoria Luise*, the *Hansa*, and the *Sachsen* will show how rapidly the German people were familiarised with the Zeppelin, and how safe air-travel became, when safety was essential, as it is in all passenger-carrying enterprises. The *Viktoria Luise* made her first trip on the 4th of March 1912, with twenty-three passengers on board, from Friedrichshafen to Frankfort-on-the-Main—a distance of about two hundred miles, which she covered in seven and a half hours. She made her hundredth trip on the 23rd of June 1912; her two-hundredth on the 21st of October in the same year; in the following year her three-hundredth trip was made on the 30th of June, and her four-hundredth on the 26th of November.

In these four hundred trips she carried 8,551 persons and travelled 29,430 miles. Some of them were made over the sea; on the 27th of June, for instance, she left Hamburg in the morning, and reached Cuxhaven in about two hours. There she picked up with a Hamburg-America liner starting for New York, and accompanied the steamer for some distance; then she steered for Heligoland, and flying round the island very low was greeted with cheers by the inhabitants. Part of her return journey was made against a headwind of sixteen miles an hour, and she reached Hamburg after a voyage of eight hours, during which she had covered a distance of about two hundred and fifty miles.

The *Hansa*, beginning in July 1912, by the end of 1913 had made two hundred and seventy-five trips, carrying 5,697 persons and travelling 22,319 miles. The *Sachsen*, beginning in May 1913, before the end of the year had made two hundred and six trips, carrying 4,857 persons and travelling about 13,700 miles. A wrecked Zeppelin is such a picture of destruction, such a vast display of twisted metal and rags lying wreathed across a landscape, that those who see it are apt to get an exaggerated idea of the dangers of airship travel. With all his misfortunes, it was Count Zeppelin's luck for many years that no life was lost among those who travelled in his ships.

In May 1906, before Count Zeppelin's enterprise had received the stamp of Imperial and national approval, there was formed, under the inspiration of the German Emperor, a society for airship development. The success of the Lebaudy airship in France prompted the construction in Germany of two types of semi-rigid airship—the Parseval and the Gross. Only four of the latter type were built, and all four suffered mishap; the last and best of them, built in 1911, is said to have shown a better performance than the best contemporary Zeppelin.

The Parseval was designed in 1906 by Major August von Parseval, of the Third Bavarian Infantry Regiment, who retired from the German Army in 1907 in order to devote himself entirely to scientific work. He was already famous for the kite balloon, which he had invented in collaboration with Hauptmann Bartsch von Sigsfeld, who died in 1906. The Parseval kite balloon was adopted or imitated by all other nations during the war. The Parseval airship was as good an airship, of the non-rigid type, as had ever been built; it was supplanted, later on, by the rigid type, because an airship's lift depends on its size, and very large airships could not be built without a rigid framework. The society for airship development bought up Major von Parseval's plans, and began to construct Parseval airships.

The statutes of the society forbade it to sell ships for profit, so an allied company was formed, the Luftfahrzeugbau-Gesellschaft, with works at Bitterfeld, and a subsidiary company, the L.V.G., or Luftverkehrs-Gesellschaft, to exploit Parseval airships for passenger-carrying, with its headquarters at Berlin and sheds at Johannisthal. Two passenger-carrying ships were built, the *Stollwerk* in 1910, and the *Charlotte* in 1912. The Parseval ships, perhaps because, being non-rigid, they were held to be inferior to the Zeppelins, were freely sold to foreign powers—one to the Austrian Army in 1909, one to the Russian and one to the Turkish Army in 1910, one to the Japanese army in 1912, another to the Russian and two to the Italian Army in 1913; last of all, in the same year, one to the British Admiralty.

Some eighteen Parseval airships were built and launched between 1909 and 1913. The third great airship-building company in Germany was the Schütte-Lanz Company, with its factory in Mannheim. It was named from Heinrich Lanz, the founder of machine works near Mannheim, who supplied the money, and Professor Schütte, of the Technical University, Danzig, who supplied the skill. Its rigid airships were made of wood; they were built from 1912 onwards expressly for the uses of the army and navy, and they played a great part in the war.

Those who were responsible for the development of the airship in Germany took the people into partnership, and devoted themselves largely to passenger-carrying. The airship became popular; and the officers and men who worked it were practised in navigation all the year round. The people, for their part, regarded the Zeppelin with the enthusiasm of patriotic fervour. France had taken the lead and had shown the way with the dirigible, but Germany, by recruiting the people for the cause, soon outdistanced her. The passenger ships served as training-ships for crews, and, if occasion should arise, were readily convertible to warlike purposes.

Yet things changed and moved so fast, that before the war broke out, although the German people still believed that the Zeppelin gave them the sovereignty of the air, the German Government had been troubled by doubts, had changed its policy, and was striving hard to overtake the French in the construction and manning of army aeroplanes. The consequence was that the war found Germany better provided with aeroplanes for use on the western front than with airships for operations oversea. The German Emperor, speaking to a wounded soldier, is reported to have said that he never willed this war.

One proof that this war was not the war he willed may be found in the state of preparation of the German air force. If war with England had been any part of the German plan, German airships would have been more numerous, and would have been ready for immediate action, as the armies that invaded Belgium were ready. The German theory was that England was not prepared for war, which, with certain brilliant and crucial exceptions, was true, and that therefore England would not go to war, which proved to be false. The French were supplying themselves with a great force of aeroplanes, and for all that could be known, air operations on the western front might determine the fortunes of the campaign. So, the German Government turned its attention to machines that are heavier than air.

What had brought about this situation was the rapid and surprising development of the aeroplane by France. Here it is necessary to go back and take up the story again at the beginning of those few and headlong years.

French aviation derives directly from Lilienthal and collaterally from the Wrights. The blood of the martyrs is the seed of the Church; but the martyrs, for the most part, die in faith, without assurance of the harvest that is to come. When Lilienthal was killed he can hardly have known that his example and his careful records would so soon bear fruit in other countries. He was regarded by his fellow-countrymen as a whimsical acrobat, who took mad risks and paid the price. But as soon as he was dead, the story of what he had done got abroad, and began to raise up for him disciples and successors, who carried on his experiments.

The chief of these in France was Captain F. Ferber, an officer of artillery and a student of science, who from 1896 onwards was a teacher in the military school at Fontainebleau. It was in 1898 that he first came across an account of Lilienthal; the reading of it impressed him as deeply as it impressed the Wrights. Here was a man, he thought, who had discovered the right way of learning to fly; if only the way were followed, success was sure. Like the Wrights, Ferber lays stress chiefly on practice. It was he, not Lilienthal, who was the author of the saying:

> To design a flying machine is nothing; to build one is nothing much; to try it in the air is everything.

In the book on aviation which he wrote shortly before his death in 1909 he expounds his creed and narrates his experiences. His mathematical knowledge, he says, served him well, for it saved him from being condemned as an empiric by those dogmatic men of science, very numerous in France (and, he might have added, in the universities of all countries), who believe that science points the way to practice, whereas the most that science can do, says Ferber, is to follow in the wake of practice, and interpret it. So, he set himself to work on a plan as old as the world—first to create the facts, and then to expound them in speech and writing.

He began to build gliders, but had no success with them until he found out for himself what he had not gathered from his reading of Lilienthal—that an up-current of wind is necessary for a prolonged glide. His first successful flight was made with his fourth glider on the 7th of December 1901. He got into touch with Mr. Chanute, another of Lilienthal's scattered disciples, and through him was supplied with papers and photographs concerning the gliding experiments of the Wrights. These were a revelation to him, and he used them in making his fifth glider, which was a great improvement on its predecessors. He lectured at Lyons to the Aero Club of the Rhone on the progress of aviation by means of gliding, and published his lecture in the *Revue d'Artillerie* of March 1904.

About this time the air was full of rumours of flight. M. Ernest Archdeacon, of Paris, took up the subject with ardour, wrote many articles on it, and encouraged others to work at it. A young man, called Gabriel Voisin, who heard Captain Ferber lecture at Lyons, came on to the platform after the lecture and declared that he wished to devote his life to the cause of aviation. The next morning, he started for Paris, and with the help of M. Archdeacon founded the earliest aeroplane factory in France—the firm of the brothers Voisin, which became the mainstay of early French aviation.

Ferber himself was carrying out a series of experiments at Nice with an aeroplane which he fitted with a six horse-power engine and suspended from a tall mast, when he was invited by Colonel Renard to help with the work of the official research laboratory at Chalais Meudon. He joined the staff, but found that the officials of a Government organisation are as ill qualified as the theorists of a university for progress in practical invention. The lower members of the hierarchy are men under orders, who do what they are told to do; the higher members are hampered by having to work through subordinates, who often do not understand their aims and take no particular interest in the work in hand.

Nevertheless, he improved his aeroplane, stabilising it by means of a long tail, and fitting it with wheels for landing, in place of the skids which were used by the Wrights. Then, like those who had gone before him, he was held up by the question of the engine. Engineers are a conservative race of men, and perhaps the perfected aeroplane would still be waiting for a suitable engine if they had not been prompted to innovation by the fashion of motor-racing. There are strange links in the chain of cause and effect; the pneumatic tyre made the motor-bicycle possible; for motor-bicycle races a light engine was devised which later on was adapted to the needs of the aeroplane.

Ferber made acquaintance with M. Levavasseur, who had invented an engine of eighty horsepower weighing less than five pounds per horse-power, and had won many races with it. This engine was named the *Antoinette* in honour of the daughter of M. Gastambide, a capitalist, who had supplied the inventor with funds. The most famous of early French aviators, Santos Dumont, Farman, Blériot, Delagrange, and others, owed much to this engine. Ferber might have had it before any of them, for M. Levavasseur offered to build it for him—twenty-four horse-power with a weight of about a hundred and twelve pounds—but public moneys could not be advanced for an engine that did not exist, so the other pioneers, who had followed Ferber in gliding experiments, preceded him in flying.

In 1906 Ferber obtained Government permission to join the Antoinette firm for a period, and by 1908 he was flying in an aeroplane of his own design. He was killed in September 1909, on the aerodrome of Beuvrequen, near Boulogne, by capsizing on rough ground in the act of alighting. His own estimate of his work was modest; he had acted, he said, as a ferment and a populariser, and had helped to put France on the right track; but it was his pride that he belonged to the great school, the school of Lilienthal, Pilcher, Chanute, and the Wrights, who went to work by a progressive method of practical experiment, who combined daring with patience, and found their way into the air.

Ferber, after his visit to America, had failed to induce the French authorities to purchase the Wright aeroplane, which he had never seen, but which, from descriptions and photographs, he was able to reconstruct, much as a geologist reconstructs an animal from fossil bones. The refusal of the French Government to purchase and the withdrawal of the Wrights from their public experiments gave France a period of respite for two years, during which time French aviation rapidly developed on lines of its own.

At the back of this movement was M. Archdeacon, who as early as 1903 had established a fund and had offered a cup as a prize for the first officially recorded flight of more than twenty-five metres. The Voisin brothers, Gabriel and Charles, having set up their factory at Billancourt-sur-Seine, built machines for him, box-kites and aeroplanes. After a time, the Voisin brothers went into business on their own account, and employed M. Colliex as their engineer. Their earliest customers, Léon Delagrange, who had been trained as a sculptor, and Henri Farman, who had combined the professions of cyclist, painter, and motor-racer, were distinguished early French flyers. That both these men had been artists seems to bear out the favourite contention of Wilbur Wright and of Captain Ferber.

To be an artist a man must create or initiate; the accumulation of knowledge will do little for him. A politician or a lawyer can reach to high distinction in his profession without the power of initiating anything. It is enough for him to handle other men's ideas, to combine them and balance them, to study and conciliate other men, and to suggest a compromise. But the artist, like the scientific discoverer, must act on his own ideas, and do battle, singlehanded, with the nature of things.

The earliest experiments of M. Archdeacon and the Voisins were made with man-carrying Hargrave box-kites, or with gliders made on the same principle, which were towed in the air behind a fast motor-boat travelling down the Seine. The next step was to fit an aeroplane with an engine and wheels so that it might attempt to rise from the ground. The Voisins collaborated with most of the early French aviators, with Louis Blériot and Robert Esnault-Pelterie, as well as with Farman and Delagrange. At one time they were closely associated with Blériot, at another time with Farman. Their first machines depended for lateral stability on the vertical panels of the box-kite structure. This was insufficient, and the French designers had to grapple, one by one, with all the difficulties that had been met and conquered by the Wrights.

They had this advantage, that the design of the Wrights' machine was, though not exactly, yet in its main features known to them. All the early aeroplanes which mounted their elevators in front of the machine may, without much doubt, be affiliated to the Wrights. The elevator is not best placed in front; its action in that position is too quick and violent, but it is under the eye of the operator, and with cool nerves he can learn to work it. While the group of enthusiasts who gathered round the Voisins were designing and experimenting, Santos Dumont, having turned his attention to machines heavier than air, suddenly appeared among them, made the first successful flight over French soil, and carried off the Archdeacon prize. His machine was a biplane, built on the box-kite principle, with three vertical panels on each side between the planes, and a box-kite elevator projecting far in front.

The wings were fixed at a considerable dihedral angle, and the engine was a twenty-four horse-power Antoinette. In his first trial, which took place at Bagatelle on the 23rd of July 1906, Santos Dumont attached a spindle-shaped balloon to the upper surface of the machine, to help it into the air. The combination of the two modes he soon found to be impossible; with the balloon attached to it the machine could not develop speed enough to support itself in the air. His next step was to practise the machine by running it down an inclined cable; then he discarded as much weight as he could, doubled the horse-power of the motor, and began to taxi freely along the ground.

On a day in September the machine raised itself for a very short space into the air. The first officially witnessed flight, of about eighty yards, took place on the 23rd of October 1906, and gained the Archdeacon Cup. About a month later he made a flight of more than a furlong. Thereafter he established himself at Saint-Cyr and developed a machine of the monoplane type, with a long tail. But he was too far from the resources of Paris, and when, on the 13th of January 1908, Henri Farman overtook his records and won the Deutsch-Archdeacon prize for a flight of one kilometre in a closed circuit, Santos Dumont lost his leading position in the world of aviation, after a brief and meteoric career which has stamped his name on history.

During these early years the Voisin brothers had the foresight and wisdom to put themselves wholly at the service of others. The promise of flight had taken hold of many minds in France and there was no lack of inventors and would-be inventors who wished to test their own ideas and to have machines built to their own designs. If the Voisins had refused to gratify them, these clients would have disappeared; and the work done for them, though much of it was done in the old blind alleys of horizontal elevating airscrews and wing-flapping machines, yet had this advantage, that it kept the workshop active and made it self-supporting.

Inventors are a difficult and jealous people; they received every indulgence from the Voisins. The machines built for them were named after them, though most of the skill and experience that went to the making came from the factory. In the same way M. Archdeacon gave up all practical experiment after 1905 and was content to play the part of the good genius of aviation, presiding at the Aero Club, offering prizes for new achievements, bringing inventors together and encouraging the exchange of ideas. The rapidity of French progress was not a little due to this self-effacing and social instinct, so characteristic of the French spirit, which kept the patron and the engineers in the background, and brought order and progress out of the chaos of personal rivalry.

Progress was slow at first. The experiments made in 1906 by Blériot in conjunction with the Voisins were made, for safety, on the water of the Lake of Enghien, but it proved impossible to get up sufficient speed on the water to rise into the air. In 1907 a greater success attended the experiments made at Vincennes, at Bagatelle, and at Issy-les-Moulineaux, where Henri Farman had obtained permission to use the army manoeuvre ground and had built himself a hangar, or shed, for his aeroplane. On the 30th of March, at Bagatelle, the Delagrange aeroplane made a flight of sixty metres.

A few months later, Farman, on a similar machine fitted with landing-wheels which worked on pivots, like castors, began to make short flights. On the 30th of September he flew for eighty metres. Seeing is believing, but many of those who saw Farman fly did not believe. The machine, they said, was only hopping into the air with the speed it had gathered on the ground; it would never fly. When, on the 26th of October, Farman made a flight of more than seven hundred metres the pessimists found another objection. The machine, they said, would never be able to turn; it could only continue in a straight line. They had hit on a real difficulty, but the Voisins and Farman himself, who, starting without any knowledge of aeroplanes or flying, had soon developed practical ideas of his own, were hard at work to meet it.

The Wrights had simplified the handling of a machine by combining the control of the vertical rudder with the control of the wing-warping. In the early Voisin machines there was no wing-warping, and the pilots had to attempt to balance and turn the machine without it; but a rod with a wheel attached to it was used to control both the elevating plane in front and the vertical rudder behind. By turning the wheel, the rudder was operated, by moving the rod the elevator was raised or lowered. It was on a machine of this kind that Farman began to practise gradual turning movements. The lateral inclination of the machine was feared and, as much as possible, avoided in these first experiments, though it is not only harmless in turning movements, but is necessary for their complete success, just as the banking of a motor race-track is necessary to keep the machines on the course.

Farman made rapid progress; and, as has been said, by the beginning of 1908 he gained the two thousand pound Deutsch-Archdeacon prize for a closed circuit of one kilometre in length. The wonderful skill of this achievement will be fully appreciated only by the best modern pilots, who would not like to be asked to repeat it on a machine unprovided with ailerons (that is to say, hinged flaps on the trailing edge of the planes), and controlled only by the elevator and the rudder. There is nothing very extravagant in dating the conquest of the air, as some French writers have dated it, from the circular flights of Farman. It is true that the Wrights had attained a much higher skill in manoeuvring, but they had retired, like Achilles, to their tent, whereas Farman's flight showed the way to many others.

In the spring of the same year Delagrange began to execute turning flights; on the 6th of July Farman gained the prize offered by M. Armengaud, the president of the society of aerial navigation, for a flight of a quarter of an hour's duration, and after the arrival of Wilbur Wright at Le Mans progress became so rapid that records were broken week by week and almost day by day. In January 1909 the Aero Club of France issued their first list of pilots' certificates. Eight names, all famous, made up the list—Léon Delagrange, Alberto Santos Dumont, Robert Esnault-Pelterie, Henri Farman, Wilbur Wright, Orville Wright, Captain Ferdinand Ferber, Louis Blériot. To make this a list of the chief French pioneers, the names of the Wrights would have to be omitted, and the names of some who were not famous pilots but who did much for flying, especially the names of M. Ernest Archdeacon and Gabriel Voisin, would have to be included.

These men, and those who worked for them, gave to France her own school of aviation. Louis Blériot and Robert Esnault-Pelterie broke away from what, since the days of Francis Wenham, had been accepted as the orthodox doctrine of the biplane, and, taking the bird for master, devised swift, light, and easily handled monoplanes. The Blériot monoplane, which first flew the Channel; the R.E.P. (or Robert Esnault-Pelterie) monoplane; the Antoinette monoplane, on which Hubert Latham performed his exploits; the small and swift Demoiselle monoplane, designed and flown by Santos Dumont; and the Tellier monoplane, which for a time held the record for cross-country flight—all these made history by their performances in the crowded years from 1908 to 1910.

The monoplane is, without any doubt, the prettiest of machines in the air. When Captain Ferber gave this reason to Mr. Chanute for preferring it to the biplane, Mr. Chanute, he says, laughed a good deal at an argument so characteristically French. But there is sense and weight in the argument. No flying animal is half so ugly as the early Wright biplane. In the world of natural fliers beauty and efficiency are one. Purity of line and economy of parts are beautiful and efficient. A good illustration of this may be found in the question of the airscrew.

The early French biplanes of the Voisin and Farman type were what would now be called 'pusher' machines; their airscrews operated behind the main planes, and their tails were supported by an open structure of wood or metal which left room for the play of the screw. In this ugly arrangement the loss of efficiency is easy to see. The screw works in a disturbed medium, and the complicated metal-work presents a large resistance to the passage of the machine through the air. The monoplane, from the first, was a 'tractor' machine; its airscrew was in front of the planes, and its body, or fuselage, was covered in and streamlined, so as to offer the least possible resistance to the air.

A later difficulty caused by the forward position of the airscrew had nothing to do with flying. When the war came, and machine-guns were mounted on aeroplanes, a clear field was needed for forward firing. This difficulty was ultimately met by the invention of a synchronizing gear, which timed the bullets between the strokes of the airscrew-blades. In all but a few types of machine the airscrew is now retained in the forward position. The debate between monoplane and biplane is not yet concluded; the biplane holds its own because with the same area of supporting surface it is much stronger and more compact than the monoplane.

Instead of wing-warping, which puts a strain on the supporting surfaces and is liable to distort them, the French (to whom Blériot is believed to have shown the way) introduced ailerons, that is, small subsidiary hinged planes attached to the extremities of the wings. By controlling these, one up and the other down, in conjunction with the rudder, the pilot can preserve his lateral balance, and turn the machine to right or left. Later on, these ailerons, when they were borrowed by the Voisin and Farman biplanes, were not fitted to the extremities of the planes, but became hinged flaps forming the extreme section of the trailing edge; and this position they have kept in all modern aeroplanes.

An even greater advance was made by the French school in its device for the control of the machine. The machine which Wilbur Wright flew in France was controlled by two upright levers, grasped by the pilot, one in either hand. The left-hand lever moved only backwards and forwards; it controlled the elevator and directed the machine upwards or downwards. The right-hand lever controlled the rudder and the warping of the wings. By moving it backwards or forwards the pilot turned the machine to right or left; by moving it sideways he warped the wings. There is nothing instinctive or natural in these correspondences; the backward and forward movement which in one lever spells up and down in the other spells right and left. It is a testimony to the extraordinary cool-headed skill of the Wrights, and to their endless practice and perseverance, that they were able to fly such a machine in safety, and to outfly their rivals.

The French school centralised the control in a single lever with a universal joint attachment at the lower end. The movements of this lever in any direction produced the effects that would instinctively be expected; a backward or forward movement turned the machine upwards or downwards, a sideways movement raised one wing or the other so as to bank the machine or to bring it to a level position again. The vertical rudder was controlled either by a wheel attached to this central lever, or by the pressure of the pilot's feet on a horizontal bar. The French moreover improved the means of taking off and alighting.

The early Wright machines were launched on rails, and alighted on skids attached to the machine like the skids of a sledge. To rise into the air again after a forced landing was impossible without special apparatus. By means of wheels elastically fixed to an under-carriage the French inventors made the aeroplane available for cross-country journeys. But the greatest difference between the two types of aeroplane, the American and the French, was their difference in stability. The Wright machine demanded everything of the pilot; it could not fly itself. If the pilot relaxed his attention for a moment, or took his hands from the levers, a crash was the certain result. The machine was a bird which flew with extended bill and without a tail; whereas the French machines had a horizontal tail-plane, which, being held rigidly at a distance from the main planes, gave to the machine a far greater measure of longitudinal stability.

All these advantages told in favour of French aviation, and secured for it progress and achievement. A few dates and facts may serve to show its rapid progress at a time when it was making history week by week. On the 30th of September 1908 Henri Farman made the first cross-country flight, from Châlons to Rheims, a distance of twenty-seven kilometres, which he covered in twenty minutes. Three days later, at Châlons, he remained in the air for just under threequarters of an hour, covering twenty-five miles, that is, about forty times the distance that had won him the Deutsch-Archdeacon prize in January. Between April and September of the same year Léon Delagrange had four times in succession raised the world's official records (which, of course, took no note of the Wrights) for duration of flight.

On the 31st of October Louis Blériot made the first cross-country circuit flight, from Toury to Artenay and back, a distance of about seventeen miles, in the course of which flight he twice landed and rose again into the air. All these and many similar achievements were dwarfed by Wilbur Wright's performance at the Hunaudières race-course near Le Mans. His first flight, on Saturday the 8th of August, lasted one minute and forty-seven seconds. Three days later, though he flew for only four minutes, the figures of eight and other manoeuvres which he executed in the air caused M. Delagrange, who witnessed them, to remark, '*Eh bien. Nous n'existons pas. Nous sommes battus.*'

On the last day of the year he flew for two hours and twenty minutes, covering seventy-seven miles. In the intervening time he had beaten the French records for duration, distance, and height. Cross-country work he did not attempt; his machine at that time was ill-fitted for it. During the winter he went to Pau to instruct his first three pupils—the Count de Lambert and MM. Paul Tissandier and Alfred Leblanc.

At the beginning of the year 1909 the mystery and craft of flying was still known only to the few. In the two years that followed it was divulged to the many, and became a public spectacle. The age of the designers was followed by the age of the performers. Flying machines and men who could fly them rapidly increased in number. A man working in a laboratory on difficult and uncertain experiments cannot engage or retain the attention of the public; a flying man, who circles over a city or flies across great tracts of populated country, is visible to all, and, when he is first seen, excites a frenzy of popular enthusiasm. These years were the years of competition and adventure, of races, and of record-breaking in distance, speed, duration, and height.

Flying was the newest sport; and the aviator, whose courage, coolness, and skill carried him through great dangers, was the hero of the day. The press, with its ready instinct for profitable publicity, offered magnificent encouragement to the new art. Large money prizes were won by gallant deeds that have made history. The *Daily Mail*, of London, offered a prize of a thousand pounds for the first flight across the English Channel. Hubert Latham, in his Antoinette monoplane, attempted this flight on the 19th of July from the neighbourhood of Calais, but the failure of his sparking plugs brought him down on to the water about six miles from the French coast, where he was picked up by his accompanying destroyer.

He was preparing another attempt when Louis Blériot, suddenly arriving at Calais, anticipated him. At half-past four on the morning of Sunday, the 25th of July, Blériot rose into the air on his monoplane, furnished with an Anzani engine of twenty-five horse-power, and headed for Dover. He flew without map or compass, and soon outdistanced the French destroyer which had been appointed to escort him. For ten minutes he lost sight of all land, but he corrected his course by observing the steamers below him, and landed in the Northfall meadow behind Dover Castle after a flight of forty minutes.

Two other newspaper prizes, one of ten thousand pounds offered by the London *Daily Mail* for a flight from London to Manchester, in three stages, the other of ten thousand dollars offered by the New York *World* for a flight from Albany to New York, were won in 1910. The first of these flights was attempted on the 24th of April by an Englishman, Claude Grahame-White, who flew a Farman biplane, but was compelled by engine trouble to descend near Lichfield, where his machine was damaged by wind in the night. Three days later Louis Paulhan, also mounted on a Farman biplane, covered the whole distance to Manchester in something over four hours, with only one landing.

Paulhan had first learned to fly in July 1909; Grahame-White had obtained his pilot's certificate from the French Aero Club as late as December 1909. The flight of a hundred and twenty miles from Albany to New York, down the Hudson River, was achieved on the 29th of May in two hours and thirty-two minutes by Glenn H. Curtiss, one of the most distinguished of American pioneers. Later on in 1910 a prize of a hundred thousand *francs* was offered by the Paris newspaper, the *Matin*, for what was called the *Circuit de l'Est*, a voyage from Paris and back by way of Troyes, Nancy, Mézières, Douai, and Amiens, a distance of four hundred and eighty-eight miles, to be completed in six stages, on alternate days, from the 7th of August to the 17th of August.

This competition was won by Wilbur Wright's pupil, Alfred Leblanc, on a Blériot monoplane. The eastern part of this circuit, a territory not much larger than Yorkshire, has since been made famous and sacred by the Battles of the Marne and Verdun and a hundred other places.

Of more value for the furtherance of the art than any of these individual exploits were the series of meetings which brought aviators together in friendly rivalry, to see and to be seen. The most notable of these meetings was also the first, the Champagne Week of Rheims, which was organised by the Marquis de Polignac, and was held, during the last week of August 1909, on the Bétheny Plain, near Rheims. The number of spectators, day by day, was from forty to fifty thousand, and the gate-money taken during the week was about £35,000. Henri Farman, Hubert Latham, and Glenn Curtiss earned among them almost £6,000 in prizes.

The Grand Prix de la Champagne for the flight of longest duration was won by Farman, who remained in the air, plodding steadily round the course, for more than three hours. He also won the passenger-carrying prize in a flight which carried two passengers round the ten-kilometre course in about ten minutes and a half. Latham gained the altitude prize by flying to a height of more than five hundred feet.

The Gordon Bennett Cup, for the best speed over two rounds of the course, was won by Curtiss in fifteen minutes fifty and three-fifths seconds, with Blériot only some five seconds behind him. There were many other prizes distributed among the more fortunate of the competitors. Perhaps the greatest gain of the meeting was that it did away with the notion that the aeroplane is a fair-weather toy. There was rain and storm, and Paulhan flew in a wind of twenty-five miles an hour. The meeting witnessed the first public success of the most famous (and most revolutionary) of aeroplane engines—the rotary Gnome engine, in which the cylinders rotate bodily round a fixed crank-shaft.

This engine was built by the brothers Louis and Laurent Seguin, who had a small motor factory in Paris. Most of the regular aviators looked askance at it, but Seguin offered to install it in a Voisin biplane of the box-kite pattern which had just been won as a prize by Louis Paulhan. In the result the old box-kite flew as never box-kite flew before, and produced a great impression at the Rheims meeting. The Gnome engine was also mounted by Henri Farman on one of the machines that he flew at Rheims, and by the solitary English competitor, Mr. G. B. Cockburn, who, according to Mr. Holt Thomas, was the first to use this engine in the air.

Other meetings followed in rapid succession, gaining recruits for the new art and converting the nations to a belief in it. Two of these, held simultaneously at Blackpool and Doncaster, soon after the Rheims meeting, were spoilt by bad weather and high winds, but at Blackpool Hubert Latham gave a marvellous display on his Antoinette machine by flying in a wind of about forty miles an hour, when no one else ventured the attempt. During 1910 aviation weeks were held in February at Heliopolis, Egypt, and in April at Nice. In October of the same year an International Aviation Tournament was held in America at Belmont Park, Long Island, where the highest honour, the prize for the Gordon Bennett speed contest, was won by Claude Grahame-White on a Blériot machine.

In Great Britain many meetings were held during the summer of 1910: one at Wolverhampton; another at Bournemouth, where the Hon. C. S. Rolls, who a month before had flown across the Channel and back without alighting, was killed; another at Lanark; and yet another at Blackpool, where George Chavez flew to a height of 5,887 feet. In the following month Chavez flew across the Alps, over the Simplon Pass, into Italy, but was fatally injured in alighting at Domodossola. These are specimen deeds only, taken from a story of adventure and progress, danger and disaster, which, if it were fully told, would fill volumes. Records, as they are called, were made and broken so fast that the heroic achievement of the spring became the daily average performance of the ensuing autumn. The movement was fairly under way, and nothing could stop it.

CHAPTER 3

Flight in England

In all these doings England bore but a small part. English aviators were few; and those who distinguished themselves in public competition had learned their flying in France. To speak of England's share in these amazing years of progress is to tell the history of a backward parish, and to describe its small contribution to a great world-wide movement. Yet the story, for that very reason, has an extraordinary interest. England never has been cosmopolitan. All her beginnings, even where she has led the way and set the fashion to the world, were parochial. If a change is in question, England makes trial of it, late and reluctantly, on a small scale, in her own garden.

All the noisy exhortations of a thousand newspapers cannot touch her apprehension or rouse her to excitement. Next year's fashions do not much preoccupy her mind; she knows that they will come to her, in due time, from France, to be taken or rejected. When a change is something more than a fashion, and vital conditions begin to be affected, her lethargy is broken in a moment and she is awake and alert. So, it was with the fashion of air-travel. The first aviator's certificate granted by a British authority was issued by the Royal Aero Club of the United Kingdom to Mr. J. T. C. Moore-Brabazon in March 1910, when already the exploits of flying men were the theme of all the world.

By the 1st of November in the same year the Royal Aero Club had issued twenty-two certificates; that is to say, twenty-two pilots, some of them self-taught, and some trained in France, were licensed by the sole British authority as competent to handle a machine in the air. Eight years later, in November 1918, when the armistice put an end to the active operations of the war, the Royal Air Force was the largest and strongest of the air forces of the world. We were late in beginning, but once we had begun we were not slow. We were rich in engineering skill and in material for the struggle.

Best of all, we had a body of youth fitted by temperament for the work of the air, and educated, as if by design, to take risks with a light heart—the boys of the Public Schools of England. As soon as the opportunity came they offered themselves in thousands for a work which can never be done well when it is done without zest, and which calls for some of the highest qualities of character—fearlessness, self-dependence, and swift decision. The Germans, before the war, used to speak with some contempt, perhaps with more than they felt, of the English love of sport, which they liked to think was frivolous and unworthy of a serious nation. Their forethought and organisation, which was intensely, almost maniacally, serious, was defeated by what they despised; and the love of sport, or, to give it its noblest name, the chivalry, of their enemies, which they treated as a foolish relic of romance, proved itself to be the most practical thing in the world.

The English pioneers of flight, who had learned their flying abroad, brought back their knowledge, and did what they could to arouse their country to effort. What their success would have been if the peace of Europe had continued unbroken and unthreatened it is impossible to say, but progress would probably have been slow—an affair of sporadic attempts and scattered adventures. The two strongest motives, patriotic devotion and commercial gain, would have been lacking. The English have never been good at preparing for a merely possible war; they are apt, indeed, to regard such preparation as ill-omened and impious. This strenuous and self-dependent breed of men, being conscious that they do not desire war, and believing that he is thrice armed who has his quarrel just, have always been content, in the face of many warnings, to repose their main confidence in the virtue of their cause and the strength of their character.

The risks that they run through this confidence have often been pointed out, but it should also be remembered that by their reluctance to act on theory they have often been saved from the elaborate futility and expense of acting on a false theory. The disaster which has befallen Germany cannot but strengthen them in their belief that it is dangerous to devote care and thought to preparing for all imaginable conflicts. So also in the activities of civil life, before they undertake a large outlay they ask to be assured of solid gains. They leave it to the adventurers, who have never failed them, to blaze the track for commerce. Where a new science is concerned, this mode of progress is slow. Private enterprise and personal rivalry too often bring with them the tactics of secrecy.

Science is not an individual possession, and the man who tries to appropriate it to himself often sterilises his work and forfeits his place in the history of progress. In his anxiety to assert his own claims he forgets that his work has been made possible only by what has come to him as a free gift from others, that his own contribution to human knowledge is a slight thing, that in protecting himself against imitators he is also depriving himself of helpers and pupils, and is bartering the dignity of science for the rewards of a patentee. The Wrights in America and Captain Ferber in France left behind them a full and frank record of all their doings, thereby conferring an enormous benefit on others, and securing for themselves an unassailable position in the history of flight.

Much may be said in favour of the traditional English doctrine of free competition. Where knowledge is readily accessible, and the field is open to all, free competition stimulates and rewards industry and skill. On the other hand, where a new science is struggling into being, commercial competition often retards it by a network of restrictions and concealments, and converts knowledge, which ought to be a public trust, to the darker purposes of private gain. The coming of the war burst these bonds, and immensely quickened the progress of the science of flight. Inventors, who are usually poor men, so soon as their country called on them, put themselves at her disposal, and found their chief reward in helping to save her at her need.

The course of events during the early years of the twentieth century left England no time for developing the art of flight in her own tentative and permissive fashion. The coming of the new art coincided with the rapid gathering of the storm-cloud that was to burst in the Great War. In 1903 the Wrights first flew in a power-driven machine. In 1909 the achievements of the Rheims meeting marked the end of the infancy of the art. In 1912 the Royal Flying Corps was formed. During this same period of ten years armaments were being piled up by all the greater European countries, international tension was increasing, and ominous events, small in themselves, but impressive by the gravity and solemnity with which they were regarded by the chancelleries of Europe, recurred in a series of growing intensity and significance.

Germany was not threatened in any part of the world, but Germany was known to believe in war, and many responsible observers were uneasily and reluctantly forced to the conviction that Germany intended war, and would make war for unlimited purposes on any small occasion created or chosen by herself. The Royal Flying Corps was formed not for far-sighted ulterior ends, as an instrument of progress and research, but for a very present need, as a weapon to be placed in the hands of the country on the day when battle should be joined. Two years before the corps was formed the aeronautical force at the disposal of the nation was centred in the balloon factory and balloon school at Aldershot.

The naval and military officers who had interested themselves in aeronautics were few, but they were competent and enthusiastic; they believed in the air, and were quick to recognise inventions of promise. The consequence of this was that the aeroplane and the airship in England, from the very first, grew up more or less tended by the government, and received as much encouragement as could possibly be given under the severe restrictions of parliamentary finance. Almost every airship that was built was built by the government. Almost every pioneer of flight in England sooner or later came into touch with the government, and did work for the nation.

As early as 1904 Mr. S. F. Cody, who had been connected in early life with the theatrical profession in America, and had made many experiments in aeronautics, was supplying kites to the balloon factory. In 1906 he was appointed chief instructor in kiting, and in 1908 he built for himself an aeroplane, similar in type to the machine of Mr. Glenn H. Curtiss, and made many experimental flights over Laffan's Plain. He was a picturesque and hardy individualist of the old school; though he had had no technical training as an engineer, his wide practical knowledge, his courage, and his exuberant vitality made him a man of mark, and engaged the admiration of the public. Most of his work was official; he was killed by the breaking of his machine in the air while flying over Laffan's Plain, in August 1913.

Another early inventor, Lieutenant J. W. Dunne, joined the balloon factory in 1906, and at once began to carry out systematic trials with gliders. Encouraged by Colonel J. E. Capper, who was in charge of the factory, and assisted by Sir Hiram Maxim, he devised a biplane glider with a box-kite tail, which when it was suspended from a kind of revolving gallows at the Crystal Palace attained a speed in the air of seventy miles an hour and rose to a height of seventy feet. Later on, the experiments were transferred to Blair Atholl in Perthshire, where the power-driven Dunne aeroplane was produced and flown. It had backward sloping wings which performed the function of a stabilizing tail.

Most aeroplanes are modelled more or less closely on flying animals; the Dunne aeroplane took hints from the *zannonia* leaf, which, being weighted in front by the seed-pod, and curved back on either side, becomes, as the tips of the leaf wither and curl, a perfectly stable aerofoil for conveying the seed to a distance. The gliding powers of the *zannonia* leaf were first noticed by Ahlborn of Berlin, and several foreign aeroplanes were modelled on it. The stability of the Dunne machine was surprising, and it performed many good flights before the war, but it sacrificed speed and lifting power to stability, so that its history in the war is a blank. Stability spells safety, and safety is not the first condition insisted on by war.

An obstinately stable machine is good for trudging along in the air, but it is not easy to manoeuvre in face of the enemy. The Dunne machine adjusted itself more readily to the gusts and currents of the air than to the demands of the pilot. Skilled war-pilots prefer to handle a machine which is as quick as a squirrel and responds at once to the pressure of a finger on the control. If the aeroplane had been developed wholly in peace, some of the stable machines of the early inventors would have come into their own, and would have had a numerous following.

The first flight ever made over English soil was made by Mr. A. V. Roe, in a machine of his own construction. Mr. Roe began life as an apprentice at the Lancashire and Yorkshire Railway Locomotive Works, and very early distinguished himself in cycle racing. He then qualified as a fitter at Portsmouth Dockyard, studied naval engineering at King's College, London, and spent three years, from 1899 to 1902, in the merchant service as a marine engineer. The seagulls and the albatross of the southern seas set him thinking, and he began to make model gliders. Returned home again, he spent some time as a draughtsman in the motor industry.

The news of the Wrights' achievements found in him a ready believer, and he wrote to *The Times* to combat the prevailing scepticism. His letter was printed, with a foot-note by the engineering editor to the effect that all attempts at artificial flight on such a basis as Mr. Roe described were not only dangerous to human life, but were foredoomed to failure from the engineering standpoint. From 1906 onwards Mr. Roe devoted all his time and all his savings to aviation.

In 1907 he made a full-size flying machine and took it to the

Brooklands motor track. He had no sufficient engine power, and while he was waiting many months for the arrival of a twenty-four horsepower Antoinette engine from France he induced sympathetic motorists to give him experimental towing flights. It was difficult, he says, to induce the motorists to let go at once when the machine began to swerve in the air; they often held on with inconvenient fidelity, and many of the experiments ended in a dive and a crash. In the spring of 1908 his Antoinette engine arrived, and on the 8th of June he made the first flight ever made in England, covering some sixty yards at a height of two feet from the ground. Then he received notice to quit Brooklands. He had never been much favoured by the management, who perhaps thought that the wreckage of aeroplanes would not add to the popularity of a motor-racing track, and his experiments had been made under very difficult conditions, for he was not allowed to sleep in the shed where his machine was housed, nor to practise with the machine during the hours when the track was in use.

He applied to the War Office for leave to erect his shed by the side of Mr. Cody's at Laffan's Plain, but was refused. He then consulted a map of London, and pitched upon Lea Marshes, where there were some large fields open to the public, and some railway arches, a couple of which he rented and boarded up. In the stable of a house at Putney belonging to one of his brothers he had already built a tractor triplane which he now removed to Lea Marshes.

Under the stress of his misfortunes he had parted with his Antoinette engine, so he had nothing better for his triplane than a nine horse-power J.A.P. motorcycle engine designed by John Alfred Prestwich. With this, the lowest-powered engine that has ever flown in England, he made, in June 1909, the first successful flight on an all-British aeroplane. Thereafter he made many flights; the earliest of these were short and low, earning him the name of 'Roe the Hopper', but before long he was making flights of three hundred yards in length at a height of from six to ten feet.

One day in the summer of 1909 a young woman who had come down to commit suicide in the River Lea saw his machine skimming about and went home; then she wrote to Mr. Roe urging him to let her take his place as pilot and so save his life at the expense of hers. Mr. Roe very tactfully replied that he would gladly let her fly the machine when he had perfected it, thus offering her something to look forward to. But his chief troubles were with the local authorities, who employed a bailiff to watch him and prevent his flying. At Brooklands

Mr. Roe had become accustomed to early rising, and it was some time before the bailiff caught him in the act of preparing to fly, but he was caught at last, and police-court proceedings were instituted.

Just at that time Blériot flew the Channel, and the case was dropped, so that the authorities were not called upon to decide whether flying is legal or illegal. As for Mr. Roe, he moved on to Wembley Park, where he flew with steadily increasing success. In 1910 he made an aviation partnership with his brother, who had prospered as a manufacturer of webbing in Manchester. In the same year he had his revenge on Brooklands, for the new manager, Major Lindsay Lloyd, saw the possibilities of aviation, and converted the centre of the track into an aerodrome. There the Roes were welcomed, and there they produced and flew their thirty-five horse-power tractor triplane.

After a visit to America they settled down to their work and had their revenge on the War Office by producing the famous Avro machine, so named after its inventor. In its original form it was a tractor biplane with a Gnome engine of fifty horse-power, shortly afterwards increased to eighty horse-power. It became, and has remained, the standard training machine for the Royal Air Force. It is sufficiently stable, and yet sensitive, and can fly safely at high or low speeds.

It set the fashion to the world in tractor biplanes. Mr. Roe had never believed in the front elevators of the early American and French aeroplanes, with the pilot sitting on the front edge of the plane, exposed to the air; nor in the tail held out by booms, as it is in the pusher machines, with the airscrews revolving between the body of the machine and the tail. For his perfected machine of 1913 he had the advice of experts and mathematicians, but the general design of the machine was his own, worked out by pure air-sense, or, in his own words, by 'eye and experience'.

Early in 1914 the German Government bought an Avro seaplane, which soon after was the first heavier-than-air machine to make the voyage from the mainland to Heligoland. No machine designed in the early days of flying can compare with the Avro. As it was in 1913, so, but for improvements in detail not easy to detect, it remained throughout the war. Its achievements in the field belong to the beginnings of the war; it raided the airship sheds at Friedrichshafen, and, handled by Commander A. W. Bigsworth, it was the first of our machines to attack and damage a Zeppelin in the air. For fighting purposes, it has had to give way to newer types, but as a training machine it has never been superseded, and even those aeroplanes which surpass it in fighting quality are most of them its own children.

The early history of Mr. A. V. Roe has been here narrated, not to praise him, though he deserves praise, nor to blame the government, though it is always easy to blame the government, but to show how things are done in England. His career, though distinguished, is typical; many other pioneers and inventors, whose story will never be written, faced difficulties as he did, and helped to lay the foundations of their country's excellence in the newly-discovered art. It has become almost usual, among those who do nothing but write, to insist that the duty of officials, and other persons publicly appointed, is to save Englishmen the trouble of thinking and acting for themselves.

If the nation were converted to this belief, the greatness of England would be nearing its term. But the nation stands in the old ways, and clings to the old adventurous instincts. As it took to the sea in the sixteenth century to defeat the Spanish tyranny, so it took to the air in the twentieth century to defeat the insolence of the Germans. The late Mr. Gladstone once explained, in the freedom of social conversation, that it is the duty of a progressive party leader to test the strength of his movement by leaning back, so that he may be sure that any advance he makes is adequately supported by the pressure of the forces behind him. It is not the most heroic view of the duties of a leader, but it has in it some of the wisdom of an old engineer, whose business compels him to measure forces accurately.

Queen Elizabeth, if she never expounded the doctrine in relation to the leadership of a nation, at least acted on it. The English people have always proved themselves equal to the demand thus made upon them; if initiative be lacking in the leaders, there is plenty of it among the rank and file. The leaders themselves, once they are buoyed up and carried forward by the rising tide, often seize their opportunity, and surpass themselves.

The history of flight in England from 1908, when Mr. Roe and Mr. Cody first flew, to 1912, when flying became a part of the duty of the military and naval forces of the Crown, is the history of a ferment, and cannot be exhibited in any tight or ordered sequence of cause and effect. Before the government took in hand the building up of an air service, there were many beginnings of private organisation. A man cannot fly until he has a machine and a place for starting and alighting. These are expensive and elaborate requirements, not easily furnished without co-operation.

The Aeronautical Society did much to make flight possible, but its labours were mainly scientific and theoretical. In 1901 Mr. F. Hedges Butler earned his place among the pioneers of the air by founding the Aero Club of the United Kingdom. This club has played a great and honourable part in the promotion of aerial navigation. When it was founded no power-driven aeroplane had as yet carried a man in the air, and the original interest of its members was in the airship, which had been brought into high credit by M. Santos Dumont; but they were quick to recognise the coming of the aeroplane, and the Hon. C. S. Rolls, who helped Mr. Butler to found the club, was one of the boldest and most skilful of early pilots.

The club brought together inventors and sportsmen, and supplied them with a suitable ground for their experiments. It undertook the training of aviators, and from 1910 onwards, issued its certificates, which, when the Government began to build the Flying Corps, were officially recognised as a warrant of proficiency in the new art. An immense service was rendered in these early years by gentlemen adventurers, engineers and pilots, who, all for love and nothing for reward, built machines and flew them. Some of these, when the storm broke, became the mainstay of the national force. To take only two names out of the first hundred to whom the Aero Club granted its certificate—a list crowded with distinction and achievement—it is not easy to assess the national debt to Mr. T. O. M. Sopwith and Mr. Geoffrey de Havilland.

It was in the latter part of 1911 that Mr. Sopwith, having flown with skill and distinction on the machines which he had bought, began to build an aeroplane from his own designs. At that time there were no aeroplane draughtsmen, and he had to stand by and instruct his mechanics point by point. He could not afford to rent a proper workshop; the machine was built in a rough wooden shed, unsupplied with water, and lighted after dark by paraffin lamps. Six men built the machine, and Mr. Sopwith flew it from the ground on which the shed stood. Its performance was better than had ever been obtained from a machine of equal horse-power. It was subsequently bought by the Admiralty, and Mr. Sopwith began to build another aeroplane of higher power, and a flying boat. In 1912 he took premises at Kingston, and there finished these two machines.

The aeroplane was successful; the flying boat was smashed during its trial flight. Another was put in hand, and was bought by the Admiralty. Aeroplane designing was in its experimental stage, so that no large orders were obtainable, and even where three of a kind were ordered, numerous alterations, demanded during the process of construction, prevented three of a kind from being built. These were the beginnings of the famous Sopwith machines, and especially of the single-seater biplane scout type, with its many varieties. The Sopwith 'Tabloid', the Sopwith 'Pup', the Sopwith 'Camel', and, last and best of all, the Sopwith 'Snipe', which was new at the front when the war ended—all these were engines of victory.

So were the equally famous machines designed for the Government by Mr. de Havilland, of which the D.H. 4 is perhaps the greatest in achievement. Mr. de Havilland built his first machine early in 1910, at his own cost. On its trial it travelled some forty yards down a slope under its own power, then it rose too steeply into the air, and when it was corrected by Mr. de Havilland, who piloted it, the strain proved too great for the struts, which were made of American whitewood; the left main plane doubled up, and the machine, falling heavily to the ground thirty-five yards from its starting-point, was totally wrecked. The great things of the air have most of them been done by survivors from wrecks. Mr. de Havilland went to work again on a much improved machine, designed to be an army biplane; in December 1910 he became a member of the staff of the balloon factory at Farnborough, and had a main hand, as shall be told hereafter, in the best of the Government aeroplane designs.

These are instances only; the story of progress is everywhere the same. The wonderful national air force was built by the skill and intelligence of a few men out of the mass of material offered to them by the private pioneers. The work of these pioneers can best be concisely described in connexion with the various centres, or aerodromes, where they gathered together to put their ideas to the test of practice. Not all the early experimenters were attracted to these communities; some preferred to work in secret; but the most fruitful work was done in open fellowship.

Among those who, in the days before aerodromes, devoted time and effort to the problem of flight, Mr. Jose Weiss deserves more than a passing mention. After experimenting with models, he devised a man-carrying bird-like glider, twenty-four feet in span, and in the year 1905, while flight was still no more than a rumour, flew it successfully on the slopes of Amberley Mount, between Arundel and Pulborough. His pilots were Mr. Gordon England and Mr. Gerald Leake. The former of these, in a wind of about twenty-five miles an hour, rose some hundred feet above his starting-point and then glided safely to earth again. The machine, says Mr. Weiss, who, shortly before his death in 1919, kindly furnished this account, had no vertical rudder, and relied on ailerons only, so that it was difficult to steer, he adds:

> The combination of ailerons with the vertical rudder introduced by the brothers Wright was the factor which determined the advent of the aeroplane.

The advent of the aeroplane and its development for war purposes has given an air of antiquity to the researches of Mr. Weiss. Yet many subtle and delicate problems connected with soaring and gliding flight are still unsolved; there was no time for them during the war. Mr. Weiss was firmly convinced that in moving currents of air flight without an engine is possible, though he did not under-estimate the difficulties to be surmounted. His glider was inherently stable, and had funds been available, might have been made into an efficient power-driven machine. The Etrich glider, which was invented at about the same time in Austria and closely resembles the Weiss machine, became the model and basis for the famous German Taube type of monoplane.

Once flying had begun in England it was not very long before home-built aeroplanes were obtainable. Most of the pioneers built their own machines. The first aeroplane factory for the supply of machines to customers was set up by Mr. T. Howard Wright in two of the arches of the London, Chatham and Dover Railway at Battersea, alongside of certain other arches occupied by the balloon factory of Messrs. Eustace and Oswald Short, who were at that time the official balloon constructors to the Aero Club. Like the Voisins in France Mr. Howard Wright put his skill at the service of others. During the winter of 1908-9 he was engaged in building experimental aeroplanes of strange design, chiefly for foreign customers. His own biplane, which resembled the Henri Farman machine, made its appearance in 1910.

He also built a type of monoplane, known as the Avis, for the Scottish Aviation Company, a firm in which the Hon. Alan Boyle and Mr. J. Herbert Spottiswoode were interested. On this monoplane Mr. Boyle made the first cross-country trip in England; the trip lasted for five minutes, and was made over the ground just outside the Brooklands track. It was on this monoplane also that Mr. Sopwith, who understood motor racing, rapidly learned to fly, and a little later, before he became a designer and manufacturer, it was on a Howard Wright biplane that he flew from Eastchurch to a point in Belgium, thus winning Baron de Forest's prize for the longest flight into the continent of Europe.

After a time Mr. Howard Wright joined the Coventry Ordnance Works, where he built a machine for the Military Trials of 1912, and he subsequently took charge of the aviation department of the torpedo-boat firm of Messrs. J. S. White and Co. of Cowes.

The Short brothers followed suit. After seeing Wilbur Wright fly at Le Mans, in 1908, Mr. Eustace Short engaged the help of his brother, Mr. Horace Short, who was an expert in steam-turbines, and they established a primitive aerodrome at Shellness, on the marshes of the Isle of Sheppey, near the terminus of the Sheppey Railway. Here the more enthusiastic of the members of the Aero Club set to work with aeroplanes.

The leading pioneers were Mr. Frank McClean, Mr. Alec Ogilvie, Mr. Moore-Brabazon, and Mr. Percy Grace, all of whom at a later date held commissions in one or other of the national air services; and two more, who held no such commissions, because before the Flying Corps was in being they had given their lives to the cause—Mr. Cecil Grace and the Hon. Charles Rolls. None of these men was in the business for profit, they were sportsmen and something more than sportsmen; they loved the new adventure and they spent their own money freely, but pleasure was not their goal; they understood what flying meant for the welfare of their country, and they worked for the safety and progress of the British Empire.

It was at Shellness in October 1909 that Mr. Moore-Brabazon, on a machine designed and built by Mr. Horace Short and fitted with a Green engine, flew the first circular mile ever flown on a British aeroplane. There were many other experiments and achievements at Shellness. These were the days, says Mr. C. G. Grey (to whose knowledge of early aviation this book is much indebted), when the watchers lay flat on the ground in order to be sure that the aeroplane had really left it. At the close of 1909, Mr. Frank McClean, who devoted his whole fortune to the cause of aviation, purchased a large tract of ground, level and free from ditches, in the middle of the Isle of Sheppey, close to the railway station at Eastchurch, and gave the use of it free to the Aero Club.

To this ground the Short brothers, who, besides building their own machines, had taken over the Wright patents for Great Britain, removed their factory, and Eastchurch very quickly became the scientific centre of British aviation. Early in 1911 the Admiralty were persuaded to allow four naval officers to learn to fly. The machines on which they learned were supplied free of cost by Mr. McClean, and another member of the Aero Club, Mr. G. B. Cockburn, who was the solitary representative of Great Britain at the Rheims meeting of 1909, supplied the tuition, also free of cost. The instructor naturally marked out for this purpose, says Mr. Cockburn, was Mr. Cecil Grace, a fine pilot, a great sportsman, and a man quite untouched by the spirit of commercialism, but only a few weeks earlier he had been lost while flying over the Channel from France to England.

So Mr. Cockburn undertook the task, and for about six weeks took up his residence at Eastchurch. The four naval officers were Lieutenants C. R. Samson, R. Gregory, and A. M. Longmore, of the Royal Navy; and Captain E. L. Gerrard, of the Royal Marine Light Infantry. They were keen and apt pupils, as they needs must have been to qualify for their certificates in six weeks of bad weather, which included one considerable snow-storm. Instruction in those days was no easy matter; the machines were pushers; the pilot sat in front with the control on his right hand, the pupil sat huddled up behind the instructor, catching hold of the control by stretching his arm over the instructor's shoulder, and getting occasional jabs in the forearm from the instructor's elbows as a hint to let go.

Mr. Cockburn weighed over fourteen stone, and Captain Gerrard only a little less, so the old fifty horsepower Gnome engine had all it could do to get the machine off the ground. In a straight flight along the aerodrome the height attained was often no more than from twenty to thirty feet; then the machine had to make a turn at that dangerously small elevation, or fly into the trees at the end. Fortunately, the aerodrome was clear except for a few week-end pilots who practised on Saturdays and Sundays; the instructor and his pupils were energetic, flying at dawn and at dusk to avoid the high winds; and the training was completed with only two crashes, neither of them very serious.

The navy pupils were encouraged throughout by frequent visits from their senior officer at Sheerness, Captain Godfrey Paine, who befriended aviation from the first. Eastchurch soon became the recognised centre for the training of naval officers in the use of aeroplanes, and when, upon the death of Mr. Horace Short, in 1917, the Short brothers vacated Eastchurch, and concentrated at their Rochester works, Eastchurch passed wholly under naval control. No honour or reward that could be given to the members of the Royal Aero Club, and especially to Mr. McClean and Mr. Cockburn, can possibly equal this, that they were part founders of the Naval Air Service.

If Eastchurch was the earliest centre of scientific experiment and practical training in aviation, it was at the great Brooklands aerodrome that flying first became popular. Mr. Roe had been allowed to use a shed in the paddock for his first aeroplane, and had made his first flight there, at a very humble elevation, but the conversion of the centre of the track into an aerodrome was not effected till late in 1909. The motor-racing track, about three and a half miles in length, enclosed a piece of land which was partly farmland and partly wilderness, watered by the river Wey. On the west side of it there was the Weybridge sewage farm, which, when flying began, added new terrors to a forced descent.

When Mr. Henri Farman visited England, in January 1908, he inspected Brooklands and expressed an unfavourable opinion of its fitness as a site for an aerodrome. So, nothing was done until the visit of M. Louis Paulhan, late in 1909. The performances of M. Paulhan at the Rheims meeting, and later at the Blackpool meeting, excited much admiration, and Mr. G. Holt Thomas, who had long studied aviation, and never grew tired of advocating its claims, determined to engage popular interest and, if possible, official support by bringing Paulhan to London, there to display his powers. By arrangement with Mr. Locke King, the proprietor of Brooklands, and Major Lindsay Lloyd, the new manager, one of the fields of the farm was cleared of obstacles and was mowed and rolled, as a landing ground for Paulhan.

There in the closing days of October 1909 Paulhan gave many exhibition flights on a Farman biplane. The longest of these, which lasted nearly three hours and covered ninety-six miles, was made on the 1st of November and was witnessed by Lord Roberts. The exhibition was not a financial success; thousands of spectators watched the flying from outside the ground, without contributing to the expenses; but it impressed the committee of the Brooklands Automobile Racing Club, and they resolved to turn the interior of their track into an aerodrome. Obstacles were removed, pits and ponds were filled in, the solider portions of the ground were furnished with a fairly good grass surface, rows of wooden sheds were erected, and the pioneers of the new art were invited by public advertisement to become their tenants.

By the spring of 1910 many aeroplanes were at work on the Brooklands ground, most of them running about it in the earnest endeavour to get up sufficient speed to rise into the air. There were no instructors. Among the earliest of the pioneers was the Hon. Alan

Boyle, and an account which he has kindly supplied, telling how he learned to fly his little Avis machine, describes the usual method of the learners, he says:

> I asked Mr. Howard Wright to build me this monoplane, which we placed upon the market as proprietors. . . . She was fitted with an Anzani engine of nominal twenty-five horsepower, but which really gave about eighteen to twenty horse-power. . . . She usually ran for about five minutes, and then got overheated and tired and struck work. . . . . I took my little Avis to Brooklands about February 1910, after it had been exhibited at the Aero Show. I partitioned off a corner of my shed, and slept in a hammock, so that I was able to take advantage of the still hours in the early morning. It is amusing to look back now and remember how I used to watch anxiously a little flag which I flew above my shed, to see what strength of wind was blowing. At first, I never used to go out until the flag was practically hanging from the mast, or was only flapping very gently in the light air, which occurred usually in the very early morning. At that time there were at Brooklands, I think, the following: Grahame-White, who was even then a comparatively experienced pilot; Charles Lane, who like me had brought out a monoplane, but with a curious tail, a fixed cambered surface with another elevating plane above and within eight inches or so of it. However, it flew very steadily indeed, when it was tested some months later. . . . . A.V. Roe was also there experimenting with his triplanes. Later on, he got them flying well. He did the most astonishing things with them.
>
> They were beautiful little machines and beautifully built, and it was a delight to watch them in the air. It was wonderful the way in which they answered to the helm. He used to go straight to a point, put his rudder over, and without any fuss or "bank" or anything, you would suddenly find the machine pointing in the exact opposite direction. . . . Then there were also there, with Blériot machines, Messrs. James Radley and Graham Gilmour. The latter was afterwards killed. Radley got his certificate on the same day as I. We were all learners at Brooklands in those days: I am the possessor of a silver cup kindly presented by the Brooklands Race Club authorities for making a circular flight, which shows we were not very advanced. In fact, no one except

Grahame-White and A.V. Roe knew anything about it at all, and they didn't know much.

I started by simply rolling about the ground in the ordinary way, and then in a short time opened her out and made short hops in an endeavour to get off the ground. I remember quite well, after I had been out, walking along my wheel tracks and examining them, and being fearfully pleased when I saw them disappear for a yard or two. That showed that I had flown.

After I had done this sort of thing for about a month, Mr. Manning came down and produced a larger jet for my engine, and warned me that if the machine would fly, she would do so now with the extra power the new jet would give the engine. He then sat down to pick up the pieces, and off I went! After making a few hops to get my hand in I opened her out and made a long steady flight of about a hundred yards, six feet up, and landed shouting. I had waited and worked for that for some time, so you can imagine my delight.

I did "straights" for some weeks and then started to do curves, and of course the banking of the machine terrified me. However, I grew used to that, and made my curves shorter and shorter until at last I thought I would try for a circle. I pointed the Avis to a part of the ground which had not yet been levelled, and of course once I was over that I jolly well had to get round somehow: so I made my first circuit. After I had been doing circuits for some time and had begun to have a little confidence in myself, I decided that it was necessary to do a *volplane*. I made inquiries and was told that immediately I shut off the engine it was necessary to put the nose of the machine down to approximately her gliding angle, otherwise she would "stall" and glide back on her tail.

You will sympathise with me when I say that I preferred to avoid this latter alternative, although as a matter of fact, having a flat tail which carried no weight, she would no doubt have taken up her gliding angle naturally. Anyway, I didn't know this, and in April (I think) in some trepidation I got over that step in my progress. I confess that I went four times round Brooklands with my hand on the switch before I could make up my mind to do the deed, and of course when I did so, I found there was nothing in it, and realised the delight of coming down without the noise of the engine in my ears. So much for learning to fly.

Brooklands was a well-known place; large crowds of people had often visited it to see the motor races; and it was near London; so that from the first it attracted sportsmen and aeroplane designers. It became the experimental ground of the British aircraft industry. Among its early tenants were the British and Colonial Aeroplane Company, founded by the late Sir George White of Bristol, and commonly known as the Bristol Company; Messrs. Martin and Handasyde, the makers of the Martinsyde machines; Mr. A. V. Roe; the Scottish Aviation Company, with their Avis monoplanes; Mr. J. V. Neal, who, in the endeavour to avoid the Wrights' patents, produced a curious biplane with a new system of control, and many others.

Sheds were occupied by Mr. Douglas Graham Gilmour, one of the finest pilots in his day that this country had produced, who was killed in an accident at Richmond, and by Mr. F. P. Raynham, who became notable as a test-pilot. Many sportsmen rented sheds and tried their hands at building machines. Mrs. Hewlett, the wife of the novelist, having learned to fly, started a school at Brooklands in partnership with M. Blondeau, a French engineer and pilot. Her son, like the swallows, was taught to fly by his mother. By the middle of 1911 a whole village of sheds had grown up. Most of the tenants were men of means, but they spent so much money on their experiments that they had very little left for the amenities of life. Mr. C. G. Grey remembers men, the possessors of comfortable incomes, who lived for years on thirty or forty shillings a week, and spent the rest on their aeroplanes.

It was a society like the early Christians; it practised fellowship and community of goods. To the eyes of a casual visitor there was no apparent difference between the owner of an aeroplane and his mechanics; all alike lived in overalls, except in hot weather, when overalls gave place to pyjamas. If anyone lacked tools or materials he borrowed them from another shed; they were lent with goodwill, though the owner knew that his only chance of seeing them again was to borrow them back. The social centre of the place was a shed in the middle of the front row, which was let by Major Lindsay Lloyd as a restaurant, and was called 'The Blue Bird'.

This restaurant was run by the wife of one of the community; it united in itself all the utilities of a public-house, a club, a parliament, and a town-hall. Living as they did for ends of their own and apart from the great world, the brotherhood naturally took pride in themselves as a chosen people, dedicated to high purposes, and they scorned the Philistines who came in crowds to see the motor racing.

On race days the Philistines were permitted, for reasons connected with the balance sheet, to have tea at 'The Blue Bird'; some of them would wander over the aerodrome, and even into the sheds, to ask the sort of question that is often asked by those who will not undertake the liabilities but think it graceful to assume the airs of a patron.

After a few years, when aeroplane construction and design settled down into a regular industry, the glory of this primitive Arcadian community passed away, and its members were scattered far and wide. Brooklands became a place of business; in one row of sheds the Bristol Company, in another Messrs. Vickers, established schools where many distinguished pilots who served their country in] the war learned to make their first flights. Before the war broke out the British branch of the Blériot Company had also taken a number of sheds, and had transformed them into a regular aircraft factory; the Martin and Handasyde firm had adapted three or four sheds, and were building a couple of monoplanes for a transatlantic attempt by that brilliant flyer, the late Mr. Gustav Hamel. In June of 1914 he was drowned in flying the English Channel, and the firm suffered a severe set-back.

Lastly, when the war came, the Brooklands aerodrome, with all its flyable machines, was taken over by the military authorities, and the days of ease and innocence were ended. A large Vickers factory was built, and turned out many machines for the Flying Corps; the Blériot and the Martinsyde firms also continued their activities for a couple of years, and then moved, the one to Addlestone, the other to Woking. During the war Brooklands was used as a training station, a wireless experimental depot, and an acceptance park by the Royal Flying Corps, which permitted the use of it, for experimental flying, to the Vickers, Martinsyde, and Blériot firms.

Other early aerodromes, almost contemporary with Brooklands, were Hendon, in the northern suburbs of London, and Larkhill, on Salisbury Plain, a few miles from Amesbury. The Hendon aerodrome, like Brooklands, owed its first fame to the initiative of Mr. Holt Thomas. After the Brooklands adventure he kept in touch with M. Louis Paulhan, and in April 1910 persuaded him to make an attempt to win the £10,000 prize offered by the *Daily Mail* for a flight from London to Manchester.

During the previous winter M. Paulhan had been flying with success in America, while his rival, Mr. Grahame-White, had been busy with his flying school at Pau, in the south of France. Mr. Grahame-White brought a Farman biplane to London, and obtained permission to use Wormwood Scrubs for his starting-place. Mr. Holt Thomas, looking for a starting-place for Paulhan, heard of a field at Hendon which was being used by a firm of electrical engineers for experiments with a small monoplane, and got leave to start Paulhan thence. After Paulhan's success, Mr. Grahame-White and his business partner, the late Mr. Richard T. Gates, visited Hendon, and finding that the field was one of a number bordering the Midland Railway without any roads cutting across them, fixed on the place as the site of what was afterwards called the London aerodrome. Here the Grahame-White Aviation Company made it their business, from 1911 onwards, to familiarise Londoners with the spectacle of flying and with its practice.

They built a number of sheds and let them to manufacturing firms. One of these was the Aircraft Manufacturing Company, formed in 1911 by Mr. Holt Thomas, who at that time was working the British rights for the French Farman Company. Another was the W. H. Ewen Aviation Company, which subsequently became the British Caudron Company. A third was the British Deperdussin Company; the wonderful little Deperdussin monoplane, in the 1912 Gordon Bennett Trials at Rheims, carried its pilot, M. Vedrines, at a speed of nearly two miles a minute for a flight of over an hour. Hendon, moreover, laid itself out to attract spectators. There were stands and enclosures, with prices of admission to suit all purses. Aeroplane racing was a regular feature of the meetings.

As early as 1911 about a hundred and twenty members of the two Houses of Parliament paid a visit to the place by invitation and were some of them taken into the air. In July 1911 two great races, modelled on the *Circuit de l'Est* of 1910, made Hendon one of their stages. The earlier of these, somewhat magniloquently called the 'Circuit of Europe', was organised by a syndicate of newspapers. The appointed course was from Paris to Paris by way of Liège, Utrecht, Brussels, and London—a distance of about a thousand miles. The second, not many days later, organised by the *Daily Mail* newspaper, and called the 'Circuit of Britain', laid its course from Brooklands to Brooklands, by way of Edinburgh and Glasgow, Exeter and Brighton, with Hendon as the first stopping-place on the outward journey.

Both competitions were won by Lieutenant Conneau of the French Navy, who flew under the name of 'Beaumont'. Whether because only one Englishman (Mr. James Valentine) took part in the earlier competition, or because the second was better advertised and first awoke the public to the significance of aviation, it was to witness the second that enthusiastic crowds first flocked to Hendon. Mr. Holt Thomas, who helped to organise the 'Circuit of Europe', found a stolid indifference in the English public.

As he drove to Hendon along the Edgware road he noticed that the people on their way to the aerodrome were mostly French. Indeed, he adds, at the aerodrome itself there were almost more police than public to witness what was a great event in the history of flight. For the 'Circuit of Britain', on the other hand, an enormous crowd gathered at Hendon. The fields on Hendon Hill were black with spectators. One farmer, remembering to make hay while the sun shone, erected a canvas screen all along the upper part of his field, and by charging threepence for admission to the other side reaped a good harvest.

The competitors arrived on a Saturday afternoon, and left again for the north early on the Monday morning. Thousands of spectators spent Sunday night in the fields, gathering round bonfires or singing to keep themselves warm. In this competition the French monoplane pilots carried off the honours; Beaumont was first, and Vedrines second. The only competitor who completed the full course on a British-built machine was the stalwart and persevering Mr. Cody on his own biplane.

The man who makes a machine and the man who flies one are the heroes of the epic of flight. Next to them, all credit must be given to the public-spirited financiers and patrons who encouraged flight, especially to those of them who were not deceived, and knew that they are the servants, not the masters, of the conquerors of the air. As a promoter of flight Mr. Holt Thomas deserves more than a passing mention. He worked early and late for the progress of the art and for its recognition by the government. He was fond of calling attention to comparative figures, pointing out, for instance, in April 1909, that the sum already spent by Germany on military aeronautics was about £400,000; by France about £47,000; and by Great Britain about £5,000.

He befriended and rewarded distinguished aviators. In September 1910 he attended the military manoeuvres in France, the first in which aeroplanes were used for reconnaissance, and there, among the experts of many nations, came across no other Englishman. He also attended the British manoeuvres of the same year, where Captain Bertram Dickson made some reconnaissance flights. In 1911 he founded the Aircraft Manufacturing Company. He foresaw a great future for military aviation and constantly did battle with the argument, fashionable among some soldiers, that the British Army, being a small army, required only a small air force.

He held, from the first, that a national air force had many tasks to fulfil other than reconnaissance, and that it should be a separate organisation, distinct from both army and navy. Men like Mr. Thomas, who, though they had no official standing, devoted study and effort to the problems of military aviation, were not a little serviceable to the country; they agitated the question, and kept it alive in the public mind. When the Royal Flying Corps at last was formed they might justly claim that they had helped it into existence.

The only other aerodrome which need here be mentioned is the Larkhill aerodrome, often called the Salisbury Plain aerodrome, or the Bristol Flying School. Eastchurch saw the beginnings of naval flying; Larkhill was the earliest centre of military flying. In 1909 Captain J. D. B. Fulton, of the Royal Field Artillery, was stationed at Bulford camp. M. Blériot's cross-Channel flight, in July of that year, excited his interest, and he set himself to build a monoplane of the Blériot type. This proved to be a slow business, so he bought from the Grahame-White firm a Blériot machine fitted with a twenty-eight horse-power Anzani engine, and began to experiment with it on the plain.

Captain Fulton was a highly skilled mechanical engineer; some of his patents for improvements in field guns had been adopted by the War Office, and from the proceeds of these he was able to meet the costs of his experiments. His title to be called the founder of military aviation in Great Britain must be shared with others, especially with Captain Bertram Dickson, also of the Royal Field Artillery, who was the first British officer to fly. After seeing the flying at the Rheims meeting in August 1909, Captain Dickson procured a Henri Farman biplane, and learned, at Châlons, to fly it. He was a natural flyer, as Captain Fulton was a natural engineer.

During 1910 he attended many aviation meetings in France; at Tours and elsewhere he held his own in competition with some of the most famous of French aviators. His ruling passion was not sport, but patriotism; he was chiefly concerned to put the aeroplane as a weapon into the hands of his country. In the summer of 1910 he made the acquaintance of Sir George White of Bristol, and joined the staff of the British and Colonial Aeroplane Company At the army manoeuvres of that autumn he appeared, a herald of the future, on a Bristol biplane, but found some difficulty in persuading the officers in command to make use of his services. The cavalry, in particular, were not friendly to the aeroplane, which, it was believed, would frighten the horses; and when a reconnaissance flight was arranged and had to be put off because the wind was high and gusty, aviation fell in esteem.

Nevertheless, some of Captain Dickson's flights served to show how an aeroplane might help an army. It was natural enough that the cavalry should prefer to carry on the work of reconnaissance in the usual way. Men believe in the weapons they are skilled to handle. When the rapier was introduced into England in the sixteenth century, it found no friends among the masters of the broadsword; its vogue was gained among young gentlemen educated in France and Italy. To let an aeroplane, attempt their work would have seemed to the cavalry like dropping the bone to catch at the shadow. But youth will be served, and in a very few years the shadow cast by Captain Dickson's aeroplane spread and multiplied and covered the field of battle.

His own career came to an untimely end. A few weeks after the manoeuvres he suffered a severe accident at the Milan aviation meeting, where he performed some of those admirable glides from a height, with the engine off, for which he had become famous. Just after one of these he had opened the throttle of his engine, and was rising again, when another aviator, called Thomas, who was rapidly planing down on an Antoinette, crashed into him from above. He lay between life and death for some weeks, and in his delirium talked incessantly of his work, and of the War Office, and of what he hoped to do for it. His health had been severely strained by the early work he had done in tropical countries, where he had been employed in exploration and the delimitation of boundaries; though he recovered from his accident and flew again, he grew steadily worse, and died in Scotland on the 28th of September 1913.

Along with Captain Fulton and Captain Dickson a third army aviator must be mentioned—Lieutenant Lancelot Gibbs, who also learned to fly at Châlons, and was present, on a Farman biplane, at the manoeuvres of 1910. At the Wolverhampton meeting, earlier in the same year, he had had a slight accident which injured his spine, so that before very long he had to give up flying. He had flown at many early meetings, and had distinguished himself in duration flights. The dangers encountered by these pioneers may be illustrated from the experiences of Lieutenant Gibbs in Spain. He had arranged to give an exhibition of flying at Durango, near Bilbao, in April 1910.

The delivery of his machine, which was sent from Paris by the

Spanish railways, was delayed, and many hours of work had to be spent on it before it could fly, so that the thirty thousand people who had assembled were kept waiting for more than an hour. They grew impatient, and when the machine was wheeled out of its shed, so that they might see the work of preparing it, they crowded round it and handled it roughly. It had to be taken back into the shed again. Thereupon they began to throw stones, which disabled the mechanic and broke the shed. One of them advanced to Lieutenant Gibbs with a drawn knife and said that flying was an impossibility, there was no such thing as aviation, and therefore they were going to knife him. The crowd shouted 'Down with science, long live religion!' Lieutenant Gibbs saved himself by his courage and calm, and was taken away by an escort, under a heavy shower of stones, to the judge's house. Within half an hour the shed, with all it contained, was burned to the ground.

These three soldiers, Captain Fulton, Captain Dickson, and Lieutenant Gibbs, have earned their place in history as the first British military aviators. Of the three Captain Fulton had most to do with Salisbury Plain and the beginnings of the air force. Some civilians were also at work. During the manoeuvres of 1910 Mr. Robert Loraine, in a Bristol machine fitted with transmitting apparatus, succeeded in sending wireless messages, from a distance of a quarter of a mile, to a temporary receiving station rigged up at Larkhill. The earliest permanent establishment at Larkhill seems to have been an aeroplane shed tenanted by Mr. H. Barber, who subsequently held a commission in the Air Force.

Mr. Barber was a man of independent means, and being convinced that flying would play a great part in war, he spent his time in devising aeroplanes for naval and military purposes. He founded a firm of his own, called 'The Aeronautical Syndicate', and produced a type of monoplane with elevator in front, which, in its later development, was named the 'Valkyrie'. He taught a good many people to fly, but none of them, except himself, became expert pilots.

The 'Valkyrie' was the last survivor of the earliest type of flying machine, often called the 'Canard' type, because the elevator is extended in front like the head of a duck in flight, and serves to balance the machine. When this type of machine was at last superseded by the more shapely modern design, Mr. Barber's syndicate died a natural death. At the outbreak of war, he joined the Royal Flying Corps, and became one of its leading technical instructors, with the rank of captain.

The second shed erected at Larkhill was built by the War Office and was intended for the use of the Hon. C. S. Rolls, so that he might give instruction to army pilots. The death of Mr. Rolls at the Bournemouth meeting in July 1910 (one of the heaviest losses that aviation has suffered in this country) put an end to that scheme, and the shed was assigned, later on, to Captain Fulton. The third shed was erected by Mr. G. B. Cockburn, who on his return from France applied to the War Office for leave to carry on at Larkhill. Mr. Cockburn was the first, he says, actually to fly over Salisbury Plain. He worked hand in hand with Captain Fulton, to whom he lent his Farman machine (the first machine built by Henri Farman after he left the Voisin firm) in order that Captain Fulton might pass the tests for the pilot's certificate in November 1910. The two together did much good work at Larkhill, and were successful in gaining a certain measure of recognition for the aeroplane among the army units on the plain.

From these beginnings Larkhill rapidly developed. Towards the end of 1910 the Bristol Company, having come to an agreement with the War Office, established themselves at Larkhill in a solidly built row of sheds. The government were not as yet prepared to undertake any large expenditure upon aeroplanes; their attitude was tentative; they had been advised by the Committee of Imperial Defence that the experiments with aeroplanes, hitherto carried out at the balloon school, should be discontinued, but that advantage should be taken of private enterprise in this branch of aeronautics.

Accordingly, the Bristol Company opened at Larkhill the Bristol School of Aviation, which remained in existence until the outbreak of the war. The chief instructor was M. Henry Jullerot, one of the best pilots in France; he was assisted by Mr. Gordon England, who had shown so much skill in handling the gliders of Mr. Weiss, and by Mr. Harry Busteed, the first notable Australian pilot. Salisbury Plain is perhaps the best stretch of country in England for the training of aviators; the school grew and prospered; the Bristol machine proved to be excellently well fitted for the purposes of instruction, and the pupils, being relieved from the dangers that attend a forced landing in populous country, distinguished themselves by their bold flying.

There were many camps of soldiers in the neighbourhood, so that the work done at Larkhill did much to convert the army to a belief in aviation. The tokens of the conversion were soon visible. On the 28th of February 1911 an Army Order was issued, creating the Air Battalion of the Royal Engineers. It ran as follows:

With a view to meeting army requirements consequent on recent developments in aerial science it has been decided to organiss an Air Battalion, to which will be entrusted the duty of creating a body of expert airmen. . . . The training and instruction of men in handling kites, balloons and aeroplanes, and other forms of aircraft, will also devolve upon this battalion. The establishment of this battalion will be organised into (1) headquarters and (2) two companies. . . . The officers will be selected from any regular arm or branch of the Service on the active list. . . . A selected candidate will, on joining the Air Battalion, go through a six months' probationary course. . . . An officer who satisfactorily completes the probationary period will be appointed to the Air Battalion for a period of four years. . . . The Warrant officers, non-commissioned officers, and men will be selected from the Corps of Royal Engineers. The existing Balloon School will be superseded by the Air Battalion, and the new organisation will be regarded as taking effect from April 1st, 1911.

The formation of the Air Battalion was a great step in advance. Up to this time flying had been a hobby or fancy of individual men; it was now organised and provided for as a part of the duty of the army. The battalion was duly formed under the command of Sir Alexander Bannerman, with Captain P. W. L. Broke-Smith, of the Royal Engineers, as adjutant. Airships were assigned to No. 1 Company and aeroplanes to No. 2 Company. This latter company, commanded by Captain Fulton, went into camp at Larkhill about the end of April.

When Mr. Cockburn, after completing the course of instruction that he gave at Eastchurch, returned to Larkhill, he found the battalion in process of formation. Its history, and its development, a year later, into the Royal Flying Corps, must be narrated in the next chapter, and the steps traced by which a small balloon factory at Chatham, started in the year 1882, was transformed into the Air Force of today. A few words may here be added concerning Captain Fulton and Mr. Cockburn, who bore so large a part in the creation of an air force. While he held his command in the Air Battalion, Captain Fulton did all he could to get it recognised as a separate branch of the army, distinct from the Royal Engineers.

When the Royal Flying Corps was formed he was appointed to the Central Flying School as instructor, and was put in charge of the workshops there. Thence he passed to the aeronautical inspection department, which was placed entirely under his control and became, what it has remained, one of the foundations of the strength and efficiency of the air force. He could not be spared from this work for combatant service, so he saw little of the war at the front; but more flying officers than ever heard his name owe him a debt of gratitude for his faithful work in providing for their safety. He died of an affection of the throat in November 1915. Mr. Cockburn, who was continuously at work on Salisbury Plain for a period of something like four years, continued, as a civilian, to give his help, first in the aeronautical inspection department, and, later on, in the investigation of aeroplane accidents.

The account which has now been given of the early years of flying in England may serve to show what a wealth of private enterprise lay ready to the hand of the government when the building of the air force began. The Royal Air Force, like the tree of the Gospel parable, grew from a small seed, but it was nourished in a rich soil. The great experiment of flying attracted a multitude of adventurous minds, and prepared recruits for the nation long before the nation asked for them.

This early predominance of private enterprise, it is worth remarking, told in favour of military rather than naval flying, and, when the Flying Corps was formed, started the Military Wing at an advantage. Little has been said as yet, because in truth there is little to say, of pioneer work in the air done by sailors. Yet no one would dare to assert that the average sailor is less resourceful, less inventive, less open to new ideas, than the average soldier. No doubt there were many senior officers in the navy, as there were many in the army, who in the early days regarded aviation with professional impatience and scorn.

Further, the higher command of the navy were not quick, when aircraft became practically efficient, to divine or devise a use for them. The difficulty of employing them over the sea was formidable, and none of their uses was quite so obvious as their use (questioned by more than one distinguished army general) for reconnaissance in a land campaign. But the real difference which told in favour of military aviation lay in the nature of the services. A sailor is attached to his ship, and flying is an art which of necessity must be practised and developed, in its beginnings, over wide level tracts of land.

The value of the airship for distant reconnaissance at sea is now fully recognised, but airship building is not a possible hobby for a young naval officer. Those naval officers who believed in the future of the new weapon were reduced to attempting to influence the government, so that it might undertake the necessary work. While the army officer could attend aviation meetings and demonstrate his opinions in practice, his less fortunate brother in the navy had no resource but to engage in a melancholy course of politics, with small prospects of public result, and smaller prospects of private advancement.

The consequence of all this is that the history of the work done by the navy with aeroplanes and airships is essentially a history of official decisions and official acts. Great credit must be given to individual navy men for their insight and persistence in advocating the claims of the air, but the history of the work done can be fully narrated, without further preamble, in an account of the origin and growth of the national air force.

Chapter 4

The Beginnings of the Air Force

Those who fear, or pretend to fear, that England may witness a revolution like the French Revolution of the eighteenth century or the Russian Revolution of the twentieth century would be well advised to compose their minds by the study of English history. That history, in all its parts, shows the passion of the English people for continuity of development. The first care of the practical Englishman who desires change is to find some precedent, which may serve to give to change the authority of ancient usage. Our laws have always been administered in this spirit; we are willing to accept, and even to hasten, change, if we can show that the change is no real change, but is only a reversion to an older practice, or a development of an established law.

It was a saying of King Alphonso of Aragon that among the many things which in this life men possess or desire all the rest are baubles compared with old wood to burn, old wine to drink, old friends to converse with, and old books to read. The English people are of a like mind; what they most care for is old customs to cherish. The very rebels of England are careful to find an honourable pedigree for their rebellion, and to invoke the support of their forefathers. A revolution based only on theory, a system warranted only by thought, will never come home to Englishmen.

The national love for continuity of development is well seen in the history of the genesis of the national air force. The whole of that force, aeroplanes, airships, kite balloons, and the rest, must be affiliated to a certain small balloon detachment of the Royal Engineers at Chatham. Little by little, very slowly and gradually at first, while only the balloon was in question, with amazing rapidity later, when the aeroplane and the airship came into being and were needed for the war, that single experimental unit of the Royal Engineers grew and transformed itself into a vast independent organisation. Names and uniforms, constitutions and regulations, were altered so often that the whole change might seem to be an orgy of official frivolity if it were not remembered that the powers brought within reach of man by the new science were increasing at an even greater speed. But there was no breach of continuity; the process was a process of growth; the new was added, and the old was not abolished.

From the days of the Montgolfiers for more than a century the value of the balloon in war was a matter of debate and question and experiment. At the Battle of Fleurus, in 1794, the triumphant French republican army used a captive balloon, chiefly, perhaps, as a symbol and token of the new era of science and liberty. Balloons were used in the Peninsular Campaign, but Napoleon's greatest achievements owed nothing to observation from the air. Even in the American Civil War, where the Federals certainly derived some advantage from their use, balloons were criticized and ridiculed more than they were feared. In Great Britain military experiments with balloons began at Woolwich Arsenal in 1878.

In the following year Captain R. P. Lee, of the Royal Engineers, reporting on the work done at the arsenal, stated that they had a thoroughly sound and reliable fleet of five balloons, and a few trained officers and men, competent to undertake their management. One of these balloons accompanied the troops on manoeuvre at the Easter Volunteer Review at Brighton. Captain H. Elsdale, of the Royal Engineers, who was in charge of the party, took part in the final march past; he was in the car of the balloon at a height of two hundred and fifty feet, while Captain J. L. B. Templer, a militia officer, managed the transport on the ground.

A balloon section was present at the Aldershot manoeuvres both in 1880 and in 1882; it was judged a success, and instructions were issued in the autumn of 1882 that the Balloon Equipment Store, as the establishment at Woolwich was called, should be removed to the School of Military Engineering at Chatham, where a small balloon factory, depot, and school of instruction was established in 1883.

The practice with the balloons was under the charge of Major Lee, and in that year Major Templer came to Chatham to carry out certain experiments in the manufacture of balloons. He brought with him a family of the name of Weinling, to construct balloons on a system devised by himself. The fabric of the balloons was the internal membrane of the lower intestine of the ox, sometimes called gold-beater's skin. The Weinling family had a secret, or what they believed to be a secret, for the secure joining together of the pieces of this skin. As they held for some time an unchallenged monopoly in the manufacture of aircraft for the British Empire, they have earned the right to a niche in the temple of Fame.

They were five in number—Mrs. Weinling and her elder son Fred, who were the first to arrive at Chatham, her two daughters, Mary Anne and Eugene, and a younger son Willie, who was about eighteen years old and was subject to fits. Their work was carried on not without interruption. In November 1883 Major Templer wrote a letter to the president of the Royal Engineer Committee, stating that he was delayed in the completion of the skin balloon by the principal workman having been sentenced to three months' imprisonment for an assault on the police.

As the Weinling family were the only persons who had ever worked in skin-balloon manufacture, and as he himself was the only other person acquainted with the art, Major Templer asked and obtained leave to have two sappers trained to the work. But this new departure led before long to further troubles. The family were very jealous of their secret, and when the balloon factory began to be enlarged it was only with the greatest difficulty that the members of the family could be induced to give instruction to other workers.

Nevertheless, in the course of a year, several balloons were made, of three sizes, the largest size having ten thousand cubic feet of capacity, and the smaller sizes seven thousand and four thousand five hundred cubic feet. When, in the autumn of 1884, an expedition was sent to Bechuanaland under Sir Charles Warren, to expel the filibusters who had raided the territory, to pacificate the country, and to reinstate the natives, a balloon detachment under Major Elsdale and Captain F. C. Trollope, of the Grenadier Guards, attached to the Royal Engineers, was included in the expedition. They took with them in the detachment three balloons, and a staff consisting of fifteen non-commissioned officers and men. There was no fighting.

At Mafeking, which was then a native village, it was found that owing to the elevation above sea-level neither of the two smaller balloons had lift enough to raise a man into the air, and that the largest balloon could take up only one observer. A native chief, Montsiou by name, went up a short distance in the balloon. The remark that he made serves to show the value of aircraft in impressing primitive peoples:

If the first white men who came into this country had brought a thing like that, and having gone up in it before our eyes, had then come down and demanded that we should worship and serve them, we would have done so. The English have indeed great power.

The chief was right. For any nation to which is entrusted the policing and administration of large tracts of uncivilized country, an air force, civil and military, is an instrument of great power.

Balloons were used again on active service in the following year, 1885, in the Soudan. A small detachment, under Major Templer with Lieutenant R.J.H.L. MacKenzie, of the Royal Engineers, and nine non-commissioned officers and sappers, accompanied the expeditionary force. The best of the material had been sent to Bechuanaland, so the equipment was very imperfect, but ascents made in a balloon of one of the smaller types, at El Teb and Tamai, and elsewhere, proved useful for reconnaissance.

On the return of these two expeditions no attempt was made to keep up a regular balloon section. What was done must for the most part be credited to the energy of those few officers who believed in the future of balloons. Majors Elsdale and Templer ran the factory for building balloons and making hydrogen, and a few non-commissioned officers, trained in balloon work, were held on the strength of depot companies. Most of the practice, in observation of gun-fire and the like, was carried out with captive balloons; the few trips adventured in free balloons were undertaken only when the gas had so deteriorated that the balloon had not lift enough for captive work.

Major Elsdale did what he could to improve equipment, and urged that two or three officers should be appointed to give their whole time to balloons and to form the nucleus of a balloon corps. He is himself remembered for his pioneer experiments in aerial photography; he sent up cameras attached to small free balloons, with a clockwork apparatus which exposed the plates at regular intervals and which finally ripped the balloon to bring it to earth again. Major Templer, for his part, took a house at Lidsing, about four miles from Chatham and the same distance from Maidstone, and, in 1887, started a small summer training camp for balloon work in one of the fields adjoining his house.

Lieutenants G. E. Phillips and C. F. Close, of the Royal Engineers, attended this camp, which was held again in the following years. In

1889 Lieutenants B. R. Ward and H. B. Jones, also of the Royal Engineers, joined it, and the authorities were soon faced with the necessity of coming to a decision whether balloons should be introduced as a definite part of the service. In that year Lieutenant-General Sir Evelyn Wood was in command of the Aldershot Division; he arranged for a balloon detachment, consisting of Lieutenants Ward and Jones, Sergeant-Major Wise, and some thirty non-commissioned officers and men, to be sent to Aldershot early in the summer to take part in the annual manoeuvres.

The experiment was a success. The balloons operated with a force which marched out from Aldershot against a flying column of the enemy encamped near the Frensham ponds. A fortunate piece of observation work is believed to have won Sir Evelyn Wood's favour for the new arm. The balloons were asked to answer the question, 'Has the enemy any outposts in rear of his camp?' Lieutenant Ward made an ascent, and though it was getting dusk and the country was not very open, he was able to see the enemy placing pickets round his camp on the nearer side, but could detect no movement beyond the camp. He reported that there were no outposts in rear of the camp; and a night attack sent out from Aldershot was a complete success.

The German Emperor was present at these same manoeuvres, and a march past on the Fox Hills was organised for his benefit. The balloon detachment was ordered to take part in it. Balloons, being an un? recognised part of the army, were not hampered by any of those regulations which prescribe the etiquette to be observed on formal occasions. Lieutenant Ward, who was in command of the detachment, resolved that he would march past in the air, at an altitude of about three hundred feet, in a balloon attached to the balloon wagon. The weather was fine and calm, and the balloon sailed by in state, with the result that the spectators all gazed upwards and had not a glance to spare for the horse artillery, the cavalry, or any other arm of the service.

Sir Evelyn Wood reported favourably on the use of balloons, and in 1890 a balloon section was introduced into the British Army as a unit of the Royal Engineers. The question of a site for the depot caused some delay. Opinion favoured Aldershot, but the General Officer Commanding objected that Aldershot should be reserved for military training. Major Templer was in favour of Lidsing, where for several years he had carried on at his own costs. In the result the depot moved to Aldershot, and having taken over a piece of very soft ground at South Farnborough, near the canal, began to erect sheds. The contractor for a balloon shed was nearly ruined by the expense of making foundations. So, things fluctuated; the factory remained at Chatham, and the depot and section, after a summer spent at Aldershot, collected at Chatham again for the winter of 1890-1.

In 1892 a definite move was made to Aldershot, which continued thereafter to be the centre for balloon work. In 1894 the balloon factory, under the superintendence of Colonel Templer, was fully established at South Farnborough. Finally, in 1905, a new and better site was found for it in the same neighbourhood, and by successive additions to the sheds and workshops then erected the present Royal Aircraft Establishment came into being. Some difficulty is presented to the historian by the chameleon changes of official nomenclature, which disguise a real identity and continuity. The Balloon Equipment Store at Woolwich became the untitled factory at Chatham, which in its turn became the balloon factory at South Farnborough.

In 1908 it was decorated, and became His Majesty's Balloon Factory; a little later it was named the Army Aircraft Factory; and, later again, in 1912, the Royal Aircraft Factory. So, it continued until far through the war, when, its initials being required for the newly-welded Royal Air Force, it was renamed yet again, and was called the Royal Aircraft Establishment. These changes in nomenclature were, of course, office-made, and have none of the significance that attaches to the history of popular names. But the Royal Aircraft Establishment itself was a natural growth, and derives, without break, from the unofficial establishment of balloons at Woolwich.

In 1899 the South African War began. Four balloon sections took an active part in the campaign. The first section, commanded by Captain H. B. Jones, operated with the troops under Lord Methuen, and proved its value at the Battle of Magersfontein. The second section, commanded by Major G. M. Heath, was with Sir George White throughout the siege of Ladysmith. An improvised section, commanded by Captain G. E. Phillips, was raised at Cape Town, and joined Sir Redvers Buller's force at Frere Camp, for the relief of Ladysmith. The regular third section, commanded by Lieutenant R. D. B. Blakeney, embarked for South Africa early in 1900, and joined the Tenth Division at Kimberley.

It is not easy to make a just estimate of the value of the balloons in this war. Some commanding officers were prejudiced against them, and the difficulties and miscarriages which are inevitable in the use of a new instrument did nothing to remove the prejudice. The steel tubes in which the hydrogen was compressed were cumbrous and heavy to transport. The artillery were not trained to make the fullest use of the balloons; the system of signalling by flags was very imperfect; and the signallers in the air often failed to attract the attention of those with the guns. For all that, the balloons proved their value.

The Ladysmith balloon did good service in directing fire during the battle of Lombard's Kop, and, more generally, in reporting on the Boer positions. Later on, in the siege it was impossible to get gas, and the balloons fell out of use. At Magersfontein it was by observation from the air that the howitzer batteries got the range of the enemy's ponies concealed in a gully, and accounted for more than two hundred of them. On the 26th of February 1900 an officer in a balloon reported on General Cronje's main position at Paardeberg, and the report was of value in directing the attack on the position.

These operations put a heavy strain on the factory. Its normal output of one balloon a month was increased during the war to two balloons a month, and new buildings at a cost of more than four thousand pounds were proposed in 1900, and approved by the Aldershot Command. Even during the South African War there were other calls on the factory. In the summer of 1900 a balloon section, under the command of Lieutenant-Colonel J. R. Macdonald, was embarked for China; in the following year the factory supplied two balloons and stores for the Antarctic Expedition of Captain Scott. These demands interfered with experimental activities, which when the war was ended, and especially when the new factory was built in 1905, were renewed with great zest.

As early as January 1902 Colonel Templer, having visited Paris to report on the doings of M. Santos Dumont, recommended that experiments with dirigible balloons should be carried out at once, but received from the War Office the reply that the estimates for the year, which, apart from these experiments, amounted to £12,000, must be cut down to half that sum. Nevertheless, from time to time grants were obtained for the construction of elongated balloons, for a complete wireless telegraphy equipment, and, in 1903, for a dirigible balloon. The factory was a small place, but it was full of energy.

In 1904 experiments were carried out with man-lifting kites, with photography from the air, with signalling devices, with mechanical apparatus for hauling down the balloons, and finally with petrol motors. It must always stand to the credit of those who were in charge of the factory that when the new era came, revolutionizing all the conditions, and when, not many years later, the Great War made its sudden and enormous demands, they rose to the occasion. Up to May 1906 Colonel Templer was superintendent of the balloon factory. He was succeeded by Colonel J. E. Capper, who held the position till October 1909.

During these early years the balloon factory and balloon school, though nominally separate, were under the same control. The chief point of difference was that the factory employed some civilians, whereas the school was wholly in the hands of the military. Mr. Haldane decided to separate them, and in 1909 appointed Mr. Mervyn O'Gorman superintendent of the balloon factory, while Colonel Capper, who was succeeded within a year by Major Sir Alexander Bannerman, Bart., took over the command of the balloon school. Colonel Capper was a firm believer in the future of the aeroplane, and a true prophet.

In a lecture on military ballooning, delivered at the Royal United Service Institution in 1906, just before he was appointed superintendent of the balloon factory, he concluded with a forecast.

> There is another and far more important phase of aerial locomotion, which in the near future may probably have to be reckoned with.... In a few years we may expect to see men moving swiftly through the air on simple surfaces, just as a gliding bird moves.... Such machines will move very rapidly, probably never less than twenty and up to a hundred miles per hour; nothing but the heaviest storms will stop them. They will be small and difficult to hit, and very difficult to damage, and their range of operations will be very large.

Colonel Capper acted on this belief, and during his time at the factory did what he could with meagre funds to encourage aviation. The policy which, in the spring of 1908, he recommended to the War Office was to buy any practicable machines that offered themselves in the market, and at the same time not to relax effort at the factory. The attempts of Lieutenant Dunne and Mr. Cody to construct an efficient aeroplane seemed hopeful, and the factory took them under its wing. Lieutenant Dunne worked at Blair Atholl from 1907 onward, and Mr. Cody, in the winter of 1907-8, began to construct his machine at Farnborough.

In the autumn of 1908 the Hon. C. S. Rolls offered to bring to Farnborough a biplane of the Farman-Delagrange type, and to experiment with it on behalf of the government, in return for the necessary shed accommodation. The acceptance of this proposal had been authorized when an accident to Mr. Cody, caused by want of space, discredited the fitness of the factory ground for aeroplane work, and the arrangement with Mr. Rolls was deferred. He renewed his proposal in the spring of 1909, this time with the offer of a Wright machine, and he had established himself at Farnborough, when his death, at the Bournemouth meeting of 1910, cut short a career of brilliant promise, for Mr. Rolls was not only one of the best of practical aviators, but was alert in all that concerned the science of his craft.

At the factory the experiments of Mr. Cody and Lieutenant Dunne were supported and continued, but progress was slow and uncertain, and when, early in 1909, the two machines between them had involved an expense of something like £2,500, further experiments with them were abandoned for a time. Their performance did not seem to warrant a large national outlay, and the bulk of Colonel Capper's work was devoted to what seemed the more promising task of supplying airships for the army. The earliest of these had been designed by Colonel Templer, and two envelopes of gold-beater's skin were ready by 1904, but the cost of making them had been so great that further progress on the ship was arrested until 1907.

In September of that year the first British Army airship, the *Nulli Secundus*, sausage-shaped, about a hundred and twenty feet long and less than thirty feet in diameter, took the air and passed successfully through its trials. It was driven by an Antoinette engine of from forty to fifty horse-power, and attained a speed of about sixteen miles an hour.

On the 5th of October the ship flew from Farnborough to London, circled round St. Paul's Cathedral, manoeuvred over the grounds at Buckingham Palace, and, on her return journey, as she could make no headway against the wind, descended in the centre of the cycle-track at the Crystal Palace, having been in the air for three and a half hours. Five days later, to avoid damage by a squall, the ship was deflated, packed up, and returned to Farnborough by road. Colonel Capper, influenced doubtless by the success of the Lebaudy airship in France, decided to rebuild *Nulli Secundus* as a semi-rigid, but funds were short, and work could not be commenced on her until the following year. In the reconstruction every possible portion of the original ship was ingeniously utilised.

The reconstructed ship was taken out for her first trial in the air on the 24th of July 1908. During this flight of four miles, lasting eighteen minutes, she suffered various mishaps.

After two more short flights she was deflated at the end of August, and the career of the *Nulli Secundus* was ended. Another smaller and fish-shaped airship, nicknamed the *Baby*, was put in hand during the autumn of 1908, but was not completed until the following spring. To enable her to carry a more powerful engine the *Baby* was enlarged by cutting the envelope in half and introducing a wide belt of goldbeater's skin in the middle. Rechristened the *Beta*, she was ready for flight at the end of May, and on the 3rd of June 1910 made a successful night-flight from Farnborough to London and back, covering a distance of about seventy miles in just over four hours.

The output of the factory was small, almost insignificant, compared with the efforts being made by foreign nations. Colonel Capper preferred not to attempt the construction of rigid airships till more was known of them. The Zeppelins were the only reputed success, and no Zeppelin, at that time, had succeeded in making a forced landing without damage to the ship. But the output of the factory is no true measure of the progress made. The officers in charge worked with an eye to the future. Early in 1906 a proposal was put forward by Brevet Colonel J. D. Fullerton, Royal Engineers, and was warmly supported by Colonel Templer, for the appointment of a committee consisting of military officers, aeronauts, mechanical engineers, and naval representatives, to investigate the whole question of aeronautics.

A modified form of this proposal was put forward three years later, in 1909, by Mr. Haldane, then Secretary of State for War. He invited Lord Rayleigh and Dr. Richard Glazebrook, the chairman and the director of the National Physical Laboratory, to confer with him, and asked them to prepare for his consideration a scheme which should secure the co-operation of the laboratory with the services, thus providing scientific inquiry with opportunities for full-scale experiment. A scheme was drafted; it was discussed and approved at a conference held in the room of the First Lord of the Admiralty, and was submitted to the Prime Minister, Mr. Asquith, who took action on it, and appointed 'The Advisory Committee for Aeronautics', under the presidency of Lord Rayleigh.

Seven of its ten members were Fellows of the Royal Society. The chairman was Dr. Glazebrook. The army was represented by Major-General Sir Charles Hadden, the navy by Captain R. H. S. Bacon, the Meteorological Office by Dr. W. N. Shaw. The other members were

Mr. Horace Darwin, Sir George Greenhill, Mr. F.W. Lanchester, Mr. H. R. A. Mallock, and Professor J. E. Petavel. To these, soon after, were added Mr. Mervyn O'Gorman, when he took over the charge of the balloon factory, and Captain Murray F. Sueter, R.N., who deserves not a little credit for his early and persistent efforts to foster aeronautics in the navy. The great value of this committee was that it brought together the various bodies concerned with aeronautics, and combined their efforts. In particular, it gave to the new science the highly skilled services of the National Physical Laboratory, which organised at Teddington a new department, with elaborate plant, for the investigation of aeronautical questions.

From this time onward, the National Physical Laboratory worked in the closest co-operation with the balloon factory. Mathematical and physical investigations were continuously carried on at the laboratory, and improvements suggested by these researches were put to the practical test at the factory. Questions of air resistance, of the stresses and strains on materials, of the best shape for the wing of an aeroplane and the best fabric for the envelope of an airship—these and scores of other problems were systematically and patiently attacked. There were no theatrically quick results, but the work done laid a firm and broad base for all subsequent success.

Hasty popular criticism is apt to measure the value of scientific advice by the tale of things done, and to overlook the credit that belongs to it for things prevented. The science of aeronautics in the year 1909 was in a very difficult and uncertain stage of its early development; any mistakes in laying the foundations of a national air force would not only have involved the nation in much useless expense, but would have imperilled the whole structure. Delay and caution are seldom popular, but they are often wise. Those who are stung by the accusation of sloth are likely to do something foolish in a hurry. Nothing is more remarkable in the history of our aeronautical development than its comparative freedom from costly mistakes. This freedom was attained by a happy conjunction of theory and practice, of the laboratory and the factory.

The speculative conclusions of the merely theoretical man had to undergo the test of action in the rain and the wind. The notions and fancies of the merely practical man were subjected to the criticism of those who could tell him why he was wrong. The rapid growth in power and efficiency of the British air force owed much to the labours of those who befriended it before it was born, and who, when it was confronted with the organised science of all the German universities, endowed it with the means of rising to a position of vantage.

The same sort of credit belongs to the conduct of the balloon factory under Mr. Mervyn O'Gorman, who had charge of it during that very crucial period from the autumn of 1909 to the summer of 1916. When he took over the factory he found at Farnborough one small machine shop, one shed for making balloons, and one airship shed. The workers were about a hundred in number, fifty men and fifty women. Seven years later, when Lieutenant-Colonel O'Gorman was appointed to the Air Board as consulting engineer to the Director-General of Military Aeronautics, the hundred had swollen to four thousand six hundred, and the buildings situated on the forest land of Farnborough had increased and multiplied out of all recognition.

This development was made necessary by the war, but it would have been impossible but for the foresight which directed the operations of the period before the war. The factory, working in close co-operation with the Advisory Committee and the National Physical Laboratory, very early became the chief centre for experimental aviation with full-sized machines. Systematic and rapid advance was hardly to be hoped for from unaided private initiative. Many private makers of machines were zealous and public-spirited, but there was no considerable private demand for aeroplanes, and a firm of manufacturers cannot carry on at a loss. Poor though it was in resources, and very meagrely supported by government grants, the factory was what the country had to depend on; and it rose to its opportunities.

Aviation, in its early stages, was cramped and harassed by engine failure. The improvement of the light engine, in design and construction, was the most pressing of needs; but no sufficiently rapid improvement could be hoped for except by the encouragement of private enterprise. For some years the factory refrained from producing any official engine design, and the superintendent attempted to encourage the efforts of private firms. In order to specify the conditions which makers must observe, and to apply proper tests to the engines supplied, it was thought desirable to build an engine laboratory.

Accordingly, an engine test plant was devised and installed. It was set in a wind-tunnel, where by steeply tilting the engine both sideways and lengthways, in varying currents of air, the actual flying conditions could be imitated, and the performance of the engine measured. This plant for the testing of engines might have been used with valuable results, but for one hindrance—the makers of engines were unwilling to send them to the factory to be tested, and the plant remained idle. There was a misunderstanding, which after a time became acute, between the factory and the private makers of aircraft. The factory, zealous for the public interest, believed that it could best serve' their interest by encouraging, supervising, and co-ordinating the efforts of the makers.

The makers, jealous of supervision and control, did not accept that view. A wise judgement will be slow to blame either. The officials of the factory were strong in the knowledge that their work was disinterested and aimed only at the public good. The makers, remembering that progress in aviation had come chiefly by way of private enterprise, feared the paralysing effect of official control, and the habitual tendency of officials, especially of competent officials, to extend their ambitions and their powers. The makers, in short, dreaded a government monopoly. A difference of this kind, even when it is gently and considerately handled, always furnishes a happy hunting-ground for the political agitator and the grievance-monger.

The thing came to a head during the war, when the success of the Fokkers, which reached its height during the early months of 1916, made the public uneasy. The Fokkers late in 1915 had been fitted with guns which fired through the airscrew. This was the secret of their success, which was short-lived, but was made the occasion, in Parliament and elsewhere, for a long array of charges against the administration and command of the Royal Flying Corps. A parliamentary committee, under the chairmanship of Mr. Justice Bailhache, was appointed to investigate these charges. Their report vindicated the Royal Flying Corps and the Royal Aircraft Factory, and expressed admiration for the work done by both under the stress and strain of war. The charges, it should be added, were not supported by the private makers, or 'the trade', as they are called; none of them made any complaint, and some of them went out of their way to record their gratitude for the help they had received from the factory.

Nevertheless, the uncertainty of its relations with the trade caused the factory, in its early days, to undertake a great diversity of business. The designing of aircraft was plainly a matter of the first importance, and for this designing it was necessary to collect a trained staff. The difficulty here was that there were no professional designers; the aeronautical world was a strange ferment of inventors, amateurs, enthusiasts, heretics of all sorts, wedded to their own notions, and mutually hostile. The factory decided to employ only those designers who had

had a solid course of training in engineering shops. By degrees engineers trained in shipyards and officers skilled in motor-car design were added to the staff of the drawing office until, by 1916, it had increased from some half-dozen to two hundred and seventy-five.

When the war came this drawing office proved its value. An immense number of aeroplanes was required, and many firms had to be employed to make them. Some of these firms were well staffed; others not so well. The factory made elaborate detailed dimensioned drawings, marked with every permitted kind and degree of variation—as many as four hundred drawings to a single aeroplane. With the help of these drawings all kinds of firms—organ-builders, makers of furniture, or pianos, or gramophones, or motor-cars—could be turned on to aeroplane manufacture. In the course of two years half a million drawings were issued to various firms; and those firms to whom the whole business of engineering was strange were successfully initiated in one of its most delicate and difficult branches.

Here, too, the outcry was raised, in the newspapers and in Parliament, that the factory was attempting to make a government monopoly of aircraft design and air-engine design. The accusation was disproved; it would probably never have been made but for the admirable efficiency of the factory in rising to meet a national crisis. National defence, it is agreed, cannot safely be left wholly to private enterprise, even in England. The factory carried out an immense number of experiments in connexion with aeroplanes and airships. The quest for stability, longitudinal and lateral, in aeroplanes was the chief preoccupation of these early years. Powerful engines are useless in a ship which cannot be trusted to keep afloat.

It was this quest, as much as anything, which drew the factory into designing aeroplanes. The various types of aeroplane designed at the factory bear names which consist of a pair of initial letters, with a number affixed. The letters indicate the type of the machine; the number indicates its place in the series of continually improving variants of the same type. Three of these types were gradually being evolved at the factory in the course of the year 1911. The earliest to attain to practical success was the B.E. type of machine. Every pilot who had his training in the early days of the war was familiar with this machine, though not every pilot knew that the initials are a monument to Louis Blériot, who first flew the Channel.

His achievement gave a great vogue to his monoplane, which was imitated by many designers; and when the factory produced a biplane fitted, like all monoplanes, with a tractor airscrew, in front of the machine, the biplane was called the Blériot Experimental. The F.E. type is the Farman Experimental, a pusher biplane, which for a long time held its own by virtue of two advantages. The observer, being seated in the very prow of the machine, could fire a gun forward without being obstructed by the airscrew. This advantage disappeared after 1915, when, by the invention of synchronizing gears, which timed the bullets to pass between the revolving blades of the screw, tractor machines were enabled to fire directly ahead.

But another advantage persisted. In night-flying, when the eyes are strained to pick up dim shapes in the dark, a clear field of vision is all-important, and the F.E. type of machine continued to be used in night raids throughout the war. The third type was the S.E., or Scouting Experimental. The fifth variant of this type, the S.E. 5, gained an enormous reputation in the war as a fighting machine, and indeed was preferred by some pilots to the best scout machines of private makers.

A fourth factory machine, produced just before the war, and no less famous than the other three, was called the R.E., or Reconnaissance Experimental. It was the first almost completely stable machine. Stability is not of the first importance to a righting scout, whose attention is concentrated on his own manoeuvres, but where a machine is used for observation, and the pilot must needs pay heed to all that is visible on the earth beneath, stability is essential. A perfectly stable machine maintains an even keel in varying gusts of wind. If it is tilted, it rights itself. If it is nose-dived, the pilot has only to let go of the control, and after a descent of some hundreds of feet it comes out of the dive and resumes its horizontal flight.

The perfecting of this type of machine was achieved at the factory, and was the work of many minds. On the mathematical side the theory of stability was investigated by Mr. F. W. Lanchester, an authority on the theory of flight, and by Professor G. H. Bryan, a great pioneer, who in 1911 produced his book on *Stability in Aviation*. He had long been interested in the subject; his work, which is recognised as epoch-making, laid a sound mathematical basis for the theory of flight, and directed the work of others along the lines of fruitful experiment.

The theoretical conclusions of Professor Bryan were reduced to a practical form by Mr. Leonard Bairstow and the members of the staff of the National Physical Laboratory, who put the doctrine to the proof of experiment, at first with models, and then with full-scale machines. The dangerous work of trying conclusions with the air fell to the young men of the factory. A brilliant young Cambridge man, Mr. E. T. Busk, of King's College, who had been trained in the laboratory of Professor Bertram Hopkinson, joined the staff of the factory in the summer of 1912, having previously spent a month at the National Physical Laboratory, to acquaint himself with the work there. He understood the theoretical basis of aeroplane design, and he was a daring and skilful pilot.

The R.E. machine was designed by the staff of the factory; Mr. Busk, in collaboration with Mr. Bairstow, worked at the problem of giving it stability. He cheerfully took all risks in trying the full-sized machines in the air. When the R.E. 1 had been theoretically warranted, by experiments with models, to right herself after a nose-dive, he tested the theory by flying the machine to a great height, turning her nose down and letting go the controls. As he expected, she righted. To test the machine, he flew her in all weathers, hurling her against the wind storms. For the purposes of these practical tests he invented an instrument of his own called the Ripograph, which recorded on a single strip all the pilot's movements in warping and steering, as well as the speed, inclination, and roll of the machine.

This machine, when the rudder was turned right or left, automatically banked itself; and when the engine was cut off, took the angle of gliding flight. It was a later variant of the same machine, an R.E. 8 belonging to the Australian Flying Corps, of which it is told that, when the pilot and observer had both been shot dead, in December 1917, the machine continued to fly in wide left-hand circles, and ultimately, when the fuel was exhausted and the engine stopped, fell near St. Pol, some thirty miles from the scene of combat, without completely wrecking itself.

When the war broke out Mr. Busk was more than ever needed at the factory. On the 5th of November 1914 he mounted in an experimental B.E. 2c machine to a height of about eight hundred feet. Exactly what happened will never be known; the petrol vapour must have been ignited by a spark; the machine burst into flames, and after drifting aimlessly for a time, fell on Laffan's Plain. The death of such men as Charles Rolls and Edward Busk was a part of the heavy price that had to be paid for victory, before victory was in sight. There was no other way; the work that they did could not be spared, and could never have been even attempted except by the quiet of absolute courage.

The business undertaken by the factory, apart from its main business of research and experiment, was almost bewildering in its diversity. From the first the officials of the factory insisted on maintaining a high standard of workmanship, which spells safety in the air. This question of workmanship became doubly important during the war, when, in order to improve the performance of machines, all avoidable weight had to be sacrificed, and the factor of safety, as it is called, reduced to the lowest permissible limit. The breaking of a spar or a wire, the failure of a bolt or a nut, may mean a fatal accident.

Further, the factory did what it could to standardise the component parts of an aeroplane, so as to facilitate repair; and this, before the war came, had been largely achieved. It designed and fitted up the instruments necessary for the pilot's use, which record for him his speed through the air, the consumption of his fuel, the rate of revolutions of his airscrew, the height attained, and other essentials.

The average pilot, it is well known, is supplied with more instruments than he uses, but it is true nevertheless that familiarity with the use of instruments has often staved off disasters. At first the factory had refrained from initiating engine designs, but when competition and trial had shown that there was no immediate prospect of obtaining a thoroughly satisfactory engine from English makers, it asked permission of the War Office, and in 1913 designed its own engine. Among its notable devices one or two may be mentioned.

The mooring-mast for airships, to which they can be tethered in the open, was invented at the factory, and developed independently for naval work, by the Admiralty. The fair-shaped wires and struts, to decrease air resistance, were a great improvement. These parts of an aeroplane offer so considerable a resistance to its passage through the air, that when their transverse section, instead of being round, is streamlined, the speed of the machine is increased by several miles an hour. In short, during those early years the factory, which directly or indirectly had to supply most of the requirements of the balloon school, the Air Battalion, and the Royal Flying Corps, combined in itself all the functions of what later on were highly organised separate Government departments—inspection, stores, repairs, the testing of inventions, and the like.

From what has been said it will be seen that the factory continued, as it began, in close relations with the army. It had been founded, under army auspices, at an important inland military centre, and it was not so well adapted, by its history or situation, to serve the navy. The results obtained by research at the National Physical Laboratory, and by experiment at the factory, furthered the science of aviation, and were open to all. But when flight began, a united national air force was not thought of by any one, or was thought of only in dreams.

Meantime the new invention offered to the navy, no less than to the army, new opportunities of increasing the power of its own weapon. The problems of the navy were not the problems of the army, and a certain self-protective jealousy made the two forces keep apart, so that each might develop unhampered by alien control. The navy trusted more to private firms, and less to the factory. It was a difference of tendency rather than a clean-cut difference of policy. Both army and navy made use of the results obtained at the laboratory and the factory.

The army employed many private makers for the supply of machines and engines, and the navy, in the course of the war, ordered a very large number of that most famous of factory machines—the B.E. 2c. But the navy stood as far aloof from the factory as possible, and looked mainly to private firms not only for the supply of machines and engines, but for much of its experimental work. Several of the firms who devoted themselves to the needs of naval aviation did excellent service as pioneers. The most distinguished of these was the firm of the Short brothers—that is, of Messrs. Oswald, Eustace, and Horace Short. The impulse of their work was scientific, not commercial.

As early as 1897 Mr. Eustace Short was an amateur balloonist, and his younger brother Oswald, at the age of fifteen, began to accompany him on his voyages. In a public library they came across that celebrated record of balloon voyages, *Travels in the Air*, by James Glaisher, and made up their minds to construct a balloon of their own. Success led them on step by step; in 1905 they contracted to supply captive war balloons for the Government of India, and in 1906 they became the club engineers of the newly formed Royal Aero Club. The reported successes of the Wright brothers in America shifted the interest of the club, and of the club engineers, from balloons to flying machines; in 1908 they built their first glider—a complete miniature Wright machine, without the power plant—for the Hon. C. S. Rolls.

At about this time they were joined by the eldest of the three brothers, Mr. Horace Short, an accomplished man of science and a lover of adventure; from this time onward, the firm of the Short brothers never looked back. From sketches made by Mr. Horace Short, they built six biplanes to the order of the Wrights. They constructed, in 1909, the aeroplane on which Mr. J. T. C. Moore-Brabazon won the prize offered by the *Daily Mail* for the first all-British machine which should fly a circular mile. They made the outer cover, gas-bags, valves, pressure-gauges, and controlling rudders for the first rigid airship constructed to the order of the Admiralty.

Their early work was done at Shellness, the flying centre for members of the Royal Aero Club, but in 1909 they moved their sheds to Eastchurch in the Isle of Sheppey, which thereafter became the flying centre of the navy. It was here that the first four naval aviators were taught to fly. The tale of the successes of the various Short machines would make something not unlike a complete history of early naval aviation. The first landing on the water by an aeroplane fitted with airbags, the first flight from the deck of a ship, the first flight up the Thames, not to mention many other incidents in the progress of record-making, must all be credited to the Short factory. The brothers held that the right way to advance aviation was to strengthen the resources of the aeroplane-designing firms, so that they might carry out their ideas without being dependent on Government demands, and the extraordinary success of the Short designs for aeroplanes and seaplanes did much to promote that creed.

At the factory the work with airships was continued, though it languished somewhat as interest in aviation grew. England had shown the way in the use of goldbeater's skin, which is greatly superior in endurance and impermeability to any other fabric, but the knowledge leaked through to Germany, and when the price of the skin, always high, suddenly rose higher from heavy German buying, England fell back on rubbered cotton. The *Baby*, altered and enlarged, was rechristened the *Beta*, and a new ship, called the *Gamma*, made of rubbered fabric, was added in 1910. The *Gamma*, though twice reconstructed and altered, was never satisfactory. In 1912 *Beta* No. 2, built in streamline shape, about a hundred feet long, stiffened at the nose with ribs like umbrella-ribs, and driven by a forty-five horse-power Clerget engine, was more of a success. Other airships, the *Delta* and *Epsilon*, of increased size and engine-power, were designed between 1911 and 1913.

In this latter year the Air Committee, a body appointed in 1912 by the Committee of Imperial Defence, advised that the navy, that is to say, the Naval Wing of the newly-formed Royal Flying Corps, should take over the development of all lighter-than-air craft. This advice, which was carried into effect by the end of the year, put an end to military experiments with airships, and supplied the navy with the nucleus of that airship force which during the war did so much good service, in convoy, in scouting for submarines, and in patrolling the coast and the English Channel.

The earliest experiments undertaken by the Admiralty with craft lighter than air had been ambitious and unfortunate. It was always recognised by those who gave thought to aeronautics that for naval purposes the airship has some advantages over the aeroplane. It can remain longer in the air, so that its range of action is greater; it can easily carry wireless apparatus both for transmitting and for receiving; it can take up a stationary point of vantage where the aeroplane must needs keep moving; it can lift a' greater weight; and (not least important) it can enormously add to the efficiency of the observer by supplying him with comfortable and habitable quarters.

These things did not escape the attention of the small and enthusiastic band of naval officers who from the first were believers in the air. Their ideas took shape in proposals which were submitted by the Director of Naval Ordnance (Captain Bacon) to the First Sea Lord (Lord Fisher) on the 21st of July 1908. What was proposed, in effect, was that Messrs. Vickers, Son & Maxim, who had been so successful in the design and manufacture of submarines, should be asked to undertake the construction of a large rigid airship of the Zeppelin type. After many meetings of the Committee of Imperial Defence, at which Captain Bacon propounded his views with great vigour, the committee recommended that the sum of £35,000 should be placed in the Navy Estimates for 1909-10, for the construction of an airship to be designed and built under Admiralty supervision.

The Treasury agreed, and Messrs. Vickers's tender for the airship was accepted on the 7th of May 1909. The huge Cavendish Dock at Barrow-in-Furness was appropriated to the work, and the greatest possible secrecy was observed in all the preparations. A special section was formed to assist in the construction of the ship—Captain Murray F. Sueter, R.N., and, with him, Lieutenant Neville Usborne, Lieutenant C. P. Talbot, and Chief Artificer Engineer A. Sharpe. For two years public curiosity was kept alive on a diet of conjecture. A good part of this time was taken up in improvements and modifications of the design of the ship.

When at last in May 1911 the shed was opened and the huge airship was brought out to her mooring-mast in the dock, those who had expected a larger and better Zeppelin seemed justified in their belief. The ship was 512 feet long and 48 feet in diameter, with a blunt bow and a pointed stern. Her capacity was approximately 700,000 cubic feet. The framework was made of a new alloy called 'duralumin', nearly as strong in tension as mild steel and not much heavier than aluminium. It was covered with 46,000 square yards of water-tight silk fabric, so treated with aluminium dust and rubber that the upper surface of the hull, which had to resist the rays of the sun, showed the silver sheen of a fish, while the lower surface, which had to resist the damp vapours of the water, was of a dull yellowish colour. The hydrogen was contained in seventeen gas-bags of rubbered fabric.

The ship was fitted with two Wolseley motors of one hundred and eighty horse-power each, and with a whole series of vertical and horizontal rudders. She was popularly called the *Mayfly*—a name which, both in and out of Parliament, suggested to bright wits an ill-omened pun. She never flew. For four days she remained tethered to the mooring-mast in the centre of the Cavendish Dock, and successfully completed her mooring trials. During this time the wind was rough, reaching in gusts a velocity of forty-five miles an hour. This wind, being a severer test than any previous airship had successfully encountered when moored in the open, proved the strength of the ship.

But her very strength, and the completeness of her fittings, told against her in another way; the lift of an airship, consisting as it does of a small excess of buoyancy over weight, is always a matter of the most delicate and difficult calculation, and her lift proved to be insufficient. She was taken back into her shed, without mishap, and alterations were at once put in hand. On the 24th of September 1911 she was again drawn out of her shed to be transferred to the mooring-post; in the process she broke her back, and became a total wreck. The ensuing court of inquiry pronounced that the accident was due to structural weakness; the naval officers and men were exonerated from all blame.

This accident had a far-reaching effect. It disappointed public hopes and strengthened the case of objectors. There are always critics who take a certain mild pleasure in failure, not because they prefer it to success, but because they have predicted it. The pioneers of aeronautics could not afford to lose friends; they had none too many. The men in high authority at the Admiralty were not convinced that airships were a desirable and practicable addition to naval resources. They would all have died to save England, but they held that she was to be saved in the old way, on the sea. One gallant and distinguished admiral, when he first saw the *Mayfly*, said, 'It is the work of a lunatic'.

The consequences of the failure were soon apparent. The president of the court of inquiry recommended to the First Sea Lord (Sir A. K. Wilson) that the policy of naval airship construction should, for the time, be abandoned. At a conference held on the 25th of January 1912, in the First Sea Lord's room at the Admiralty, it was decided, in accordance with this recommendation, that the airship experiments should be discontinued. Moreover, the special section, the nucleus of a naval air service, was, by the decision of the Admiralty, broken up, and Captain Sueter and his officers were returned to general service. When the construction of rigid airships was at last taken up again early in 1914, they were too late for the market; the heavy demands of the war delayed their completion, and no British rigid airship was in use at the time of the Battle of Jutland.

It is to the credit of the pioneers of the Naval Air Service that when they were faced with this disaster, after years of fruitless effort, they did not lose heart or hope, but held on their course. Time was on their side. In the later autumn of 1911 the Committee of Imperial Defence, as shall be explained in the next chapter, appointed a technical sub-committee to give advice on the measures which should be taken to secure for the country an efficient aerial service. On the 5th of February 1912 Captain Sueter gave evidence to this body of experts, and sketched in broad outline his ideas for the development of a naval air service. Airships and aeroplanes, he said, were both required, and neither of them should be developed at the expense of the other.

An airship had the great advantage that she could carry long-distance wireless apparatus, and could send or receive a message over a space of three hundred miles. She could stop her engines and drift over suspected places, for the detection of submarines and mines. The seaplane, he maintained, should also be developed, and he saw no insuperable difficulties in devising a machine that should be able to alight on either water or land and to rise again into the air from either, he said:

> I think you have got a certain amount of intellect in the navy to do it, and I think you have got a certain amount of intellect in the army to do it. The two together, with the Advisory Committee—there are talented people there—and the manufacturers in the country; between us all we could devise something. We did not have great difficulty with the submarine boats; and that was all new at first.

The problem of the air, he held, was vital for the navy; and when he was asked whether we must try to command the air as well as the sea, he replied:

I think it will come to that. I do not say that we wish to do so, but I think we will be forced to do so.

In a memorandum submitted to the same sub-committee by Captain Bertram Dickson the meaning of the command of the air is more fully explained, he writes:

> In the case of a European war between two countries, both sides would be equipped with large corps of aeroplanes, each trying to obtain information of the other, and to hide its own movements. The efforts which each would exert in order to hinder or prevent the enemy from obtaining information ... would lead to the inevitable result of a war in the air, for the supremacy of the air, by armed aeroplanes against each other. *This fight for the supremacy of the air in future wars will be of the first and greatest importance*, and when it has been won the land and sea forces of the loser will be at such a disadvantage that the war will certainly have to terminate at a much smaller loss in men and money to both sides.

The whole matter is clearly stated in these passages. The people of Great Britain live in an island. They do not desire—they have never desired—to dominate the world, or to dictate to other peoples how they shall live. They do desire to be free of the world, and to take their luck in it, passing to and fro without hindrance. This freedom of theirs has repeatedly been imperilled by foreign powers, who have always desired a greater degree of uniformity and control than is tolerable to Britain. In order to keep their doors open, the people of this island have been compelled to fight at sea, and have attained a measure of naval power which is sometimes called the mastery of the seas, but which, in essence, is no more than the obstinate and resolute assertion of their right to be the masters of themselves.

They have been adventurers and pirates; they have never been tyrants. They fight desperately because they know that even on distant seas they are fighting for their lives, and for all that makes their lives worth living. Their many victories, under, which they groan, have compelled them to learn the imperial art, an art which they practise not without skill, but reluctantly, and without zest. With the conquest of the air their task of self-defence has been doubled. It is not to be wondered at that those who were responsible for keeping open the gates of the sea should turn their eyes away from the new duty. But the new duty—command of the air, so to call it—was plainly visible to those who once looked at it. We must keep the highways open, or our freedom is gone. We must command the air. Captain Sueter said:

> I do not say that we wish to do so, but I think we shall be forced to do so.

The whole of our naval history is summed up in that sentence; and the whole of our air policy is foretold.

The force that was to compel us was already in being. The science of aeronautics had passed from the experimental to the practical stage, and foreign powers were rapidly building up very formidable air forces. Of these foreign forces we naturally knew most of the French, for France was both our neighbour and our friend. In October 1911 a very full and illuminative report was supplied to the government by Lieutenant Ralph Glyn, an officer attached to the newly-formed Air Battalion. It described, with reasoned comments, the aeronautical exercises carried out by the French air corps at the Camp de Châlons during the previous August.

At that time the French War Ministry had at its disposal, so far as could be ascertained, something between two hundred and two hundred and twenty aeroplanes. The biplanes were all Farmans. The monoplanes, which were on the whole preferred by expert opinion to the biplanes, were of many types, all famous for achievement—Nieuports, Blériots, Deperdussins, R.E.P.'s, Antoinettes, and others. The methods of training were elaborate and complete, and the air corps were continually practised in co-operation with all other arms—infantry, cavalry, and artillery. The writer says:

> There is no doubt at all but that the Germans have suddenly realised that the French Army since the general employment of aeroplanes with troops has improved its fighting efficiency by at least twenty *per cent*. . . . For the last five years the Germans have concentrated their whole attention upon the building, manoeuvring, and employment with troops, of dirigibles. They have gained a slight advance over France, in fact, in this branch of aeronautics; but they have quite dropped behind in the question of heavier-than-air machines. France now after an equal period has just, and only just, formed a really efficient fighting aerial corps; and this lead of five years she is determined to maintain.

This is not an over-statement. From the first the French, who had thought out the whole business, laid great stress on reconnaissance and control of artillery fire as the main uses of aircraft. For reconnaissance the aeroplanes were practised to co-operate with cavalry. For fire control official maps, divided into geometrical squares, so that a pair of numbers will identify a position within a score or so of yards, were supplied in duplicate to the pilots of the aeroplanes and to the commanding officers of batteries. The system of signalling employed was mostly primitive, but already in 1911, the French were experimenting with captive balloons which received the messages from the aeroplane, and by wireless, or some kind of visible signal, transmitted them to the guns. Lieutenant Glyn says:

> Practice has made almost perfect a remarkable system which renders the efficient French artillery more formidable than ever.

Further, infantry were trained to co-operate with aircraft, so as to learn to take advantage of the new arm; and aerial photography was practised, under strict conditions of secrecy, with a surprising degree of success. In short, almost all the uses which later became the commonplaces of the war were exemplified in the French manoeuvres of 1911. Battle in the air and the use of aircraft as a weapon of direct offence were later developments.

In October and November of the same year Captain F. H. Sykes, of the General Staff, and Captain J. D. B. Fulton, of the Air Battalion, visited many of the French military and civil aerodromes, and were present at the military aeroplane competition at Rheims. Captain Sykes says:

> The trials held at Rheims are considerably in advance of anything yet attempted.

The machines were flown by the best available pilots, and were under the personal supervision of the makers and designers. Aerodromes were better and more numerous than in England; many of them were situated in wide plains, so that the learner could make his first cross-country flights over good even landing ground. Captain Sykes, in his report, suggests that aeroplane sheds should be erected and flying schools started at stations not very far apart from one another in England, so that cross-country training may be facilitated.

> These stations should be as near as possible, to where troops are quartered, so as to afford an opportunity for aeroplanes to work with troops on field days. The cost would, I think, be inconsid-

erable in comparison to the value gained.

This suggestion was carried out, but not until the war had compelled an immense expansion of the air force. The French, then, were ahead of us, and were showing us the way. Of German preparations less was known, and estimates of the German air force, even when made by experts, were largely guesswork. The Zeppelin airships enjoyed a world-wide fame, and there is good reason to think that the German Government practised a certain measure of frankness with regard to their airship establishment in order the more effectively to shroud the very resolute effort they were making to overtake the French in the production of aeroplanes. If ever they thought that the airship alone would do their business, that dream soon passed away.

A good deal of valuable information concerning the German air force was obtained in the summer of 1912, just after the formation of the Royal Flying Corps. In June of that year the Technical Sub-committee of the Committee of Imperial Defence (a body whose cumbrous name does no justice to its swift decisions) dispatched two of its members, Captain Sueter and Mr. O'Gorman, to France, Austria, and Germany, to report, primarily, on the whole airship question. In Germany these delegates took occasion to visit five aeroplane factories—the Rumpler, Etrich, Albatross, Harland, and Fokker, besides inspecting various flying grounds and wireless stations. Their report is full of interest.

> No year passes in which orders equal to our total equipment are not placed by Germany, France, and Italy.

In Germany they found there were thirty airships available, and a large Government factory for rigids 'only thinly pretending to be a private speculation.' They append a list of no fewer than twenty-eight military flying grounds at which there were flying camps. They were deeply impressed by the evidence of large expenditure, direct and indirect, on aerial preparation, and the systematic manner of that expenditure.

> The position of Germany appeared to us to be widely different from what it is described in the English press ... and far more active.

During their trip in the Zeppelin airship *Viktoria Luise* they were struck with the fervour of popular enthusiasm.

On passing over villages, isolated farms, &c, everybody turned out and cheered and waved.

This popular enthusiasm was further demonstrated by the substantial evidence of large subscriptions from municipal bodies and private persons. Everywhere they found reason to suspect a certain amount of concealed Government support and subsidy underlying ostensibly private ventures.

This report was presented in July 1912. The technical sub-committee, at a later date, drew some further lessons from it.

> The report shows that German airships have, by repeated voyages, proved their ability to reconnoitre the whole of the German coastline on the North Sea. In any future war with Germany, except in foggy or stormy weather, it is probable that no British war vessels or torpedo craft will be able to approach within many miles of the German coast without their presence being discovered and reported to the enemy. Unless we had obtained command of the air, any idea that our torpedo craft could seek shelter among the Frisian Islands and remain there undetected must be abandoned. . . . The report also shows that German airships have covered a distance equal to the distance from Germany to the British coast without replenishing fuel. . . In favourable weather the German airships can already be employed for reconnaissance over vast areas of the North Sea, and one airship, owing to the extended view from high altitudes under favourable weather conditions, is able to accomplish the work of a large number of scouting cruisers. It is difficult to exaggerate the value of this advantage to Germany. By a systematic and regular patrol of the approaches to the coast, it will be possible in fair weather for German airships to discover the approach of an enemy and to give timely warning of attack, and if the approaches are reported free from the enemy the defenders of the ports and the crews of ships in these ports will be relieved for many hours from the intense and harassing strain caused by uncertainty as to the probability of attack.

Further, the sub-committee point out that the great continental airships, which can easily carry thirty persons, can certainly carry a sufficient weight of bombs to destroy torpedo-craft, dock gates, power stations, magazines, and the like; and that they are far less dependent on favourable weather than is generally supposed.

In short, every one of the strategical and tactical advantages which the Committee of Imperial Defence anticipated in 1909 when recommending the construction of a rigid airship for the Navy, has been, or is in a fair way of being, realised by the German airships. These results have only been attained by perseverance under the most discouraging conditions of disaster and loss.

The total air force possessed by Great Britain, to set over against these great foreign organisations, consisted of two small army airships, named *Beta* and *Gamma*, and a very small number of aeroplanes.

The report of Captain Sueter and Mr. O'Gorman put the whole matter in a new light, and showed the need for action. In regard to aeroplanes, this action had already been taken. In the winter of 1911-12 the subcommittee had recommended the formation of a corps of aviators; and this recommendation, as shall be told in the next chapter, had been promptly carried into effect. As for airships, which chiefly concerned the navy, the question was now not whether the Admiralty were willing to take up experimental work with a new-fangled invention, but whether they could afford to neglect a weapon of certain value, which might prove to be a determining factor in war.

Airships of the largest size and power must be provided, said the subcommittee, in the near future. But to build these airships at once, they were agreed, would be to court disaster. A large airship is of little use to men who have had no training in the handling and navigation of airships. Such experience as was available was to be found at the Royal Aircraft Factory, which had produced and flown airships for military purposes. The Admiralty responded at once; in September 1912 the naval airship section, which had been disbanded earlier in the year, was reconstituted, and Commander E. A. D. Masterman, Lieutenants N. F. Usborne, F. L. M. Boothby, and H. L. Woodcock, and a small number of ratings were attached to the airship squadron of the Military Wing at Farnborough, to gain experience of work with airships.

The airships themselves were to be supplied from various sources. The factory was to build a new airship of the *Gamma* type. A small Willows airship, which happened to be on the market, though it had no military value, was held to be worth its cost for training purposes. The sub-committee also recommended the purchase of two foreign airships. Here there were difficulties. The best airships of Germany were the rigid Zeppelin and the semi-rigid Parseval. The Zeppelin Company was forbidden by the German Government to sell its ships to foreigners; but negotiations for the purchase of a Parseval airship were successful. An Astra-Torres non-rigid airship of about 400,000 cubic feet of capacity was acquired from France in the course of the year 1913.

In July of the same year Mr. Winston Churchill, the then First Lord of the Admiralty, who regularly gave his strong support to naval aeronautics, approved of the construction of two rigid airships and six non-rigid airships. Treasury sanction was obtained for this programme. The rigid airships were to be built by Messrs. Vickers at Barrow-in-Furness. Of the six non-rigids, three were to be of the Parseval type, and three of the Forlanini type. One of the Parsevals was to be built in Germany, and two by Messrs. Vickers, who had succeeded in obtaining a licence for the construction of this type of ship; one of the Forlaninis was to be built in Italy, and two by Messrs. Armstrong Whitworth.

When the war broke out, the Parseval airship completing in Germany was confiscated by the German Government; and the Forlanini airship, under process of construction in Italy, was retained by the Italian Government. The building of one of the rigid airships had just begun, and work on it was for a time abandoned. It is necessary thus to anticipate later events, in order to show how it came about that no airships of the larger type, suitable for distant reconnaissance with the fleet, were in the service of Great Britain during the war.

The building and manoeuvring of airships is not a pastime within the reach of a private purse. The British Government had taken advantage of the enterprise and rivalry of private makers of aeroplanes, whom it wisely permitted to run the risks and show the way. No such policy was possible in the manufacture of airships, which is essentially a Government business. There was therefore, it is perhaps not fanciful to say, something agreeable to the German temper, and disagreeable to the English temper, in the airship as a weapon of war. The Germans put an absolute trust in their government.

Yet, after all, it is the spirit of a people that matters; the most magnificent and exclusive of government organisations will fail through weakness if it is not ultimately based on the voluntary efforts and ingrained habits of the people who stand behind the government and support it. The German Navy was a powerful and splendid growth, fostered by the government. But it was a forced growth, and the failure of the German operations at sea, regarded broadly, must be credited not to the British navy, but to the whole body of British seamen, naval and civilian. The British navy was at its appointed stations; the temper of a seafaring people, self-reliant, resourceful, and indomitable, was everywhere, and shone like a phosphorescence over thousands of unregarded acts of sacrifice.

The private enterprises of officers and men in the navy are limited by the conditions of the service, but such opportunities as could be found or made were not neglected. While the *Mayfly* was building at Barrow-in-Furness Commander Oliver Swann purchased an Avro aeroplane and with the help of subscriptions from other officers and officers' wives made many experiments with a view to adapting it for work over the water. He tried different types of floats on the machine, and at last, on the 18th of November 1911, he succeeded in getting off the water for a very short flight. He was the first in England to achieve this feat, and from that time forward the development of seaplanes progressed rapidly. A full account of these experiments was sent by Captain Sueter to Lord Rayleigh's Advisory Committee, and thereafter a valuable series of researches was conducted at the National Physical Laboratory by Mr. G. S. Baker and others. One result of these researches was the development of a boat-shaped type of float, with flared bows, in addition to the toboggan shape.

Experiment was active also at Eastchurch. During the summer of 1911 the four naval officers whom Mr. Cockburn had taught to fly continued to make practice flights on the two machines supplied by Mr. McClean. In October Lieutenant Samson succeeded in persuading the Admiralty to buy the two aeroplanes and to send to Eastchurch twelve naval ratings, as the basis of a naval flying school. The experiments of this little band of pioneers were all directed to adapting the aeroplane to naval work. Lieutenant Longmore and Mr. Oswald Short designed and tested airbags, by the aid of which a machine successfully alighted on the water. Lieutenant Samson designed and got leave to build in Chatham Dockyard a platform with a double trackway for starting aeroplanes from the decks of ships.

The idea at this time was that the machine should start from the ship and by the aid of the airbags should alight on the water under the lee of the ship, whence it could be lifted on board. The platform was erected on board H.M.S. *Africa*, and Lieutenant Samson made a successful flight from it in December 1911. Thereafter, with the help of Mr. Horace Short, he worked out a design for a seaplane; the machine was completed in March 1912 and its first flight was made at Portland.

On this seaplane Lieutenant Samson flew, first and last, for about a hundred and fifty hours, without breaking a strut or a float, which is a signal testimony to the merits of both the design and the construction.

The Royal Aircraft Factory, working for the Air Department of the Admiralty, also produced a seaplane, which was successfully tested on Fleet Pond. Meantime the first flying boat had been designed by Mr. Sopwith, so that all the material requisite for naval aviation was rapidly making its appearance. If the number of aviators was still very small, that was due to lack of opportunity, not to lack of zeal among naval officers. When the original four were taught to fly their names were selected from a list of about two hundred, all of whom had volunteered for the new service.

Scattered incidents and experiments, like those narrated above, are what make up the history of the beginnings of the national air force. In such a story no closely-knit dramatic sequence is possible. The history of the growth of an oak tree from an acorn may perhaps be told in dramatic form, but who can tell the history of the obscure workings of yeast, or of the growth of a field of grass? The earliest aviators were self-willed and diverse. As Captain Bertram Dickson remarked, when he was questioned concerning their enrolment for the national service:

> One man is a rich man; another man is an artist, or he is an actor; another man is a mechanic. They are funny fellows. You will get a certain number if you pay them well, because they are out for making money; you will get others who will do it for sport, and others who will do it for the advertisement.

The problem for the government and for those who advised the government was how to make a united body out of these odds and ends; how to reduce these talented, excitable, artistic, highly individual elements to the discipline and purpose of a great service. Two admirable instructors were at hand—the army and the navy. The thing had to be done quickly, and most of those soldiers and sailors who realised the importance of the problem were agreed in thinking that the only right way was to get the army and the navy each of them to develop its air service. Some others, looking at the thing in a broader light, held that the air should have its own service. The laws and habits of the land, they argued, are not the laws and habits of the sea; surely the air differs from both of them as much as they differ from each other.

But this opinion could not be acted on at short notice. A great service cannot be built up from the beginning in one year, or even in the lifetime of one generation of men. Time is needed; and time was what was lacking. The only resource for immediate purposes was to engage the sympathies of the army and the navy, who are always willing to cooperate, though never to coalesce, and let each of them build up its own air service after its own fashion. A certain formal unity, which might by degrees become a real unity, could be given to the two air services by the magic of a uniform and a name.

Meantime, what of the Air Battalion, which was formed in the spring of 1911, and continued in being until it was annulled and superseded by the formation of the Royal Flying Corps in the spring of 1912? The Air Battalion numbered among its officers, men distinguished for their achievement, but it was born out of due time. These years, 1911 and 1912, were years of divided counsels and uncertain policy. Rumours and reports of the passenger-carrying flights of the Zeppelin, which by this time had outlived its early misfortunes, and of the formidable development of the French military aeroplane, distracted opinion and paralysed effort. The old debate between heavier than air and lighter than air was reopened.

England could not hope to overtake Germany in the construction of airships; could she hope to match France in the production of aeroplanes? And if she could, was there not a chance, after all, that the future, even for military purposes, lay with the airship? The very composition of the Air Battalion reflected these uncertainties. Its headquarters were at Farnborough; the flying camp for aeroplanes was at Larkhill. Sir Alexander Bannerman, who was in command, was a balloon expert, with a distinguished record in the South African and Russo-Japanese wars.

At a later date, in April 1912, he qualified as an aviator on a Bristol biplane at Brooklands. His adjutant, Captain P. W. L. Broke-Smith, had been an instructor at the balloon school, and was a skilled military airship pilot. Of the officers attached, Captain J. D. B. Fulton, of the Royal Field Artillery, and Captain C. J. Burke, of the Royal Irish Regiment, have inscribed their names on the history of aviation; Captain A. D. Carden, of the Royal Engineers, and Captain E. M. Maitland, of the Essex Regiment, were apostles of the airship. Captain Carden was an expert in meteorology, and Captain Maitland's name will long be remembered in connexion with the first airship flight across the Atlantic, achieved by the R 34, piloted by Major G. H. Scott, in July 1919.

The gradual rise in esteem of aviation is witnessed by the fact that during the last days of the Air Battalion's short career not only Sir Alexander Bannerman but also Captain Broke-Smith and Captain Carden were engaged in qualifying for the aviation certificate of the Royal Aero. Club. There is, of course, no inconsistency in the union of the two methods; the Air Battalion took all aeronautics for its province; there need be no falling out between the aeroplane pilot and the airship pilot so long as each recognises and believes in the other. What most delayed progress was that the higher authorities did not know what to encourage.

The most valuable work done for the national air force in the winter of 1911-12 was done in committee at Whitehall, where the whole matter was conscientiously investigated, and the scheme of the Royal Flying Corps was prepared. Meantime the Air Battalion, in view of its probable speedy extinction, received very little support. The number of aeroplanes supplied to the flying camp at Larkhill was almost ludicrously small, and a large proportion of the time spent in training was devoted to theory and observation work.

The difficulties of the position appear in a memorandum sent by the commandant on the 25th of August 1911 to the chief engineer at Aldershot. This memorandum discusses the employment of the battalion during the coming winter, and recommends that No. 2 Company (that is, the aeroplane company) be recalled to Farnborough for a time, 'in order that the men may live in barracks, do a little drill, and be generally smartened up'. But as some new machines will need trying during the winter, a detachment of the company, it is suggested, should be kept on Salisbury Plain, and its members changed from time to time, so as to prevent the discipline of the company from becoming too lax.

Further it is urged that extra leave for a period of two months should be granted to officers, so that they may go abroad and see what is being done in foreign countries. In discussing the question of special pay for officers the *commandant* remarks that there is a tendency to devote attention solely to aeroplanes.

> At present there are, I believe, forty applicants for vacancies with the aeroplanes, and as far as I know none for work with the dirigibles.
>
> If the rates of pay were made less for dirigibles than for aeroplanes, as is done in foreign countries, this difficulty, he says, would be accentuated.

These misgivings were justified by the event. The recommendations of the commandant were, in the main, carried out, but the conditions during the winter made progress almost impossible. There were no proper living quarters at Larkhill, so officers and men lived at Bulford—the officers at the Royal Artillery Mess—and went to and from their work in horsed transport wagons. As they used to go down to Bulford for dinner at midday, the actual work done in the sheds was inconsiderable.

A further very real difficulty was inevitable, and might be compared to the growing pains of any healthy organism. The air forces of Great Britain took their origin, as has been explained, from the Royal Engineers. For a very long time—something over a quarter of a century—the Royal Engineers had the monopoly of the air. When science quickened new growth, this new growth was still attached by habit and tradition to the old body. In March 1912 eight out of fourteen officers of the Air Battalion were members of the Royal Engineers. The remainder, including some of the keenest students of aviation—Captain Fulton, Captain Burke, Captain Maitland, Lieutenant Barrington-Kennett—were, in a regimental sense, interlopers. Those who understand the strength and virtue of regimental society and regimental tradition will easily understand also how in a mixed body the old loyalty and the new pull different ways and impede the smooth working of the machine.

All these difficulties deserve mention if only because they did in fact make the work on Salisbury Plain poor and ineffective during the winter of 1911-12. But they are not the whole of the story. Keats once wrote to a friend:

> The first thing that strikes me on hearing of trouble having befallen another is this—"Well, it cannot be helped, he will have the pleasure of trying the resources of his spirit."

That pleasure was enjoyed by the little band of stalwarts who about the end of April 1911 went into camp at Larkhill as No. 2 Company, Air Battalion. If they received scant encouragement, they got to work without waiting for more. When Mr. Cockburn, after instructing the naval officers at Eastchurch, returned to Larkhill to find his old machine, he found the company in possession on the plain. Captain Fulton was in command. Most of the officers had had some little experience of flying. Mr. Cockburn says:

> Captain Fulton had had some practice on my machine; Lieu-

tenant Conner had had some also, but not nearly so much. Captain Burke had learnt in France, and was about on a par with Captain Fulton. These two were certainly the best pilots at that time. Lieutenant Barrington-Kennett had had a short course on a Blériot some time before, but had not flown for some months. Lieutenant Cammell was flying a Blériot of weird and wonderful type, his own property. These were the originals, but Captain Loraine and Lieutenant Hynes joined soon afterwards.

To these names should be added another—Lieutenant H. R. P. Reynolds, of the Royal Engineers.

Having taught the navy to fly, Mr. Cockburn now lent his help to the army, he says:

> The machines, with the exception of the Blériot were either Farmans or Bristol box-kites. . . . Lieutenant Barrington-Kennett had no experience on these, and Lieutenant Reynolds had no experience on anything. The experience of the remainder was not sufficient to admit of their acting as Instructors, so Captain Fulton got permission for me to carry on and take Barrington-Kennett and Reynolds in hand. This was an easy business compared with Eastchurch—a three miles' straight with good landing all the way made the first flights an easy matter. There were no incidents, except in a joy-ride for Lieutenant Cammell when his cap blew off and back into the propeller, causing a most tremendous noise which scared us badly, me particularly, as I didn't know the cause. . . . Progress was good; everyone was very keen; and the Air Battalion soon developed into quite respectable pilots without any accidents.

The company had a glorious and adventurous summer. It is strange to compare their doings with the elaborate exercises which were being practised at the same time by the French air corps at the Camp de Châlons. On Salisbury Plain very little effort was made to co-operate with other arms, except spasmodically. The pilots were new to their work, and the triumph was to get into the air at all. The first united effort of the battalion, says Mr. Cockburn, was to fly from Larkhill to Farnborough.

> It was a most exciting event; they went off at intervals, and every one of them got there. It was a very creditable performance both for them and for their mechanics. It must be remembered

that the latter were all inexperienced, but what they lacked in experience they made up for in zest, always ready to learn, and as keen as possible to go up. One of them at this time was the eldest of the McCuddens, and many of the others are now (1918) officers holding considerable positions in the Royal Air Force. They were a fine lot of men, and deserve their success as pioneers.

The higher grade Aero Club certificate was obtainable by the successful performance of a cross-country flight to a destination named a short time before the start. Cross-country flights were much in fashion, so that pilots were away from the battalion for about half their time. They flew in mufti; Lieutenants Barrington-Kennett and Reynolds more than once got. into trouble for being away as much as a week at a time. These absences were sometimes due to engine failure, sometimes (it was believed) to the discovery of a well-provided country house and kind hosts.

The army manoeuvres of August 1911, appointed to be held in Cambridgeshire, were the event of the summer; and the Air Battalion was detailed to take part in them. Owing to the shortage of water in that droughty summer the event never came off, but the aeroplane company started from Larkhill, and met with plenty of incident on the way. Air Commodore Brooke-Popham, who was at that time attached to the company from the Staff College, has very kindly set down his memories of the flight. He started from Larkhill with Captain Burke on the old Farman, with the object of making Oxford, but owing to a slight adverse wind and the low speed of the machine, which made only thirty miles an hour in a calm, they had to be content with Wantage, and got to Oxford the next morning.

Lieutenant Barrington-Kennett, with a mechanic, made a forced landing in the neighbourhood of Burford, but with the assistance of Captain Brooke-Popham and Lieutenant Hynes, who went to his rescue in the only motor vehicle possessed by the company, he got into the air again, and also reached Oxford. Meantime Lieutenant Conner had had a crash in a fog, without hurting himself, on high ground at West Ilsley, south of Oxford. Maps, in those days, were mostly provided by the officers themselves, and Lieutenant Conner had steered himself successfully by the aid of a map torn out of a Bradshaw Railway Guide.

Eventually the mobilised military air force of the British Empire, that is to say. Captains Burke, Brooke-Popham, and Massy, Lieutenants Barrington-Kennett and Reynolds, arrived in Oxford, at the end of the first stage. Here there were no tools available for repair, the few belonging to the company having been dispatched, by orders given at cross-purposes, straight to Cambridge. Nevertheless, the little band of enthusiasts bravely started on the last stage of their journey. Captains Burke and Brooke-Popham had engine failure about ten miles out of Oxford, and, landing in a ridge-and-furrow field, broke a tail skid.

Most of the day was consumed in getting this skid mended, patchwork fashion, by a coachbuilder in Oxford, to procure whose aid Captain Brooke-Popham returned to Oxford by earth. When the machine flew again it was forced to land at once, this time with serious damage. The other three officers had all been compelled by the bumpy weather to land not many miles away. In the evening they started again. Captain Massy had engine trouble fifty yards from the start, and completely wrecked his machine without hurting himself at all. Lieutenant Reynolds, who was the next to go, ran into a thunderstorm. His famous accident deserves to be recorded in his own words:

> That evening, soon after seven o'clock, I started again, it was warm and fine but rather suggestive of thunder; the air was perfectly still. I scarcely had occasion to move the control lever at all until I got to Bletchley, where it began to get rather bumpy; at first, I thought nothing of this, but suddenly it got much worse, and I came to the conclusion it was time to descend. A big black thunder-cloud was coming up on my right front; it did not look reassuring, and there was good landing ground below.
> At this time, I was flying about 1,700 feet altitude by my aneroid, which had been set at Oxford in the morning. I began a glide, but almost directly I had switched off the tail of the machine was suddenly wrenched upwards as if it had been hit from below, and I saw the elevator go down perpendicularly below me. I was not strapped in, and I suppose I caught hold of the uprights at my side, for the next thing I realised was that I was lying in a heap on what ordinarily is the under surface of the top plane. The machine in fact was upside-down.
> I stood up, held on, and waited. The machine just floated about, gliding from side to side like a piece of paper falling. Then it over-swung itself, so to speak, and went down more or less

vertically sideways until it righted itself momentarily the right way up.

Then it went down tail first, turned over upside-down again, and restarted the old floating motion. We were still some way from the ground, and took what seemed like a long time in reaching it. I looked round somewhat hurriedly; the tail was still there, and I could see nothing wrong. As we got close to the ground the machine was doing long swings from side to side, and I made up my mind that the only thing to do was to try and jump clear of the wreckage before the crash. In the last swing we slid down, I think, about thirty feet, and hit the ground pretty hard.

Fortunately, I hung on practically to the end, and, according to those who were looking on, I did not jump till about ten feet from the ground.

Those who were looking on were two men, stark naked, who had been bathing nearby. About fifty or sixty people soon collected, and some time passed before it occurred to anyone to remark that these two men had no clothes on.

The military air force of the Empire had now been reduced to two serviceable aeroplanes which got to Cambridge, one piloted by Lieutenant Barrington-Kennett, the other by Lieutenant Cammell, who had been delayed at Larkhill for some days but had flown by way of London without mishap. These officers were well received and entertained by the resident members of the University.

Later in the autumn the government bought some new machines for the battalion. In one of these, a two-seater Nieuport monoplane, with a fifty horsepower Gnome engine, Lieutenant Barrington-Kennett made a record passenger-carrying flight. On the 14th of February 1912 he flew 249½ miles in four hours thirty-two minutes. In a rapidly advancing tide every wave makes a record, which is obliterated by the next wave. But the use of the word 'record', so frequent in the annals of aviation, does convey some sense of the exhilaration of the pioneers. Another of the machines supplied by the government was a Bréguet biplane with a sixty horse-power Renault engine. Mr. Cockburn says:

> It was a most unwholesome beast, with flexible wings, steel spars, and wheel control.
>
> It required enormous strength to steer it, and was perseveringly

and valorously flown by Lieutenant Hynes. There was also a Deperdussin two-seater monoplane, which Captain Fulton flew; and the earliest of the B.E. machines from the Aircraft Factory, which fell to the lot of Captain Burke. The battalion was much impressed by the number of instruments fitted to their new machines. In the machines they were accustomed to there was nothing but a revolution counter, and sometimes, though not always, a compass.

If the pilot's scientific ambitions went beyond this simple outfit, he carried a watch on his wrist and an aneroid slung round his neck. The risks that these early pilots cheerfully faced at the call of duty were serious enough, and it is surprising that their casualties were so few. The only fatal accident in the Air Battalion was the death of Lieutenant R. A. Cammell, R.E., who was killed while flying a Valkyrie monoplane at Hendon on the 17th of September 1911. The machine was not familiar to him, and it is believed that he forgot to work the forward elevator; at the height of about ninety feet the monoplane tilted to one side, and fell with a crash.

Lieutenant Cammell was one of the pioneers of British military aviation. So early as June 1910 he had been sent to France to take over a Blériot machine. He attended the Rheims meeting of that year and sent home some valuable reports. He was a daring and skilful aviator, and had qualified also as an airship pilot.

The story of Great Britain's apprenticeship in the air has now been brought down to the point at which the Royal Flying Corps, famous on every battle front of the world war, makes its first appearance. So far it has been a story of small things, of interrupted experiments and tentative advances; of the caution of the government, and the boldness of the private adventurer. There is nothing new in the story; the air was attacked and mastered in the English fashion. When we are confronted with great issues, it is our habit, or so we are fond of saying, to 'muddle through'. Foreign nations, and especially enemy nations, do not so describe our activities. But we are great self-critics, and not free from that kind of inverted self-esteem which makes a man speak of his own achievements with deceitful and extravagant modesty.

The business of history is to tell the truth; the truth is that we muddle through with amazing success. This success we affect to regard as an undeserved reward bestowed by Providence on improvidence. But is the law of cause and effect really made void on our behalf? The people of the island, it is true, are slow to make up their minds; their respect for experience and their care for justice make them distrust quick action if it is not instinctive action. They are unimaginative in this sense, that they are not very readily excited by the theatrical exhortations which are addressed to them from day to day. In a much deeper sense they are imaginative; they have a sure instinct for the realities of life. When they are presented with a doubtful novelty, they prefer to wait; and they can afford to wait, for they know that their young will be eager to show the way, and, in the meantime, they are not afraid.

CHAPTER 5

The Royal Flying Corps

In November 1911 the Prime Minister requested the standing sub-committee of the Committee of Imperial Defence, under the chairmanship of Lord Haldane, to consider the future development of aerial navigation for naval and military purposes, and the measures which might be taken to secure to this country an efficient aerial service. Things had moved fast since 1908, when a distinguished general had expounded to a similar committee the futility of observation from the air. This time the committee came to a quick decision, and recommended immediate action. The chief of their recommendations were as follows:

The creation of a British Aeronautical Service, to be regarded as one, and to be designated 'The Flying Corps'.

The Corps to consist of a Naval Wing, a Military Wing, and a Central Flying School for the training of pilots.

The Flying Corps to be kept in the closest possible collaboration with the Advisory Committee for Aeronautics and with the Aircraft Factory, so that the work of experiment and research should have its due influence on practice.

A permanent consultative committee, named 'The Air Committee', to be appointed, to deal with all aeronautical questions affecting both the Admiralty and the War Office.

The preparation of a detailed scheme was delegated to a technical sub-committee consisting of Colonel the Right Hon. J. E. B. Seely, as chairman, Brigadier-General G. K. Scott-Moncrieff, Brigadier-General David Henderson, Commander C. R. Samson, R.N., Lieutenant R. Gregory, R.N., and Mr. Mervyn O'Gorman, with Rear-Admiral Sir C. L. Ottley and Captain M. P. A. Hankey as secretaries. The deliberations of this body were remarkable for agreement and dispatch;

their report was ready by the 27th of February 1912; it passed through its successive stages with very few alterations, and was approved by the Committee of Imperial Defence on the 25th of April.

The Royal Flying Corps was constituted by a Royal Warrant on the 13th of April 1912; a special Army Order was issued two days later setting up the necessary regulations, and on the 13th of May the old Air Battalion and its reserve were finally absorbed by the new body.

The advantage of government by committee is that it obtains, by successive stages, the sanction and support of the many for the plans initiated by the few. Nothing was ever created by eight men. But eight or more men, expert in various ways, can render invaluable service by listening, criticizing, and befriending. The plans which were considered and adopted by the technical sub-committee had been prepared in private by a small informal body of three, that is to say, by Brigadier-General David Henderson, Captain F. H. Sykes, and Major D. S. MacInnes.

Brigadier-General David Henderson had served at the Battle of Khartoum in 1898, and had distinguished himself in the South African War. He was the author of a book on *The Art of Reconnaissance*, which ran through several editions. His interest in reconnaissance, and his appreciation of its importance in war, made him a friend to aviation. In 1911, at the age of forty-nine, he had learned to fly at Brooklands, and thereafter, as Director of Military Training at the War Office, did all in his power to encourage the new movement. Captain Frederick Hugh Sykes was a General Staff officer who had seen service in many lands.

In the South African War, he served with the Imperial Yeomanry, and was severely wounded. In 1901 he joined the 15th or King's Hussars, and for two years was stationed in West Africa. Thereafter he was attached to the Intelligence Department at Army Headquarters in India, passed the Staff College, and in February 1911 became General Staff officer in the Directorate of Military Operations under Brigadier-General Sir Henry Wilson.

It was in July and August 1904, while he was on leave from West Africa, that he made his first acquaintance with the air. He obtained permission to be attached to the balloon units training with the army on Salisbury Plain; made many ascents, and went through the course and examination at the Farnborough balloon school. Thenceforward he took every possible opportunity, to improve his knowledge of aeronautics. He was quick to discern the significance of aviation. When, in 1910, he saw flight in France, he recognised that the work of cavalry in distant reconnaissance was dead and done with.

During his time at the War Office he spent the mornings, before breakfast, in learning to fly, and in June 1911 took his pilot's certificate on a Bristol biplane at Brooklands. Within the office he insisted on the importance of military aeronautics, and when the Committee of Imperial Defence took up the question he was naturally chosen to serve on the committee which prepared a draft organisation. Associated with him was Major Duncan Sayre MacInnes, of the Royal Engineers, who had been through the South African War, and at the time of the formation of the Flying Corps was serving with the Military Training Directorate.

Only those who worked with him will ever know how great a debt the Flying Corps owes to his industry and devotion. During the war he was employed under the Directorate of Military Aeronautics, and in 1916 was made Director of Aircraft Equipment, with the rank of brigadier-general. He wore himself out in the service of the country, and died in May 1918. These three men laid the groundwork of the plans which were approved by the technical sub-committee.

The record of the preliminary meetings of the subcommittee, and of the evidence given by witnesses, is full of interest, and shows history in the making, the chairman said:

> It has been suggested to me, that the Royal Flying Corps is a better name than 'the Royal Air Corps.'

And again, when the name for the tactical unit of the force was under consideration, and objection was taken to the words 'company' and 'group'—'Why not squadron?' said the chairman. It is the happiness of the small technical subcommittee that the scheme which they approved was equal to the strain of an unexampled war, and that the very names which they chose are now engraved on the history of the nation.

The choice of the squadron, consisting of three flights of aeroplanes, with four machines to a flight, as the unit of the new force was judicious and farsighted. In France the unit was the *'escadrille'*, consisting of six machines, and roughly corresponding to what we call a flight. This precedent was rejected. Not enough competent officers, it was feared, were available to command a large number of small independent units. On the other hand, if too large a unit had been chosen, it would have been difficult to put the air service at the disposal of the various army formations which might ask for assistance from the air.

The squadron, when it was created, was elastic and manageable, and secured for the air force, as the war has proved, that corporate spirit and that pride in history and tradition which are the strength of the regimental system.

The deliberations of the sub-committee were conducted in a severely practical spirit. Many of the constructive problems which came before them still remain problems, and might have been debated, with much to be said on both sides, till the conversion of the Jews; but the pressure of time made itself ominously felt in all their proceedings. The country, as a whole, was not awake to the German menace. The sudden appearance of the German gunboat *Panther* at Agadir in July 1911 ought, it may be said, to have awakened it. But the average Englishman could hardly bring himself to believe that a great European nation would seek war as a duellist seeks a quarrel, from sensitive vanity and pride in his own fighting skill.

The army and the navy were quicker to discern the reality of the threat. The military machine that was to supply the small expeditionary force was working at high pressure, and the air was tense. If Germany intended to make her bid for the mastery of Europe, it was recognised that she had every reason for making it soon. The chairman, at a meeting in January 1912, said:

> All the heads of departments are very anxious to get on with this—Lord Haldane told me so last night, Mr. Churchill told me so two or three days ago, and the Chancellor of the Exchequer himself is anxious to see it done, and wisely: but what is the best method to pursue in order to do in a week what is generally done in a year?

He said later:

> At the present time in this country, we have, as far as I know, of actual flying men in the army about eleven, and of actual flying men in the navy about eight, and France has about two hundred and sixty-three, so we are what you might call behind.

Moreover, the committee realised that an air service would be needed by the army of Great Britain more than it is needed by the armies of foreign powers. In a memorandum by the War Office, drawn up in the same month of January 1912, it is pointed out that a British expeditionary force might have to operate as a detached force, and that to such a force information is all-important. The need for haste appears in many of the recommendations of the committee.

For the supply of trained flyers to the army and the navy, and for the formation of a reserve, the first necessity was to start work at the Central Flying School, for which a site had been chosen on the Upavon Downs of Salisbury Plain, north of the Upavon-Everley road. The buildings necessary for this school could not be ready till the end of June, so the committee recommended that the work of the school should, in the meantime, be carried on in canvas tents and sheds.

Some problems of wide import forced themselves on the attention of the committee, and were of necessity settled with a view to immediate results and immediate efficiency. When shelter is needed from a pitiless storm, the leisurely plans of the architect must give way. One of these problems was the rank of pilots. Should every pilot be an officer, or should we follow the example of France, and train some mechanics to the work of piloting? From the first, Mr. Churchill was in favour of admitting to the State school of aviation not only a proportion of officers of both services, but also petty officers, non-commissioned officers and men, as well as civilians. In the report of the technical sub-committee the war establishment for an expeditionary force is planned on these lines.

The Military Wing of the Royal Flying Corps was to contain seven aeroplane squadrons, each squadron to number twelve machines, with an additional machine for the commanding officer. Two pilots were allowed for each aeroplane, and, in addition, to provide for the wastage of war, an equal number in reserve. The war establishment, calculated on this basis for the purposes of the expeditionary force, required the services of three hundred and sixty-four trained pilots, of whom, it was suggested, one hundred and eighty-two should be officers, and one hundred and eighty-two non-commissioned officers.

This part of the scheme cannot be said to have failed in practice: it never reached the test of practice. The surest and readiest way to obtain the services of skilled flyers was to offer them commissions in the Flying Corps, and it was felt to be invidious that some pilots should enter the corps as officers, while others, of equal skill, should enter in the non-commissioned ranks. Some of the witnesses were of the opinion that not many men of the skilled mechanic class would be ready or willing to risk their lives as pilots.

The experience of the war has disproved this forecast; an observer in war must have at least as cool a head and as stout a heart as a pilot, and everyone who has flown on the western front knows that among the very best observers not a few were non-commissioned officers. But the fact is that the question was settled by lack of time. To give effect to the scheme outlined in the report of the technical sub-committee would have required much time and experiment and adjustment; in practice the simpler way was chosen, and the business of piloting was reserved, in the main, for commissioned officers. Courage is found everywhere among English-speaking peoples; the real point to secure is that the pilots of one squadron, or the pilot and observer of one machine, should not only meet on duty, but should live together. That perfect understanding and instant collaboration which spells efficiency in the air is the product of habitual intimacy and easy association during leisure hours.

In the early days of the Royal Flying Corps a certain small number of non-commissioned officers were trained to do the work of piloting, so that the officers who new with them in two-seater machines might be freed for the more important work of observation. This experiment was not favourably reported on, and the opinion has often been expressed that men chosen from the non-commissioned ranks of the army or the lower-deck ratings of the navy do not make good pilots. A wise judgement on the question will consider all the circumstances. Promotion in both army and navy was slow before the war, so that a non-commissioned officer or petty officer was often a married man, considerably in advance of the age at which the most successful war pilots are made.

The inspired recklessness of youth does not long persist among those who from boyhood up have to earn their living by responsible work. Moreover, commanding officers, whether in the army or the navy, were naturally reluctant to let their skilled men be taken from them, so that the men whom they sent to be trained as pilots were too often men for whom no other good use could be found. One naval officer said:

If they don't break their necks, it will wake them up.

Again, in 1918, when cadets, after a preliminary technical training, were graded as officer cadets or non-commissioned officer cadets, all the more promising men were given commissions, so that only men of inferior intelligence were left to become non-commissioned pilots. It is surely rash to lay stress on vague class distinctions. A stander-by who happened, during the war, to witness the management of an Arab camel convoy by a handful of British private soldiers, remarked that though these soldiers knew no language but their own, their initiative and tact, their natural assumption of authority, and their unfailing good temper, which at last got the convoy under way, showed that they belonged to an imperial race.

The question of the rank of pilots is really a social question, a question, that is to say, not of individual superiority but of smooth collaboration. If a whole squadron of the Flying Corps had been staffed, as was at one time suggested, by men picked from the non-commissioned ranks, there can be no doubt that it would have made a name for itself among the very best.

The largest question of all in the making of the Flying Corps was the question whether the air service was to be a new and independent service, taking rank with the army and the navy, or was to be, for the most part, divided between the army and the navy, and placed under their control. This question, it might seem, was settled by the opening words of the sub-committee's recommendations:

> The British Aeronautical Service should be regarded as one, and should be designated "The Flying Corps".

But subsequent developments soon showed that this settlement was not accepted on all hands. The navy never fully accepted it. The British navy is a body enormously strong in its corporate feeling, conscious of its responsibilities, proud of its history, and wedded to its own ways. Its self-reliant character, which had made it slow to recognise the importance of the air, made it slow also, when the importance of the air was proved, to allow a weapon necessary for naval operations to pass out of its own control. When the active combatant service of the Royal Flying Corps came into being, it consisted of a Naval Wing and a Military Wing.

The Naval Wing had its headquarters at Eastchurch, where the Naval Flying School had been established. For administrative purposes the Naval Flying School was placed under the orders of the captain of H.M.S. *Actaeon*, and all officers and men were to be borne on the books of the *Actaeon*. Experiments with seaplanes and flying boats were still in their infancy, and the organisation of the Naval Wing was wisely left undetermined for the time.

The distribution of the aeroplane squadrons of the Military Wing was left for the consideration of the War Office, but the sub-committee recommended that one squadron should be stationed at Salisbury Plain, within reach of the Central Flying School, and one at Aldershot, in the neighbourhood of the Aircraft Factory. All recruits training as pilots, whether for the Naval Wing or the Military Wing, were to graduate at the Central Flying School, and thence were to be detailed to join either the Naval Flying School at Eastchurch, for a special course of naval aviation, or one of the military aeroplane squadrons, for a special course of military aviation.

That was the plan. So far as the Military Wing was concerned, it was punctually carried out. In the Naval Wing a certain centrifugal tendency very early made itself felt. The official name 'Royal Flying Corps, Naval Wing', after making its appearance in a few documents, dropped out of use, and its place was taken by a name which in process of time received the stamp of official recognition—'The Royal Naval Air Service'. Thereafter the words 'Military Wing', though they were still used, were no longer required, and 'The Royal Flying Corps' became a sufficient description of what was a distinctively military body. The Admiralty from the first worked independently. Soon after the Naval Wing of the Royal Flying Corps was created the First Lord of the Admiralty set up a new department to supervise it, and placed Captain Murray Sueter in charge, as Director of the Air Department.

At an earlier date Commander C. R. Samson had been placed in charge of the Naval Flying School. The energies of the school, pending the establishment of the Central Flying School, were devoted mainly to elementary training in flying. By the provisions of the original scheme this elementary training belonged to the joint Central Flying School, while the Naval Flying School was to be used for experiment and for specialised training in naval air work. But the Naval Flying School continued throughout the war to train naval flying officers from the beginning, teaching them the art of flying as well as its special applications for naval purposes.

The question whether there should be a single air service, specialised in its branches, or separate air services, organised for mutual assistance, is a question that stirs deep feeling, so that the very virtues which make men serviceable to their country are ranged in opposition one to another. The old allegiances are not easily forgotten; when a sailor learns to fly he remains a sailor, and the air for him is merely the roof of the sea. The knowledge, moreover, gained from his life at sea is knowledge not only useful but essential to him if he is to do good work in the Naval Air Service.

He must be able to recognise the various types of war vessels, and the various nationalities of vessels of the merchant marine. He must know all about the submarine, the mine, and the torpedo. He must be well versed in weather observation, and able to navigate safely without the aid of landmarks. He must understand naval tactics, and must be able to bear a part in them. All this, it has been urged by many sailors, is a much more complicated and experienced business than the mere flying of an aeroplane. The Naval Air Service, they contend, should be a part of the navy.

There is force and weight in these contentions, yet they are not conclusive. If the navy were itself a new invention, a very similar kind of argument might be used to subordinate it to the army. The main business of the navy, it might be said, is to supply the army with transport facilities and mobile gun-platforms. But this is absurd; the sea will not submit to so cavalier a treatment. Those who believe in a single air force base their opinion on certain very simple considerations. As the prime business of a navy is the navigation of the sea, so, they hold, the prime business of an air force is the navigation of the air; all its other activities depend on this.

The science of aeronautics is yet in its childhood; its development must not be cramped by tying it too closely to a service which works under narrower conditions. If there should be another great war (and though no one desires it, no one dares to think it impossible), the fittest man to hold the command of united land and sea forces might well be a Marshal of the Air. But the strongest argument for a single air force is not so much an argument as an instinct. Every kind of warfare develops in men its own type of character. The virtues of the soldier and the virtues of the sailor are not the same; or, if they are the same (for courage and duty can never be superseded), they are the same with surprising differences. The soldier is drilled to fight men when the occasion arises; the sailor is at war all his life with the sea. The character of the sailor—his resourcefulness and vigilance, his patience and stoicism, his dislike of formality—is put upon him by his age-long conflict with his old enemy.

In seafaring men there is a temper of the sea, admired by all who have ever made acquaintance with it. Those who were privileged to watch the performance of our flying men in the war know that there is developed in them a temper not less remarkable and not less worthy of cultivation—the temper of the air. War in the air demands a quickness of thought and nerve greater than is exacted by any other kind of war. It is a deadly and gallant tournament. The airman goes out to seek his enemy: he must be full of initiative. His ordeal may come upon him suddenly, at any time, with less than a minute's notice: he must be able to concentrate all his powers instantaneously to meet it. He fights alone.

During a great part of his time in the air he is within easy reach of safety; a swift glide will take him far away from the enemy, but he must choose danger, and carry on. One service cannot be judged by the standards of another service. A soldier who knows nothing of the sea might easily mistake naval discipline for lack of discipline. A like mistake has often been made by those who are brought into casual relations with the air force. But the temper of the air force is a new and wonderful thing, born of the duties and dangers which war in the air has brought with it. To preserve that temper as a national inheritance is the dearest wish of those who covet for the air force a place beside the navy and the army.

Now that the officers for the air force are being trained, as officers for the navy and the army have long been trained, at a cadet college with its own traditions, the question will solve itself. The necessity for collaboration during the war did something to unite the branches of the force. But perfect unity can be attained only by men who have lived and worked together. Men who have lived apart speak different languages. In April 1918, when the Royal Naval Air Service and the Royal Flying Corps were united in the Royal Air Force, it was found necessary to deal with this language difficulty.

The Naval Air Service and the Flying Corps used different names for the same thing. The Naval Air Service used the names they would have used aboard ship. The officers' mess they called 'the ward-room mess', and the dining-room 'the mess deck'. The cookhouse with them was the galley; rations were victuals; and kit was gear. In July 1918 an order was issued by the Air Ministry prescribing the terms to be adopted in the new force. The use of starboard and port for right and left was ordered as a concession to the sailors; and at all air stations the time of day was to be denoted, as onboard ship, by the sounding of bells. In some few cases the naval and military usages were both discarded in favour of a new term proper to the air force.

Thus, non-commissioned officers and men, who are described in the navy as 'ratings' and in the army as 'other ranks', were named, in accordance with a practice which had already grown up, 'airmen'. Names are full of compliment and fantasy: 'airman' is the official name for those members of the air force who spend their time and do their work on the ground.

These are not light matters. One of the strongest bonds of human sympathy is community in habits of speech. Divergences in speech are fruitful in every kind of hostility. It was a Scottish captain of the merchant marine who expressed a dislike for the French, and when called on for his reasons, replied that as a people they are ridiculous, for they call a boy a 'mousse'.

The navy and the army have always been loyal comrades, ready to help each other at short notice. These relations persisted between the two branches of the air force. In the scheme for the Royal Flying Corps it had been provided that each branch of the service should be treated as a reserve to the other branch. Thus, in a purely naval war the whole of the Flying Corps was to be available for the navy, and in a war, that should call for no assistance from the navy (if such a war can be conceived) the whole of the corps was to be available for the army. In accordance with these ideas machines flown by naval officers played a very successful part in the army manoeuvres of 1912 and 1913.

Further, in order to co-ordinate the efforts of the Admiralty and the War Office, a permanent consultative committee, called the Air Committee, was provided for in the original scheme, and held its first meeting in July 1912. This committee was a kind of nucleus of an Air Ministry; the importance attached to it may be judged from its composition. Colonel Seely, by this time Secretary of State for War, was its first chairman, and later on Vice-Admiral Sir John Jellicoe, the Second Sea Lord of the Admiralty, became its vice-chairman. The officers in command of the Central Flying School, of the Naval Wing, and of the Military Wing had seats on it. So had the Director of Military Training, the Director of the Air Department, and the Superintendent of the Royal Aircraft Factory.

The committee proved its value as a place of conference, where those who were responsible for aerial development in its various branches might compare their ideas. But it had no executive powers, so that its success in promoting an active policy automatically diminished its own importance. It could consider and advise, but the decision rested with the Admiralty and the War Office. It was useful at an early stage; then, like the Ghost in *Hamlet*, having prompted others to action, it faded away.

The need for a central controlling body, that is to say, for an Air Ministry, was soon to be acutely felt. The naval and military air forces were friends, but they were also rivals. In so far as this rivalry prompted them to compete in skill and valour, it was wholly good. But rival orders for munitions of war, and especially for aeroplanes, given to manufacturing firms by two branches of one service, are not so good. The output of the factories was not unlimited, and only a central authority could determine how that output might be best used for the nation's need.

The activities of the Naval Air Service, from the time it came into being until the outbreak of war, were very largely experimental. Those who were responsible for naval operations had at first no complete, definite, and practical scheme for the employment of aircraft in naval warfare. It would have been difficult for them to produce such a scheme; opinion was fluctuating and divided, and the progress of aeronautical science supplied improved machines and opened out new possibilities every month. The time of the service was spent in demonstrating these new possibilities, rather than in organising and training their forces for the needs of a definite programme. Nevertheless, this experimental period witnessed rapid growth and prepared the way for surprising achievements by the Naval Air Service during the war.

The uses of the Military Wing, on the other hand, were definitely conceived from the first. It was brought into being to fulfil a certain purpose. Its officers knew when and where and how their services would be required. They knew, that is to say, that on the outbreak of war they would be mobilised, that they would operate with an expeditionary force, and that their business would be, by observation from the air, to keep the commanders of that force acquainted with the movements and dispositions of the enemy. The constitution of the Military Wing was elastic, so that its numbers could be increased and its uses multiplied, but its original purpose, to supply the needs of an expeditionary force, dictated its first establishment and its early training.

Its first duty was reconnaissance. All its other and later uses were consequences of this central purpose, and were forced on it by the hard logic of events. The full establishment of the Military Wing was to comprise a headquarters, seven aeroplane squadrons, and one airship and kite squadron (providing two airships and two flights of kites). Later in the year there was also established at South Farnborough what was then called a Flying Depot, Line of Communications, but was afterwards named an Aircraft Park. Its duties were the maintenance of a reserve of aeroplanes, and the carrying out of such repairs as were beyond the powers of the squadron workshops yet were not serious enough to compel the return of the machine to its maker.

In its beginnings and during its early years the Military Wing was greatly indebted to the technical knowledge and the inventive skill of the Royal Engineers. It was they who had produced the army balloon and the army airship. Before the Royal Flying Corps was founded they had devised a practicable and efficient aeroplane, and they had been chiefly responsible for the organisation of the Air Battalion. The best tribute that could be paid to their fostering care was paid by the Royal Flying Corps when, being fully fledged, it started on its great career.

The building up of the Military Wing to fit it for its purpose was not a light task. Skilled officers, skilled men, an adequate supply of the best machines, suitable flying grounds in various parts of Great Britain, a well-staffed central school for training—these were some of the first necessities. After two years, when war came, only four out of the seven squadrons were ready for instant service in France. But the value of this little force was out of all proportion greater than its numerical strength. Through all the difficulties and delays that clog a new movement it had kept a single purpose in view and had worked for it. The great achievements of the Royal Flying Corps during the war may seem to make its early history and early efforts a trivial thing in the comparison. But the spirit was there; and some of the merits of the later performance may be detected in the tedious and imperfect rehearsals, the long hours of duty-flights and experiment, demanding that three-o'clock-in-the-morning kind of courage which is willing to face danger in the midst of a world at ease.

In March 1912 Colonel Seely had announced in the House of Commons that there would be required at once for the Military Wing a hundred and thirty-three officers, and for the Naval Wing about thirty or forty officers. It was not proposed at first to teach all these officers at the Central Flying School. They would learn to fly privately, and would go to the school for more advanced instruction. The skilled men required were of many kinds. The most important of these were mechanics, men who had served at full pay in engineering workshops, who had some knowledge of electricity, and could make intelligible sketches of machinery.

A list of some other classes whose services were invited proves that though the air service was small its needs were many and complex. Men of the following trades were to be enrolled, by enlistment or transfer, in the Military Wing: blacksmiths, carpenters and joiners, clerks, coppersmiths, draughtsmen, electricians, fitters, harness-makers, instrument repairers, metal-turners, painters, patternmakers, photographers, riggers, sail-makers, tinsmiths, turners, wheelwrights, whitesmiths, wireless operators, wood-turners. Men of the following minor trades were also invited: cable-jointers, chauffeurs, drillers, dynamo attendants, electric-bell fitters, joiners' helpers, machinists, motor fitters, plumbers' mates, switchboard attendants, tool-grinders, wiremen. Last, a welcome was promised to men above average intelligence whose education at school had reached what is called the Fifth Standard.

When an aeroplane glides down to earth as easily as a bird, and comes to rest, a chance onlooker would hardly guess what a world of intricate labour and pains has gone to the attainment of that beautiful simplicity. It is the workshop which gives safety in flight; and because the workshop needs highly skilled men, whose services are in demand, at high wages, for many other purposes, an air force must always be difficult and expensive to maintain in time of peace.

Captain F. H. Sykes was given the command of the Military Wing on its formation. His adjutant was Lieutenant B. H. Barrington-Kennett. Captain H. R. M. Brooke-Popham in March of that year joined the Air Battalion, and was serving at Farnborough when the Royal Flying Corps came into being. Most of the aeroplane company were then at Larkhill, but Captain C. J. Burke, with his B.E. machine, and Captain A. G. Fox, of the Royal Engineers, with a Bristol box-kite, were at Farnborough. Some of the officers of the airship company were making strenuous and successful efforts to get the aviation certificates which were demanded from officers of the new formation.

In April and May about a dozen officers from various units joined at Farnborough. One of the first of these was Captain Patrick Hamilton, of the Worcestershire Regiment, who had done much flying in the Argentine (and, incidentally, had been stoned by the human herd for refusing to give an exhibition flight in impossible weather). He was a keen and skilled aviator; he had made more than two hundred flights, and had had some narrow escapes—one particularly, when his machine capsized and glided a hundred feet upside-down, at a sharp angle to the ground. By the two strong masts of the monoplane and by the breaking of the machine he was preserved unhurt. He remarked that it was a good lesson, for 'to an aviator experience is everything'.

He brought with him to Farnborough his two-seater Deperdussin monoplane with a sixty horse-power Anzani engine. Others who joined about the same time were Major H. R. Cook of the Royal Artillery, who became instructor in theory at the Central Flying School, Captain E. B. Loraine of the Grenadier Guards, Captain C. R. W. Allen of the Welch Regiment, Captain G. H. Raleigh of the Essex Regiment, Lieutenant C. A. H. Longcroft of the Welch Regiment, and Lieutenant G. T. Porter of the Royal Artillery. A sort of class was held at Farnborough for these early recruits; they heard lectures, and did practical work in the overhaul of engines.

There were only four serviceable machines available at that time, one B.E., one Bréguet, and two Bristol box-kites, so the recruits, who wanted above all things to fly, were disappointed. They were taken up in the baskets of captive spherical balloons, where they spent hour after hour sketching the various parts of Farnborough, counting the cows on the common, and writing descriptions of what they could see from the balloon. The labours of the pencil and the pen are not easily carried on in the basket of a captive balloon: it swings and twirls in a breeze, and very often produces air sickness. This form of instruction was relieved by an ascent in the airship *Gamma*, and by occasional trips in free balloons.

Towards the end of April Captain H. R. M. Brooke-Popham took over from Captain Fulton the command of the old aeroplane company on Salisbury Plain, and on the 13th of May, when the Royal Flying Corps was formed, this company became No. 3 Squadron of the new formation. No. 2 Squadron was formed from the nucleus of aeroplane pilots at Farnborough, and was placed under the command of Captain C. J. Burke. In August the Central Flying School was started at Upavon, with Captain Godfrey Paine, R.N., as commandant.

The airship company at Farnborough, being lineally descended from the old balloon school, became No. I Squadron of the Royal Flying Corps Military Wing. The command of this squadron was given to one of the earliest of aeronautical-pioneers, Captain E. M. Maitland, who, almost alone among the pioneers, preferred the airship to the aeroplane. Edward Maitland Maitland, after being educated at Haileybury and Trinity College, Cambridge, joined the Essex Regiment as a second lieutenant in 1900. He served in the South African War, and in the spring of 1908 turned his attention to ballooning.

On the 18th of November in that year, along with Mr. C. C. Turner and the late Professor A. E. Gaudron, he ascended from the Crystal Palace in the *Mammoth*, a balloon of more than a hundred thousand cubic feet in capacity, supplied by the enterprise of the Daily *Graphic*, and travelled in the air to Mateki Derevni in Russia, a distance of 1,117 miles, which was traversed in thirty-six and a half hours. His main interest was not in Russia, but in the air, and he returned to England at once. When in 1919 he accompanied the airship R 34 on the first famous air voyage across the Atlantic, he remained in America for only a few hours. During the years 1909 and 1910 he was attached to the balloon school at Farnborough, and carried out aeroplane experiments at his own costs. He piloted a Voisin biplane in 1909 at the Doncaster meeting, which, because it started the day before the Blackpool meeting, may be called the first flying meeting in England.

In August 1910 he flew a Howard Wright biplane at Larkhill when there were only two other machines there, namely, Captain Fulton's Blériot and the first biplane of the Bristol Company. On this occasion he crashed and broke both his ankles. When the Air Battalion was formed in 1911 he chose to work with airships, and was given the command of the airship company. His courage and gallantry were unfailing, and his parachute descents were legion. When Professor Gaudron fell ill, and was prevented from giving his exhibition descents in a parachute at the Alexandra Palace, Captain Maitland took his place. He was the first to make a parachute descent from an airship; this was from the airship *Delta*, in 1913.

In 1915, for the purpose of experiment, he descended in a parachute liberated from a spherical balloon at a height of 10,500 feet. In 1917 he jumped, with his parachute, from an airship over the sea at a height of a thousand feet. He believed that the parachute is a necessary adjunct to the airship, and that by practice and experience it can be brought into safe habitual use. So, he did not sit on a fence and watch the thistledown, but took every opportunity that presented itself for a parachute descent. One such opportunity he refused. When, on the 24th of August 1921, he was killed in the disaster to the R 38, he spent his last moments in endeavouring to check and control the fall of the airship. He was free from self-regard, and had the devotion of all who served with him.

His life, though it ended in its prime, was surprisingly long, for he had made danger his friend, and in the advancement of the cause to which he dedicated himself had welcomed every risk. Under Major Maitland's command the airship squadron—that is to say, No. 1 Squadron—grew in strength and efficiency, but it was cut off in its youth from the aeroplane squadrons. Expert opinion, which was divided on the military value of airships, was united on their naval value.

Not without protest the decision was made to hand over all the airships to the navy, and at the close of the year 1913 this was done.

An airship is much more costly than an aeroplane, whether to construct or to work, and when it flies at a moderate height for the purposes of military reconnaissance, it is much more vulnerable. This, no doubt, was the consideration which determined the severance of the airships from the army. Yet the airships, during their brief period of service with the Military Wing, had demonstrated in the most convincing fashion the enormous value of aerial reconnaissance, and, more important still, had put the whole Flying Corps in their debt by adapting wireless telegraphy to the uses of aircraft.

The value of this work was not at once apparent. The time before the war was spent chiefly in experiment. During the retreat from Mons no ground receiving stations could be established. But when the German rush was beaten back, and the opposing armies were ranged along a fixed line, wireless telegraphy became a necessity for aeroplanes. The machines and the plant needed for this new development were not in existence; but a good deal of the preliminary work, much more troublesome and uncertain than the multiplication of a pattern, had been done. In a very short time there appeared at the front large numbers of machines fitted with wireless. The credit of this sudden apparition belongs, in part at least, to the Royal Engineers, and to their child, the balloon school, which by a steady process of growth had been transformed into the airship squadron of the Royal Flying Corps.

The power of sending messages through space, in any direction, over great distances, is so enormous an addition to the utility of aircraft that a few words must here be said about wireless telegraphy. The discovery was made by the gradual researches of men of science. These researches had their beginning in a famous paper by James Clerk Maxwell, who subsequently became the first professor of experimental physics at Cambridge. His paper, *On a Dynamical Theory of the Electro-Magnetic Field*, read to the Royal Society in 1864, contains a theoretical demonstration that electro-magnetic action travels through space in waves with the velocity of light.

Twenty-three years later, in 1887, Heinrich Rudolf Hertz, of the University of Bonn, published the results of his experiments in producing these waves by means of oscillating currents of electricity. His investigations confirmed what Clerk Maxwell had proved mathematically. Thereafter progress was rapid, and during the closing years of the nineteenth century the problem of subduing the waves to the service of man was attacked and solved. In 1889 Professor Oliver Lodge was measuring electrical radiation. At Liverpool University College he constructed a Hertz radiator to emit the waves, and received them at various points of the building. Edouard Branly's invention of the 'coherer', an instrument designed to receive Hertzian waves, was communicated to the British Association at Edinburgh in 1893. During the same year Nikola Tesla published his researches on high frequency currents; on these much of the later work on wireless telegraphy was based.

In 1895-6 William Rutherford set up at the Cavendish Laboratory apparatus by which he received signals in distant parts of Cambridge up to a distance of half a mile from the oscillator. Many other men of science, among whom was Captain H. B. Jackson, of the Royal Navy, were at work on the problem, when in 1896 Signor Guglielmo Marconi arrived in England with an apparatus of his own construction which ultimately brought wireless telegraphy to the stage of practical and commercial utility. By 1899 signals had been transmitted across the English Channel.

Man has no sense organs which record the impact of electrical waves, but he has succeeded in devising instruments which register that impact, and which make it perceptible to the organs of sight or of hearing. The operation of the electrical waves may be best explained, perhaps, by the analogy of sound. When the string of a piano is struck by its hammer it vibrates, and communicates its vibrations to the surrounding air; these vibrations, travelling outwards in waves, produce corresponding vibrations in the ear-drum of a listener. The string is tuned, by its tension and its weight, to a single note; the ear can adapt itself to receive and transmit to the brain only a limited range of notes.

There are many vibrations in the air which are too rapid or too slow for reception by the human ear. The sound-waves of the piano-string produce their effect on any neighbouring body which is capable of vibrating at the same rate as the incoming waves, as, for instance, another string tuned to the same note, or a volume of air enclosed in a vessel which vibrates in correspondence. These are in 'resonance' with the vibrating string; they repeat the original disturbance and reinforce its effect.

So, it is with electricity. If the electricity with which any conducting body is charged be suddenly disturbed, electrical waves are generated which travel outwards in all directions with the velocity of light. The problem of wireless telegraphy is the problem of producing these waves by means of an instrument called a transmitter, and of recording their impact at a distance by means of an instrument called a receiver. In its simplest form the transmitting instrument consists of two conducting bodies, or plates, charged the one with positive the other with negative electricity, separated from each other by air or some other insulating material, and connected by a coil of wire called an inductance coil.

To explain the how and why, so far as these questions can be explained, would involve a whole treatise on electricity; for the present purpose it is enough to say that when the two plates are connected through the coil, the electrical discharge is oscillatory in character, as the current runs to and fro between the one plate and the other, and that these oscillations are radiated into space in the form of waves. The frequency of the waves, the rapidity, that is, with which wave follows wave, depends on the size and proximity of the plates and on the length and form of the coil which connects them. The receiving instrument is similarly constructed, and can be so adjusted that the waves which it would generate if it were a transmitter would have the same frequency as those it is to receive. It is thus in resonance with the transmitter, and the effect of the incoming impulses is greatly enhanced.

If the waves produced are to be perceptible at any considerable distance, the transmitting instrument must be capable of absorbing a large amount of energy and radiating this energy into space in the form of waves.

The storing capacity of the instrument is increased by having large plates close together, but its radiating properties are impaired if the plates are too close.

The chief advance made by Signor Marconi lay in his use of the earth as one of the plates. In his wireless installation, a network of insulated wires, suspended in the air above, is one plate, the earth is the other; and the two are connected by an inductance coil. This device cannot be applied to aircraft, for obviously no connexion with the earth is possible. Both of the plates, or networks of wire, have to be carried on the airship or aeroplane. No great weight could be carried on the early type of aeroplane, and no great space was available.

This brief and imperfect description has been given in order to make clear some of the difficulties which attend the application of wireless telegraphy to aircraft, and especially to aeroplanes.

The theory of flight was worked out by men of science in the laboratory; flight itself was first achieved by men who had had no systematic scientific training, but who endeavoured to acquaint themselves with scientific results, and to apply them, as best they might, to the difficulties with which they were familiar in practice. So, it was also with the application of wireless telegraphy to aircraft. The men of the laboratory were not familiar with all the conditions which had to be observed, nor with all the unforeseen obstacles which present themselves in practice. It remained for those who knew the conditions and the obstacles to work out the practical problem for themselves. The vibration and noise, which make it difficult in an aeroplane to hear anything but the engine, the risk of fire, and the imperfect protection of the instruments from splashes of oil and the rush of the air—all these things complicated the problem.

As early as 1907 Captain Llewelyn Evans, who commanded the 1st Wireless Company of the Royal Engineers at Aldershot, lent his help to Colonel Capper of the balloon school in devising wireless communication between aircraft and the ground. The apparatus had to be extemporized. The first experiments were made by Lieutenant C. J. Aston, R.E., in a captive balloon. In May 1908 a free run was made in the balloon Pegasus, in. which a receiving set of wireless had been installed. When the balloon was over Petersfield, Lieutenant Aston received very good signals from the Aldershot wireless station twenty miles distant. During the same month the sending of messages from the balloon was also tried with promising results.

These experiments soon came to an end. The time was not ripe for further developments. No airships or aeroplanes were as yet in use in England, and all available energy had to be concentrated on producing wireless telegraphy sets for the use of the army. In October 1909 Captain H. P. T. Lefroy, R.E., was placed in charge of all experimental work in wireless telegraphy for the army. This appointment he retained until the outbreak of the war. He had been commissioned in the Royal Engineers in 1899, and had begun to study wireless at Gibraltar in 1905. Approaching the question from the service side, he was able to do much to adapt wireless telegraphy to the new conditions presented by the conquest of the air.

As soon as the army airship *Beta* was available he had her equipped with wireless apparatus, and on the 27th of January 1911 went up in her from Farnborough. Many messages were sent from the airship to the ground station up to a range of thirty miles, and for a short time, while the airship engine stopped running, it was found possible to receive messages from the ground. In the roar of the engine nothing could be heard.

In the summer of 1911 Captain Lefroy spent much of his time in designing a transmitting apparatus for aeroplanes. In January 1912 he went up with Mr. Geoffrey de Havilland in the first B.E. machine, to test its suitability for wireless. In May 1912 he set about fitting the same machine, which was then being flown by Major Burke, with a generator driven from the engine crank-shaft by bicycle-chain gear. These experiments prepared the way for later achievement.

In the same year the Naval Wing of the Royal Flying Corps began to experiment with a light wireless set for aeroplanes. As no machines were available for fitting, a station was constructed on Burntwick Island, the conditions being as nearly as possible the conditions in an aeroplane. Stray signals were received from this station by H.M.S. *Actaeon*, about one mile distant. In June 1912 Commander Samson, flying the first Short seaplane, fitted with a practice wireless set such as used in destroyers, succeeded in sending messages a distance of three, four, and, on occasions, of ten miles.

In August 1912 Lieutenant Raymond Fitzmaurice, R.N., who had served as a wireless telegraphy officer with the fleet, was appointed to arrange for the installation of wireless apparatus in naval aircraft. A few days after his arrival at Eastchurch he was ordered to go to Farnborough to take charge of the wireless in the airship *Gamma* on the defending side in the forthcoming army manoeuvres. Captain Lefroy was to take charge of the wireless in the airship *Delta*, which was intended to operate on the attacking side. Both these airships had been equipped with wireless apparatus by Captain Lefroy, on instructions from the War Office, to ascertain what could be done by wireless from aircraft in the manoeuvres.

The set of wireless for the *Gamma* had to be improvised from odds and ends—an old magneto and some Moscicki jars. The 'aerial', which does the work of one of the plates of a condenser, was a double trailer of wire let down from the bottom of the car off two drums; the 'earth', which does the work of the other plate, was made of insulated wires triced out to the bow and stern of the gas-bag. The magneto was run by a belt from one of the ballonet blowers. Receiving instruments were also installed, but these could only be used when the engine was stopped.

As soon as the weather was favourable the two airships sailed from

Farnborough; the *Gamma* for Kneesworth camp, on the defending side, the *Delta* for Thetford, on the attacking side. The *Delta* broke down over North London, but so successful was the wireless installation that her messages reporting the break-down were received near Thetford and at Portsmouth by H.M.S. *Vernon*; the *Beta* took her place, but was too small to carry the wireless installation. The *Gamma* was thus the only craft fitted with wireless, and the efforts of the attacking side were devoted to intercepting her messages at a ground station. The *Gamma* was an unqualified success. Her signals came in strong and loud from a distance of thirty-five miles to a station at Whittlesford fitted with naval service receiving apparatus. Speaking of the work of aircraft, General Grierson, who commanded the defending force, says:

> The impression left on my mind is that their use has revolutionized the art of war. So long as hostile aircraft are hovering over one's troops all movements are liable to be seen and reported, and therefore the first step in war will be to get rid of the hostile aircraft. He who does this first or who keeps the last aeroplane afloat will win, other things being approximately equal. . . . The airship, as long as she remained afloat, was of more use to me for strategical reconnaissance than the aeroplanes, as, being fitted with wireless telegraphy, I received her messages in a continuous stream and immediately after the observations had been made. . . . It is a pity that the airship cannot *receive* messages by wireless, but doubtless modern science will soon remedy this defect.

This was the first triumph of aerial reconnaissance in England. Every morning the *Gamma* went out at daybreak and scouted over the enemy; within half an hour the general in command was in receipt of very full information which enabled him to make out his dispositions and movements for the day. Some attempts were made to conceal troops at the halt from the view of aircraft; but, as General Grierson remarks, for troops on the move there is only one certain cover—the shades of night. So complete was the information supplied from the air that the commander of the defending force was enabled to organise his attack and end the manoeuvres a day sooner than was expected.

After the manoeuvres the *Gamma* flew by night over Cambridge and bombarded that seat of learning with Very lights. It took three hours to fly twenty miles, from Kneesworth to Cambridge, against a strong head wind, and at one o'clock at night the mechanic informed Major Maitland, who commanded the *Gamma*, that only one-quarter hour's supply of lubricating oil remained. So, the ship had to shut off her engines and float on the tide of the air. By throwing out all her ballast she kept afloat till dawn, and made a safe landing in the neighbourhood of Bristol. Captain Fitzmaurice says:

> I don't think I shall ever forget the feeling of perfect peace and quiet one experiences when ballooning by night.

The same feeling was experienced by Lunardi during his first ascent in a balloon. The history of aeronautics, if it could be fully written, is in the main a history of Peace in the air.

The two years before the war were years of progress. In 1912 M. Lucien Rouzet invented a transmitting apparatus which, in proportion to its power, was lighter in weight than anything that had previously been in use; a number of these sets were purchased by the Naval and Military Wings to be used in aircraft. During May 1913 successful wireless trials were carried out by Lieutenant Fitzmaurice in a Short seaplane piloted by Sub-Lieutenant J. T. Babington.

During one of these a flight was made along the coast from the Isle of Grain to the North Foreland, the seaplane being in communication with the receiving stations at Grain and Eastchurch and with ships at sea during the whole of its flight. Its signals were read up to a distance of forty-five miles. During this flight the seaplane signalled a wireless salute to the royal yacht, which was taking the king and queen to Flushing on a visit to Germany. In the naval manoeuvres of the summer, Lieutenant Fitzmaurice and Commander Samson were sent out to scout over the sea due east from Yarmouth in the latest Short seaplane, No. 81. Her engine failed, and she was compelled to come down on the sea, but the wireless messages which she had sent to H.M.S. *Hermes* served to locate her, and when the *Hermes* went to look for her she was found near the expected place on board a German timber boat which had come to her assistance.

The airships *Delta* and *Eta* were both equipped with wireless for the army manoeuvres of 1913, and were based on Dunchurch, near Rugby. In all, *Delta* sent sixty-six messages during her seven voyages, and on the 24th of September carried out a successful night reconnaissance. The *Eta*, owing to engine trouble, played no effective part in the manoeuvres, but during her journey from Farnborough to Dunchurch she maintained wireless communication with Aldershot till she reached Woodstock, when she called up Dunchurch and kept in communication for the remainder of the voyage. Captain Lefroy in his report says:

'It seems probable that H.M. Airships *Delta* and *Eta* can exchange messages with each other when 100 miles apart in the air, which may prove useful for organisation purposes, &c. I received clear signals from the North Foreland station (and a ship to which she was talking) when 130 miles N.W. of it, and whilst H.M.A. *Eta* was cruising northwards at touring speed.'

Just before the 1913 army manoeuvres, Lieutenant B.T. James, piloting a B.E. aeroplane, succeeded in receiving wireless signals with the engine running at full power. To enable him to do this his machine was fitted with Captain Lefroy's new receiving set in which magneto disturbances were screened off and the signals strengthened by Brown relays, that is, microphones invented by Mr. S. G. Brown. In June 1914 Lieutenants D. S. Lewis and B. T. James flew from Netheravon to Bournemouth each in a B.E. aeroplane equipped with sending and receiving apparatus; they flew about ten miles apart, and kept in close communication with each other the whole way.

Captain Lefroy continued to act as wireless expert to the Royal Flying Corps up to the outbreak of the war. The work done by him and by Lieutenant Fitzmaurice was of great value. When the war broke out wireless sets had been fitted to sixteen seaplanes, as well as to the two airships *Astra-Torres* and *Parseval*, which did good service in patrolling the Channel during the passage of the Expeditionary Force.

The development of wireless telegraphy for the uses of aircraft was only one small part of the work which had to be arranged and supervised by the headquarters staff at Farnborough. They had to recruit, organise, and train the new force. Energy, faith, and self-sacrifice were asked for, not in vain, from the officers and men who came into the corps. The headquarters staff was small, but with the help of the officers commanding the squadrons and the staff of the flying school at Upavon, they inaugurated a great tradition. There were no precedents. The staff had first to invent their work, and then to do it. The details of supply and transport, the ordering of machines from the makers, the training and equipment of every recruit—all these things had to be thought out in advance.

The official text-books, regulations, and standing orders, which were all complete and ready for issue when the war came, bear witness to the foresight and initiative of Major Sykes and the small staff who worked under him at headquarters. The Flying Corps resembles the navy in this respect, that its daily work in time of peace is not very much unlike its daily work in time of war, so that if the work is hard and incessant, at least it is rewarded by the sense of achievement.

One particular achievement was greater than all the rest. When flight began it attracted men of romantic and adventurous temper, some of whom were much concerned with their own performances and had a natural liking for display. If these tendencies had been encouraged, or even permitted, they would have ruined the corps. The staff, to a man, set their faces like flint against all such indulgences. Publicity, advertisement, the rubbish of popular applause, were anathema to them. What they sought to create was a service temper, and they were so successful that the typical pilot of the war was as modest and dutiful as a lieutenant of infantry. The building up of the Flying Corps on these lines, remote from the public gaze, deprived it of popular support, but it gained for it what was a thousand times more valuable—a severe code of duty, a high standard of quiet courage, and an immense corporate pride. To have kept the infant corps and all its doings in the public eye would have been as disastrous an experiment as to attempt to educate a child on the music-hall stage.

A great part of the early work of the Flying Corps was experimental. Various kinds of experiment were assigned by the corps headquarters to the several squadrons, and the headquarters staff took care that any success achieved by one squadron should become the rule for the betterment of all. An experimental branch of the Military Wing was formed in March 1913 under Major Herbert Musgrave; it dealt, among other things, with experimental work in connexion with ballooning, kiting, wireless telegraphy, photography, meteorology, bomb-dropping, musketry, and gunnery, and co-operation with artillery.

Major Musgrave deserves more than a passing mention in any military history of the air. After serving throughout the South African War as a lieutenant in the Royal Engineers he had passed through the Staff College. The possibilities of aviation very early took possession of his mind. In 1909, from the cliffs of Dover, he saw M. Blériot arrive in a monoplane, and was so impressed by the sight that he went straight to the War Office to draw attention to the military significance of this portent, and its threat to our insular security.

From this time forward his mind was set on aeronautics. He applied for military aviation service before the Flying Corps was formed, and in May 1912 repeated his application. He noted in his diary:

A staff officer should know the capabilities of aviation. He should be able to observe from an aeroplane and to travel by aeroplane with dispatches.

At last, in October 1912, during a short period of leave, he learned to fly at the Bristol Flying School on Salisbury Plain. In the following spring he was gazetted a squadron commander in the Royal Flying Corps. He was at once appointed assistant *commandant* and officer in charge of experiments. His utility to the Flying Corps, while it was in the making, was immense. He urged that new squadrons should be formed even while machines were lacking, so that the organisation and discipline should be perfected in advance. The flying training of the corps, he insisted, should always have a clear military purpose in view.

He was no militarist, but he was a good soldier, and he knew the imminence of war with Germany. As early as December 1911, in a lecture which he delivered in Malta, he predicted the war.

> When it comes, be assured it will come suddenly. We shall wake up one night, and find ourselves at war.... Another thing is certain. This war will be no walk-over.... In the military sphere it will be the hardest, fiercest, and bloodiest struggle we have ever had to face; let us fully make up our minds to that, and probably every one of us here tonight will take part in it. We need not be afraid of overdoing our preparations.

For two years Major Musgrave worked hard in helping to prepare the Flying Corps for its coming ordeal. In the spring of 1914 a headquarters flight was placed at his disposal for technical work in many kinds. Up to this time there had been two kinds of experimental work; the National Physical Laboratory was responsible for purely scientific experiments, while the commanders of squadrons tested new ideas in practice. But these two sets of men worked under very different conditions, and neither of them fully understood the aims and difficulties of the other branch.

The headquarters flight was intended to serve as a link between theory and practice. Major Musgrave gave special attention to wireless telegraphy, and with the assistance of Lieutenants D. S. Lewis and B. T. James, both also of the Royal Engineers and both pioneers of wireless, he made good progress in its practical application to the needs of the Flying Corps. When the war came, the headquarters flight was broken up in order to bring the four original squadrons up to strength, but the wireless section was attached for a time to No. 4 Squadron, and in September 1914 a headquarters wireless unit was formed at Fère-en-Tardenois in France, with Major Musgrave in command.

From this unit the whole wireless telegraphy organisation of the Royal Flying Corps was gradually developed. In December 1914 the unit was enlarged, and became No. 9 Squadron stationed at headquarters. Having worked out all details for the supply of wireless machines to the squadrons in the field, Major Musgrave in March 1915 left the Royal Flying Corps to take up duty with the staff of the army. He was severely wounded in August 1916. Almost two years later, on the night of the 2nd of June 1918, having persuaded a battalion commander to let him accompany a patrol, he was killed by a rifle grenade, inside the German lines. He desired no personal advancement, and would have thought no other honour so great as to die for his country. Such men, though the records of their lives are buried under a mass of tedious detail, are the engineers of victory.

When the airships were handed over to the navy, it became necessary to reorganise No. 1 Squadron as an aeroplane squadron. This was put in hand on the 1st of May 1914, and was not completed when the war broke out. The senior aeroplane squadrons of the Military Wing were, therefore, No. 2 Squadron under Major Burke, and No. 3 Squadron under Major Brooke-Popham.

The officers of these squadrons, to whom it fell to set the example and to show the way, were a remarkable group of pioneers. Some of them were accomplished flyers, who took delight in the mastery of the air. But none of them practised the art for the art's sake. They were not virtuosos, bent on exhibiting the heights to which individual skill can attain. They did not play a lone hand. The risks that they took were the risks, not of adventure, but of duty. They were soldiers first. One and all they were impressed with the importance of military aviation for their country's need. Captain Patrick Hamilton said:

It has got to come, and we have got to do it.

Their lives were pledged to their country, and until their country should call for them, were held in trust, not to be lightly thrown away. Some were called early, during the exercises of peace; others during the war. Others again, a minority, were marked down for a third chance, and were given the duty of carrying on, through the war and after it. The time of the call, early or late, made no difference; the work of the corps was not interrupted. When Captain Eustace Loraine, the first to go, was killed with his passenger, Staff-Sergeant R. H.V.Wilson, near Stonehenge, on the 5th of July 1912, the order was issued that flying would go on as usual that evening.

An order like this not only creates a tradition, it pays the right honour to the dead, who died on duty no less than if they had been brought down by the guns of the enemy. The casualties of the first summer were not light in proportion to the strength of the corps, and in one respect were very heavy, for almost all of those who were killed were creators and founders, whose work and influence would have been invaluable in building up the corps. They could ill be spared. They left nothing but their example; yet anyone who remembers what the Flying Corps achieved during the war may well wonder whether that example does not count for as much as a long life of devoted service.

Captain Eustace Broke Loraine had served with the Grenadier Guards in the South African War. His great-grandfather was the famous British admiral, Sir Philip Broke, who in 1813 commanded H.M.S. *Shannon*, and after a fifteen minutes' battle outside the port of New York compelled the surrender of the United States frigate *Chesapeake*. That battle, it has been truly said, was won before it was fought; the *Shannon* had been many years cruising at sea; she was in perfect fighting trim, her men were disciplined and her gunners practised. The men of the *Chesapeake* were fresh from the shore, strangers to each other and to their officers, so that the heavier armament of the *Chesapeake* was of no avail.

When Captain Loraine joined the Flying Corps he applied his great-grandfather's methods, and set himself by study, care, discipline, and skill to prepare the materials of victory. He was a highly skilled pilot, perhaps overbold. The machine he was flying on the 5th of July was the fast two-seater Nieuport monoplane on which Lieutenant Barrington-Kennett had achieved some records. It seems that he attempted too sharp a turn, lost flying speed, side-slipped, and nose-dived. He was only a few hundred feet up, and there was no time to save the crash. Those who knew him believe that he would have done much for the Flying Corps. He spared no pains to understand his business, and to make theory and practice help each other. Staff-Sergeant Wilson, who was killed with him, was the senior technical non-commissioned officer of No. 3 Squadron, a first-class man, and a heavy loss.

Other fatalities were to follow. On the 6th of September Captain

Patrick Hamilton and Lieutenant A. Wyness-Stuart, flying a hundred horse-power Deperdussin monoplane on reconnaissance duties connected with the cavalry divisional training, crashed and were killed at Graveley, near Hitchin. Four days later Lieutenant E. Hotchkiss and Lieutenant C. A. Bettington, flying an eighty horse-power Bristol monoplane from Larkhill to Cambridge, crashed and were killed at Wolvercote, near Oxford.

A committee was appointed to investigate these accidents, and in the meantime an order was issued by the War Office forbidding the use of monoplanes in the Royal Flying Corps. This order altered the scheme for the army manoeuvres, where it had been intended to allot a squadron of monoplanes to one force and a squadron of biplanes to the other, in order to compare results. No. 3 Squadron, nevertheless, assembled near Cambridge in such strength as it could muster; there were Major Brooke-Popham, Captain Fox, and Second Lieutenant G. de Havilland of the squadron; these were joined by Mr. Cody, who came as a civilian with his own machine, and by officers of the Naval Air Service, who flew Short biplanes.

The ban on monoplanes, it may be remarked in passing, was a heavy blow to one of the earliest pioneers of aviation in this country. Mr. L. Howard Flanders, who had worked with Mr. A. V. Roe at Lea Marshes, and had designed the 'Pup' monoplane for Mr. J. V. Neale at Brooklands, had subsequently formed a company for the building of aeroplanes, with works at Richmond. He obtained a War Office contract for four monoplanes, but when, after trial, he was engaged in reconstructing the under-carriages, the use of the monoplane was forbidden to army pilots. This and other disappointments put an end to Mr. Flanders's building activities, but his name deserves record among the pioneers.

When Lieutenant B. H. Barrington-Kennett of the Grenadier Guards became adjutant of the Military Wing of the Royal Flying Corps he made a vow that the corps should combine the smartness of the Guards with the efficiency of the Sappers. In spite of difficulties and disasters, the corps went far, in the first two years of its existence, towards attaining that ideal. In the summer of 1912 the Central Flying School at Upavon got to work, and thenceforward supplied a steady stream of trained reinforcements for the corps. There was inevitable delay at first; but as soon as some of the new wooden buildings were nearing completion they were taken over, and on the 19th of June the school was opened.

The plan was that there should be three courses every year, each of them lasting three months and passing on its graduates for further training either with the military squadrons or at the naval school. The first course began on the 17th of August 1912, and was not completed until the end of December, but the subsequent courses were punctually completed in the time prescribed. The delay in the first course was due chiefly to a shortage of machines. The use of monoplanes was forbidden, and the nineteen pupils who presented themselves in August had to be instructed on the only four available biplanes, which were soon damaged by, the maiden efforts of the learners.

For a short time, the pupils were sent on leave, and the school was closed; then new machines and new recruits began to arrive, and the work of education went forward. Besides the main business of flying, the pupils were instructed and examined in map-reading and signalling, the management of the internal-combustion engine, and the theoretical aspects of the art of reconnaissance. Of a total of thirty-four pupils who were examined at the end of the course, only two failed to pass. During the next year and a half, up to the very eve of the war, the work of the school went on steadily, with improving material and increasing efficiency.

There were three fatal accidents: on the 3rd of October 1913 Major G. C. Merrick was killed on a Short biplane; on the 10th of March 1914 Captain C. P. Downer, on a B.E. biplane; and on the 19th of March 1914 Lieutenant H. F. Treeby, on a Maurice Farman biplane.

On an average about thirty officers passed out from the school, into one branch or another of the service, at the end of each course. Most of these were army officers, but there was also a fair number of naval officers, marine officers, and naval volunteer and civilian reservists. The school was run on army lines, so that a good deal of adjustment and tact were called for in dealing with the navy pupils, who were accustomed to a more generous scale of allowances and a different system of discipline. But the resolve to make a success of the new air force prevailed over lesser difficulties, and harmony was maintained.

The steady flow of recruits from Upavon soon enabled the Military Wing of the Royal Flying Corps to form new squadrons. These squadrons all started in the same fashion; they hived off, so to say, from the earlier squadrons. As early as September 1912, a part of Major Burke's squadron, stationed at Farnborough, was detached, and became the basis of No. 4 Squadron, commanded by Major G. H. Raleigh, of the Essex Regiment, who had joined the Air Battalion just before the birth of the Royal Flying Corps. In August 1913 a single flight of Major Brooke-Popham's squadron became the basis of No. 5 Squadron, under Major J. F. A. Higgins. In January 1914 No. 6 Squadron, under Captain J. H. W. Becke, of the Notts, and Derby Regiment, and in May 1914 No. 7 Squadron, which was commanded later by Major J. M. Salmond, began to be formed at Farnborough.

The history of the Military Wing of the Royal Flying Corps before the war may be best illustrated by a more detailed account of the doings of the two earliest squadrons, commanded by Major Brooke-Popham and Major Burke. These showed the way to the others. There was no generally recognised orthodox method of training flying men for the purposes of war. Most of the work of the early squadrons was, in the strictest sense of the word, experimental. There was at first a vague idea, expressed in the Army Estimates of 1912, that the Royal Aircraft Factory was responsible for experiments, and that the squadrons had only to apply methods and use machinery already tested and approved by others.

But it was soon found that the problems of the air could not be effectively anticipated in the laboratory. They were many of them soldiers' problems. The man who is to meet the enemy in the air, and to be shot at, has a quick imagination in dealing with such matters as the protective colouring of aircraft, their defences against enemy bullets, or the designing of them so as to give a good field of fire to any weapon that they carry; and he takes a lively personal interest in such questions as stability, speed, rate of climbing, and ease in handling. The ultimate appeal on the various devices for the use by aircraft of musketry, gunnery, photography, wireless telegraphy, bomb-dropping, and signalling, must in the long run be made to the pilot. If he is prejudiced, and sometimes prefers a known evil to an unknown good, his hourly experiences and dangers are a wonderful solvent of that prejudice. It is not in the laboratory that the Derby is won, or the manoeuvres and tactics of the air worked out.

Major Brooke-Popham's squadron on Salisbury Plain was the first to get to work. In its origin, as has been told, it was the old aeroplane company of the Air Battalion, so that it was free from some of the difficulties which attend the creation of a new unit. It had at its disposal about ten machines of various types, and, for transport, one Mercedes car belonging to Captain Eustace Loraine and another belonging to the government. Besides instructional flights and practice in reconnaissance, which were of course a regular part of the business of the squadron, it devoted its attention at once to co-operation with other arms, and especially to the observation of artillery fire.

It was fortunate in getting the wholehearted support of Colonel the Hon. F. Bingham, who was at that time commandant of the school at Shoeburyness, and chief instructor of the artillery practice camp at Larkhill. The great difficulty was to devise a sufficient method of signalling to the guns. Wireless telegraphy, which was destined to provide the solution of this problem, was then at an early stage of its development, and the apparatus was too cumbrous and heavy to be carried on the machines. Experiments were made with flags, with written messages carried back and dropped to the gunners, and finally with coloured Very lights. Progress was slow. Only a small amount of ammunition was allowed to the gunners. On windy days flying was far from safe; on calm days there was sometimes fog, or, if the weather was hot, the air became dangerously bumpy.

Nevertheless, the squadron flew in strong winds, and took every opportunity of demonstrating to the troops on the plain that it was worth their while to cultivate relations with the new arm. Towards the end of May there was a big field day, and though the wind was almost a gale, four machines went up, flown by Major Brooke-Popham, Captain Fox, Captain Hamilton, and by Major Burke, who had come over from Farnborough on purpose. The important thing at this time, and for long after, was to show the infantry what aeroplanes could do for them. At a later time, during the war, it became necessary to teach the infantry what aeroplanes could not do for them—that they could not, for instance, supply them with a complete defence against enemy aircraft.

At the beginning of August 1912 Military Aeroplane Trials took place on Salisbury Plain. These trials were competitions, arranged by the War Office, to determine the type of aeroplane best suited to the requirements of the army. One competition, with a first prize of £4,000, was open to the world; the other, with a first prize of £1,000, was limited to aeroplanes manufactured wholly, except for the engines, in the United Kingdom. The judges were Brigadier-General Henderson, Captain Godfrey Paine, Mr. Mervyn O'Gorman, and Major Sykes. The tests imposed and the award of the prizes showed clearly enough that what the military authorities were seeking was a strong, fairly fast machine, a good climber, able to take off and alight on uneven ground and to pull up within a short distance after alighting. Further, a high value was attached to range of speed, that is, to the power of flying both fast and slow, and to a free and open view from the seat of the observer. Both the first prizes were won by Mr. Cody on his own biplane, which was of the 'canard', or tail-first type, and was fitted with an Austro-Daimler engine of a hundred and twenty horse-power. The winning machine did not in the end prove to be suitable for army purposes, and only a few were ordered, but the trials gave timely and needed encouragement to the aeroplane industry. The army machines and the army pilots were, of course, not eligible for these competitions, but the factory machine B.E. 2 made a great impression on those who saw it fly.

It was in this machine that Mr. G. de Havilland, with Major Sykes as passenger, created a British record by rising to a height of 9,500 feet in one hour and twenty minutes. A few years later, when the war had quickened invention, a good two-seater machine could rise to that height in less than ten minutes. The only engine of British manufacture which completed all the trials was a sixty horse-power Green engine, fitted in an Avro machine.

Certainly, the British public did not know what was being done for them, against the real day of trial, by the handful of officers who foresaw that that day would soon come, and who strove unceasingly to be prepared for it. About two hundred members of Parliament came down to Salisbury Plain on the 8th of August to witness the competition of the aeroplanes in the Military Trials. The wind was judged to be too tempestuous for flying, and the flights were limited to a few short circuits round the aerodrome in the afternoon. On the morning of that same day a brigade of territorials, training at Wareham, asked for a couple of military machines to co-operate with them. Major Brooke-Popham and Lieutenant G. T. Porter started off in an Avro, and, a little later, Captain Hamilton followed in his Deperdussin.

The wind was so strong that Captain Hamilton could make no headway, and was obliged to turn back. Major Brooke-Popham and Lieutenant Porter battled their way to Wareham, but could not get farther to co-operate with the troops, and flew back to the plain in the afternoon. On their arrival there they found that the wind had abated a little, and that flying had just begun in the trials. The next day the newspapers published long accounts of the exhibition flying over the aerodrome, with a single line at the end recording that 'military airmen also flew'.

In the early days of September No. 3 Squadron co-operated in the cavalry divisional training, but without much success. The weather was bad, and the cavalry, being preoccupied with their own work, had not much attention to spare for the aeroplanes. In France, a year earlier, aeroplanes had been systematically practised with cavalry, sometimes to direct a forced march, sometimes to detect dummy field works, prepared to deceive the cavalry and to lead them into a trap.

But if their co-operation with the cavalry was imperfect and disappointing, the work done by aeroplanes a few days later, during the army manoeuvres, was a complete vindication of the Flying Corps. There were two divisions on each side; the attacking force, under Sir Douglas Haig, advanced from the east; the defending force was commanded by General Grierson. The services rendered to the defence by the airship Gamma have already been described. The fatal accidents of the summer and the consequent prohibition of monoplanes diminished the available force of aeroplanes, but a squadron of seven was allotted to each side. Major Burke's squadron, with its headquarters at Thetford, operated with the attacking force; Major Brooke-Popham was with the defence at Cambridge.

Operations started at six o'clock on the morning of Monday, the 16th of September. At a conference on Sunday afternoon, General Briggs, who commanded the cavalry on the side of the defence, told General Grierson that the forces were far apart, and he could not hope to bring in any definite information till Tuesday. General Grierson was then reminded by his chief staff officer that he had some aeroplanes.

'Do you think the aeroplanes could do anything?' he asked of Major Brooke-Popham, and on hearing that they could, ordered them to get out, 'and if you see anything, let us know.'

Monday morning was fine and clear; the aeroplanes started at six o'clock; soon after nine o'clock they supplied General Grierson with complete, accurate, and detailed information concerning the disposition of all the enemy troops. During the rest of the manoeuvres he based his plans on information from the air. On his left flank there were only two roads by which the enemy could advance; he left this flank entirely unguarded, keeping one aeroplane in continual observation above the two roads, and so was able to concentrate the whole of his forces at the decisive point. In the course of a few days the aeroplanes rose into such esteem that they were asked to verify information which had been brought in by the cavalry.

Air Commodore C. A. H. Longcroft, who flew in Major Burke's squadron on the attacking side, has kindly set down some of his memories of this time. The work of the Flying Corps, he says, was impeded by the enormous crowds which used to collect round the hangars. But the weather was good, and it was soon found that no considerable body of troops could move without being seen from the air. To avoid observation the troops moved on either side of the road, under the hedges. They even practised a primitive sort of camouflage, covering wagons and guns with branches of trees, which, while they were on the road, made them more conspicuous than ever.

This first experience of moving warfare taught many lessons. The difficulty of communication between pilot and observer when the voice is drowned in the noise of the engine was met by devising a code of signals, and many of these signals continued in use throughout the war, after speaking-tubes had been fitted to machines. The selection of landing grounds when moving camp, the methods of parking aeroplanes in the open, and the means of providing a regular supply of fuel, were all studied and improved.

In another way these manoeuvres, which were witnessed by General Foch, were a date in the progress of army aviation. No weapon, however good, can be of much use in the hands of those who have not learned to trust it. The progress of the aeroplane was so rapid that the education of commanding officers in its use became a thing of the first importance. Some of them, even when war broke out, had had but few opportunities of testing the powers of aeroplanes.

After the manoeuvres No. 3 Squadron returned to Larkhill, to do battle all the winter with the old difficulties. The officers were accommodated at an inn called the 'Bustard', about two and a half miles to the west of the Larkhill sheds; the men were at Bulford camp, three miles to the east of the sheds. After a time, the men were shifted to the cavalry school at Netheravon, which, though it was a little farther off, gave better quarters. Meantime a new aerodrome was being made, with sheds complete, at Netheravon, for the use of the squadron. The winter was passed in the old exercise of co-operation with the artillery and in new experiments. At Easter a 'fly past' of aeroplanes took place at a review of a territorial brigade on Perham Down. General Smith-Dorrien, who reviewed the troops, took the salute from the aeroplanes. There was a cross-wind, so that the symmetry of the spectacle was a little marred by the crab-like motion of the aeroplanes, which had to keep their noses some points into the wind to allow for drift.

Several officers joined during the winter, and the squadron began to be better supplied with machines. For the manoeuvres of 1913 it was made up to war strength both in aeroplanes and transport. These manoeuvres, however, did not give much opportunity to aeroplanes; the idea was that four divisions, and with them No. 3 Squadron, should operate against a skeleton army. The squadron had next to nothing to observe; the other side had plenty to observe, but could not get full value out of their skeleton force. The tactics of the air had hardly reached the point at which a theoretic trial of this kind might have been of value. Yet a good deal was learnt by the Flying Corps from these manoeuvres.

Major Brooke-Popham drew up a very full report on them, and in the following winter Lieutenant Barrington-Kennett, under the title *What I learnt on Manoeuvres, 1913*, brought together the information he had obtained as adjutant from the talk and written statements of those who took part in them. Both reports show a relentless attention to detail, and an unfailing imagination for the realities of war. The squadron had twelve machines at work during the manoeuvres. Of these one was wrecked. Two had to be brought home by road, one for lack of spare parts, the other because it had been taken over with a damaged engine—both avoidable accidents. The one wrecked machine, Major Brooke-Popham remarks, does not represent the loss that would have occurred on a campaign. Four machines had to land, and would have been captured in war. That is to say, the loss amounted to five machines in four days, or one-tenth of the force every day.

One of the lessons learnt at the manoeuvres was that accurate observations could be made from a height of at least six thousand feet. This was one of those many things which, having been habitually ridiculed by theorists, are at once established by those who make the experiment. So high flying came into fashion, and brought with it a new set of problems concerning the effect of atmospheric height on the human body and on the aeroplane engine.

The total mileage covered by the machines on divisional and army manoeuvres was 4,545 miles on reconnaissance and 3,310 miles on other flights. Among the many suggestions made by Major Brooke-Popham for improving the efficiency of the corps, some of the most important have been vindicated by the subsequent experience of the war. It is necessary, he says, that the Flying Corps should be taken seriously by commanders and their staffs. The work of the flying officers involves strain and danger; it is not enough that they should be praised for skill and daring; they must feel that their information is wanted, that an accurate report will be used, and that failure to obtain information from the air will be treated as worthy of censure. If a squadron commander finds that no one cares for the information he brings, he will keep his machines on the ground in rough weather. On divisional manoeuvres the Flying Corps were not always made to feel that they were wanted.

No great stress, perhaps, should be laid on this complaint; it belongs to the early days of military flying, and its date is past. A new invention is often slow in gaining recognition. When its utility is as great as the utility of flying a little experience soon converts objectors. What was important was that the experience should be gained before the war. Observers in the early months of the war sometimes found it difficult to convince the military command that their reports were true.

The value of information, says Major Brooke-Popham, depends also upon the rapidity with which it is handed in to the proper quarters:

> More than once movements of a hostile cavalry brigade were seen within a few miles of our own troops. The information was not of great value to the commander-in-chief, but was of great importance to the advanced guard or cavalry commander, yet by the time it had got out to him from headquarters probably two hours or more had elapsed.

This delay was sometimes avoided on manoeuvres by dropping messages from the air, but the whole large question of the relations of the Flying Corps to the various army commands and the organisation of the machinery of report was left until the pressure of war compelled an answer. Then, during the first winter of the war, when the growth of the Flying Corps allowed of more complex arrangements, the machinery was decentralised, and subordinate commanders were furnished directly with the information most needed by them.

Lieutenant Barrington-Kennett's essay well illustrates his keenness and foresight in preparing the corps for their ordeal of 1914. He was a great disciplinarian, he knew every officer and man individually, he was universally liked, and he did more perhaps than anyone else to hold the corps together and to train it in an efficient routine. He knew—no one better—that the corps, though it did its work in the air, had to live on the ground, and that its efficiency depended on a hundred important details. Here are some of his suggestions:

Landing-grounds should be chosen, if possible, from the air, to avoid the employment of numerous parties of officers touring the country in cars. The drivers of lorries and cars should be trained in map-reading. Semaphore signalling should be taught to all ranks, to save the employment of messengers. There should be oil lorries for the distribution of petrol, and leather tool-bags to be carried on motor-bicycles to the scene of an engine breakdown. Acetylene and petrol are better illuminants than paraffin for working on machines by night. Experiments should be made in towing aeroplanes, swinging freely on their own wheels, behind a motor-lorry; they are often damaged when they are carried on lorries.

Recruits for the motor transport should be taught system in packing and unloading, and should be trained in march discipline. All recruits should be drilled in the routine of pitching and striking camp. All ranks should know something of field cookery. The main lessons of the manoeuvres, the writer says, are first, that subsidiary training in the business of soldiering is of enormous importance; and, second, that responsibility must be regularly distributed, and duties allotted, so that when the strain of war comes, the whole burden shall not crush the few devoted officers who have been eager to shoulder it in time of peace. The work of the pilots and mechanics of the British air service, he remarks in conclusion, is second to none; if only this work can be fitted into a solid framework of systematic administration and sound military discipline, the British Flying Corps will lead the world.

These are not the matters that a lover of romance looks for in a history of the war in the air. But they are the essentials of success; without them the brilliancy of individual courage is of no avail. War is a tedious kind of scholarship. When Sir Henry Savile was Provost of Eton in the reign of Elizabeth, and a young scholar was recommended to him for a good wit, he would say:

> Out upon him, I'll have nothing to do with him; give me the plodding student. If I would look for wits, I would go to Newgate; there be the wits.

It was by the energy and forethought of the plodding student that the Flying Corps, when it took the field with the little British Expeditionary Force, was enabled to bear a part in saving the British Army, and perhaps the civilization of free men, from the blind onrush of the German tide.

The work of Major Brooke-Popham's squadron, during these years of preparation, included a great diversity of experiment. With the progress of flight, it began to be realised that fighting in the air was, sooner or later, inevitable, and in the winter of 1913 a series of experiments was carried out at Hythe, by a single flight of No. 3 Squadron, under Captain P. L. W. Herbert, to determine the most suitable kind of machine-gun for use in aeroplanes. A large number of types were tested, and the Lewis gun was at last chosen, with the proviso that it should go through a series of tests on the ground. These took a long time, and it was not till September 1914 that the first machines fitted with Lewis guns reached the Flying Corps in France.

From the beginning of 1914 onwards, No. 3 Squadron also began a whole series of experiments in photography; Government funds were scanty, and the officers bought their own cameras. There was no skilled photographer among them, but they set themselves to learn. They devised the type of camera which was used in the air service until 1915, when Messrs. J.T.C. Moore-Brabazon and C. D. M. Campbell brought out their first camera. They would develop negatives in the air, and, after a reconnaissance would land with the negatives ready to print. In one day, at a height of five thousand feet and over, they took a complete series of photographs of the defences of the Isle of Wight and the Solent.

From time to time there were a good many adventures by members of the squadron outside the daily routine. The first night flight made by any officer of the Military Wing was made on the 16th of April, 1913, by Lieutenant Cholmondeley, who flew a Maurice Farman machine by moonlight from the camp at Larkhill to the Central Flying School at Upavon, and back again. Later in the year Commander Samson, of the Naval Wing, successfully practised night flying, without any lights on the machine or the aerodrome; but as a regular business night flying was not taken in hand by the squadrons until well on in the war.

During the month of July 1913 Lieutenants R. Cholmondeley and G. I. Carmichael became evangelists for the Flying Corps; they went on a recruiting tour to Colchester, and gave free passenger trips to all likely converts among the officers of the garrison there. Long before this, in 1912, the squadron had begun to train non-commissioned officers to fly. The first of these to get his certificate was Sergeant F. Ridd. He had originally been a bricklayer, but after joining the Air Battalion had developed an extraordinary talent for rigging, and became an all-round accomplished airman. Others who were taught to fly soon after were W. T. J. McCudden, the eldest of the four brothers of that name, and W. V. Strugnell, who, later on, became a flight commander in France.

The most famous of the McCuddens, James Byford McCudden, V.C., who brought down over fifty enemy aeroplanes, joined the squadron as a mechanic in 1913, and became a pilot in the second year of the war. In his book, *Five Years with the Royal Flying Corps* (1918), he says:

> I often look back and think what a splendid Squadron No. 3 was. We had a magnificent set of officers, and the N.C.O.'s and men were as one family.

The other of the two pioneer aeroplane squadrons was formed at Farnborough in May 1912, and was put under the command of Major Charles James Burke, of the Royal Irish Regiment. Major Burke rendered enormous service to the cause of military flying. He took it up because he fully realised the importance of the part it was destined to play in war. He had served in the ranks in the South African War, and at the close of the war was commissioned in the Royal Irish Regiment, becoming captain in September 1909. In 1910 he learned in France to fly a Farman biplane, and obtained the aviation certificate of the French Aero Club.

Thereafter he was employed at the balloon school, and in 1911 was attached to the newly-formed Air Battalion. He was something of a missionary, and in that same year contributed two papers to the Royal United Service Institution, one on *Aeroplanes of Today and their Use in War*, the other on *The Airship as an aid to the solution of existing strategical problems*. On the formation of the Royal Flying Corps he was given command of No. 2 Squadron, which, after a time at Farnborough, was stationed as a complete unit at Montrose on the east coast of Scotland. He brought his squadron to a high state of efficiency, and on the outbreak of war flew with it to France. There he did good service, till he was invalided home in the summer of 1915 and became temporary commandant of the Central Flying School.

In 1916 he was again in France. The war was taking a huge toll, and he rejoined his old regiment, which was in straits for officers. In the previous year Major Barrington-Kennett, under the same pressure, had returned to duty with the Grenadier Guards, and had been killed in action near Festubert. Colonel Burke rejoined the Royal Irish Regiment in the summer of 1916, and was killed on the 9th of April 1917, on the first day of the Arras offensive.

He impressed those who knew him by his character. He was not a good pilot, and was almost famous for his crashes. He was not a popular officer. He was not what would be called a clever man. But he was single-minded, and utterly brave and determined, careless alike of danger and of ridicule. There is often granted to singleness of purpose a kind of second sight which is denied to mere intelligence. Major Burke (to give him his earlier title) knew many things about military aviation and the handling of a squadron which it was left for the war to prove, and which, even with the experience of war to teach them, some commanding officers were slow to learn. A paper of 'Maxims' which he jotted down as early as 1912 contains many wise and practical remarks. Some of them are of general application, as, for instance, these:

> *When things are going well, the man in charge can give play to his fears.*
> *Nothing is ever as good or as bad as it seems.*
> *If you know what you want, you can do your part, and get others to do theirs. Most people don't know what they want.*

But by far the greater number of them deal with aviation and its problems. Here are some worthy of remembrance:

> *Time in the air is needed to make a pilot.*
> *In training pilots, no machine should go out without knowing what it is to do, do that and that alone, then land.*
> *No young pilot should be allowed out in 'bumps' until he has done fifteen hours' piloting.*
> *An aeroplane will live in any wind and a lifeboat in any sea, but they both want good and experienced men at the tiller.*
> *When on the ground everyone overrates his capacity for air work.*
> *A squadron commander should want a good squadron, and not to be able to break records.*
> *Waiting about on an aerodrome has spoilt more pilots than everything else put together.*

This last truth will come home to all pilots who have flown on the war front. To have discovered it shows an instinct for command. Flying is a nervous business; there is no wear and tear harder on a war pilot than to be kept in attendance on an aerodrome, with the nerves at a high degree of tension, and perhaps to be dismissed in the end. A skilful and imaginative commander will use all possible devices to avoid or diminish these periods of strain.

Any account of Major Burke would be incomplete if it contained no mention of his famous machine, the first B.E. This machine was familiarly known to the officers of the early Flying Corps, most of whom—Sykes, Brancker, Brooke-Popham, Raleigh, Carden, Ashmore, Longcroft, and many others—had occasionally flown it. It was an experimental two-seater tractor biplane, designed as early as 1911 at the factory. At that time no funds were available for constructing aeroplanes of factory design.

This difficulty was overcome by an expedient well known to all students of law. There was no money for construction, but there was money for repairs and overhaul. The first B.E. was created by the drastic repair and reconstruction of another machine. A Voisin pusher with a sixty horse-power Wolseley engine had been presented to the army by the Duke of Westminster, and was sent to the factory for repair. When it emerged, like the phoenix, from the process of reconstruction, only the engine remained to testify to its previous existence, and even that was replaced, a little later, by a sixty horse-power Renault engine. It was now the B.E. tractor, and in March 1912, some two months before the formation of the Royal Flying Corps, it was handed over to the Air Battalion, and was assigned to Captain Burke.

It had a long and adventurous career, and was often flown at Farnborough for the testing of experimental devices. When at last it was wrecked, beyond hope of repair, in January 1915, it had seen almost three years of service, and had perhaps known more crashes than any aeroplane before or since. It was frequently returned to the factory for the replacement of the undercarriage and for other repairs. The first machine of its type, it outlived generations of its successors, and before it yielded to fate had become the revered grandfather of the whole brood of factory aeroplanes.

Many of the records of the early work of No. 2 Squadron, commanded by Major Burke, are missing. This was the first squadron sent out from Farnborough to occupy a new station, and to carry on its work as an independent unit. It may safely be presumed that a great part of the time spent at Farnborough was devoted to organisation, and to preparation for the new venture. The shortage of machines was the main obstacle to early training.

In May 1912 Captain G. H. Raleigh and Lieutenants C. A. H. Longcroft and C. T. Carfrae were sent for a month to Douai in France, to pick up what knowledge they could at the workshop where Bréguet machines were being constructed for the Flying Corps. They then returned to Farnborough, where they began to practise cross-country flying. Much initial training was necessary before the squadron could be fitted for independence.

In January 1913 it began to move north, by air and road and rail; by the end of February it was installed in its new quarters at Montrose. Five of the officers flew all the way: Captain J. H. W. Becke and Lieutenant Longcroft on B.E. machines, Captains G. W. P. Dawes and P. L. W. Herbert, Lieutenant F. F. Waldron on Maurice Farmans. The first stage of the flight was to Towcester on the 17th of February. One machine, piloted by Captain Becke, arrived at its destination that night. The others were stranded by engine failure, loss of direction, and the like. Lieutenant Longcroft had a forced landing at Littlemore, near Oxford, and spent the night in the Littlemore lunatic asylum. By the 20th all five machines had reached Towcester, and started on their next stages—to Newark and York.

At Knavesmire racecourse, near York, part of a morning was spent in writing autographs for boys, some of whom, perhaps, may have become pilots in the later years of the war. On the 22nd the squadron moved off for Newcastle. It was a day of fog and haze; only two of the pilots found the landing-ground at Gosforth Park that night, and these two had to land many times to get their bearings. The directions given them would have been helpful to foot-travellers; but turnings in the road and well-known public-houses are not easy to recognise from the air. On the 25th the squadron moved to Edinburgh, and on the following morning to Montrose.

At both places they were tumultuously received and liberally entertained. The mechanics in charge of the machines and transport did their business so well, often working at night, in the rain, with no sort of shelter, that both the transport lorries and the machines arrived at Montrose in perfect order.

At their new quarters training in flight and reconnaissance was strenuously carried on, and the squadron flew on an average about a thousand miles a week. Many non-commissioned officers and warrant officers were instructed in aviation. Some thirty miles south of Montrose, across the Firth of Tay, there is a three miles stretch of level sand at St. Andrews, and this was used for instruction in aviation—not without trouble and difficulty from the irresponsible and wandering habits of spectators. The more skilled of the pilots gained much experience in long-distance flying. All deliveries of new machines were made by air. Inspecting officers and other visitors to the camp were commonly met at Edinburgh in the morning, were then flown to Montrose to spend the day, and back again to Edinburgh in time to catch the night mail for the south.

In August 1913 Captain Longcroft, with Lieutenant-Colonel Sykes as passenger, flew from Farnborough to Montrose in one day, landing only once on the way, at Alnmouth. The machine was a B.E. fitted with a special auxiliary tank under the passenger's seat, and the time in the air for the whole journey was seven hours and forty minutes. In September 1913 six machines of the squadron took part in the Irish Command manoeuvres. The outward and homeward journeys by air, of about four hundred miles each way in distance, including the crossing of the Irish Sea, were the severest part of the test. The manoeuvre area was bad for aviation owing to the scarcity of good landing-grounds and the prevalence of mist and rain. Moreover, the opposing armies were separated by too small a distance to give full scope to the aeroplanes.

The principal battle took place in a mountain defile. Each of the machines flew on an average about two thousand miles, that is to say, about a thousand miles in reconnaissance, and about a thousand in the journey to and fro. There was no case of engine failure, and no one landed in hostile territory. A statistical account of the work of the squadron from May 1913 to June 1914 shows that, during that time, of eighteen machines in constant use and subject to great exposure only three were wrecked. This fact speaks volumes for the efficiency of the squadron. They flew in all weathers, sometimes even when the wind was faster than the machines. More than once 'tortoise races' on Maurice Farmans were organised; the winner of these races was the machine that was blown back fastest over a given course.

The longest flight of all was made by Captain Longcroft in November 1913. In the front seat of a B.E. machine First-Class Air Mechanic H. C. S. Bullock fitted a petrol tank of his own design, estimated to give at least eight hours' fuel for the seventy horse-power Renault engine. On the 22nd of November Captain Longcroft started on this machine, and flew from Montrose to Portsmouth and back again to Farnborough in seven hours twenty minutes, without once landing.

Major Burke has left a diary for 1914; some of the entries in it go far to explain the causes of the efficiency of the squadron. No detail was too small for his attention; the discipline that he taught was the discipline of war.

In practice, a man cannot always be on the job that will be given him on active service, but he should be trained with that in view, and every other employment must be regarded as temporary and a side issue. Further, though barracks must be kept spotlessly clean, this work must be done by the minimum number of men, in order to swell the numbers of those available for technical work and instruction.

The importance of the main issue was ever present to his mind. In another entry he records how he reproved a young lieutenant, telling him that:

He must take his work seriously and make himself older in character.'

Map-reading, signalling, propeller-swinging, car-starting, military training, technical training, the safety of the public, the prompt payment of small tradesmen ('which defeats accusation of army unbusinesslike methods'); these and a hundred other cares are the matter of the diary. That they were all subordinate to the main issue appears in the orders which he gave to some of the pilots of No. 6 Squadron, at Dover, in the summer of 1914. Any pilot who met a Zeppelin, and failed to bring it down by firing at it, would be expected, he said, to take other measures, that is to say, to charge it. Not a few of the early war pilots were prepared to carry out these instructions.

The work done by the other early squadrons was similar in kind. No. 4 Squadron was formed at Farnborough in the autumn of 1912 under Major G. H. Raleigh, of the Essex Regiment, who had served with distinction in the South African War. After completing its establishment, it moved to Netheravon, where it carried on practice in reconnaissance, co-operation with artillery, cross-country flying, night flying, and all the business of an active unit. The record of miles flown during 1913 by No. 4 Squadron hardly falls short of the record of the two senior squadrons; all three flew more than fifty thousand miles.

When No. 5 Squadron was formed under Major Higgins a part of it was stationed for a time at Dover, and the squadron moved to new quarters at Fort Grange, Gosport, on the 6th of July, 1914, a month before the war. No. 6 Squadron was nearly complete when the war came, but No. 7 Squadron was very much under strength. Thus, in August of that year four aeroplane squadrons were ready for war, another was almost ready, and another was no more than a nucleus. The rest of the magnificent array which served the country on the battle fronts was yet to make.

The month of June in 1914 was given up to a Concentration Camp at Netheravon. The idea of bringing the squadrons together in this camp seems to have originated with Colonel Sykes, whose arrangements were admirable in their detailed forethought and completeness. The mornings were devoted to trials and experiments, the afternoons to lectures and discussion on those innumerable problems which confront an air force. Tactical exercises, the reconnaissance of stated areas in the search for parties of men or lorries, photography, handling balloons, practice in changing landing-grounds, and the like, were followed by discussions of the day's work. Lieutenant D. S. Lewis and Lieutenant B. T. James took every possible opportunity, during the discussions, to urge the development of wireless telegraphy. In the speed and climbing tests the greatest success was achieved by a B.E. machine fitted with a seventy horse-power Renault engine.

Much attention was paid to reconnaissance and to co-operation with other arms. There was a natural rivalry among the squadrons. Major Burke's squadron was reputed to have the best pilots, while the Netheravon squadrons had had more training in co-operation with other arms, and in the diverse uses of aeroplanes in war. But the unknown dangers which all had to share were a strong bond, and the spirit of comradeship prevailed. The officers and men of the Royal Flying Corps were makers, not inheritors, of that tradition of unity and gallantry which is the soul of a regiment, and which carries it with unbroken spirit through the trials and losses of war.

The single use in war for which the machines of the Military Wing of the Royal Flying Corps were designed and the men trained was (let it be repeated) reconnaissance. There had been many experiments in other uses, but though these had already reached the stage of practical application, it was the stress of the war which first compelled their adoption on a wide scale.

The Military Wing was small—much smaller than the military air forces of the French or the Germans—it was designed to operate with an expeditionary force and to furnish that force with eyes. Its later developments, which added the work of hands to the work of eyes, were imposed on it by the necessities of war. Even artillery observation, which is the work of eyes, was at first no regular part of its duty. When the Germans were driven back from the Marne, and the long line of the battle front was defined and fixed, the business of helping the artillery became a matter of the first importance.

Many of the functions brilliantly performed during the course of the war by aeroplanes had been claimed, during the early days of aviation, as the proper province of the airship. A wireless installation for receiving and sending messages was too heavy for an aeroplane; it must be carried by an airship. No sufficient weight of bombs could be carried by an aeroplane; the airship was the predestined bombing machine. Machine-guns were difficult to work from an aeroplane; they were the natural weapon of the airship. Photography was a hope worthy of experiment, but even photography was thought to be best suited to the airship, and internal accommodation for a camera was not asked for or provided in an aeroplane.

At the back of all this lay the strongest argument of all: the value of reconnaissance to the army was so great, and our military aeroplanes were so few, that it was impossible to spare any of them for less essential work. As the Flying Corps grew in numbers and skill it found breathing space to look around and to claim the duties that had been judged to be outside its scope.

As a nation we distrust theory. We learn very quickly from experience, and are almost obstinately unwilling to learn in any other way. Experience is a costly school, but it teaches nothing false. A nation which attends experience could never be hurried into disaster, as the Germans were hurried by a debauch of political and military theory, subtly appealing to the national vanity. To insure themselves against so foolish a fate the British are willing to pay a heavy price. They have an instinctive dislike, which often seems to be unreasonable in its strength, for all that is novel and showy. They are ready enough to take pleasure in a spectacle, but they are prejudiced against taking the theatre as a guide for life.

This is well seen in the disfavour with which the practical military authorities regarded the more spectacular developments of aviation, which yet, in the event, were found to have practical uses. Looping the loop, and other kinds of what are now called 'aerobatics', were habitually disparaged as idle spectacles. Yet the 'Immelmann turn', so called, whereby a machine, after performing half a loop, falls rapidly away on one wing, was a manoeuvre which, when first used by the enemy, proved fatal to many of our pilots. The spin, at the outbreak of the war, was regarded as a fault in an aeroplane, due chiefly to bad construction; later on, Dr. F. A. Lindemann, by his researches and courageous experiments at the Royal Aircraft Factory, proved that any aeroplane can spin, and that any pilot who understands the spin can get out of it if there is height to spare.

During the war the spin was freely used by pilots to break off a fight, to simulate defeat, or to descend in a vertical path. Similarly, little stress was laid, at the beginning, on speed, for speed was not helpful to reconnaissance, or on climb and height, for it was believed that at three thousand feet from the ground a machine would be practically immune from gun-fire, and that reconnaissance, to be effective, must be carried on below the level of the clouds. These misconceptions were soon to be corrected by experience. Another, more costly in its consequences, was that a machine-gun, when carried in an aeroplane, must have a large arc, or cone, of fire, so that the gun might be fired in any direction, up, down, or across. To secure this end guns had to be carried in the front of a pusher machine, which is slower and more clumsy than a tractor.

But the difficulty of accurate firing from a flying platform at an object moving with unknown speed on an undetermined course was found to be very great. The problem was much simplified by the introduction of devices for firing a fixed machine-gun through the tractor screw, so that the pilot could aim his gun by aiming his aeroplane, or gun-platform, which responds delicately and quickly to his control.

When the war began we were not inferior in aerodynamical knowledge to the Germans or even to the French. Speaking at the Aeronautical Society in February 1914, Brigadier-General Henderson said,

> If anyone wants to know which country has the fastest aeroplane in the world—it is Great Britain.

This was the S.E. 4, a forerunner of the more famous S.E. 5. If more powerful engines had been installed in the British machines of 1914, they would have given us a speed that the enemy could not touch. But we were preoccupied with the needs of reconnaissance, and we cared little about speed. In the early part of the war we hampered our aeroplanes with fitments, cameras, and instruments, which were attached as protuberances to the streamlined body of the aeroplane and made speed impossible. In the Flying Corps itself an aeroplane thus fitted was commonly called a Christmas tree. We thought too little of power in the engine, a mistake not quickly remedied, seeing that the time which must elapse between the ordering of an engine and its production in quantity is, even under pressure, a period of about twelve months.

The engines available at the outbreak of the war for British military aircraft were the seventy horse-power Renault and the eighty horse-power Gnome. In Germany airship engines of two hundred horse-power and more, easily modified for use in aeroplanes, were available in quantity some time before the war. For military machines we were satisfied with smaller engines, which worked well, and enabled our aeroplanes to accomplish all that at that time seemed likely to be asked of them. If we were wrong we were content to wait for experience to correct us.

The problems presented to the Naval Wing of the Royal Flying Corps were widely different from those which engrossed the attention of the soldiers. The difference, to put it briefly, was the difference between defence and attack. The British Army does not fight at home, and this privilege it enjoys by virtue of the constant vigilance of the British navy. The ultimate business of the British navy, though it visits all the seas of the world, is home defence. Yet that defence cannot be effectively carried out at home, and when we are at war our frontiers are the enemy coasts and our best defence is attack. This old established doctrine of naval warfare is the orthodox doctrine also of aerial warfare.

A mobile force confined to one place by losing its mobility loses most of its virtue. The fencer who does nothing but parry can never win a bout, and in the end, will fail to parry. The recognition of this doctrine in relation to aerial warfare was gradual. When the Royal Flying Corps was established and the question of the defence of our coasts by aircraft first came under discussion, our available airships, aeroplanes, and seaplanes, though their development had been amazingly rapid, were weapons without much power of offence. The main thing was to give them a chance of proving and increasing their utility.

In October 1912 the Admiralty decided to establish a chain of seaplane and airship stations on the east coast of Great Britain. The earliest of these stations, after Eastchurch, was the seaplane station of the Isle of Grain, commissioned in December 1912, with Lieutenant J.W. Seddon as officer in command. This was followed, in the first half of 1913, by the establishment of similar stations at Calshot, Felixstowe, Yarmouth, and Cromarty. H.M.S. *Hermes*, in succession to H.M.S. *Actaeon*, was commissioned on the 7th of May 1913 as headquarters of the Naval Wing, and her commanding officer, Captain G. W. Vivian, R.N., was given charge of all coastal air stations.

For airships a station at Hoo on the Medway was established with two double sheds of the largest size; it was called Kingsnorth, and was completed in April 1914, by which time all military airships had been handed over to the Admiralty. All the seaplane stations were in a sense offshoots of Eastchurch, which continued to be the principal naval flying school. Except for some valuable experimental work, not very much was done before the war at the seaplane coast stations. The supply of machines was small, and when the bare needs of Eastchurch and Grain had been met, not enough remained for the outfit of the other stations. Nevertheless, the zeal of the naval pilots, encouraged and supported by the First Lord of the Admiralty (Mr. Winston Churchill) and by the Director of the Air Department (Captain Murray Sueter), wrought good progress in a short time.

The first successful seaplane was produced at Eastchurch, as has been told, in March 1912. Just before the war, the Naval Wing of the Royal Flying Corps had in its possession fifty-two seaplanes, of which twenty-six were in flying condition, and further, had forty-six seaplanes on order. Those who know how difficult it is to get new things done will easily recognise that this measure of progress, though perhaps not very impressive numerically, could never have been achieved save by indomitable perseverance and effort. Sailors are accustomed to work hard and cheerfully under adverse conditions.

In the naval manoeuvres of July 1913, the *Hermes*, carrying two seaplanes, which were flown from its launching platform, operated with the fleet. Four seaplanes and one aeroplane from Yarmouth, three seaplanes from Leven, and three from Cromarty, also bore a part. The weather was not good, and the manoeuvres proved that the smaller type of seaplane was useless for work in the North Sea. Any attempt to get these machines off the water in a North Sea 'lop' infallibly led to their destruction. Further, it was found necessary for the safety of pilots that every machine should be fitted with wireless telegraphy. A machine fitted with folding wings was flown from the *Hermes* by Commander Samson, and was found to be the best and most manageable type.

In a minute dated the 26th of October 1913 the First Lord of the Admiralty sketches a policy and a programme for the ensuing years. Aeroplanes and seaplanes, he remarks, are needed by the navy for oversea work and for home work. He recommends three new types of machine: first, an oversea fighting seaplane, to operate from a ship as base; next, a scouting seaplane, to work with the fleet at sea; and last, a home-service fighting aeroplane, to repel enemy aircraft when they attack the vulnerable points of our island, and to carry out patrol duties along the coast. The events of the war have given historic interest to all forecasts prepared before the war.

Mr. Churchill's minute is naturally much concerned with the Zeppelin, which should be attacked, he says, by an aeroplane descending on it obliquely from above, and discharging a series of small bombs or fireballs, at rapid intervals, so that a string of them, more than a hundred yards in length, would be drawn like a whiplash across the gas-bag. This is a near anticipation of the method by which Flight Sub-Lieutenant R. A. J. Warneford brought down a Zeppelin in flames between Ghent and Brussels on the 7th of June 1915. The immense improvements in construction which were wrought by the war may be measured by Mr. Churchill's specifications for the rate of climb of the two-seater aeroplanes and seaplanes—namely, three thousand feet in twenty minutes. When he drafted his scheme that was a good rate of climb; before the war ended there were machines on the flying fronts which could climb three thousand feet in two minutes.

Under the direction of the Air Department much attention was paid by pilots in the Naval Air Service to experimental work and the diverse uses of aeroplanes. So early as January 1912 Lieutenant H. A. Williamson, R.N., a submarine officer who had gained the Royal Aero Club certificate, submitted to the Admiralty a paper which anticipated some later successes. He advocated the use of aeroplanes operating from a parent ship for the detection of submarines, and showed how bombs exploding twenty feet below the surface might be used to destroy these craft. The practical introduction of depth charges was delayed for years by the difficulty of devising the delicate and accurate mechanism which uses the pressure of the water to explode the bomb at a given depth. But before the war ended the detection of submarines from the air and the use by surface craft of depth charges for destroying them had been brought to such a degree of efficiency that the submarine menace was countered and held.

The submarine learned to fear aircraft as the birds of the thicket fear the hawk. It would be tedious to attempt to describe the long series of experiments by which this result was at last attained. The earliest attempts to detect submarines from the air were made with seaplanes at Harwich in June 1912, and at Rosyth in September of the same year. The shallow tidal waters were found to be very opaque, but in clear weather a periscope could be seen from a considerable distance, and in misty weather the seaplane, when it sighted a submarine in diving trim on the surface, could swoop down and drop a bomb before the submarine could dive.

Progress in bomb-dropping was not less. Nothing is easier than to drop a detonating bomb, with good intentions, over the side of an aeroplane; the difficulty of hitting the mark lay in determining the flight of the bomb and in devising an efficient dropping gear. To drop a weight from a rapidly moving aeroplane so that it shall hit a particular spot on the surface of the earth is not an easy affair; the pace and direction of the machine, its height from the ground, the shape and air resistance of the bomb, must all be accurately known. They cannot be calculated in the air; success in bomb-dropping depends on the designing of a gear for dropping and sighting which shall perform these calculations automatically.

Very early in the history of aviation dummy bombs had been dropped, for spectacular purposes, at targets marked on the ground. The designing of an efficient dropping gear and the study of the flight of bombs were taken up by the Air Department of the Admiralty from the very first. Under their direction a very valuable series of experiments was carried out at Eastchurch, at first by Commander Samson, and later by Lieutenant R. H. Clark Hall, a naval gunnery lieutenant, who had learnt to fly, and was appointed in March 1913 for armament duties with the Royal Naval Air Service.

The whole subject was new. No one could tell exactly how the flight of an aeroplane would be affected when the weight of the machine should be suddenly lightened by the release of a large bomb; no one could be sure that a powerful explosion on the surface of the sea would not affect the machine flying at a moderate height above it. In 1912 a dummy hundred-pound bomb was dropped from a Short pusher biplane flown by Commander Samson, who was surprised and pleased to find that the effect on the flight of the machine was hardly noticeable.

In December 1913 experiments were carried out to determine the lowest height at which bombs could be safely dropped from an aeroplane. No heavy bombs were available, but floating charges of various weights, from 2¼ pounds to 40 pounds, were fired electrically from a destroyer, while Maurice Farman seaplanes flew at various heights directly above the explosion. Again, the effect upon the machines was less than had been anticipated. The general conclusion was that an aeroplane flying at a height of 350 feet or more could drop a hundred-pound bomb, containing forty pounds of high explosive, without danger from the air disturbance caused by the explosion.

A good war machine aims at combining the safety of the operator with a high degree of danger to the victim. The second of these requirements was the more difficult of fulfilment, and was the subject of many experiments. Until the war took the measure of their powers, the German Zeppelins preoccupied attention, and were regarded as the most important targets for aerial attack. The towing of an explosive grapnel, which, suspended from an aeroplane, should make contact with the side of an airship, was the subject of experiments at Eastchurch. This idea, though nothing occurred to prove it impracticable, was soon abandoned in favour of simpler methods—the dropping, for instance, of a series of light bombs with sensitive fuses, or the firing of Hales grenades from an ordinary service rifle. To make these effective, it was essential that they should detonate on contact with ordinary balloon fabric, and preliminary experiments were carried out at the Cotton Powder Company's works at Faversham in October 1913.

When two sheets of fabric, stitched on frames to represent the two skins of a rigid airship, were hit by a grenade of the naval type with a four-ounce charge, it was found that the front sheet was blown to shreds and the rear sheet had a hole about half a foot in diameter blown in it. Later experiments at Farnborough against balloons filled with hydrogen, and made to resemble as nearly as possible a section of a rigid airship, were completely successful. Firing at floating targets, and at small target balloons released from the aeroplanes, was practised at Eastchurch. It was found that, with no burst or splash to indicate where the shot hit, this practice was unprofitable. The effective use of small-bore fire-arms against aircraft was made possible by two inventions, produced under the stress of the war itself, that is to say, of the tracer bullet, which leaves behind it in the air a visible track of its flight, and of the incendiary bullet, which sets fire to anything inflammable that it hits.

At the outbreak of war, the only effective weapon for attacking the Zeppelin from the air was the Hales grenade. Of two hundred of these which had been manufactured for the use of the Naval Wing many had been used in experiment; the remainder were hastily distributed by Lieutenant Clark Hall among the seaplane stations on the East Coast.

The Naval Air Service experimented also with the mounting of machine-guns on aeroplanes. On this matter Lieutenant Clark Hall, early in 1914, reported as follows:

Machine-gun aeroplanes are (or will be) required to drive off enemy machines approaching our ports with the intention of obtaining information or attacking with bombs our magazines, oil tanks, or dockyards. . . . I do not think the present state of foreign seaplanes for attack or scouting over our home ports is such as to make the question extremely urgent, but I would strongly advocate having by the end of 1914 at each of our home ports and important bases at least two aeroplanes mounting machine-guns for the sole purpose of beating off or destroying attacking or scouting enemy aeroplanes.

From what has been said it is evident that the Naval Wing of the Royal Flying Corps paid more attention than was paid by the Military Wing to the use of the aeroplane as a fighting machine. This difference naturally followed from the diverse tasks to be performed by the two branches of the air service. The Military Wing, small as it was, knew that it would be entrusted with the immense task of scouting for the expeditionary force, and that its business would be rather to avoid than to seek battle in the air. The Naval Wing, being entrusted first of all with the defence of the coast, aimed at doing something more than observing the movements of an attacking enemy.

Thus, in bomb-dropping and in machine-gunnery the Naval Wing was more advanced than the Military Wing. Both wings were active and alive with experiment, so that after a while experimental work which had originally been assigned to the factory and the Central Flying School was transferred to the Wing Headquarters. During the year 1913 wireless experiments were discontinued at the Central Flying School, and were concentrated at the Military Wing. There was a valuable measure of co-operation between the two wings. This co-operation was conspicuous, as has been seen, in wireless telegraphy, which was first applied to aircraft at Farnborough.

The lighter-than-air craft, which belonged first to the army and then to the navy, were a valuable link between the two wings. Each wing was ready to learn from the other. In January 1914, by permission of the Admiralty, officers of the Military Wing witnessed the experiments made by the Naval Wing with bomb-dropping gear. If the Naval Wing in some respects made more material progress, it should be remembered that they received more material support. They were encouraged by the indefatigable Director of the Air Department, and received from the Admiralty larger grants of money than came to the

Military Wing. No doubt a certain spirit of rivalry made itself felt. Service loyalty is a strong passion, and the main tendency, before the war, was for the two branches of the air service to drift apart, and to attach themselves closely, the one to the army, the other to the navy.

At the end of 1913 H.M.S. *Hermes* was paid off, and the headquarters of the Naval Wing was transferred to the Central Air Office, Sheerness. All ranks and ratings hitherto borne on the books of the *Hermes* were transferred to the books of this newly created office, and Captain F. R. Scarlett, R.N., late second in command of the *Hermes*, was placed in charge, with the title of Inspecting Captain of Aircraft. He was responsible to the Director of the Air Department, and, in regard to aircraft carried on ships afloat, or operating with the fleet, was also directly responsible to the Commander-in-Chief of the Home Fleets. In some respects, the progress made by the Naval Wing of the Royal Flying Corps during 1913 had been continuous and satisfactory. Training had been carried on regularly at the Central Flying School, at Eastchurch, and, for airship work, at Farnborough.

By the end of the year there were about a hundred trained pilots. Stations for guarding the coast had been established in five places other than Eastchurch, and arrangements were in hand for doubling this number. The record of miles flown during the year by naval aeroplanes and seaplanes was no less than 131,081 miles. Wireless telegraphy had made a great advance; transmitting sets were in course of being fitted to all seaplanes, and the reception of messages in aeroplanes had been experimentally obtained. Systematic bomb-dropping had been practised with growing accuracy and success. A system for transmitting meteorological charts from the Admiralty, so that air stations and aircraft in the air should receive frequent statements of the weather conditions, had been brought into working order.

On the other hand, all these advances were experimental in character, and no attempt had been made to equip the force completely for the needs of war. In this matter there is perhaps something to be said on both sides Where munitions are improving every year, too soon is almost as bad as too late. In fact, at the beginning of the war the Naval Air Service had only two aeroplanes and one airship fitted with machine-guns. Of the aeroplanes, one carried a Maxim gun, another a Lewis gun, loaned to the Admiralty by Colonel Lucas, C.B., of Hobland Hall, Yarmouth. No. 3 Airship (the Astra-Torres) was fitted with a Hotchkiss gun. The offensive weapon carried by other machines was a rifle. The various air stations were not liberally supplied with munitions of war. The Isle of Grain had four Hales hand-grenades. Hendon (the station for the defence of London) and Felixstowe had twelve each. The other stations were supplied in a like proportion, except Eastchurch, which had a hundred and fifty hand-grenades, forty-two rifle grenades, twenty-six twenty-pound bombs, and a Maxim gun. When the war broke out, a number of six-inch shells were fitted with tail vanes and converted into bombs.

On the 1st of July 1914 the separate existence of the naval air force was officially recognised. The Naval Wing of the Royal Flying Corps became the Royal Naval Air Service, with a constitution of its own. The naval flying school at Eastchurch and the naval air stations on the coast, together with all aircraft employed for naval purposes, were grouped under the administration of the Air Department of the Admiralty and the Central Air Office. So, for a time, the national air force was broken in two. The army and the navy had been willing enough to co-operate, but the habits of life and thought of a soldier and a sailor are incurably different. Moreover, the tasks of the two wings, as has been said, were distinct, and neither wing was very well able to appreciate the business of the other.

The Naval Wing had not the transport or equipment to operate at a distance from the sea, and, on the other hand, was inclined to insist that all military aeroplanes, when used for coast defence, should be placed under naval command. The Military Wing was preoccupied with continental geography and with strategical problems. The two attitudes and two methods lent a certain richness and diversity to our air operations in the war. When Commander Samson established himself at Dunkirk during the first year of the war, his variegated activities bore very little resemblance to the operations of the military squadrons on the battle-front.

The review of the fleet by the king, at Spithead, from the 18th to the 22nd of July 1914, gave to the Royal Naval Air Service an opportunity to demonstrate its use in connexion with naval operations. Most of the available naval aircraft were concentrated at Portsmouth, Weymouth, and Calshot to take part in the review. On the 20th of July an organised flight of seventeen seaplanes, and two flights of aeroplanes in formation headed by Commander Samson, manoeuvred over the fleet. This formation flying had been practised at Eastchurch before the review.

Three airships from Farnborough and one from Kingsnorth also took part in the demonstration. Within a few weeks all were to take part in the operations of war. The aeroplanes and seaplanes flew low over the fleet. Some naval officers, who had previously seen little of aircraft, expressed the opinion that the planes flew low because they could not fly high, and that their performance was an acrobatic exhibition, useless for the purposes of war. These and other doubters were soon converted by the war.

When the review was over, the seaplanes and airships returned to their several bases. The flights of aeroplanes, under Commander Samson, went on tour, first to Dorchester, where they stayed four or five days, and thence to the Central Flying School. They had been there only a few hours when they received urgent orders to return to Eastchurch, where they arrived on the 27th of July. On the same day seaplanes from other stations were assembled at Grain Island, Felixstowe, and Yarmouth, to be ready to patrol the coast in the event of war. These precautionary orders, and the orders given by the Admiralty on the previous day, arresting the dispersal of the British fleet, were among the first orders of the war.

On the 29th of July instructions were issued to the Naval Air Service that the duties of scouting and patrol were to be secondary to the protection of the country against hostile aircraft. All machines were to be kept tuned up and ready for action. On the 30th of July the Army Council agreed to send No. 4 Squadron of aeroplanes to reinforce the naval machines at Eastchurch. Eastchurch, during the months before the war, had been active in rehearsal; fighting in the air had been practised, and trial raids, over Chatham and the neighbouring magazines, had been carried out, two aeroplanes attacking and six or eight forming a defensive screen. Work of this kind had knit together the Eastchurch unit and had fitted it for active service abroad. In the meantime, at the outbreak of the war, attacks by German aircraft were expected on points of military and naval importance.

Germany was known to possess eleven rigid airships, and was believed to have others under construction. Our most authoritative knowledge of the state of German aviation was derived from a series of competitions held in Germany from the 17th to the 25th of May 1914, and called 'The Prince Henry Circuit'. These were witnessed by Captain W. Henderson, R.N., as naval *attaché*, and by Lieutenant-Colonel the Hon. A. Russell, as military *attaché*. The witnesses pay tribute to the skill and dash of the German flying officers and to the spirit of the flying battalions. The officers they found to be fine-drawn, lean, determined-looking youngsters, unlike the well-known heavy Teutonic type. Owing partly to the monotony of German regimental life there was great competition, they were told, to enter the flying service, eight hundred candidates having presented themselves for forty vacancies.

In 'The Prince Henry Circuit', a cross-country flight of more than a thousand miles, to be completed in six days, twenty-six aeroplanes started. The weather was stormy, and there were many accidents; one pilot and three observers were killed. These were regarded as having lost their lives in action, and there was no interruption of the programme. Among the best of the many machines that competed were the military L.V.G. (or Luft-Verkehrs-Gesellschaft) biplane, which won the chief prizes, the A. E.G. (or Allgemeine Elektrizitäts-Gesellschaft) biplane, the Albatross, and the Aviatik. On the whole, said our witnesses, the Germans had not progressed fast or far in aviation. They were still learning to fly; they were seeking for the best type of machine; and had given no serious attention, as yet, to the question of battle in the air. The test that was to compare the British and German air forces was now at hand.

Chapter 6

The War: The Royal Flying Corps from Mons to Ypres

The German war of the twentieth century, like the German wars of the eighteenth and nineteenth centuries, was carefully planned and prepared by the military rulers of Prussia. To elucidate its origins and causes will be the work of many long years. Yet enough is known to make it certain that this last and greatest war conforms to the old design. The Prussians have always been proud of their doctrine of war, and have explained it to the world with perfect frankness. War has always been regarded by them as the great engine of national progress. By war they united the peoples of Germany; by war they hoped to gain for the peoples of Germany an acknowledged supremacy in the civilized world. These peoples had received unity at the hands of Prussia, and though they did not like Prussia, they believed enthusiastically in Prussian strength and Prussian wisdom.

If Prussia led them to war, they were encouraged to think that the war would be unerringly designed to increase their power and prosperity. Yet many of them would have shrunk from naked assault and robbery; and Prussia, to conciliate these, invented the fable of the war of defence. That a sudden attack on her neighbours, delivered by Germany in time of peace, is a strictly defensive act has often been explained by German military and political writers, never perhaps more clearly than in a secret official report, drawn up at Berlin in the spring of 1913, on the strengthening of the German Army.

A copy of this report fell into the hands of the French.

The people must be accustomed to think that an offensive war on our part is a necessity. . . . . We must act with prudence in order to arouse no suspicion.

The fable of the war of defence was helped out with the fable of encirclement. Germany, being situated in the midst of Europe, had many neighbours, most of whom had more reason to fear her than to like her. Any exhibition of goodwill between these neighbours was treated by German statesmen, for years before the war, as a covert act of hostility to Germany, amply justifying reprisals. The treaty between France and Russia, wholly defensive in character, the expression of goodwill between France and England, inspired in part by fears of the restless ambitions of Germany, though both were intended to guarantee the existing state of things, were odious to Berlin. The peace of Europe hung by a thread.

On Sunday, the 28th of June 1914, the Archduke Francis Ferdinand, heir to the throne of Austria, and his wife, the Duchess of Hohenberg, paid a visit to Serajevo, the capital of Bosnia, and were there murdered by Bosnian assassins. It has not been proved that Germany had any part in the murder, but she was quite willing to take advantage of it. The Kiel canal, joining the Baltic with the North Sea, had just been widened to admit the largest battleships, and the German Army had just been raised to an unexampled strength. The gun was loaded and pointed; if it was allowed to be fired by accident the military rulers of Germany were much to blame. They were not in the habit of trusting any part of their plans to accident.

But the excitement caused by the archduke's murder was allowed to die away, and an uneasy calm succeeded. On the 23rd of July the Austrian Government, alleging that the Serajevo assassinations had been planned in Belgrade, presented to Serbia, with the declared approval of Germany, an ultimatum, containing demands of so extreme a character that the acceptance of them would have meant the abandonment by Serbia of her national independence. Serbia appealed to Russia, and, acting on Russia's advice, accepted all the demands except two. These two, which involved the appointment of Austro-Hungarian delegates to assist in administering the internal affairs of Serbia, were not bluntly rejected; Serbia asked that they should be referred to The Hague Tribunal. Austria replied by withdrawing her minister, declaring war upon Serbia, and bombarding Belgrade.

This action was bound to involve Russia, who could not stand by and seethe Slavonic States of southern Europe destroyed and annexed. But the Russian Government, along with the Governments of France,

Great Britain, and Italy, did their utmost to preserve the peace. They suggested mediation and a conference of the Powers. Germany alone refused. Alleging that Russia had already mobilised her army, she decreed a state of war, and on Saturday, the 1st of August, declared war upon Russia. France by her treaty with Russia would shortly have become involved; but the German Government would not wait for her. They judged it all-important to gain a military success at the very start of the war, and to this everything had to give way.

They declared war on France, and massed armies along the frontier between Liége and Luxembourg, with the intention of forcing a passage through Belgium. England, who was one of the guarantors of the integrity of Belgium, was thus involved. At 11.0 p.m. on the 4th of August, Great Britain declared war on Germany, and the World War had begun.

The events of the twelve days from the 23rd of July to the 4th of August, when they shall be set forth in detail, will furnish volumes of history. Those who study them minutely are in some danger of failing to see the wood for the trees. The attitude of the nations was made clear enough during these days. When Austria issued her ultimatum, many people in England thought of it as a portent of renewed distant trouble in the Balkans, to be quickly begun and soon ended. It was not so regarded in Germany. The people of Germany, though they were not in the confidence of their Government, were sufficiently familiar with its mode of operation to recognise the challenge to Serbia for what it was, Germany's chosen occasion for her great war.

The citizens not only of Berlin, but of the Rhineland, and of little northern towns on the Kiel canal, went mad with joy; there was shouting and song and public festivity. Meantime in England, as the truth dawned, there were hushed voices and an intense solemnity. The day had come, and no one doubted the severity of the ordeal. Yet neither did any one, except an unhappy few who had been nursed in folly and illusion, doubt the necessity of taking up the challenge. The country was united. Not only was the safety and existence of the British Commonwealth involved, but the great principle of civilization, difficult to name, but perhaps best called by the appealing name of decency, which bids man remember that he is frail and that it behoves him to be considerate and pitiful and sincere, had been flouted by the arrogant military rulers of Germany.

Great Britain had a navy; her army and her air force, for the purposes of a great European war, were yet to make. The motive that was to supply her with millions of volunteers was not only patriotism, though patriotism was strong, but a sense that her cause, in this war, was the cause of humanity. There are many who will gladly fight to raise their country and people in power and prosperity above other countries and other peoples. There are many also among English-speaking peoples who are unwilling to fight for any such end. But they are fighters, and they will fight to protect the weak and to assert the right. They are a reserve worth enlisting in any army; it was by their help that the opponents of Germany attained to a conquering strength.

The systematic cruelties of Germany, inflicted by order on the helpless populations of Serbia and Belgium and northern France, are not matter of controversy; they have been proved by many extant military documents and by the testimony of many living witnesses. They were designed to reduce whole peoples to a state of impotent terror, beneath the level of humanity. The apology made for them, that by shortening resistance to the inevitable they were in effect merciful, is a blasphemous apology, which puts Germany in the place of the Almighty. The effect anticipated did not follow. The system of terrorism hardened and prolonged resistance; it launched against Germany the chivalry of the world; it created for use against Germany the chivalry of the air; and it left Germany unhonoured in her ultimate downfall.

The German plan of campaign, it was rightly believed, was a swift invasion and disablement of France, to be followed by more prolonged operations against Russia. By this plan the German Army was to reach Paris on the fortieth day after mobilisation. There was no promise that Great Britain would help France, but the attitude of Germany had long been so threatening that the General Staffs of the two countries had taken counsel with each other concerning the best manner of employing the British forces in the event of common resistance to German aggression. It had been provisionally agreed that the British Army should be concentrated on the left flank of the French Army, in the area between Avesnes and Le Cateau, but this agreement was based on the assumption that the two armies would be mobilised simultaneously.

When the principal British Ministers and the leading members of the naval and military staffs assembled at Downing street on the 5th and 6th of August, we were already behindhand, and the whole question of the employment and disposition of the expeditionary force had to be reopened. It was expected by some soldiers and some civilians that the little British Army would be landed at a point on the coast of France or Belgium whence it could strike at the flank of the German invaders. The strategic advantages of that idea had to yield to the enormous importance of giving moral and material support to our Allies by fighting at their side; moreover, there could be no assurance that the coast of Belgium would not fall into the hands of the Germans at a very early stage in the campaign. Accordingly, it was agreed to ship our army to France, and to leave the manner of its employment to be settled in concert with the French.

The original British Expeditionary Force, under the command of Field-Marshal Sir John French, began to embark on the 9th of August; by the 20th its concentration in a pear-shaped area between Maubeuge and Le Cateau was complete. It consisted of the First Army Corps, under Lieutenant-General Sir Douglas Haig; the Second Army Corps, under Lieutenant-General Sir James Grierson, who died soon after landing in France and was succeeded by General Sir Horace Smith-Dorrien; and the Cavalry Division, under Major-General E. H. H. Allenby.

The Germans made no attempt to interfere with the transport of the expeditionary force from England to France. They had many other things to think of, and there is evidence to show that they viewed with satisfaction the placing of that admirable little force in a situation where they hoped that they could cut it off and annihilate it. That they were disappointed in this hope was due not a little to the activity and efficiency of the newest arm, numbering about a thousand, all told, the Royal Flying Corps.

The Royal Flying Corps took the field under the command of Brigadier-General Sir David Henderson. It consisted of Headquarters, Aeroplane Squadrons Nos. 2, 3, 4, and 5, and an Aircraft Park. Fairly complete arrangements, thought out in detail, had been made some months earlier for its mobilisation. Each squadron was to mobilise at its peace station, and was to be ready to move on the fourth day. On that day the aeroplanes were to move, by air, first to Dover, and thence, on the sixth day, to the field base in the theatre of war. The horses, horse-vehicles, and motor-bicycles, together with a certain amount of baggage and supplies, were to travel by rail, and the mechanical transport and trailers by road, to the appointed port of embarkation, there to be shipped for the overseas base.

The Aircraft Park, numbering twelve officers and a hundred and sixty-two other ranks, with four motor-cycles and twenty-four aeroplanes in cases, were to leave Farnborough for Avonmouth on the seventh day. Instructions were issued naming the hour and place of departure of the various trains, with detailed orders as to machines, personnel, transport, and petrol. On the second day of mobilisation a detachment from No. 6 Squadron was to proceed to Dover, there to make ready a landing-ground for the other squadrons, and to provide for replenishment of fuel and minor repairs to aircraft. Squadron commanders were urged to work out all necessary arrangements for the journey.

How carefully they did this is shown by some of the entries in the squadron diaries. In the diary of No. 2 Squadron (Major C. J. Burke's) a list is given of the articles that were to be carried on each of the machines flying over to France. Besides revolvers, glasses, a spare pair of goggles, and a roll of tools, pilots were ordered to carry with them a water-bottle containing boiled water, a small stove, and, in the haversack, biscuits, cold meat, a piece of chocolate, and a packet of soup-making material.

The programme for mobilisation was, in the main, successfully carried out. The headquarters of the Royal Flying Corps left Farnborough for Southampton on the night of the 11th of August, their motor transport having gone before. They embarked at Southampton, with their horses, and reached Amiens on the morning of the 13th. The movements of the Aircraft Park, though it was the last unit to leave England, may be next recorded, because it was in effect the travelling base of the squadrons. The personnel and equipment were entrained at Farnborough during the evening of Saturday, the 15th of August, and travelled to Avonmouth. Of the twenty machines allotted to them only four, all Sopwith Tabloids, were actually taken over in cases.

Of the other sixteen (nine B.E. 2's, one B.E. 2 c, three B.E. 8's, and three Henri Farmans) about half were used to bring the squadrons up to establishment; the remainder were flown over to Amiens by the personnel of the Aircraft Park, or by the spare pilots who accompanied the squadrons. The Aircraft Park embarked at Avonmouth very early on the morning of the 17th, arriving at Boulogne on the night of the 18th. They disembarked, an unfamiliar apparition, on the following morning. The landing officer had no precedent to guide him in dealing with them. Wing Commander W. D. Beatty tells how a wire was dispatched to General Headquarters:

B.E. 2 c 1914

B.E. 2 a 1914

B.E. 8 1914

Sopwith Camels

SOPWITH CAMEL

BLERIOT XI

An unnumbered unit without aeroplanes which calls itself an Aircraft Park has arrived. What are we to do with it?

If the question was not promptly answered at Boulogne it was answered later on. The original Aircraft Park was the nucleus of that vast system of supply and repair which supported the squadrons operating on the western front and kept them in fighting trim.

On the 21st of August the Aircraft Park moved up to Amiens, to make an advanced base for the squadrons, which were already at Maubeuge. Three days were spent at Amiens in unloading, unpacking, and setting up workshops. Then, on the 25th, they received orders to retire to Le Havre. The retreat from Mons had begun, and Boulogne was being evacuated by the British troops. How far the wave of invasion would flow could not be certainly known; on the 30th of August, at the request of the French admiral who commanded at Le Havre, the machines belonging to the Aircraft Park were employed to carry out reconnaissances along the coast roads; on the following day German cavalry entered Amiens.

There was a real danger that stores and machines landed in northern France for the use of the Royal Flying Corps might fall into the hands of the Germans; accordingly, a base was established, for the reception of stores from England, at St.-Nazaire, on the Loire. The advanced base of the Aircraft Park moved up, by successive stages, as the prospects of the Allies improved, first from Le Havre to Le Mans, then, at the end of September, to Juvisy, near Paris; lastly, in mid-October, the port base was moved from St.-Nazaire to Rouen, and at the end of October the advanced base left Juvisy for St.-Omer, which became its permanent station during the earlier part of the war.

The squadrons flew to France. No. 2 Squadron, at Montrose, had the hardest task. Its pilots started on their southward flight to Farnborough as early as the 3rd of August; after some accidents they all reached Dover. Their transport left Montrose by rail on the morning of the 8th of August and arrived the same evening at Prince's Dock, Govan, near Glasgow, where the lorries and stores were loaded on S.S. *Dogra* for Boulogne. No. 3 Squadron was at Netheravon when war broke out; on the 12th of August the machines flew to Dover and the transport moved off by road to Southampton, where it was embarked for Boulogne. The squadron suffered a loss at Netheravon. Second Lieutenant R. R. Skene, a skilful pilot, with Air Mechanic R. K. Barlow as passenger, crashed his machine soon after taking off;

both pilot and passenger were killed. No. 4 Squadron on the 31st of July had been sent to Eastchurch, to assist the navy in preparations for home defence and to be ready for mobilisation. From Eastchurch the machines flew to Dover and the transport proceeded to Southampton. By the evening of the 12th of August, the machines of Nos. 2, 3, and 4 Squadrons were at Dover. At midnight Lieutenant-Colonel F. H. Sykes arrived, and orders were given for all machines to be ready to fly over at 6.0 a.m. the following morning, the 13th of August.

The first machine of No. 2 Squadron to start left at 6.25 a.m., and the first to arrive landed at Amiens at 8.20 a.m. This machine was flown by Lieutenant H. D. Harvey-Kelly, one of the lightest hearted and highest spirited of the young pilots who gave their lives in the war. The machines of No. 3 Squadron arrived safely at Amiens, with the exception of one piloted by Second Lieutenant E. N. Fuller, who with his mechanic did not rejoin his squadron until five days later at Maubeuge. One flight of No. 4 Squadron remained at Dover to carry out patrol duties, but a wireless flight, consisting of three officers who had made a study of wireless telegraphy, was attached to the squadron, and was taken overseas with it. Some of the aeroplanes of No. 4 Squadron were damaged on the way over by following their leader, Captain F. J. L. Cogan, who was forced by engine failure to land in a ploughed field in France.

No. 5 Squadron moved a little later than the other three. It was delayed by a shortage of shipping and a series of accidents to the machines. When the Concentration Camp broke up, this squadron had gone to occupy its new station at Gosport. On the 14th, when starting out for Dover, Captain G. I. Carmichael wrecked his machine at Gosport; on the same day Lieutenant R. O. Abercromby and Lieutenant H. F. Glanville damaged their machines at Shoreham, and Lieutenant H. le M. Brock damaged his at Salmer. The squadron flew from Dover to France on the 15th of August; Captain. Carmichael, having obtained a new machine, flew over on that same day; Lieutenant Brock rejoined the squadron at Maubeuge on the 20th; Lieutenants Abercromby and Glanville on the 22nd. Lieutenant R. M. Vaughan, who had flown over with the squadron, also rejoined it on the 22nd; he had made a forced landing near Boulogne, had been arrested by the French, and was imprisoned for nearly a week.

The transport of the squadrons, which proceeded by way of Southampton, was largely made up from the motorcars and commercial vans collected at Regent's Park in London during the first few days of the war. The ammunition and bomb lorry of No. 5 Squadron had belonged to the proprietors of a famous sauce: it was a brilliant scarlet, with the legend painted in gold letters on its side—*The World's Appetiser*. It could be seen from some height in the air, and it helped the pilots of the squadron, during the retreat from Mons, to identify their own transport.

The names of the officers of the Royal Flying Corps who went to France, the great majority of them by air, deserve record. They were the first organised national force to fly to a war overseas. The following is believed to be a complete list up to the eve of Mons, but it is not infallible. Officers and men were changed up to the last minute, so that the headquarters file, having been prepared in advance, is not authoritative. The squadron war diaries are sometimes sketchy. Even when surviving pilots set down what they remember, the whole war lies between them and those early days, and their memory is often fragmentary. The following list is compiled, as correctly as may be, from the diary of Lieutenant B. H. Barrington-Kennett (a careful and accurate document), the war diaries of Squadrons Nos. 2, 3, 4, and 5, which were kept in some detail, the headquarters' records, and the reminiscences of some of the officers who flew across or who travelled with the transport.

HEADQUARTERS

Brigadier-General Sir David Henderson, K.C.B., D.S.O.; Commander, Royal Flying Corps.
Lieutenant-Colonel F. H. Sykes, 15th Hussars; General Staff Officer, 1st Grade.
Major H. R. M. Brooke-Popham, Oxfordshire and Buckinghamshire Light Infantry; Deputy Assistant Quartermaster-General.
Captain W. G. H. Salmond, Royal Artillery; General Staff Officer, 2nd Grade.
Lieutenant B. H. Barrington-Kennett, Grenadier Guards; Deputy Assistant Adjutant and Quartermaster-General.

attached.

Captain R. H. L. Cordner, Royal Army Medical Corps.
Captain C. G. Buchanan, Indian Army.
Lieutenant the Hon. M. Baring, Intelligence Corps.
2nd Lieutenant O. G. W. G. Lywood, Norfolk Regiment (Special Reserve); for Wireless duties.

NO. 2 SQUADRON
Squadron Commander.
Major C. J. Burke, Royal Irish Regiment.
Flight Commanders.
Captain G. W. P. Dawes, Royal Berkshire Regiment.
Captain F. F. Waldron, 19th Hussars.
Captain G. E. Todd, Welch Regiment.
Flying Officers.
Lieutenant R. B. Martyn, Wiltshire Regiment.
Lieutenant L. Dawes, Middlesex Regiment.
Lieutenant R. M. Rodwell, West Yorkshire Regiment.
Lieutenant M. W. Noel, Liverpool Regiment.
Lieutenant E. R. L. Corballis, Royal Dublin Fusiliers.
Lieutenant H. D. Harvey-Kelly, Royal Irish Regiment.
Lieutenant W. R. Freeman, Manchester Regiment.
Lieutenant W. H. C. Mansfield, Shropshire Light Infantry.
Lieutenant C. B. Spence, Royal Artillery.
Captain A. B. Burdett, York and Lancaster Regiment.
Captain A. Ross-Hume, Scottish Rifles.
Lieutenant D. S. K. Crosbie, Argyll and Sutherland Highlanders.
Lieutenant C. A. G. L. H. Farie, Highland Light Infantry.
Lieutenant T. L. S. Holbrow, Royal Engineers.
2nd Lieutenant G. J. Malcolm, Royal Artillery.
Supernumerary.
Major C. A. H. Longcroft, Welch Regiment; Squadron Commander.
Captain U. J. D. Bourke, Oxfordshire and Buckinghamshire Light Infantry; Flight Commander.
Captain W. Lawrence, 7th Battalion, Essex Regiment (Territorial Force); Flight Commander.
Attached.
Lieutenant K. R. Van der Spuy, South African Defence Forces.

NO. 3 SQUADRON
Squadron Commander.
Major J. M. Salmond, Royal Lancaster Regiment.
Flight Commanders.
Captain P. L. W. Herbert, Nottinghamshire and Derbyshire Regiment.
Captain L. E. O. Charlton, D.S.O., Lancashire Fusiliers.

Captain P. B. Joubert de la Ferté, Royal Artillery.
Flying Officers.
2nd Lieutenant V. H. N. Wadham, Hampshire Regiment.
Lieutenant D. L. Allen, Royal Irish Fusiliers.
Lieutenant A. M. Read, Northamptonshire Regiment.
Lieutenant E. L. Conran, 2nd County of London Yeomanry.
Lieutenant A. Christie, Royal Artillery.
Lieutenant A. R. Shekleton, Royal Munster Fusiliers.
2nd Lieutenant E. N. Fuller, Royal Flying Corps, (Special Reserve.)
Lieutenant W. C. K. Birch, Yorkshire Regiment.
Lieutenant G. F. Pretyman, Somerset Light Infantry.
Lieutenant W. R. Read, 1st Dragoon Guards.
2nd Lieutenant A. Hartree, Royal Artillery.
Lieutenant V. S. E. Lindop, Leinster Regiment.
Lieutenant G. L. Cruikshank, Gordon Highlanders (Special Reserve).
Lieutenant W. F. MacNeece, Royal West Kent Regiment.
2nd Lieutenant L. A. Bryan, South Irish Horse.
Major L. B. Boyd-Moss, South Staffordshire Regiment.
2nd Lieutenant E. W. C. Perry, Royal Flying Corps, (Special Reserve).

NO. 4 SQUADRON
Squadron Commander.
Major G. H. Raleigh, Essex Regiment.
Flight Commanders.
Captain G. S. Shephard, Royal Fusiliers.
Captain A. H. L. Soames, 3rd Hussars.
Captain F. J. L. Cogan, Royal Artillery.
Flying Officers.
Lieutenant P. H. L. Playfair, Royal Artillery.
Lieutenant K. P. Atkinson, Royal Artillery.
Lieutenant R. P. Mills, Royal Fusiliers (Special Reserve).
Lieutenant T. W. Mulcahy-Morgan, Royal Irish Fusiliers.
Lieutenant R. G. D. Small, Leinster Regiment.
Lieutenant W. G. S. Mitchell, Highland Light Infantry.
Lieutenant G. W. Mapplebeck, Liverpool Regiment (Special Reserve).
Lieutenant C. G. Hosking, Royal Artillery.

Lieutenant H. J. A. Roche, Royal Munster Fusiliers.
Lieutenant I. M. Bonham-Carter, Northumberland Fusiliers.
2nd Lieutenant A. L. Russell, Royal Flying Corps, (Special Reserve.)

Wireless Flight.

Lieutenant D. S. Lewis, Royal Engineers.
Lieutenant B. T. James, Royal Engineers.
Lieutenant S. C. W. Smith, East Surrey Regiment (Special Reserve.)

Attached.

Captain D. Le G. Pitcher, Indian Army.
Captain H. L. Reilly, Indian Army.

NO. 5 SQUADRON

Squadron Commander.

Major J. F. A. Higgins, D.S.O., Royal Artillery.

Flight Commanders.

Captain D. G. Conner, Royal Artillery.
Captain G. I. Carmichael, Royal Artillery.
Captain R. Grey, Warwickshire Royal Horse Artillery (Territorial Force).

Flying Officers.

Lieutenant H. F. Glanville, West India Regiment.
Lieutenant F. G. Small, Connaught Rangers.
Lieutenant R. O. Abercromby, Royal Flying Corps, (Special Reserve.)
2nd Lieutenant C. W. Wilson, Royal Flying Corps, (Special Reserve.)
Lieutenant H. le M. Brock, Royal Warwickshire Regiment.
Lieutenant R. M. Vaughan, Royal Inniskilling Fusiliers.
Lieutenant L. da C. Penn-Gaskell, Norfolk Regiment (Special Reserve).
Lieutenant A. E. Borton, Royal Highlanders.
Lieutenant Lord G. Wellesley, Grenadier Guards.
Lieutenant C. G. G. Bayly, Royal Engineers.
Lieutenant C. E. C. Rabagliati, Yorkshire Light Infantry.
2nd Lieutenant A. A. B. Thomson, Royal Flying Corps, Special Reserve.
2nd Lieutenant L. A. Strange, Royal Flying Corps, Special Reserve.

2nd Lieutenant R. R. Smith-Barry, Royal Flying Corps, Special Reserve.
2nd Lieutenant D. C. Ware, Royal Flying Corps, Special Reserve.
2nd Lieutenant V. Waterfall, East Yorkshire Regiment (Special Reserve).
Captain R. A. Boger, Royal Engineers.
Captain B. C. Fairfax, Reserve of Officers.
Attached.
Lieutenant G. S. Creed, South African Defence Forces.

AIRCRAFT PARK
Squadron Commander.
Major A. D. Carden, Royal Engineers.
Flight Commanders.
Major Hon. C. M. P. Brabazon, Irish Guards.
Captain W. D. Beatty, Royal Engineers.
Captain R. Cholmondeley, Rifle Brigade.
Lieutenant G. B. Hynes, Royal Artillery.
Flying Officers.
Lieutenant G. T. Porter, Royal Artillery.
2nd Lieutenant C. G. Bell, Royal Flying Corps, (Special Reserve.)
2nd Lieutenant N. C. Spratt, Royal Flying Corps, (Special Reserve.)
Lieutenant R. H. Verney, Army Service Corps.

Something must be said of the machines which flew to France. Experience at manoeuvres had favoured the factory B.E. 2 biplane; of the other types most in use the Henri Farman had been found fatiguing to fly, and the Maurice Farman was too slow. Accordingly, in the winter of 1913-14 Lieutenant-Colonel F. H. Sykes had urged the gradual substitution of B.E. machines for the Farmans. Major W. S. Brancker, writing for the Director-General of Military Aeronautics, objected to this proposal on the ground that until a satisfactory type of righting aeroplane should be evolved, the Henri Farman was the only machine that could mount weapons effectively; and further, that a slow machine had some advantages for observation.

The first of these objections was not fully met until firing through the airscrew was introduced; the second was for a long time an accepted idea. The war was to prove that a slow machine, exposed to armed attack, cannot live in the air. The battle of the machines ended, for the time, in compromise. It was judged important that the Flying Corps should have four squadrons ready for war by the spring of 1914, and large changes would have caused delay. In the event, at the date of mobilisation, No. 2 Squadron and No. 4 Squadron were furnished throughout with B.E. 2 machines; No. 3 Squadron made use of Blériots and Henri Farmans, and No. 5 of Henri Farmans, Avros, and B.E. 8's. A single type of machine for a single squadron is a thing to be desired; the squadron is easier for the pilots and the mechanics to handle; but in the early days of the war there was no formation flying; each machine did its work alone, so that uniformity was of less importance.

When the Flying Corps arrived in France they were received by the French with enthusiasm, and had their full share of the hospitality of those days. The officers were treated as honoured guests; the men with the transport were greeted by crowds of villagers, who at all their stopping-places pressed on them bottles of wine, bunches of flowers, fruit, and eggs. At Amiens the transport and machines were parked outside the town, without cover, and the officers were billeted at the 'Hôtel du Rhin' and elsewhere. The hardships of the war were yet to come. Lieutenant B. H. Barrington-Kennett, with his mind always set on the task before them, remarks:

> There seemed to be a general misunderstanding amongst the troops as to the length of time during which rations have to last. They were apt to eat what they wanted at one meal and then throw the remainder away. R.F.C. peace training does not encourage economy with food, as the men are financially well off, and can always buy food and drink in the villages.

On. Sunday, the 16th of August, the headquarters of the Flying Corps, the aeroplanes of Nos. 2, 3, and 4 Squadrons, and the transport of Nos. 3 and 4 Squadrons moved from Amiens to Maubeuge. Second Lieutenant E. W. C. Perry and his mechanic, H. E. Parfitt, of No. 3 Squadron, who were flying a B.E. 8 machine (familiarly known as a 'bloater'), crashed over the aerodrome at Amiens; the machine caught fire, and both were killed. There was another accident on the 18th, when the aeroplanes and transport of No. 5 Squadron followed. Second Lieutenant R. R. Smith-Barry and Corporal F. Geard, also flying a B.E. 8 machine, crashed at Péronne; the officer broke several bones, and the corporal was killed. Three of these machines in all were flown over at the beginning; they had been allotted to the Aircraft Park, and

RFC Aircraft Aloft

were taken on charge of the squadrons in the field to fill vacancies caused by mishaps. The third of them was the machine flown over by Captain G. I. Carmichael.

At Maubeuge the French authorities gave all the help they could, providing blankets and straw for the troops. The Flying Corps were now in the war zone, but for the first two or three days the conditions were those of peace. They saw nothing of the British Army till one evening British troops marched through Maubeuge on their way to Mons. Wing Commander P. B. Joubert de la Ferté says:

> We were rather sorry they had come, because up till that moment we had only been fired on by the French whenever we flew. Now we were fired on by French *and* English. . . . . To this day I can remember the roar of musketry that greeted two of our machines as they left the aerodrome and crossed the main Maubeuge-Mons road, along which a British column was proceeding.

To guard against incidents like this the Flying Corps, while stationed at Maubeuge, turned to, and by working all night painted a Union Jack in the form of a shield on the underside of the lower planes of all the machines.

While the Flying Corps remained at Maubeuge and began to carry out reconnaissances over Belgium, the little British Army had moved up north to Mons, where it first met the enemy. By the 22nd of August it was in position, on a front of some twenty-five miles, the First Army Corps holding a line from Harmignies to Peissant on the east, the Second Army Corps holding Mons and the canal that runs from Mons to Condé on the west. On the right of the British the Fifth French Army, under General Lanrezac, was coming up to the line of the River Sambre.

The original German plan was broad and simple. The main striking force was to march through Belgium and Luxembourg into France. Its advance was to be a wheel pivoting on Thionville. Count von Schlieffen, who had vacated the appointment of Chief of the General Staff in 1906, had prepared this plan. He maintained that if the advance of a strong right wing, marching on Paris through Belgium, were firmly persisted in, it would draw the bulk of the French forces away from their eastern fortress positions to the neighbourhood of Paris, and that there the decisive battle would be fought. His successor, von Moltke, believed that the French, on the outbreak of war, would at once deliver a strong offensive in Lorraine and so would themselves come into the open, away from the bastion of the eastern fortresses.

He must be prepared, he thought, to fight the decisive battle either on his left wing in Lorraine, or on his right wing near Paris, or, in short, at any point that the initial operations of the French should determine. This was not the conception of Count von Schlieffen, who had intended to impose his will on the campaign and to make the enemy conform to his movements. When he was on his death-bed in 1913, his thoughts were fixed on the war. The last words he was heard to mutter were:

> It must come to a fight, only give me a strong right wing.

Von Moltke, though he did not absolutely weaken the right wing, weakened it relatively, by using most of the newly formed divisions of the German Army for strengthening the left wing.

The French, when the war came, delivered their offensive in Alsace and Lorraine as had been expected, but not in the strength that had been expected. They were held up, and retired, not without loss, to strong defensive positions covering Épinal and Nancy. Meantime, the advance of the German armies through Belgium was met by a French offensive in the Ardennes, which also failed, whereupon General Joffre ordered a retreat on the whole front, and began to move some of his forces westward, to prepare for the battle in front of Paris.

The successes won by the German left wing and centre against a yielding and retreating enemy were mistaken by the German high command for decisive actions, which they were not. The French armies which had been driven back on the Lorraine front rapidly recovered, and on the 25th of August delivered a brilliant counter-offensive, inflicting heavy losses on the Germans, and in effect upsetting all the German plans. The indecision which marked the movements of the German right wing through northern France had its origin in von Moltke's modifications of von Schlieffen's plans and in the readiness of the Germans to believe that the war was virtually won. (This brief summary is based on two admirable articles in *The Army Quarterly* for April and July 1921, compiled by the Historical Section—Military Branch—of the Committee of Imperial Defence.)

The heroic stand made by the Belgians at Liége purchased invaluable time for the preparations of the Allies. When, on the 17th of August, the last fort of Liége fell, the great wheel of the German northern armies began to revolve. Its pace was to be regulated by the pace of the armies nearest to its circumference; that is to say, the First Army, under von Kluck, and the Second Army, under von Bülow. Three divisions of cavalry were to advance against the line Antwerp-Brussels-Charleroi, moving westward across Belgium in order to discover whether a Belgian Army was still in being, whether the British had landed any troops, and whether French forces were moving up into northern Belgium.

The Belgian Army retired within the defensive lines of Antwerp, and by the 20th of August Brussels was in the hands of the enemy. By the 22nd, von Bülow's army had entered Charleroi and was crossing the Sambre. The repulse of the French centre in the Ardennes left the British Army and the French Fifth Army completely isolated on the front Mons-Charleroi. The French Fifth Army began to retreat. On Sunday morning, the 23rd of August, von Kluck's army came into action against the British position at Mons.

The British Army had taken up its position in high hopes. It was not a British defeat which began the retreat from Mons, and the troops were not well pleased when they were ordered to retire. But the retreat was inevitable, and the most that the British could do was by rear-guard actions to put a brake upon the speed of the advancing enemy until such time as they should be able to form up again in the Allied line and assail him. Much depended on their power to gain information concerning the movements of the enemy, so that they might know their own dangers and opportunities. Von Kluck had at first no definite news of the whereabouts of the British Army. As late as the 20th of August the German Supreme Command had issued a communication to the German armies stating that:

> A disembarkation of British Forces at Boulogne and their employment from the direction of Lille must be taken into account. It is the opinion here, however, that a landing on a big scale has not yet taken place.

General von Zwehl, Commander of the Seventh Reserve Corps, writing in September 1919, tells how the Germans had no reliable information concerning the British expeditionary force.

> It was only on the 22nd of August, that an English cavalry squadron was heard of at Casteau, six miles north-east of Mons, and an aeroplane of the English fifth flying squadron was shot down that had gone up from Maubeuge. The presence of the English in front was thus established, although nothing as re-

gards their strength.

The first news that reached General von Kluck of the presence of the British forces came to him from a British, not from a German, aeroplane.

The first aerial reconnaissances by the Royal Flying Corps were carried out on Wednesday, the 19th of August, by Captain P. B. Joubert de la Ferté of No. 3 Squadron, in a Blériot, and Lieutenant G. W. Mapplebeck of No. 4 Squadron, in a B.E. They started at 9.30 a.m., and flew without observers. Captain Joubert de la Ferté was to reconnoitre Nivelles-Genappe in order to report what Belgian forces were in that neighbourhood; Lieutenant Mapplebeck was to find out whether enemy cavalry were still in force in the neighbourhood of Gembloux. The machines were to fly together as far as Nivelles, 'so that if one was obliged to descend the other could report its whereabouts.' The machines lost their way and lost each other. Lieutenant Mapplebeck eventually found himself over a large town which he failed to recognise as Brussels.

Later he picked up his position at Ottignies, and soon found Gembloux, where he could see only a small body of cavalry moving in a south-easterly direction. After leaving Gembloux he was enveloped in cloud for some miles, came down to 300 feet over Namur, followed the Sambre, missed Maubeuge, and landed near Le Cateau, whence he flew back to the aerodrome at Maubeuge. He had been away from 9.30 a.m. to 12.0 midday. Captain Joubert de la Ferté, whose machine was slower than Lieutenant Mapplebeck's, attempted to steer by compass through the banks of cloud, and after two hours of wandering landed at Tournai. He made inquiries concerning the Belgian Army, but nothing was known of them.

He left Tournai at 12.15 p.m., lost his way again, and at 2.0 p.m. landed at Courtrai. Here he was told by the *gendarmerie* that the headquarters of the Belgian flying corps was at Louvain. He left Courtrai at 3.0 p.m. and passed over Ath, Hal, Braine l'Alleud, Nivelles, returning to Maubeuge at 5.30 p.m. He reported occasional trains in the main stations and pickets on the roads to Brussels.

On the 20th Major C. A. H. Longcroft, with Captain U. J. D. Bourke as observer, reconnoitred as far as Louvain and reported a force of all arms moving southwest through Tervueren, and another force moving into Wavre. They also saw an aerodrome just east of Louvain with seven machines on the ground. Lieutenant E. R. L. Corballis, who.

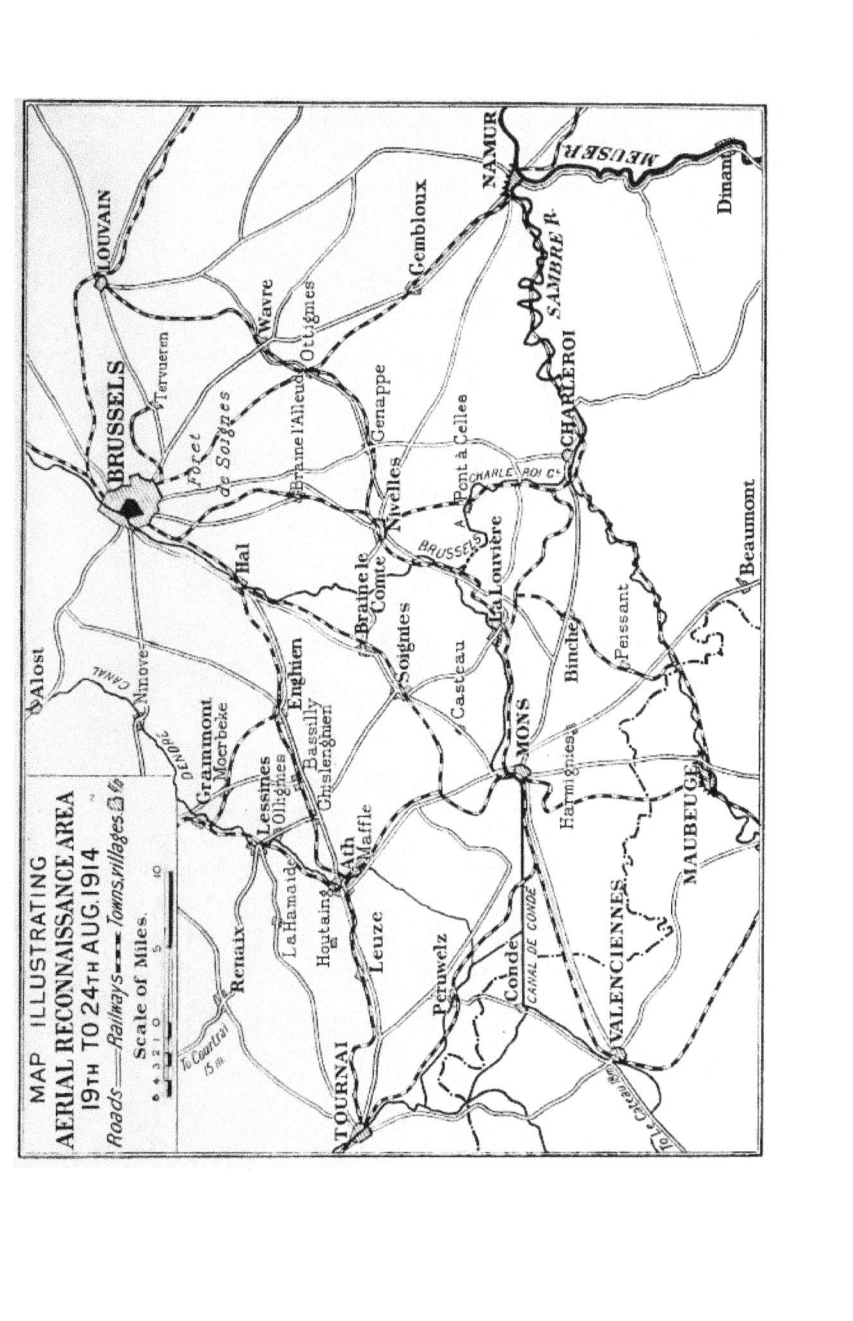

with Captain G. E. Todd, flew over the area Nivelles-Hal-Enghien, reported that there was no sign of troops and that all bridges in the area appeared to be intact. The German flood was spreading but was still some distance away.

On the following day (an important day of enemy movements) the weather in the morning was too foggy for observation, and in the afternoon, was rainy and misty. Three reconnaissances which were made in the afternoon showed that the country immediately in front of the British was very quiet, but in the wood one mile south of Nivelles Lieutenant Corballis reported a large body of cavalry with some guns and infantry (this was later identified as the German 9th Cavalry Division), and another body of infantry moving south on Charieroi. At Pont-à-Celles on the Charleroi canal, south of Nivelles, three villages were seen to be burning.

On the 22nd there were twelve reconnaissances which revealed the presence of large bodies of troops moving in the direction of the British front, and did much to dissipate the fog of war. The first machine to return came in soon after eleven. This was piloted by Captain G. S. Shephard, with Lieutenant I. M. Bonham-Carter as observer. They had landed at Beaumont (about twelve miles east of Maubeuge) for petrol. Here they were informed that French cavalry had encountered German infantry north of the Sambre canal on the previous afternoon, and had had to fall back.

The next machine to return came in at 11.50 a.m. with a wounded observer, Sergeant-Major D. S. Jillings of No. 2 Squadron. He was the first British soldier to be wounded in an aeroplane, and this casualty seemed to bring the German armies nearer than a dozen unmolested reconnaissances could have done. The machine, piloted by Lieutenant M. W. Noel, had come under heavy rifle fire first of all at Ollignies, south-east of Lessines, and then, after passing over a cavalry regiment just south-west of Ghislenghien, had been met with rifle and machine-gun fire. Frequent rifle fire was encountered all the way back to Ath, and just south-east of Ath, over Maffle, Sergeant-Major Jillings had been wounded in the leg by a rifle bullet.

Confirmation of the presence of large bodies of enemy in this area came from Captain L. E. O. Charlton flying as observer with Second Lieutenant V. H. N. Wadham. They started at 10.0 a.m. and passed over Charleroi, Gembloux, and Brussels without seeing any large movements, but reported that the northern part of Charleroi and many other towns and villages in that area were burning. From Brussels they went on towards Grammont, and landed at Moerbeke, two miles south-east of Grammont, to make inquiries. Here they received information which hastened their departure. They learnt that a force of 5,000 Germans was in Grammont, that cavalry and cyclists were in Lessines, and that cavalry were expected from Enghien to arrive in Ath that evening.

When passing over Bassilly, about half-way between Ath and Enghien, they were fired on by enemy troops which they estimated at the strength of an infantry brigade, and they drew further fire from patrols in Ath. They came in with their information at 1.10 p.m.; Lieutenant W. H. C. Mansfield just before this had reported large bodies moving into Enghien and Soignies. Afternoon reconnaissances added little that was new except that there were cavalry and infantry in the area north of the Mons-Condé canal, and cavalry as far west as Peruwelz.

The most important reconnaissance of the day is unfortunately not recorded in the war diary. The value of the report when it came in was recognised at once, and Brigadier-General Sir David Henderson took it personally to General Headquarters. It stated that a long column, whose strength was estimated to be that of an army corps, was moving westward on the Brussels-Ninove road. At Ninove the column continued south-west towards Grammont. This was von Kluck's Second Corps, and the report seemed to show an attempt at an enveloping movement. The same report confirmed what had already been seen, the presence of enemy troops moving along the great Chaussée on Soignies. This column was taking advantage of the trees on either side of the road to shield its movements.

This was the first day on which a machine failed to return from over enemy territory. Lieutenants V. Waterfall and C. G. G. Bayly, of No. 5 Squadron, started on a reconnaissance in an Avro at 10.16 a.m. and next day were reported missing. It was the bringing down of this machine, no doubt, which gave the Germans their first assurance of the presence of the British forces. The observer's report, so far as he had written it, was picked up near the wreckage of the machine by some Belgian peasants, and eventually found its way to the War Office in London. (See next page).

Sir John French on the evening of the 22nd held a conference at Le Cateau, whereat the position of the Germans, so far as it was then known, was explained and discussed. At the close of the conference Sir John stated that owing to the retreat of the French Fifth Army, the British offensive would not take place. A request from General Lan-

No. of Reconnaissance		Hour Started 10.16 a—
Date August 22		Hour Ended
Aeroplane No.	Pilot Lt C.M Wakefield Observer Lt C.G.G Bayly	

Time	Place	OBSERVATION
10.50	Mons–Soignies road	600' baggage wagon on road moving from THIEUSIS due N.E.
11.0	ENGHIEN Soignies	Cav: for Soc" in file 4 coy: inf: in fours } ENGHIEN apparently 6 four horse team } BASSILY 2 coy inf 4 four horse teams Column turning to left to right, will 6 coys mounted

RECONNAISSANCE REPORT OF LIEUTENANT C. G. G. BAYLY

rezac arrived at 11.0 p.m., asking for offensive action against the German right flank, which was pressing him back from the Sambre. This could not be undertaken, but Sir John French promised to remain in his position for twenty-four hours.

In his book, *A Staff Officer's Scrap Book*, Sir Ian Hamilton, who was attached to the Japanese Army during the Russo-Japanese War, has the following entry:

> The Russians are sending up balloons to our front, and in front of the Twelfth Division. Judging by manoeuvres and South African experiences, they should now obtain a lot of misleading intelligence.

Observation from the air, when the war broke out, had still to prove its worth. The Royal Flying Corps, though confident of its own ability, was a new and untried arm. In the early reports there are occasional inaccuracies. Some of the early observers, among those who were hastily enrolled to bring newly formed squadrons up to strength, had not much military knowledge, and were not practised in reading the appearances of things seen from the air.

At the time of the Battles of Ypres, 1914, observers of No. 6 Squadron, which had prepared itself in hot haste for foreign service, mistook long patches of tar on macadamized roads for troops on the move, and the shadows cast by the gravestones in a churchyard for a military bivouac. Mistakes like these, though they were not very many, naturally made commanding officers shy of trusting implicitly to reports from the air. Yet the early reports of the first four squadrons did show without any possibility of mistake how formidable the German movements were.

Sir John French remained at Mons and was led into fighting a battle in a perilous position against much superior forces. The air reports of the 22nd had given some hints of the success of von Bülow's army in crossing the Sambre, had indicated a possible enveloping movement from the direction of Grammont, and had revealed something of the strength of the enemy troops on the British front. On the following day the attack began on the position at Mons, and pilots and observers were flying over and behind the battlefield looking for enemy movements, and locating enemy batteries.

On the 24th the retreat was in progress. As early as the morning of the 23rd the Royal Flying Corps had begun to shift its quarters from Maubeuge to Le Cateau. The transport and machines of No. 3 Squadron moved southward on that day, and on the 24th headquarters and other squadrons also moved to Le Cateau. Major Maurice Baring says:

> We slept, and when I say we I mean dozens of pilots, fully dressed in a barn, on the top of, and underneath, an enormous load of straw. . . . Everybody was quite cheerful, especially the pilots.

On the afternoon of the 25th they moved again to St.-Quentin. The rapidity of the retreat put a heavy strain upon the headquarters of the Royal Flying Corps, which had to travel before the retreating army, to select an old aerodrome or to make a new one almost every day, and in the brief hours between arrival and departure to carry on all the complicated and delicate business of ministering to the needs of the squadrons. The places occupied by headquarters during the retreat were as follows:

Sunday, 16th August	Maubeuge
Monday, 24th August	Le Cateau
Tuesday, 25th August	St.-Quentin
Wednesday, 26th August	La Fère
Friday, 28th August	Compiègne
Sunday, 30th August	Senlis
Monday, 31st August	Juilly
Wednesday, 2nd September	Senlis
Thursday, 3rd September	Touquin
Friday, 4th September	Melun.

In some of these places regular aerodromes were available, in others a landing-ground had to be improvised. Sometimes officers of headquarters would be sent on a long way ahead in motorcars to select a landing-ground, while another officer in a motorcar was detailed to guide the transport. This he did by taking with him a small number of men and dropping them one by one at the partings of the ways. When the route was very complicated, these guides became so many that they had to be carried in a transport lorry. The transport drivers were not as yet skilled in the art of map-reading, and to lose the transport would have left the Flying Corps helpless.

Sometimes the officers who selected the landing-ground moved with the transport, and made their choice when the transport reached its destination. The only recognised French aerodromes which were used by the Royal Flying Corps during the retreat were those at

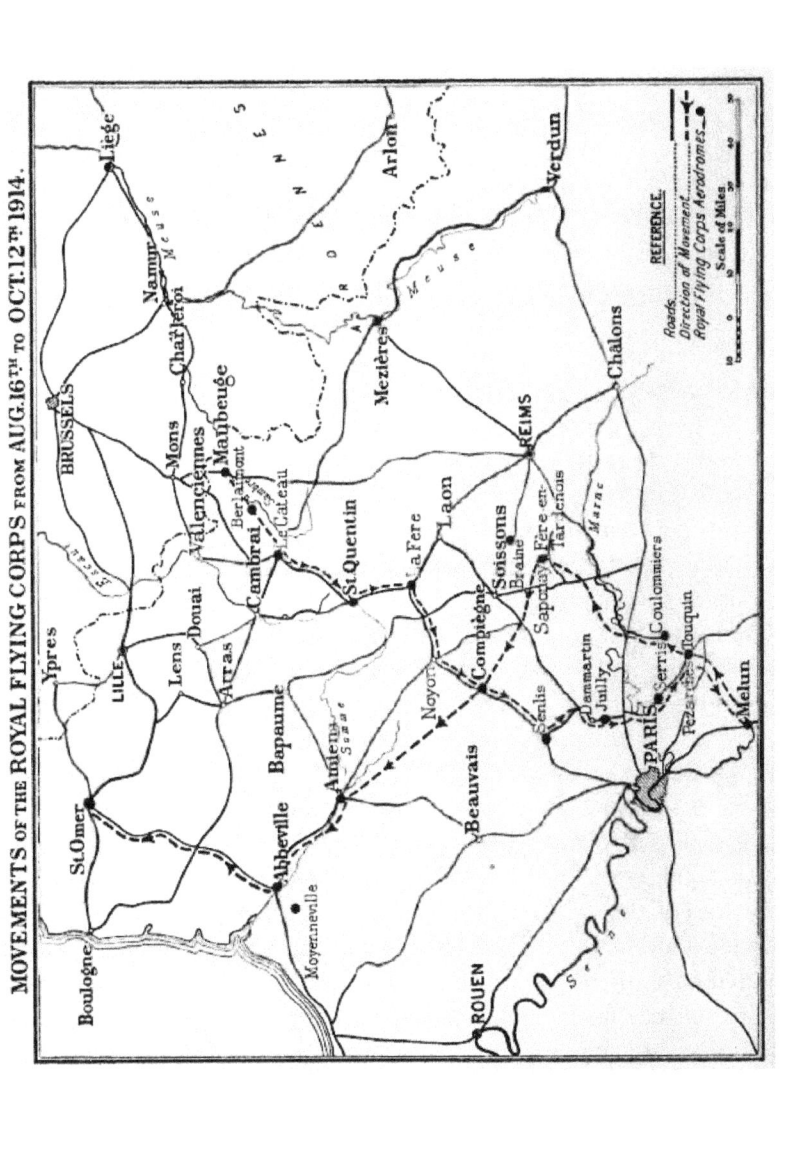

Compiègne, Senlis, and Melun.

Whilst the aerodromes were changing almost daily, the officers carried on reconnaissance, sometimes starting out not knowing whether their aerodrome would be in British or enemy hands by the time they should return. On the 24th, whilst the squadrons were moving from Maubeuge to Le Cateau, the enemy advance as seen from the air looked menacing enough. Captain G. S. Shephard and Lieutenant I. M. Bonham-Carter were watching von Kluck's right wing soon after 4.0 a.m. They returned at six o'clock with news of extensive movement about Ath and Leuze. They reported a broken column nearly ten miles long with its head pointing at Peruwelz. The column branched off the main Ath-Tournai road at Leuze. This was part of von Kluck's Second Corps, and its line of march would take it to the west of the extreme western flank of the British Army.

The news was not reassuring. Captain H. C. Jackson as observer with Lieutenant E. L. Conran went up at 8.30 a.m. and came back at 12.30 p.m. with information of long enemy columns moving from Grammont through Lessines into La Hamaide and further troops on the Ath-Leuze road. They had flown as far as Ninove and Alost, but found the country there clear. On returning over Lessines at 11.30 a.m. they saw three German aeroplanes on the ground; they dropped a bomb overboard, but missed.

In the evening of the 24th, the first day of the retreat, the position was on the whole not unsatisfactory. The British Fifth Division had not only defended six miles of front, but with the aid of the cavalry and the 19th Infantry Brigade had met and beaten off von Kluck's enveloping attack. But that attack was soon renewed. On the following morning a heavy movement of German troops southward from Marchiennes, with cavalry, guns, and transport, was reported at six o'clock. Marchiennes is almost midway between Valenciennes and Douai, to the west of the British line of retreat. This moving line of troops continued southward through Somain for a distance of about five miles, and then bent in a south-easterly direction, pointing straight at Le Cateau, until it reached Bouchain, where there were mounted and dismounted troops extending over three miles.

But Le Cateau was not the objective of these troops. General von Kluck believed that the next stand of the British Army, after Mons, would be made on a position running east and west through Bavai, and resting its right on the fortress of Maubeuge. The troops seen at Bouchain were intended to envelop it and take it in the rear. Meantime the British Army, having escaped the lure of Maubeuge, was continuing its painful march southward on both sides of the Forest of Mormal; and the claw that was extended to catch it closed upon air.

These movements of von Kluck's army on the 25th were influenced by his own air reports, which appear to have misled him. The army order issued by him from Soignies at 8.30 p.m. on the night of the 24th assumed that the British Army would accept battle on the line Maubeuge-Bavai-Valenciennes. Von Kluck was very hopeful, he says:

> The outflanking of the left of the British Army, on the assumption that it remained in position, appeared to be guaranteed.

An important air report which reached him at 1.0 a.m. on the 25th led him to suspect that the British were withdrawing on Maubeuge. Speaking of this report, he says:

> Enemy columns of all arms were in retreat on the roads Bellignies-Bavai, La Flamengrie-Bavai, and Gommegnies-Bavai. The direction in which the movement was being made beyond Bavai had not yet been determined; nevertheless, the army commander began to suspect that the British were withdrawing on Maubeuge.

He sent out orders in great haste by motorcar for the army to advance in a more southerly direction. At 9.0 a.m. however, a new air report came as a surprise. Long British columns of all arms were moving from Bavai along the Roman road to Le Cateau, and numerous small columns, single companies, batteries, squadrons, and cars were crossing the Selle, north and south of Solesmes.

> The enemy was marching in an almost opposite direction to what was supposed earlier in the morning.

A fresh order was at once sent out to attack the British and bring them to a standstill. Von Kluck does not quote these air reports. But he says enough to show that he was misled chiefly by his own preconceptions. Hope told a flattering tale, and he seems to have been possessed by the idea that the British Army would be tempted into the fortress of Maubeuge.

The whole body of information which on any one day was obtained from the reconnaissances of the Royal Flying Corps could be set out in detail only by quoting all the reports in full. That would be

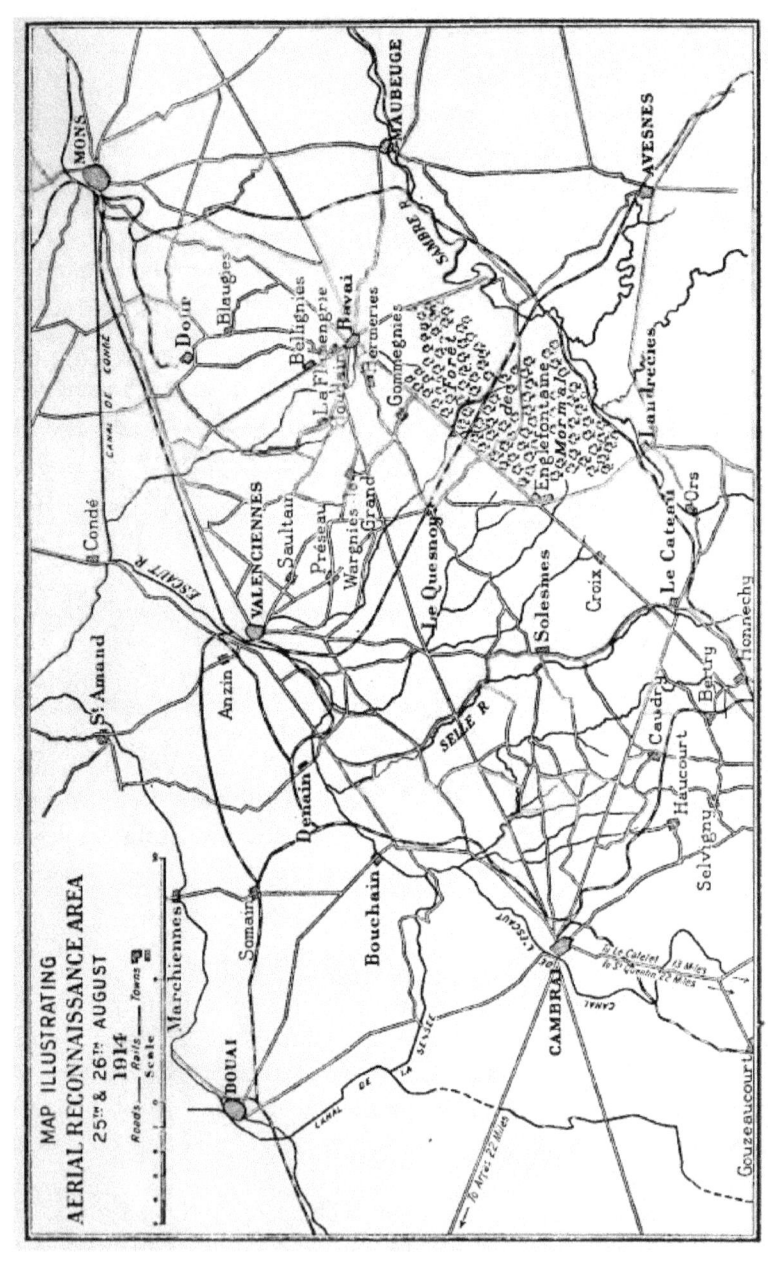

too cumbrous a method of writing history. The reports contain much that is comparatively insignificant. But the reader of this book may desire to know exactly what an air report is like, and his curiosity shall be gratified. Here is the report, of no special tactical significance, but full of incident, of a long air reconnaissance made by Lieutenant G. F. Pretyman and Major L. B. Boyd-Moss in a machine of No. 3 Squadron, on the day of the Battle of Le Cateau:

The machine, it will be seen, dropped a bomb on a park of transport vehicles, was fired at by howitzers, and was brought down by heavy infantry fire. A more dreaded enemy here makes an early appearance—the prevailing westerly wind. This wind was the heaviest trial for pilots during years on the western front; it made it easy to get at the enemy and difficult to get away from him; the road to safety always, while the west wind was blowing, lay uphill.

On this same day—the day of the Battle of Le Cateau—the First Army Corps under Sir Douglas Haig was delayed, and failed to reach its appointed position in touch with the Second Army Corps. Lieutenant A. E. Borton and Lieutenant F. G. Small were dispatched from headquarters in a machine of No. 5 Squadron to 'find Sir Douglas Haig'. With them went Lieutenant D. S. Lewis in a B.E. machine fitted with wireless apparatus. He was to report by wireless when Sir Douglas Haig was found. Lieutenants Borton and Small in their Henri Farman, being unable to find a suitable landing-ground in the rear of the First Army Corps, landed between the firing lines in a field protected by a rise in the ground from the direct fire of the enemy.

With the aid of a cavalry patrol they succeeded in delivering their message to Sir Douglas Haig, after which they returned to their machine, started up the engine, and flew away in the presence of two *Uhlans*, who had just ridden into the field. Meantime, Lieutenant Lewis, to whom they were unable to signal, lost touch with them; he circled in the air for an hour under fire, and returned with one shell splinter and four bullet-holes in his machine, and with one of his hands grazed by a bullet. Captain L. E. O. Charlton was also sent at 11.30 a.m. to report to General Smith-Dorrien at Bertry, he says:

> I found him in considerable anxiety as to his left about Haucourt and Selvigny. Having been on that flank at 9.30 a.m., I was able to reassure him as to its safety, and made another ascent to confirm my previous reconnaissance. During the reconnaissance I was able to report that the enemy had made no progress,

though their shell-fire had increased. I was sent up again to examine the right about Le Cateau, and on reporting at 2.45 p.m. the general told me that the Fifth Division had been unable to withstand a most determined artillery attack, and had come back. He added that he had no doubt he would succeed in getting them back somehow, and requested me to inform Sir Archibald Murray. I left at 3.0 p.m. and reported to General Headquarters as ordered.

General Smith-Dorrien did succeed in getting them back. The stand made at Le Cateau was a great fight against odds; and the part played in the battle by the Royal Flying Corps seems a little thing when it is compared with the gallant resistance of the infantry. But British machines were flying over the enemy, under fire, within full view of the British Army, and some British officers who took part in the battle have described how the sight of our aeroplanes above them raised the spirits of the troops and gave them a feeling of security.

Copies of the original reports made out by observers before and during the retreat from Mons are preserved in the war diary of headquarters, Royal Flying Corps. It is not possible to say when each of these reports reached General Headquarters; they were sent in as soon as possible after the machines landed—some of them at once by telephone. When the reports are systematically mapped out, day by day, they give a fairly accurate picture of the German advance and throw light on the German plans.

General von Kluck speaks more than once of driving the British Army before him, but the complete map of the German movements, as they were reported day by day from the air, shows that his predominant idea was to envelop them. Always the crab-like claw is seen extended to the west and beginning to close in on the line of the British retreat; always the British Army is already at a point farther south on the line, out of the reach of the claw. When with swollen and blistered feet and half asleep on the march, the patient British soldier carried on, he was doing more to defeat the Germans than he could have done if his dearest wish had been granted and he had been allowed to make a desperate stand. It is a wonderful army that can suffer the long depression and fatigue of such a retreat and yet keep its fighting quality unimpaired.

Von Kluck's advance after the Battle of Le Cateau was directed to the south-west. (*Guns at Le Cateau*, two accounts of the B. E. F. in the First World War—*The Royal Regiment of Artillery at Le Cateau, 26 August, 1914* by A. F. Becke & *The Stand at Le Cateau, 26th August, 1914* by C. de Sausmarez is also published by Leonaur.) Speaking of the situation on the 28th of August, he says:

> The occupation of the Somme area marked the conclusion of the fighting with the British Army for the time being. In spite of the great efforts of the First Army the British had escaped the repeated attempts to envelop them. They continued their retreat southwards.

On the same day the headquarters of the German Army propounded a new task, they wrote:

> The left wing of the main French forces is retreating in a southerly and south-westerly direction in front of the victorious Second and Third Armies. It appears to be of decisive importance to find the flank of this force, whether retreating or in position, force it away from Paris, and outflank it. Compared with this new objective the attempt to force the British Army away from the coast is of minor importance.

The German Supreme Command were giving most of their attention to the operations on their left wing, where the Fifth and Sixth German Armies were converging for the attack on Nancy, which town, when it fell, was to witness the triumphal entry of the German Emperor. Meantime, the French, trusting to the strength of their eastern fortifications, were rapidly taking troops away from their eastern armies to form a new French Army, the Sixth, which was to operate to the north of Paris and was to take part in the counteroffensive against the German First and Second Armies. This was unknown to the German Command, who thought that victory lay within the grasp of their eastern armies.

On the evening of the 30th of August General von Kluck received wireless messages from the headquarters of the Second Army reporting a decisive victory, and asking the First Army to wheel inwards towards the line La Fère-Laon in order to gain the full advantages of the victory. General von Kluck replied that the First Army had wheeled round towards the Oise and would advance on the 31st by Compiègne and Noyon to exploit the success of the Second Army. This was the much-discussed wheeling movement, or swerve, which was discovered by the British from the air.

Von Kluck had been ordered by the German Supreme Command on the 28th to continue his march towards the Lower Seine. Now, in response to von Billow's request, he wheeled his army south-eastwards towards the Oise. The German Supreme Command was informed of this, and replied:

'The movement begun by the First Army is in accordance with the wishes of the Supreme Command.'

The Royal Flying Corps reports of the 31st of August gave to the British Command the first intimation of what was happening. Here is one of them:

It will be seen that Captain E. W. Furse, when he picked up the

Date : 31.8.1914.   Pilot : Lieutenant A. E. Borton.
                    Observer : Captain E. W. Furse.
Hour at which reconnaissance commenced : 9.20 a.m.

Time.	Place.	Observation.
9.55	Villeneuve.	Motor T.
9.58	E. Roberval.	,,
10.2	At Station N. of Verberie.	Motor T. halted clear of road.
10.6	La Croix.	Cavalry and transport much opened out, head La Croix.
10.13	Compiègne.	Clear.
10.20	Chevincourt.	Cavalry about 1 Bde. moving towards Thourotte. Head near that place. More cavalry and guns following across fields. Bivouac at Chevincourt. Transport coming in from Marest road 10.25.
10.26	Mareuil.	Cavalry column still continues—opened out—new column trotting S.
10.27	Lassigny.	Artillery just S. of town moving south. Column ended just S. of Lassigny (¼ mile). Another column, tail Lassigny, was moving towards Thiescourt. Also mounted troops. About one mile N. of Lassigny mounted troops in bivouac and on road from Roye, stretching right up to Roye. Columns included guns and motor transport. Parked transport just N. of Roye.
10.50	Roye.	Three Batteries halted in field 1¼ m. S.E. of Roye. Besides the column stretching south to Lassigny, there was another column stretching S.E. on Noyon road. German aeroplane on ground S. of Roye.

10.55	Conchy.	Infantry and guns moving due east through Conchy.
	Orvillers.	Few troops in village.
11.0	Ressons.	Went up road east of railway. This was clear.
11.3	Margny.	Squadrons moving S.E.
11.7	Compiègne road 2¼ miles S.E. of Cuvilly.	Troop car moving towards Compiègne.
	Estrées-St.-Denis.	Squadrons at intervals down this road from Roye. Just S. of Estrées a Bde. of Cav. and one battery halted clear of road.
	Bazicourt.	Cav. Inf. and Transport seen. Squadron Cav. moving N. out of Bazicourt. Inf.—much opened out—moving east into Bazicourt from Rosoy. Inf. looked in dark uniform. Transport—some halted and some moving south.
11.25	Sarron.	2 Regts. Cav. moving east from Brenouille.
11.27	Pont-St.-Maxence.	Motor Transport. Some halted. Some going south. No bridges over Oise appeared to be destroyed. Some barges might have been sunk in stream at Compiègne.

(*Signed*) E. W. FURSE.

enemy, first observed Marwitz's cavalry corps which crossed the Oise at Thourotte on the morning of the 31st. He then saw part of the German Third Corps, which, after spending the night in Roye, moved on the 31st through Lassigny, crossed the Oise at Ribecourt, and in the evening reached Attichy on the Aisne. The remainder of the Third Corps moved on Noyon and at night reached Vic on the Aisne. These movements on Noyon and Ribecourt differed in direction from the previous movements of the German left wing.

The reports supplement and confirm one another. Captain D. Le G. Pitcher, of No. 4 Squadron, had gone up with Captain A. H. L. Soames soon after 7.0 a.m., and had returned at 8.40 a.m. with the news of a column stretching from Roye to Chevincourt. This information was at once telephoned from the aerodrome at Senlis to General Headquarters. The movements of some of the other formations of the German First Army were also seen to have changed direction. Lieutenant C. G. Hosking and Lieutenant K. P. Atkinson on a B.E. of No. 4 Squadron flew over Roye and Lassigny, confirming the report

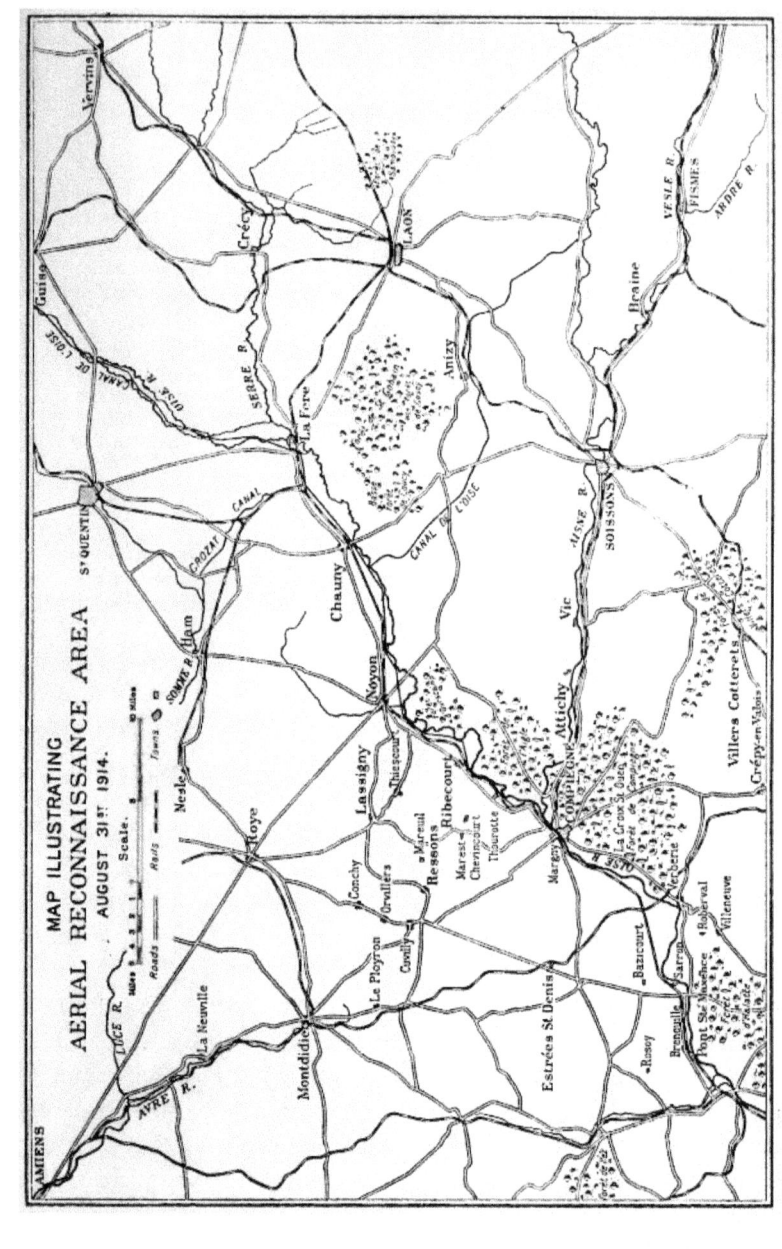

of movements in that area. Then turning west, they passed over various columns moving in a southerly direction until they reached the road that follows along the east bank of the River Avre from Amiens through Montdidier, and here they found part of the German Second Corps. The head of the main body was in Montdidier at 2.0 p.m., and its tail was in La Neuville. Flying south along the road they found the advanced guard of the column at Le Ployron.

All these air reports left little doubt as to the enemy's movements, and the operation orders sent out by General Headquarters from Dammartin-en-Goële at 8.50 p.m. on the 31st of August gave the information that the enemy appeared to have completed his westerly movement, and that large columns were advancing in a general southerly or south-easterly direction on Noyon-Compiègne. Sir John French directed that the retirement should be continued on the following day in a south-westerly direction.

Air reconnaissances of the 1st of September, whilst confirming the news of von Kluck's wheel in a south-easterly direction, also reported heavy columns as having reached Villers-Cotterets and Crépy-en-Valois. To withdraw the British out of reach of a night attack Sir John French decided to continue the retreat earlier than he had intended. The corps commanders were ordered to get clear by a night march. We know now from von Kluck's own statement that, perturbed at leaving the British Army on his flank, he determined to make another effort to catch them up. He therefore ordered his corps to turn south to settle with the British. So, on the 1st of September he was again in pursuit of the British, but the British were slipping from his grasp. There was fighting on this day, which held up the pursuit, and by the evening the German Army had made an average advance of no more than ten miles.

Von Kluck persisted on the following day, but in vain. The British escaped towards the Marne. He says:

'A chance of dealing a decisive blow against the British Army was now no longer to be hoped for, and it was therefore decided to move the two corps on the left wing, the Third and Ninth, in the general direction of Château-Thierry against the flank of the French retreating from Braisne-Fismes on Château-Thierry-Dormans in front of the Second Army.'

The air reports which came in on the 3rd of September showed much of this further change of plan. Long columns were seen marching almost due east towards the Ourcq and later in the day other col-

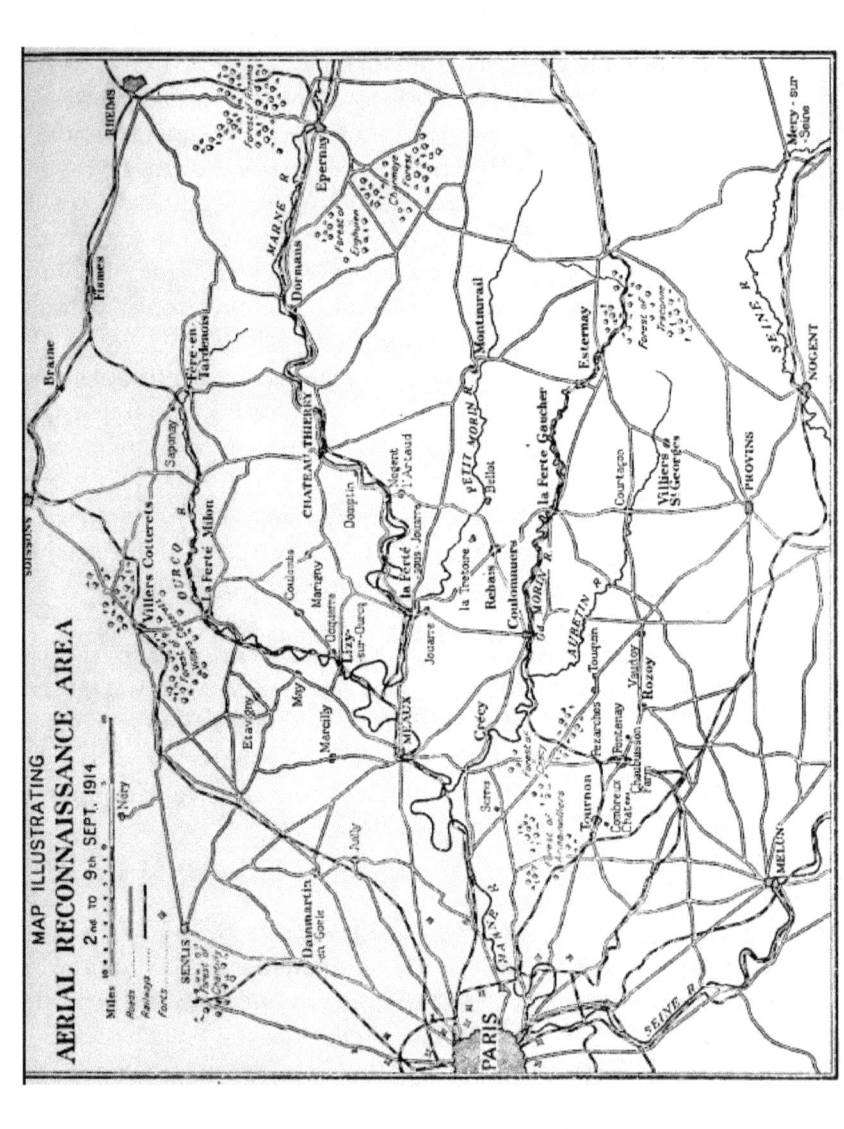

umns were nearing the Marne. Some had already crossed the Marne at Château-Thierry, whilst others were making for crossings west of that town.

At 4.35 p.m. General Headquarters sent out the following telegram:

> Present information leads to the belief that the enemy is moving from west to east and that no immediate attack is intended. Unless the situation again changes troops will remain in their present billets. The Commander-in-Chief is most anxious that the Army should have a complete rest tomorrow. No digging or other operations except those necessary for protection will be undertaken unless special orders are issued.

Pilots who went out soon after dawn on the morning of the 4th found a thick mist over the river Marne extending to the depth of a mile on either bank, but various columns were seen stirring out of bivouacs on the north of the river and there were other movements well to the south of the river. At 12.20 p.m. Lieutenant R. P. Mills saw movements between Bellot and Rebais and artillery in action on the high ground one mile south-east of Bellot. In the afternoon there came fuller reports of movements towards the Petit Morin. The situation as traced at Royal Flying Corps headquarters on the night of the 4th from observations made during the day is very accurate. It shows that the German Ninth Corps, which had secured the crossings at Château-Thierry on the previous evening, had progressed to near Montmirail; that the Third and Fourth Corps had got well clear of the Marne and were about and across the Petit Morin; and that the Second Corps and Marwitz's cavalry were held up at the Marne east of Meaux.

Von Kluck had marched into a bag between the Fifth French Army on the Marne and the newly formed Sixth French Army advancing to the Ourcq. Just at this time the German Supreme Command seems to have become aware of the danger threatening the German armies on the right wing. On the night of the 4th of September orders had been sent out from German First Army headquarters at La Ferté Milon, detailing the movements to be made on the following day. These movements had already begun when at 7.15 a.m. on the 5th fresh instructions arrived from the Supreme Command ordering the First and Second Armies to remain facing the eastern front of Paris; the First Army between the Oise and the Marne, occupying the Marne crossings west of Château-Thierry, and the Second Army between the Marne and the Seine, occupying the Seine crossings from Nogent to Méry. This led, says von Kluck, to 'the difficult backwards wheel of the First Army', and to what he calls 'the important events that occurred during the second week of September'—events known to history as the Battle of the Marne.

Von Kluck allowed the original movements ordered for the 5th to be carried out, and, he says:

> The conclusion of this advance marked the culminating point of the operations of the First Army.

On this same day General Joffre told Sir John French that he intended to take the offensive forthwith as the conditions seemed favourable, and on the morning of the 6th this offensive opened.

The main work of the Royal Flying Corps throughout the days of the retreat was reconnaissance, and enough has been said of their reports to show that Sir John French was well served by his new arm. He had been warned before the Battle of Mons, not only of the heavy movement on his front but of the enveloping attempt on his flank, and throughout the retreat he was punctually informed of von Kluck's enveloping efforts. The change of direction made on the 31st of August was immediately seen and reported. Von Kluck's renewed pursuit of the British on the two following days did not escape observation. Finally, the German swerve to the left on the 3rd of September was closely followed from the air.

These are the main conclusions that come from a study of the air reports of those days. General Headquarters were perhaps at first a little shy of trusting the air reports, but they realised their value during the retreat, and paid more and more attention to them—an attention which found practical results in the operation orders issued. The Royal Flying Corps played their part in helping the British Army to escape. Further, they were making themselves, and were improving in skill every day. The lessons learned on the retreat from Mons bore their full fruit at a later period, when the officers of the original squadrons held the command of those Flying Corps units which operated in the mobile campaigns of distant theatres of the war.

Their work during the retreat was done under difficulties. There were alarms at Compiègne of *Uhlans* seen in the vicinity of the aerodrome, and a guard was provided from the Camerons. Major B. H. Barrington-Kennett remarks on the difficulty of defending a Flying

Corps camp from attack by cavalry. It would seem advisable, he says, when camped in an open aerodrome to park the aeroplanes inside a *laager* formed by lorries and cars. The headlights of the cars would lighten a good field of fire, and would probably, if switched on at the approach of cavalry, cause the horses to stampede. The Royal Flying Corps, he adds, should be armed and practised with machineguns and rifles, so that they may protect themselves without asking for an escort.

At Juilly on the 1st of September there was another alarm. The country to the north was thickly wooded, and German cavalry, which proved later to be those escaped from the affair at Méry, were reported within a few miles, with no British troops between. General Headquarters at Dammartin-en-Goële, some two miles away, hastily took their departure, and the Royal Flying Corps transport was sent off at once to Serris. But the aeroplanes could not leave, for already it was dark. The suggestion was made that the aeroplanes should fly off in the dark, but fortunately, says Major C. J. Burke, this was not attempted.

The Flying Corps stood to arms to defend itself. A sunken road running east and west past the aerodrome was occupied, rifles and ammunition were served out to the mechanics, and machine-guns were set in position. After a time, a troop of North Irish Horse arrived, to aid in the defence. All night watch was kept, but the German cavalry did not appear. In the morning, for the first time since the beginning of the retreat, there was no ground mist, and the machines got away at once.

The history of the retreat is made up of incidents like this. Some of the flying officers have kindly communicated their memories and impressions. Wing Commander P. B. Joubert de la Ferté says:

> The extraordinary part about the retreat, was the contrasts that one experienced from day to day; one night sleeping under a hedge in a thunder-storm; the next in a comfortable private house; the third in the most modern type of hotel with every luxury and convenience, the whole forming a picture the impression of which has lasted throughout the war.... One curious thing was, unless one was brought down or left behind near the firing line one never came up against the actual unpleasantnesses of war, and it was not until the advance to the Aisne started that those of us who had not been on ground duty, or unlucky, saw any signs of fighting other than from the air. What we saw during the advance confirmed our impressions from

the air as to the unspeakableness of the Hun in his methods of dealing with the civilian population.

I saw half a dozen villages on fire during the first day of the battle, twenty miles west of Mons, where by no possible means could there have been any armed resistance to the passage of the Huns. It was simply frightfulness on the part of the *Uhlans*, and what we saw later on the ground at Pezarches, Coulommiers, and La Fère was a clear indication of wilful and unnecessary destruction of private property. The sight of a draper's shop with every window smashed, every shelf emptied, and the contents thrown into the street was quite a common one.

Major F. G. Small says, speaking of the 27th of August:

The retreat continued to Compiègne Forest, Huns pressing our troops all the while. On returning from late reconnaissances in the dusk, it was most interesting to watch the local fighting in the roads between their vanguards and our rear-guards. The spreading of fires all over the country around Compiègne Forest was a more curious sight than even the later trench offensive, the fires spreading like long flaming worms along the main road, as the Huns fired each village they went through. The northern portion of Compiègne Forest was blazing at this date.

The speed of the retreat caused some embarrassments. On the 31st of August, while the Flying Corps occupied Senlis racecourse, two officers, belonging to Nos. 4 and 5 Squadrons, motored to Paris to get some aircraft spares, and returning in the evening found the Germans in occupation. In the dusk they were mistaken for German officers and drove their car right up to the cottages which a few hours earlier had been the headquarters of the Flying Corps. Aviation teaches quick resource; the officers managed to escape.

The pilots were not downhearted. At Compiègne, where they were billeted in a school, Major Baring records that they were in tearing spirits. Besides their main duty of observation from the air, they rendered other occasional services. Wing Commander L. A. Strange says:

The usual orders on the retreat were dawn reconnaissances, dropping hand-grenades and petrol bombs on the enemy, and when it was impossible to notify pilots of the next aerodrome, the orders were to fly approximately twenty miles south and look out for the remainder of the machines on the ground, if machines had left the last aerodromes.

During the retreat the dropping of bombs was still in an early experimental stage. There were some mildly successful exploits. About dusk on the 1st of September an unnamed officer of the Flying Corps, flying over the woods north of Villers-Cotterets, noticed two columns of the enemy's cavalry converging at the angle of cross-roads. He dropped two bombs, which caused confusion and a stampede. There was no bomb-dropping gear in use at this time, but small handgrenades were carried in the pockets, and larger bombs were slung or tied about the person.

The first experience of German bombs was at Compiègne on the 29th of August; while the Flying Corps were stationed there a German machine flew over the aerodrome and dropped three small bombs, which did no harm. On our side there was no time during the retreat for experiment with new devices; it was not until the Germans took up fixed positions on the Aisne that the inventive powers of the Flying Corps got to work on the devising of bombing gear, the improving of artillery observation, and the mounting of machineguns.

The retreat also witnessed the beginnings of fighting in the air. The first German machine to be seen by the British appeared over the aerodrome at Maubeuge on the 22nd of August. There are various accounts of this. Major C. J. Burke in his diary says:

> At about 2.25 p.m. an Albatross biplane passed over the town. Major Longcroft with Captain Dawes as passenger, Lieutenant Dawes with Major Burke as passenger, on B.E.'s, gave chase. The gun machine piloted by Lieutenant Strange also went out. The machine (Albatross) had far too long a start, and got into a rain cloud.

Wing Commander L. A. Strange says:

> Chased a German Albatross machine for forty-five minutes, Lieutenant Penn-Gaskell observer, with Lewis gun. Was unable to get higher than 3,500 feet, while the Albatross was at about 5,000 feet. Observed no effect from the fire. As a result of this received orders to discard Lewis gun and mounting, and transfer the controls from rear seat to the front seat, the passenger to carry rifle in the back seat.

Major J. T. B. McCudden says:

About the 22nd August a strange aeroplane flew over us at about 4,000 feet, and the aerodrome look-out reported it to be a German machine, the first we had seen in the War. We all turned out armed with rifles, and about six machines got ready to go up in pursuit. . . . All the machines which went up were loaded with hand-grenades, as the intention then was to bring a hostile aeroplane down by dropping bombs on it. The German easily got away, although it looked at one time as if Captain Longcroft would be able to intercept him on a B.E. 2 a. About half an hour after the German had departed a Henri Farman of No. 5 Squadron, fitted with a machine-gun, was still climbing steadily over the aerodrome at about 1,000 feet in a strenuous endeavour to catch the Boche.

No. 5 Squadron from the first had been zealous in experimenting with machine-guns. Experience of fighting in the air, which began with this adventure, soon taught how enormous is the advantage, whether for attack or escape, given by superiority in height.

It was not, however, until the 25th of August that an enemy machine was brought down by a British aeroplane. Sir John French in his first dispatch, dated the 7th of September 1914, alludes to the earliest combats. His tribute must be quoted in full:

> I wish particularly to bring to your Lordships' notice the admirable work done by the Royal Flying Corps under Sir David Henderson. Their skill, energy, and perseverance have been beyond all praise. They have furnished me with the most complete and accurate information, which has been of incalculable value in the conduct of operations. Fired at constantly both by friend and foe, and not hesitating to fly in every kind of weather, they have remained undaunted throughout. Further, by actually fighting in the air, they have succeeded in destroying five of the enemy's machines.

Unfortunately, during the retreat combat reports were not made out, so that there is no account in the war diaries of the actual fighting. Some of the fights are mentioned. On the 25th of August three machines of No. 2 Squadron chased an enemy monoplane. It was forced to land; Lieutenant H. D. Harvey-Kelly and Lieutenant W. H. C. Mansfield landed near it and continued the chase on foot, but the Germans escaped into a wood. When some trophies had been taken from the machine it was burnt. Another German machine was forced to descend on the same day near Le Quesnoy, where it was captured. Aeroplanes at this time had no special armament; officers carried revolvers and sometimes a carbine; but the confidence and determination with which they attacked did the work of a machinegun, and brought the enemy down. In one instance, a little later on, a British pilot and observer, who were destitute of ammunition, succeeded by manoeuvring boldly above a German machine in bringing it to the ground and taking it captive.

On the afternoon of the 5th of September neither the German Supreme Command (which had its headquarters at Luxembourg) nor the staff of the German First Army had any idea that an offensive of the whole French Army was imminent. The Supreme Command was expecting a decisive victory in the east against the Verdun-Nancy-St.-Dié defences. They believed that the German First and Second Armies could easily hold the weak French forces around Paris until this decision should be achieved, and they did not know how great a part of the French strength had been transferred from the east to the west. From the 5th to the 9th of September they issued no orders to their First and Second Armies, who were left to fight out the decisive battle of the war, without their help and almost without their knowledge, against superior forces.

General Joffre's 'Instruction' for the offensive on the 6th was brought to British General Headquarters by a French staff officer at 3 a.m. on the morning of the 5th. Unfortunately, orders to the British Army to continue the retreat in accordance with General Joffre's previous instructions had already been given to the corps commanders. The Second Corps had moved off before midnight and the First and Third Corps a little later. Consequently, the British Army by the end of the day was some twelve to fifteen miles farther back than the French commander-in-chief expected, and although its subsequent advance across the Marne had a decisive effect, the hard fighting of the battle was borne by the French Army on the Ourcq.

During the 5th, General Maunoury, commanding the Sixth French Army on the British left, and later on General Joffre himself, visited Sir John French, and all arrangements for the morrow's offensive were discussed. Sir John French's operation orders issued at 5.15 p.m. on the 5th of September directed the army to advance eastward with a view to attacking. The preliminary movement of the British Army, a wheel to the east, pivoting on its right, was to be completed by the right wing at 9 a.m. and by the left wing at 10 a.m. on the 6th.

On the early morning of the 6th Sir John French gave verbal instructions that the Royal Flying Corps were to send aeroplanes to report for reconnaissance direct to the First and Second Corps. The officer commanding No. 5 Squadron, with three machines, was to report for tactical reconnaissance direct to Sir Douglas Haig at Chaubuisson farm, one and a half miles east of Fontenay; and the officer commanding No. 3 Squadron, also with three machines, was to report direct to Sir Horace Smith-Dorrien at Combreux Château, near Tournan. With each detachment was to go a wireless aeroplane from No. 4 Squadron to keep Royal Flying Corps headquarters informed by wireless. The machines were to return to headquarters at night.

This was the beginning of the decentralisation of the Royal Flying Corps, whereby certain squadrons, which came to be called corps squadrons, were attached to the corps commands. The German air service from the beginning had been thus organised. With the German First Army headquarters there was one aeroplane section for long-distance strategic reconnaissance and each of the corps, with the exception of the Fourth Reserve Corps, had its own section for tactical work. From Maubeuge to the Marne the squadrons of the Royal Flying Corps had been kept together under the immediate control of General Henderson. The experiment of detaching machines to report direct to the First and Second Corps worked well on the 6th of September, and Sir John French gave orders that this arrangement was to continue.

Aeroplanes which were sent out on the morning of the 6th brought information of confused movements of the German First Army. On the British front a certain amount of movement northwards was seen in the afternoon. Of the progress of the battle on his flanks Sir John French had little knowledge. Aeroplanes were sent up to reconnoitre the position. One which flew over the area of the Sixth French Army west of the Ourcq saw at about five o'clock a good deal of movement and shells bursting in the area Étavigny-Marcilly-May-en-Multien. Another machine which flew along the line of the Fifth French Army on the British right came back with the information that at four o'clock fighting was going on south of Ésternay and north of Villiers-St.-Georges.

By seven o'clock that evening Sir John French had no definite news of the progress of the French armies on his wings save what was contained in these air reports, and the orders which he issued stated simply that all troops should be ready to move at any time after 8.0

a.m. on the morrow.

Early on the 7th the situation became clearer; a general retirement of the Germans on the British front was in progress. Sir John French had issued orders at 8.0 a.m. for the advance to be continued in the direction of Rebais, the army to move in echelon from the right and to attack the enemy wherever met. Aeroplanes on morning reconnaissance returned soon after the army began to move with information of early activity behind the German lines and general movement northwards. Later in the morning columns were seen moving in a north-westerly direction towards the Ourcq. These reconnaissances seemed to show that von Kluck was hurriedly withdrawing two of his corps—the Second and the Fourth—to reinforce his right wing across the Ourcq.

Early reconnaissances on the 8th told of congested movement over the bridge at La Ferté-sous-Jouarre, south of which masses of troops were awaiting their turn to cross. But the British advance was necessarily slow. The country was well suited to rear-guard actions and skilful use was made of the ground by the German machine-gunners. By the evening the British had forced the passage of the Petit Morin, but they spent the night south of the Marne. Meantime, as air reports showed, von Kluck's right was heavily engaged by Maunoury's Sixth Army to the west of the Ourcq.

On the night of the 8th General Joffre, taking advantage of the withdrawal of the two German corps from the British front, ordered that Maunoury's army should hold the enemy troops on the right bank of the Ourcq, whilst the British on the following day should advance across the Marne between Nogent l'Artaud and La Ferté-sous-Jouarre against the left and rear of the enemy on the Ourcq. The Marne with its steep wooded sides was well suited to rear-guard actions and a stubborn resistance was expected. But air observers who came in early on the morning of the 9th brought back the news of enemy columns formed up facing in a northerly direction. Some were already on the move, and it became apparent that the enemy intended no determined, but only a delaying stand on the Marne.

Captain D. Le G. Pitcher, piloted by Lieutenant G. W. Mapplebeck, whilst reconnoitring near Château-Thierry about 12.45 p.m. saw large bodies of enemy troops in the neighbourhood of Château-Thierry and infantry moving on Domptin. This position was west of the British Third Infantry Brigade, and the whole of the First Corps was ordered to halt until the situation should be cleared up. The First

Corps did not move forward again until 3.0 p.m. By the evening of the 9th the First and Second Corps were across the Marne, but the Third Corps on the left had been held up and was mostly south of the river. General Maunoury had had a hard fight, but by the late afternoon the Germans, pressed by the advance of the British across the Marne, had begun to retire in a north-easterly direction.

Captain R. A. Boger, piloted by Captain R. Grey, brought this welcome news direct to the General Officer Commanding the Third Corps (Lieutenant-General W. P. Pulteney) at 5.0 p.m. He had seen long columns moving north-east from Lizy through Ocquerre on to Coulombs. This was believed to be von Kluck's Fifth Division. Other observers came in with similar information. By the evening of the 9th the retirement of the enemy was general from the Ourcq to Verdun. The battle of the Marne was won. The German armies retired, with no very great disorder, to strong positions along the heights of the northern bank of the river Aisne. Paris was saved; for the first time for over a hundred years an invading Prussian Army had been turned and driven back; but the war was yet to come.

During the battle the Royal Flying Corps had been active over the enemy, and, as has been shown, reported his movements fully day by day. The machines which worked direct with the corps had supplied much useful tactical information, which was passed on direct to the corps commanders as soon as the machines landed. The observers usually reported by word of mouth, and so were able to convey a full and true impression. They reported which river-bridges were broken and which intact, and they dropped messages on to the advanced British infantry in places, warning them of danger ahead. They sometimes located for corps commanders the head of the leading troops of their corps.

After a three days' stay at Melun, the headquarters of the Flying Corps moved on the 7th of September to Touquin—the first move forward since the retreat from Mons. At Pezarches, about a mile away, a field was chosen for an aerodrome. Fighting had taken place there, and small one-man trenches had to be filled in before any machine could land. On the 9th of September headquarters moved forward again to Coulommiers, and on the 12th to Fère-en-Tardenois, which place became the headquarters for the battle of the Aisne. Here the squadrons were established at Saponay, some two miles to the north-west.

For many long months and years, the Flying Corps was not again to be employed in a war of movement against a powerful European army, so that the work they did from the time when they arrived at

Maubeuge to the time when they settled at Fère-en-Tardenois has a unique value. The French commander-in-chief paid tribute to their skill. His message ran:

> Please express most particularly to Marshal French my thanks for the services rendered to us every day by the English Flying Corps. The precision, exactitude, and regularity of the news brought in by them are evidence of their perfect organisation and also of the perfect training of pilots and observers.

The weather during the early part of the Marne battle had been excellent for flying. The air had been still and the heat tropical. On the 9th of September, the critical day of the battle, the weather broke, and for the next few days there were violent storms and heavy rains which greatly impeded air work of any sort. The worst of these storms occurred on the night of the 12th of September, when the squadrons had newly arrived at Saponay. Four machines of No. 5 Squadron were completely wrecked, and others damaged. Lieutenant L. A. Strange saved his Henri Farman machine, which had made a forced landing, by pushing it up against a haystack, laying a ladder over the front skids, and piling large paving-stones on the ladder, using hay twisted into ropes for tying down the machine. A diary of No. 3 Squadron records that when the machines of that squadron arrived at Saponay, about five hours before the transport:

> A terrible storm was raging, and before anything could be done to make the machines more secure the wind shifted, and about half the total number of machines were over on their backs. One Henri Farman went up about thirty feet in the air and crashed on top of another Henri Farman in a hopeless tangle. B.E.'s of No. 2 Squadron were blowing across the aerodrome, and when daylight arrived and the storm abated, the aerodrome presented a pitiful sight. The Royal Flying Corps in the field had probably not more than ten machines serviceable that morning.... Hangars were not yet issued.

The protection of machines from accidents like this became comparatively easy when the line of battle was stabilized and fixed aerodromes were made.

On Sunday, the 13th of September, the Allied armies had crossed the Aisne, but were held up by the enemy line of defence which ran along the heights from east of Compiègne to north of Rheims. There was dogged fighting, with attacks and counter-attacks, but little or no progress was made. The Germans had regained the initiative, and the British Army was forced to dig itself in along the line of battle. On the 18th of September General Joffre changed his plans and began to push forces up on the Allied left in order to envelop the German right flank. To give this movement a chance the enemy had to be held on the front, and the cavalry were called on to take their turn in the trenches—a duty which before long became very familiar to them.

But the Germans extended and reinforced their line for a similar outflanking movement. These enveloping attempts did not cease until the opposing armies were ranged along a line of trenches stretching from the Swiss frontier to the coast of Belgium. During the battle of the Aisne, from the 12th to the 15th of September, the British forced the passage of the river and captured the Aisne heights including the Chemin des Dames. Thereafter fighting degenerated into a sullen trench warfare, culminating on the 26th of September and the two following days in a series of fierce attacks by the Germans. These attacks were repulsed and were not again renewed.

On the 12th of September Lieutenant L. Dawes and Lieutenant W. R. Freeman, of No. 2 Squadron, had a notable adventure. They left in the morning to carry out an aerial reconnaissance to St.-Quentin. A little south of Anizy-le-Château, between Soissons and Laon, their machine began to rock and vibrate in the air, as if the tail were loose. They planed down at once, and landed in a small field, finishing up in a wood, where they damaged their undercarriage, wings, and airscrew. Large German columns were on the roads on both sides of them, within about two hundred yards. Taking only a biscuit and some tubes of beef extract with them, they hid in another wood close by. Some German cavalry came up to the machine, and then went all round the first wood, but found nothing, and after an hour and a half went away.

The two officers lay hid until the evening, and then started in the direction of the Aisne, some eight miles distant. During the night they passed several German pickets, but the war was young, the spirit of exhilaration still prevailed in the German Army, and the pickets were making so much noise that they passed unobserved. At 3.0 in the morning they reached the Aisne, where they lay down and slept. At 6.0 they were wakened by the firing of a gun close by, and realised that they were in front of the German position. German cavalry patrolled the road in front of them, and they were under heavy shell-fire from the British. They swam the Aisne, dried their clothes in a house by the canal, and then walked to the British guns, which were still in action. They were given food by the Third Cavalry Brigade, and were taken back on a supply column to rejoin their squadron after an absence of more than two days. It might be supposed that their troubles were now at an end, but they had yet to face their squadron commander, Major Burke, who sternly rebuked them for violating the order that no two pilots should fly together in the same machine.

The work of observation now entered a new phase. When armies are in fixed positions movement behind the front and along the lines of communication does not greatly vary from day to day. The Flying Corps were employed to map out the enemy's chief railheads, his aerodromes (which were surprisingly numerous), his camps, and his dumps. They began also to observe the positions of enemy batteries in order to range them for our own artillery, and they made some attempts to take photographs from the air of the enemy trenches and lines of communication.

Maubeuge had fallen on the 7th of September and, in addition to the Seventh Reserve Corps and other troops, the siege artillery which had been used to reduce Maubeuge was brought down to the Aisne, and the British guns were outranged and outnumbered. The spotting of hostile batteries became an operation of the first importance, and the Flying Corps quickly rose to its opportunities. When trench warfare began, the aeroplanes attached to corps commands took up artillery officers daily from each division over the German batteries. The positions of these batteries were noted on maps, and the maps were sent in every day to the divisional artillery commander, who allotted the targets to his batteries.

When any part of the British lines was shelled, information was obtained from the air and orders were given to those of our batteries which could best reply, to concentrate on the enemy's guns. The wireless machines of No. 4 Squadron had been attached to the army corps direct during the battle of the Marne, but their opportunities had been few. On the Aisne they were first used to observe for the artillery. Two pioneers of wireless telegraphy are associated in work and in memory with these early attempts at wireless co-operation with the artillery—Lieutenants Lewis and James.

Donald Swain Lewis had joined the Royal Engineers in 1904, and, after qualifying as a pilot in May 1912, had transferred to the Royal Flying Corps in December 1913. By example and precept, he had done all that he could before the war to adapt wireless telegraphy to the uses of the Flying Corps and to convince others of its necessity. Before the battle of the Aisne ended he had won his victory. He was in the habit of going out alone in a B.E. machine, piloting the machine and operating the wireless at the same time. A brother officer noted of him in a diary:

> Lewis, R.E., came in from spotting with his machine shot full of holes; I believe he likes it!

Later on in the war, at home and in the field, he continued his work. In April 1915 he was appointed to command No. 3 Squadron, in succession to Major J. M. Salmond, and did much to maintain and advance the great reputation of that pioneer among squadrons. After a spell at home during the winter of 1915-16, he returned to France in February 1916, to command the Second Wing, co-operating with the Second Army in the Ypres salient. By this time, he held the rank of lieutenant-colonel, but he continued to fly over the enemy lines.

On the 10th of April 1916, flying a Morane parasol, east of Wytschaete, with Captain A.W. Gale, an officer of the Trench Mortars, as passenger, he was brought down by a direct hit from the enemy's anti-aircraft guns. He had been showing Captain Gale some of the objectives on which the trench mortar fire had been directed during the week, and was killed in action while he was carrying out the duties of that artillery observation which he had done so much to perfect.

Baron Trevenen James had been a mathematical scholar and head of his House at Harrow; in 1907 he passed into Woolwich, and two years later was commissioned in the Royal Engineers. He was early interested in aviation; in June 1912, after only three days' practice, he obtained the Royal Aero Club certificate at Hendon, flying a Howard Wright biplane. In April 1913 he joined the Military Wing of the Royal Flying Corps, and was at once employed in carrying out experiments with wireless. In December 1913 he was joined by Lieutenant Lewis, and the two became famous for the theory and practice of their craft.

On the outbreak of war Lieutenant James was attached to No. 4 Squadron for wireless duties; when in September 1914 the headquarters wireless telegraphy unit was formed, under the command of Major H. Musgrave, at Fère-en-Tardenois, Lieutenant James was attached to it, and shared with Lieutenant Lewis the duty of reporting by wireless over the fire of the enemy guns. Like Lieutenant Lewis, he was subsequently killed in the air. On the 13th of July 1915 his commanding officer reports:

He was observing from the aeroplane alone, as he generally did. He was ranging a battery, and was being heavily shelled. His machine was hit by a shell, and was seen to dive to the ground from a great height. The Germans dropped a note from one of their machines saying that he was dead when he fell. . . . He met the end I am sure he would have wished for—if it had to be—suddenly, alone, and doing his duty.

These two, then, Lieutenants Lewis and James, had been untiring in their enthusiasm and perseverance during the years before the war. On the Aisne their reward was granted them. General Sir Horace Smith-Dorrien, in a telegram dated the 27th of September 1914, says:

> I wish to express my great admiration for the splendid work the Royal Flying Corps is doing for my corps from day to day. Nothing prevents them from obtaining the required information, and they frequently return with rifle or shrapnel bullets through their aeroplane or even their clothing, without considering such, to them, ordinary incidents as worth mentioning. Today I watched for a long time an aeroplane observing for the six-inch howitzers for the Third Division. It was, at times, smothered with hostile anti-aircraft guns, but, nothing daunted, it continued for hours through a wireless installation to observe the fire and indeed to control the battery with most satisfactory results. I am not mentioning names, as to do so, where all are daily showing such heroic and efficient work, would be invidious.

Lieutenants Lewis and James are now beyond the voices of envy, and their names may fitly be recorded in the memory of their country. One of the earliest of the messages sent down by wireless from the air is dated the 24th of September 1914. It is worthy of full quotation:

4.2 p.m.	A very little short. Fire. Fire.
4.4 p.m.	Fire again. Fire again.
4.12 p.m.	A little short; line O.K.
4.15 p.m.	Short. Over, over and a little left.
4.20 p.m.	You were just between two batteries. Search two hundred yards each side of your last shot. Range O.K.
4.22 p.m.	You have them.
4.26 p.m.	Hit. Hit. Hit.
4.32 p.m.	About 50 yards short and to the right.
4.37 p.m.	Your last shot in the middle of 3 batteries in action; search all round within 300 yards of your last shot and you have them.
4.42 p.m.	I am coming home now.

The later signals directing artillery fire were not so full of colour as these early messages. They consisted of code letters. The clock code for signalling the results of artillery fire was first used in 1915 and afterwards generally throughout the war. The target was taken as the centre of a clock and imaginary lines were circumscribed around it at distances of 10, 25, 50, 100, 200, 300, 400, and 500 yards. These lines were lettered y, z, a, b, c, d, e, f, respectively.

Twelve o'clock was always taken as true north from the target and the remaining hours accordingly. An observer noted the fall of the rounds with reference to the imaginary circles and clock-hours and signalled the result, for instance, as y 4, or c 6. A direct hit was o.k., and there were other signals. Messages from the battery or any other ground station were signalled to the observer in the aeroplane by means of white strips which were laid out on the ground to form the letters of a code.

During the Battle of the Aisne, the wireless machines were few in number and other methods of signalling were mostly in use. On the 15th of September Captain L. E. O. Charlton fired Very lights over enemy guns previously observed. On the 24th of September:

> Lieutenant Allen and two others with aeroplanes indicated targets and observed fire, communication being by flash signals.

Sometimes the pilots returned and landed to report on gun positions. But when once the gunners had profited by the superior accuracy and speed of report by wireless, they were hungry for more machines.

On the 23rd of September the commander of the Second Corps telegraphed to General Headquarters:

> I hope that you will be able to spare the wireless aeroplane and receiving set to Third Division again tomorrow. The results were so good yesterday that it seems a pity not to keep it with the division, which has got accustomed to its uses and is in a position to benefit even more largely by the experience gained.

The answer was that the machine had been damaged by anti-aircraft fire, but would be ready again shortly. A wireless aeroplane was as popular as an opera-singer, and the headquarters wireless section soon developed into No. 9 Squadron of the Royal Flying Corps. The attitude of the gunners may be well seen in an entry made in the war diary of No. 3 Siege Battery, dated the 23rd of January 1915—

Airman (Captain Cherry) reported for co-operation (lamp only, alas!).

The photography was a mere beginning. On the 15th of September Lieutenant G. F. Pretyman took five photographs of the enemy positions; these were developed later on the ground, and were the forerunners of that immense photographic map of the western front in thousands of sections, constantly renewed and corrected, which played so great a part in the later stages of the war. Some other experiments had no later history. Steel darts called *'flêchettes'*, about five inches long and three-eighths of an inch in diameter, were dropped over enemy horse-lines and troops by No. 3 Squadron.

A canister holding about 250 of these darts was fixed under the fuselage; by the pulling of a wire the bottom of the tin was opened and the darts were released. To do any harm these darts had to score a direct hit on some living object, so that a whole canister of them was probably a less formidable weapon than a bomb. Even on a battlefield life is sparsely distributed on the ground.

There was hardly any fighting in the air during the Battle of the Aisne, and reconnaissance machines were not attacked by other aeroplanes. They were fired at from the ground by anti-aircraft artillery. The antiaircraft guns got their name of 'Archies' from a light-hearted British pilot, who when he was fired at in the air quoted a popular music-hall refrain—'*Archibald, certainly not!*' The Germans used kite balloons for observation. In the attempt to drop a bomb on one of these Lieutenant G. W. Mapplebeck was attacked, on the 22nd of September, by a German Albatross, and was wounded in the leg. He was the first of our pilots to be wounded in the air from an enemy aeroplane—a long list it was to be.

The Royal Flying Corps were few indeed in comparison with the air forces opposed to them, but they were full of zeal and initiative. On the 19th of September they received a valued compliment from the French General Staff, who asked the British Commander-in-Chief to permit them to carry out reconnaissances along the front of the Fifth French Army. This was already being done, but Sir David Henderson promised to take measures to make the reconnaissance more complete.

In the Battle of the Aisne the British forces were co-operating with General Maunoury's Sixth French Army on their left. The so-called race for the sea was, in fact, a race for the flank of the opposing army. On the 20th of September De Castelnau's army formed up on the left of Maunoury and at first made some progress, but was pushed back by the reinforced army of General von Bülow, and was held on a line extending from Ribecourt on the Oise to Albert. On the 30th of September General Maud'huy's army came into position on the left of De Castelnau, along a line extending from Albert to Lens, while at the same time cavalry and territorials occupied Lille and Douai on the German right. This army in its turn was opposed by the German Sixth Army sent up from Metz, which pushed the French behind Arras, occupied Lens and Douai, and began to shell Lille.

General Maud'huy could do no more than fight to hold his ground till another army should come to his relief on his left. For this purpose, the British Army was shifted from the Aisne to its natural position in defence of the Channel ports, and came into action along a line extending northwards from La Bassée. The actual line was fixed by a series of fierce engagements culminating in the Battles of Ypres, 1914.

The Allied plan was to hold the French and Belgian coast and to take the offensive in the north. With this purpose in view the Seventh Division of the British Army and the Third Cavalry Division, both of which came under the command of Sir Henry Rawlinson, were disembarked, from the 6th of October onward, at Zeebrugge and Ostend. But Antwerp was taken by the Germans on the 9th of October, and the first business of this famous force was to cover the Belgian retreat along the coast.

The German Fourth Army was being rapidly pushed forward into Belgium; Lille capitulated on the 13th of October; Zeebrugge and Ostend were occupied by the Germans on the 15th. Still the idea of a counter-offensive was not abandoned, and the works and defences of Zeebrugge were left intact in the hope of its speedy recapture.

On the night of the 1st of October, the British Army had begun to move northwards from the Aisne. By the 9th of October the British Second Corps had detrained at Abbeville and received orders to march on Béthune; on the 12th the Third Corps began detraining and concentrating at St.-Omer and Hazebrouck, and subsequently moved up to Bailleul and Armentières. A week later, on the 19th, the First Corps under Sir Douglas Haig detrained at Hazebrouck and moved on Ypres. General Headquarters left Fère-en-Tardenois on the 8th of October and after a five-days' stay at Abbeville established themselves at St.-Omer.

The Royal Flying Corps had moved north with the British Expeditionary Force, from Fère-en-Tardenois by way of Abbeville, to St.-Omer, where they were established by the 12th of October. No. 2 Squadron remained behind for a few days, to carry on with Sir Douglas Haig's corps on the Aisne, but joined up at St.-Omer on the 17th of October. In addition to the four original squadrons, No. 6 Squadron, newly arrived from England under Major J. H. W. Becke, came under Brigadier-General Henderson's orders on the 16th of October. This squadron had been stationed at South Farnborough as a reserve for the squadrons in the field. When General Rawlinson's force was sent to Ostend, to attempt the relief of Antwerp, Lord Kitchener said:

I want a squadron to go with it.

He ordered that No. 6 Squadron should be ready in forty-eight hours. The squadron was hastily completed; some pilots and machines were obtained from the Central Flying School; some machines were bought from private firms; equipment, tools, and the like were collected at night; and on the 7th of October the squadron flew to Bruges and began at once to carry out reconnaissances. On the following day they flew to Ostend, and, their transport having arrived, were concentrated on the racecourse. Five days later they retired to Dunkirk, and by the 16th of October were established at Poperinghe, where they came under the orders of headquarters at St.-Omer.

A good deal of reconnaissance was carried on by the squadrons during the northward move of the army. On the 29th of September unusual and heavy movement in a northerly and north-westerly direction had been observed behind the enemy lines on the Aisne. On the 1st of October air reconnaissances showed that the trenches in front of the British First Army Corps were unoccupied or very lightly held, and during the next few days there were many indications that one or two German Army corps were being withdrawn to the north. Meantime the enemy took more trouble than usual to interfere with our aircraft, and employed an increased number of anti-aircraft guns. In the north our strategic reconnaissances were not so successful, and the formidable enemy movement against the Ypres line developed undetected.

Not many aeroplanes were available at this time for the wider sort of strategic reconnaissance. Nos. 2, 3, and 5 Squadrons had been attached, by an order issued on the 1st of October, to the First, Second, and Third Army Corps respectively, while No. 4 Squadron was detailed for strategical reconnaissance. The General Officers Commanding army corps had learned the value of aeroplanes and demanded their assistance. Much of the country over which they were operating in Northern France and Flanders was flat and enclosed, unsuitable either way for cavalry reconnaissance.

Long-distance work was done chiefly from headquarters. On the 3rd of October, when the situation at Antwerp had become critical, Lieutenant-Colonel F. H. Sykes flew direct to Bruges from Fère-en-Tardenois, with a message from Sir John French to the Belgian Chief of Staff at Antwerp. On the following day he returned and reported that the Germans had broken through the south-eastern sector of the outer defences of Antwerp, that the Belgians were awaiting help, and that they might possibly hold out for two or three weeks. In forwarding the report to Lord Kitchener Sir John French adds:

The relief of Antwerp I regard as my first objective.

This mission was followed by others, and a few days later Sir John French speaks of reports which he is receiving daily by air from General Rawlinson.

Meantime a squadron of the Royal Naval Air Service, as shall be told in the next chapter, had been operating for some weeks from Ostend and Dunkirk with French territorial forces. The French territorials were hastily embodied troops taken from civilian life and were not of much use for a fight against odds. When the Seventh Division was landed at Ostend and Zeebrugge during the first week of October, and the improvised British Naval Division arrived at Antwerp, the situation was already out of hand. The British Army was small; it had helped to save Paris, and now paid the price in the loss of the Belgian coast.

The Seventh Division occupied Ghent, and after covering the retreat of the Belgian Army, which halted along the line of the Yser, from Dixmude to Nieuport, fell back by way of Roulers to a position east of Ypres. When the whole British force came into line, it held a front of some thirty-five miles, with Maud'huy's Tenth French Army on its right across the Béthune-Lille road. On its left the line was held, from a point north of Ypres to the sea, by the Belgian Army, assisted by four French cavalry divisions under General De Mitry. The German Army had failed to take Paris; all its efforts were now concentrated on the seizure of the Channel ports, and its pressure on the defending line was like the pressure of a great rising head of waters against the gates of a lock.

The glory of the defence belongs to the infantry. The men who flew above them could only watch them and help them with eyes. The infantry were often unconscious of this help; they disliked seeing hostile observers above them and often fired on aeroplanes with very little distinction made between friends and foes. On the 26th of October Major G. H. Raleigh, of No. 4 Squadron, reports an artillery reconnaissance as follows:

> Hosking and Crean did a tactical reconnaissance early, but were unable to locate batteries owing to clouds. They went up later and did it. The clouds were low, so it was arranged that they should fly over one of our batteries to observe for ranging. The machine came down in flames and was completely demolished. Pilot and passenger had both been wounded by our own infantry fire when at a height of about a thousand feet with the large Union Jack plainly visible.

Wing Commander W. D. Beatty tells how, before this time, the disadvantage of the Union Jack marking on the planes was becoming evident. The officer in command of an aviation camp at Paris had pointed out to him that, at a height, only the red cross of the Union Jack was clearly visible, and that it was mistaken by the French for the German marking. A suggestion was made that the British should adopt the French circular marking. The mishap of the 26th of October hastened the adoption of this suggestion, and thereafter the French target was painted on British aeroplanes, with the alteration only of blue for red and red for blue, to preserve national distinctions.

Commanding officers sometimes complained that our machines were little in evidence. The aeroplane observers, operating over enemy territory, reported to their own command, and their reports, forwarded to the proper quarters, took effect in the orders issued by Headquarters, so that crucial improvements were sometimes made in our dispositions, by information obtained from the air, though the infantry had seen no machine in the air above them. The use of machines for more local needs, such as artillery ranging, hastened the recognition of the services rendered by the Flying Corps, and brought it into closer touch with the other arms.

Photographic cameras and fittings were still very imperfect, and photography from the air was not much practised, but sketch-maps of enemy trenches and gun-pits, as located by air reconnaissances, were issued by Headquarters during the Battle of Ypres. Good work was done in directing the fire of the artillery, and the few wireless machines were much in demand. A telegram sent on the 28th of October from Sir Horace Smith-Dorrien to the Royal Flying Corps headquarters runs:

> Can you send us a second machine, with wireless installation, for use tomorrow? The aeroplane now working without wireless with Fifth Division has more to do than it can accomplish owing to observation being required for French artillery as well as our own.

But the wireless machine was required by the First Corps, at the northern end of the line, and a machine without wireless was sent instead.

The deadly and effective method of directing artillery fire on hostile batteries by means of wireless telegraphy played a great part in winning the war, but for the first battle of Ypres the wireless machines were not ready in quantity. The penalty which had to be paid for this unreadiness was heavy. Precious shells, which were all too few, had to be expended for ranging purposes. On the 4th of November Lord Kitchener wired to Sir John French:

> I have been talking to David Henderson about giving more observation to artillery by aeroplanes. As this saves the ranging ammunition, which is worth anything to us, please insist upon it.

Failing wireless, other methods of ranging had to be employed. These methods had been set forth in an official paper issued on the 28th of October. The aeroplane flies at any convenient height and when it is exactly above the target it fires a Very light. The battery range-finders, who have been following its course, then take its range and another observer with the battery takes its angle of elevation. These two observations are sufficient to determine the horizontal distance between the battery and the target. It was sometimes found difficult to take the range of an aeroplane, at a given moment, with an ordinary range-finder, and an alternative method of ranging is suggested.

By this method the aeroplane flies at a prearranged height, and, as before, fires a light exactly over the target. But this method also is liable to error, for an aeroplane determines its height by the use of a barometer, and barometers are only approximately accurate for this purpose. So, it was suggested that the two methods should be combined: the aeroplane should endeavour to fly at a fixed height, and the range-finders should, if possible, also make their calculations. These methods cannot attain to the accuracy of wireless, but they were found in practice to give fairly good results. They were not quickly or generally adopted; many battery commanders continued to prefer the reports of their trained ground observers to the indications given from the air. When wireless machines were increased in number, artillery observation from the air came into its own.

In a report dated the 5th of February 1915, Brigadier-General Stokes, commander of the 27th Divisional Artillery, lays stress on the enormous advantages of wireless. He says that the 116th Heavy Battery of the Royal Garrison Artillery, which had at its disposal an aeroplane equipped with a lamp, had succeeded in registering only three targets in fifteen days, whereas the 130th Howitzer Battery, which had a share in the services of a wireless aeroplane, had registered eight targets in seven days. The disadvantages of the older and cruder method are many; a thin mist which does not prevent the aeroplane from observing the target is enough to prevent signalling to the battery; the lamp is difficult to use on a rough day, and difficult to read against the sun; the aeroplane has to be kept under continual observation by the battery. To get better value out of our artillery, the general concludes, the wireless service must be largely increased.

Reconnaissance from the air was much impeded, during the second half of October, by low clouds and bad weather, but enough was observed to give some forecast of the tremendous attack that was impending. The Germans outnumbered the British three or four times, and threw their whole weight, now against one part, and now against another, of the thin line of infantry fighting in mud and water. Those who would judge the battle will find no escape from the dilemma; either the British defence, maintained for thirty-four days, from the 19th of October to the 21st of November, against an army which esteemed itself the best army in the world, must be given a high and honourable place among the great military achievements of history, or the German Army was disgraced by its defeat.

But the German Army was a good army, and was not disgraced. The Germans themselves respected their enemy, on the ground and in the air. On the 21st of November, at the close of the Battle of Ypres, two German second lieutenants of the air corps, called Fribenius and Hahn, were taken prisoner near Neuve-Chapelle, and were examined. They said that the performances of British aeroplanes had caused instructions to be issued that a British aeroplane was to be attacked whenever encountered. British aeroplanes, they said, were easily distinguishable from others, for they always showed fight at once. What prisoners say under examination is not evidence, but this early tribute to the fighting quality of the Royal Flying Corps is repeated in many later testimonies.

The crisis of the Battle of Ypres came on the 31st of October, when the line of the First Division was broken and the left flank of the Seventh Division exposed, at Gheluvelt, some six miles east of Ypres. The counter-attack by the First Guards Brigade and the famous bayonet charge of the Second Worcestershire Regiment retook Gheluvelt, and re-established the line. The last act of the long agony came on the 11th of November, when a great attack was delivered all along the line. The place of honour on the Ypres-Menin road was given to two brigades of the Prussian Guard Corps, who had been brought up from Arras for the purpose. The First Division of the British Army met this attack at its heaviest point of impact, and by the close of the day the Prussians had gained five hundred yards of ground at the cost of enormous losses.

The story of the battle belongs to military history; the loss and profit account can be summarised in two facts. The First Brigade, which met the Prussian spearhead, was taken back into reserve on the following day. It had gone into the battle four thousand five hundred strong; on the 12th of November there remained, of the First Scots Guards, one officer and sixty-nine men; of the Black Watch, one officer and a hundred and nine men; of the Cameron Highlanders, three officers and a hundred and forty men; of the First Coldstream Guards, no officers and a hundred and fifty men. This is not a list of the surrendered remnant of an army: it is a list of some of the victors of Ypres. The other fact is no less significant; after a week of fighting the German attack fainted and died, and when the next great assault upon the Ypres salient was delivered, in April 1915, it was led not by the Prussian Guard but by clouds of poison-gas.

No extraordinary or signal services were rendered by the Flying Corps during the crises of the battle. The weather was bad, and on some days flying was impossible. Yet by every flight knowledge was increased. When the British troops arrived in Flanders and were sent at once into the battle, the country in front of them was unknown. The dispositions of the enemy forces were not even guessed at. Then by the aid of the Flying Corps the enemy's batteries were mapped out, his trench lines observed and noted, his railheads and his roads watched for signs of movement. The reports received just before the battle do not, it is true, indicate the whole volume of movement that was coming towards the Ypres area.

The newly raised reserve corps which formed part of the German Fourth Army, the transport of which to the western front began on the 10th of October, were not definitely seen from the air until just before the battle. But observers' reports did indicate that many troops were moving on the Ypres front, and once battle was joined enemy movements were fully reported on.

When at the end of October, the Belgian Army mortgaged great tracts of their ground for many years by opening the canal sluices and letting in the sea, the Germans were enabled to divert the Third Reserve Corps southwards. The movements of troops from this area were observed by the Royal Flying Corps, and General Headquarters on the 1st of November issued this summary:

> The coast road from Ostend to Nieuport was reported clear this morning, and there are indications generally of a transference of troops from the north of Dixmude southwards.

Again, when the attack on Ypres had failed and died away, the Germans transferred many troops from the western to the eastern front; these movements also were seen by the Royal Flying Corps, who reported on the 20th of November an abnormal amount of rolling stock at various stations behind the German front. General Headquarters Intelligence Summary for the 20th of November says:

> The rolling stock formerly parked on the Ostend-Thourout and Ostend-Roulers lines has evidently been 'broken up, and distributed to a number of stations along the Lys and in the area immediately north of it, which would be suitable points of entrainment for the forces in that district..... This redistribution of the rolling stock, together with the apparent reduction in motor transport, would seem to point to some important movement away from this immediate theatre being in contemplation.

Air reports for the following day proved that much movement eastwards had already taken place.

Throughout the battle tactical reconnaissances had been maintained to a depth of from fifteen to twenty miles behind the German lines. There were some few fights in the air, and a little bombing, but observation was still the principal duty of the Royal Flying Corps. They were greatly privileged; at a time when our people at home knew nothing of what the army was doing, they, and they alone, witnessed the Battle of Ypres.

They would gladly have done more. Many of them had been infantry officers, and were eager to lend a hand to the infantry in that heroic struggle, but they lacked the means Not until the summer of 1916 were they able, by organised attacks from the air, to help to determine the fortunes of a battle.

With the close of the battle there came a lull in the fighting. This lull continued throughout the dark and damp of the first winter, and the interest of the war in the air shifts to the preparations which were being pressed forward at home for renewing the war during 1915 on a larger scale and with better material.

One incident which occurred just after the Battle of Ypres shall here be narrated; it serves to illustrate how the air work of the Germans may sometimes have been impeded by a certain defect of sympathy in the German officer class. German two-seater machines were commonly piloted by non-commissioned officers, who took their orders from the officer in the observer's seat.

On the 22nd of November Lieutenants L. A. Strange and F. G. Small, of No. 5 Squadron, were returning from a reconnaissance, flying at a height of about seven thousand feet. Their machine, an Avro, with an 80 horse-power Gnome engine, carried a Lewis gun. which had been mounted by them, against orders, on rope tackle of their own devising, just above the observer's seat. In the air they met a new German Albatross with a 100 horse-power Mercedes engine. They showed fight at once. Diving from a height of five hundred feet above the German machine, and at right angles to its line of flight, they turned underneath it and flew along with it, a little in front and less than a hundred feet below.

From this position, which they maintained while both machines made two complete turns in the air, they were able to empty two drums of ammunition into the German machine. After the second drum the German pilot lost his nerve, and the machine side-slipped away and down, landing behind our lines, close to Neuve-Église. There were twenty bullet-holes in the German machine, but the pilot and observer were both uninjured. The British officers landed close by, to claim their prisoners.

The German observer, a commissioned officer, took little notice of them; as soon as his machine landed he jumped out of it, and dragging the partner of his dangers and triumphs out of the pilot's seat, knocked him down, and began to kick him heavily about the body. If ever a collection of incidents shall be made, under the title *How the War was Lost and Won*, to illustrate the causes of things, this little drama will deserve a place in it.

CHAPTER 7

The Royal Naval Air Service in 1914

When the war broke out the Naval Wing of the Royal Flying Corps had already been separated from the Military Wing, and had become the Royal Naval Air Service. Captain Murray Sueter was Director of the Air Department, and Captain G. M. Paine was Commandant of the Central Flying School. Six officers, all pioneers of the air, held the rank of wing commander, and nineteen held the rank of squadron commander. There were twelve flight commanders, and, with the addition of some few who joined on the 5th and 6th of August, there were ninety-one flight lieutenants, flight sub-lieutenants, and warrant officers. The number of petty officers and men was approximately seven hundred.

Some of the officers and men had been appointed for special duties in connexion with gunnery, torpedo work, navigation, wireless telegraphy, and engineering. The duties which fell to the Royal Naval Air Service were naturally more various and more complicated than those which fell to the Royal Flying Corps. The Naval Air Service had to fly seaplanes and airships, as well as aeroplanes. They had made more progress than the Military Wing in fitting wireless telegraphy and in arming aircraft. They had in their possession, when war broke out, thirty-nine aeroplanes and fifty-two seaplanes, of which about half were ready for immediate use. They had also seven airships, of which one, the little Willows airship, may be left out of the reckoning, but of the others, the *Parseval, Astra-Torres*, and *Beta*, did good work in the war.

Some of the aeroplanes and most of the seaplanes were fitted with more powerful engines than any that were used by the Royal Flying Corps. Engines of two hundred horse-power were being installed in Short, Wight, and Sopwith seaplanes, with a view not chiefly to speed but to the carrying of torpedoes. These machines were not successful at first, but experiment was active. Two aeroplanes and one airship had been fitted with machine-guns; petrol incendiary bombs had been tried with success; and gear for the release of bombs was being gradually improved. More important still, wireless telegraphy plants had been set up at the various seaplane stations on the coast, and sixteen seaplanes, operating in connexion with these stations, had been fitted with transmitting apparatus.

These preparations, when they are looked back on across the years of war, may seem tentative and small, but the idea which dominated them is clear enough. Whether war would come soon was doubtful; what was certain was that war, if it did come, would come from the nation which for many long years had boasted of war, preached war, and intended war. The main concern of the Naval Air Service, in co-operation with the navy, was the defence of the East Coast from attack, whether by sea or by air, and the safeguarding of the Channel for the passage of an expeditionary force to the coast of Belgium or France. Other uses for a naval air force were a matter of time and experiment.

There was at first no general scheme, prepared in detail, and ready to be put into action, for the offensive employment of naval aircraft, so that the work of the service tended to relapse into defence. Very little had been done to provide for the co-operation of aircraft with the fleet at sea. The *Mayfly* mishap had left us unsupplied with airships of the necessary power and range for naval reconnaissance, nor were the means at hand to enable seaplanes to do scouting work for the fleet.

In December 1912 a design for a specially constructed seaplane-carrying ship had been submitted by the Air Department after consultation with Messrs. Beardmore of Dalmuir, but when the war came no such ship was in existence. The light cruiser H.M.S. *Hermes* had been adapted for seaplane carrying and had operated with the fleet during the naval manoeuvres of July 1913, but this was no more than a makeshift. The *Hermes* was refitted and re-commissioned in October 1914 to carry three seaplanes, and at the end of that month was sunk by a torpedo from an enemy submarine on her passage from Dunkirk to Dover.

War is a wonderful stimulant; and many things were done at high pressure, in the early days of August, to increase the resources, in men and material, of the Naval Air Service. The reserve was called up; in addition, a certain number of officers were entered direct from civilian

No 1 Squadron Royal Naval Air Service

ROYAL NAVAL AIR SERVICE

life, and were put to school, at Upavon or Eastchurch, to learn their new duties. Thousands of young men were eager to enter the service as pilots, but the training accommodation was wholly inadequate. The Bristol School at Brooklands, the Grahame-White School at Hendon, and the Eastbourne Aviation School were pressed into the service; in addition to these the naval air station at Calshot undertook to make seaplane pilots of some of those who had taken their flying certificates elsewhere. As was to be expected, training under these conditions proved difficult. All efficient machines were wanted for the war, so that machines which had been condemned for use on active service were sometimes employed in training new pilots.

If all those who deserve credit and praise for their part in the war in the air were to be mentioned, their names on the Roll of Honour would be thick as the motes that people the sunbeam. Most of them must be content, and are content, to know that they did their work and served their country. But here and there occurs a name which must not be passed without comment. On the 5th of August 1914 Mr. F. K. McClean, by whose help the first naval air pilots had been trained, joined the Royal Naval Air Service as a flight lieutenant. At the same time he offered to the service his three motorcars, his motorboat at Teddington, his yacht *Zenaida*, with two machines, and his private house at Eastchurch, which was converted into a hospital. A nation which commands the allegiance of such citizens need never fear defeat.

The earliest measure of defence undertaken by the Naval Air Service was the institution of a coastal patrol for the whole of the East Coast, from Kinnaird's Head, in Aberdeenshire, to Dungeness, between Dover and Hastings. This was ordered by the Admiralty on the 8th of August. The Royal Flying Corps, or rather, such incomplete squadrons of the Royal Flying Corps as were not yet ordered abroad, undertook the northern and southern extremes of this patrol, that is to say, the northern section between the Moray Firth and the Firth of Forth, from Kinnaird's Head to Fife Ness, and the southern section between the Thames and the coast of Sussex, from the North Foreland to Dungeness.

The most vulnerable part of the East Coast, from the Forth to the Thames, or from North Berwick to Clacton, was to be patrolled by the Naval Air Service. But these arrangements were soon altered. Not many days after the outbreak of war the Germans established themselves in Belgium, and it was believed that they would use Belgium as a base for formidable attacks by aircraft on the Thames estuary and London. The forces of the Naval Air Service were therefore concentrated between the Humber and the Thames, from Immingham to Clacton. The Wash was thought to be the most likely landfall for a German airship raiding London. Regular patrols of the coast were carried out in the early days of the war, to report the movements of all enemy ships and aircraft and to detect enemy submarines. But there was not much to report, and it was weary work waiting for the enemy to begin.

The British Expeditionary Force was ready for service abroad, and it fell to the Naval Air Service to watch over its passage across the Channel. A regular patrol between Westgate, close to the North Foreland, and Ostend was maintained by seaplanes, following one another at intervals of two hours. On the 13th of August a temporary seaplane base was established at Ostend under the command of Flight Lieutenant E. T. R. Chambers, but on the 22nd of August, when the expeditionary force was safely landed and the occupation of Ostend by the Germans seemed imminent, the base was withdrawn, and the men and stores were taken back to England.

An airship patrol of the Channel undertaken by airships Nos. 3 and 4 (that is to say, by the *Astra-Torres* and *Parseval*) began on the 10th of August, and was continued throughout the month. The average time of flight of a seaplane on patrol was about three hours, of an airship about twelve hours, so that the airship, which could slacken its speed and hover, had the advantage in observation. The chart following illustrates the patrols carried out by the two airships on the 13th of August 1914. Here are copies of their logs for the day:

' *Log of No. 3 Airship, 13th August* 1914.

7.10 a.m.	Rose.
7.37	Passed Sittingbourne.
7.45	Passed Teynham Station.
7.50	Passed Faversham.
8.20	Passed Canterbury.
9.0	Passed Coastguard Station.
9.49	Sighted No. 4 Airship.
10.41	Sighted seaplane on starboard quarter.
5.50 p.m.	Altered course for Coastguard Station.
6.25	Coastguard Station.
6.54	Faversham.
7.4	Sittingbourne.
7.34	Landed.

'*Log of No. 4 Airship, 13th August 1914.*

7.40 a.m.	Left Kingsnorth.
9.28	Passed Coastguard Station, shaped course for Calais.
10.35	Shaped course for Dover.
11.25	Shaped course for Calais.
11.35*	Broke one blade of port propeller, rendering it necessary to change two for new blades.
12.55 p.m.	Proceeded to Calais.
1.40	Shaped course for Dover.
2.12	Course as requisite to arrive at Calais.
2.52	,, ,, ,, ,, ,, ,, Dover.
3.20	,, ,, ,, ,, ,, ,, Calais.
4.00	,, ,, ,, ,, ,, ,, Dover.
4.45	,, ,, ,, ,, ,, ,, Calais.
5.45	,, ,, ,, ,, ,, ,, Deal.
7.30	Arrived at Kingsnorth.
7.53	Landed.

'* Off Dover at 11.35 a.m. one blade of the port propeller burst and flew off, narrowly missing damaging the rigging near the envelope. We were able to fit two new blades while under way and continue the patrol. This took one hour and twenty minutes.'

It will be seen that the *Parseval*, which could not fly for a whole day without landing for the replenishment of fuel, plied continually between Dover and Calais, while the *Astra-Torres*, which was the stronger ship, laid her course far to the east and north-east to search the Channel for the approach of hostile craft.

Once the expeditionary force was safely across the Channel, these routine patrols were discontinued, though both airships and seaplanes continued to make special scouting flights over the North Sea and Channel. The main work of the Royal Naval Air Service continued to be coastguard work. At dawn and at sunset patrols were carried out every possible day, scouting the line of the coast. The group which had its centre at the Isle of Grain was entrusted with the defence of the Thames estuary. They had to report the approach of hostile ships and aircraft, to help our submarines in attack, and to warn friendly craft. They had two sub-stations, at Clacton and Westgate, facing each other across the estuary. The monotony of the life was relieved at times by alarms.

In September a seaplane on patrol from Felixstowe sighted a Zeppelin. The news was received with enthusiasm, which was damped a little when it was learned that the pilot was some way out to sea, and

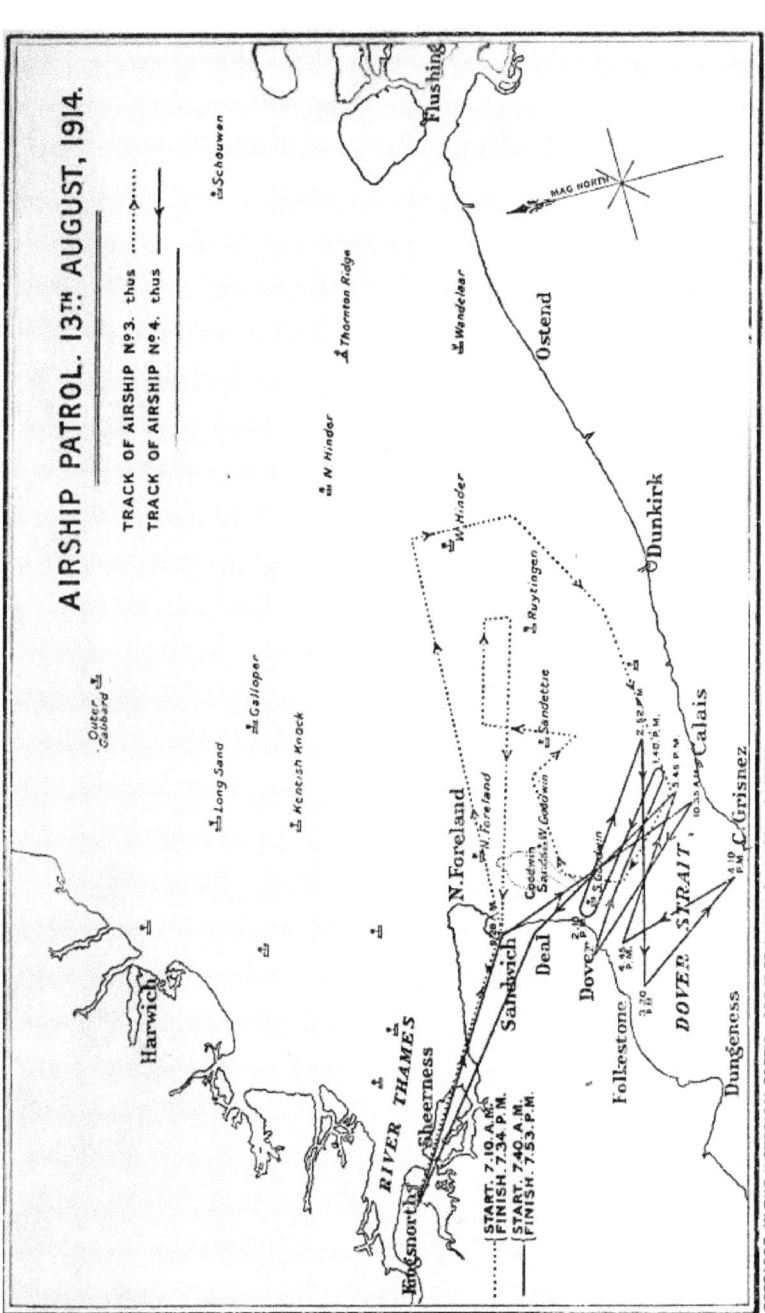

that his estimate of his distance from the Zeppelin was sixty miles. On the 17th of November the Admiralty suspected an impending raid by German warships, and ordered that all available aeroplanes and seaplanes should be in the air for the daylight patrol of Thursday, the 19th of November. But even war, as the philosopher remarked, has its seamy side, and the enemy did not appear.

This patrol work was tedious and, when the winter came, even dangerous; a few pilots were lost and some spent hours adrift on wrecked seaplanes. Here is the report of a December experience of Squadron Commander J. W. Seddon, over the North Sea:

> I have the honour to report as follows on the circumstances of my patrol flight with Leading Mechanic R. L Hartley in Seaplane No. 829 from Grain on Thursday, 17th inst., which ended with the salvage of this seaplane by the Norwegian Steamship *Orn*, who took us with the seaplane to Holland; and also on the circumstances of our detention at the Hook of Holland and subsequent release, and of the detention of the seaplane at Rotterdam.
>
> '1. *Diary of Events.*
>
> 8.10 a.m.   Left Grain. Wind Wly. moderate.
> 9.0 a.m.   Passed over Galloper, continued eastwards to investigate steamer proceeding eastwards at high speed.
> 9.10 a.m.   Steamer proved to be s.s. *Fulmar* of Liverpool. Turned back for Galloper. Wind strong Wly.
> 9.35 a.m.   Motor failed suddenly and completely. Landed, nothing in sight. Sea moderately bad. Failure due to breakage of ignition ring, and though several attempts were made and engine started on each occasion, a lasting repair could not be made. As I was not carrying an anchor seaplane commenced to drift at about 2 knots through the water E. by N. (compass).

I was feeling unwell when I left Grain and consequently was continually ill; Leading Mechanic Hartley also was seasick at first.

The seaplane commenced to settle on the port main float and about 10.30 the port wing float carried away. Leading Mechanic Hartley moved out of his seat on to the starboard plane.

The starboard wing float carried away about 11.15 a.m. and the trailing edge of the port lower plane was continually disintegrating.

About noon, or perhaps 11.30 a.m., the Flushing steamer passed from E. to W., but 7 or 8 miles to the northward, and did not see our signals.

From then onwards Hartley was continually moving slightly outwards on the plane to counteract the heel to port, and occasional heavy seas occurring every five or ten minutes accumulated small damages.

I therefore endeavoured to empty the main tank by overflowing through the gravity tank, but the 6 petrol coming back into my face made me more ill, and after half an hour I could not continue.

At 2.45 p.m., when I was expecting that a T.B.D. might appear to search for us, we sighted a small steamer to the N. Westward and making more or less towards us (some 6 miles distant). Waiting till she was abeam and only some 2 to 3 miles distant I fired my pistol and also waved. These signals did not appear to be observed at first, but finally she turned towards us about 3.15 p.m. and about 3.30 asked us if we wished to be taken off. This steamer proved to be the s.s. *Orn* (Captain Rewne). He manoeuvred and lowered a boat and took us aboard about 4.15 p.m.

I asked the captain if he could consider salving the seaplane, being worth as she was about £2,000, while the engine alone was worth £600 or £700.

He promised to try and I went away in the boat again to the seaplane.

I was not able to board the seaplane myself (going overboard while assisting one of the crew to do so), but this man got on board the seaplane successfully and made the necessary lines fast.

After some difficulty and damage to the seaplane through insufficient reach of the derrick, she was got on board and the wings folded by 6.0 p.m.; the *Orn* actually proceeding on her course shortly before this. No other vessels were sighted during these operations. We were picked up about 11 miles east from the Galloper Lightship.

The captain of the *Orn* said he could not put back to England on account of there being no lights, but otherwise would have done so.

The captain of the *Orn* did everything possible for us, supplying us with hot coffee, food, and wine, and myself with dry clothes. We arrived in Dutch waters about 3.10 a.m. and anchored off the "Hook".

After attending to the seaplane and taking all possible steps to secure its release by the Dutch Government, Squadron Commander Seddon was successful in obtaining the release of himself and his companion; on the 20th of December they sailed from Rotterdam for Harwich.

The seaplane patrols had not sufficient range to get into touch with the enemy off his own coasts, as the flying boat patrols almost always did in the later years of the war. Nevertheless, the first six months of coastguard work were of high value. They knit the service together, and produced a large body of skilled and practised pilots who prepared themselves or instructed others for later achievement.

An additional station for seaplane and aeroplane work was established at Scapa Flow to carry out patrols over the fleet. The patrols commenced on the 24th of August 1914 and continued daily in all weathers until the 21st of November, when the machines and hangars were completely wrecked in a gale. On the 27th of August 'Seaplanes Nos. 97 and 156 led the Battle Fleet to sea'. These were both Henri Farman seaplanes. There were also two Short seaplanes and a Sopwith Bat boat. A few more were added in the course of the following weeks, and so zealous and efficient were the mechanics that, with all the wear and tear of the daily patrol, not than two machines at the most were ever out of action at one time during the first six weeks. Further bases were established during the autumn of 1914 at Newcastle-on-Tyne and Dover, but the lack of serviceable machines curtailed the activities of these stations.

The real dramatic centre of England's effort in the air was to be found, during these months, not at the coastal stations, but in the training schools and workshops. The progress there made, at first invisible, was so rapid that Captain Sueter was able to say in July 1915 that every machine possessed by the Royal Naval Air Service at the outbreak of the war 'is now regarded as fit only for a museum.'

The problem of providing seaplanes with a floating base so that they might operate with the fleet at sea became urgent at once. On the 11th of August the Admiralty, realising the great utility of aerial scouting with the fleet, took over three cross-Channel steamers from the South-Eastern and Chatham Railway Company—the *Empress*, the *Engadine*, and the *Riviera*. The *Empress* was fitted out to carry machines and stores for the Naval Air Service. The *Engadine* and the *Riviera* were structurally altered at Chatham Dockyard, so that they might serve as seaplane-carriers. Later on, in October 1914, the *Empress* was also converted into a seaplane-carrier, and her work as transport and messenger vessel was taken over by the *Princess Victoria*.

The whole business of seaplanes was still in the experimental stage, and during the first twelve months of the war there were many disappointments. It was found that the seaplanes, when they were loaded with bombs, could not get off a sea that would hardly distress a picket boat. Proposals for an aerial raid on Wilhelmshaven and the Kiel canal were put forward by the Admiralty on the 13th of August, but the machinery was too imperfect, and the raid did not come off. But on Christmas Day, 1914, when the weather was propitious, a successful raid was carried out, as shall be seen, against Cuxhaven.

In the meantime much experimental work was done at high pressure, and a heavy responsibility fell on the technical staff of the Naval Air Service, who had to place definite orders, a year ahead, for engines to be developed and manufactured upon a large scale. In 1915 this policy produced the 225 horse-power Wight tractor, which could fly for seven hours at a speed of seventy knots, carrying a fair weight of bombs, and the 225 horse-power Short tractor, which could carry five hundredweight of explosives over a distance of three hundred miles. Both these machines could face broken water better than the earlier types, though it was not until the flying boat was perfected that the difficulties presented by a moderate sea were at last overcome.

It was an acute disappointment to the Naval Air Service that the enemy fleet at Wilhelmshaven and the enemy dockyards at Kiel should be left so long unmolested. The tendency to find someone to blame for lost opportunities is always strong in England. We are a strenuous and moral people, and we ask for a very formidable blend of virtues in our leaders. We are proud of the bull-dog breed and the traditions of our navy, but we demand from the bull-dog all the subtlety of the fox. We came through the war with credit not chiefly by intelligence but by character. Perhaps the two are never perfectly combined in one man. We know what it is to entrust our good name and our safety to men of stalwart and upright character, whose intelligence may in some points be open to criticism. Fortunately, we do not so well know what it is to trust our ultimate welfare to men of quick intelligence whose character is not above suspicion. The Lords of the Admiralty, like the rest of that great service, are good fighting sailors and good patriots.

What are called the principles of war, though they can be simply stated, are not easy to learn, and can never be learned from books alone. They are the principles of human nature; and who ever learned from books how to deal successfully with his fellows? War, which drives human nature to its last resources, is a great engine of education, teaching no lessons which it does not illustrate, and enforcing all its lessons by bitter penalties. One of the notorious principles of war, familiar to all who have read books about war, is that a merely defensive attitude is a losing attitude. This truth is as true of games and boxing, or of traffic and bargaining, as it is of war. Every successful huckster is thoroughly versed in the doctrine of the initiative, which he knows by instinct and experience, not by the reading of learned treatises.

A man who knows what he wants and means to get it is at a great advantage in traffic with another man who is thinking only of self-defence. Every successful boxer is an expert in military science; he tries either to weaken his adversary by repeated assaults on the vital organs, or to knock him out by a stunning blow. He does not call these operations by the learned names of strategy and tactics, but he knows all about them. The most that a book can do, for trader or boxer or soldier, is to quicken perception and prepare the mind for the teaching of experience.

The experience of the war from beginning to end taught the old lesson of the supreme value of the offensive. The lesson was quickly learned and put to the proof by our forces on the western front. The Royal Naval Air Service, from the first, sought every opportunity for offensive action. Raids over enemy centres, for the reasons which have been given, were impossible to carry out except in the best of weather. Offensive action in collaboration with ships of war was impeded by the imperfect structure of the seaplanes and the imperfect arrangements for conveying them to the scene of action.

Meantime the public, impressed by the dangers to be feared from the Zeppelin, called chiefly for defence. It has never been easy to instruct even the members of the other services concerning the right use of aircraft in war. When once they were reconciled to our aeroplanes they liked to see them in the air above them, which is the place of all places where our aeroplanes are least useful. It is greatly to the credit of those officers who commanded the Royal Flying Corps and the Royal Naval Air Service that they divined the right doctrine, and practised it, and established it in use, thereby securing for the air force the liberty to use its power to the best advantage.

The best and most highly trained of the naval air units was the first to be sent abroad. This was the Eastchurch squadron, under Wing Commander Samson. Just after the outbreak of war it had been sent to Skegness, to carry out patrol duties. On the 25th of August its commander was summoned to London by the Director of the Air Department, and was ordered to take his squadron on the following morning to Ostend, which had been chosen to serve as an advanced base for reconnaissance. They were to cooperate with a force of marines. Air Commodore Samson, in the reminiscences which he has kindly contributed for the purpose of this history, speaks with enthusiasm of the men and officers under his command.

'Never once were we let down by our men, and both in France and the Dardanelles they worked like slaves without a single complaint. It is an absolute fact that during these periods I never had to deal with a single disciplinary offence. They were the very pick of the Royal Naval Air Service.'

The pilots, after receiving their orders, were kept waiting for a day at Eastchurch, to give time for the landing of the Marine Brigade. Air Commodore Samson says:

> This depressed everybody, as we were all suffering from the fear of the war being over before we could get a chance to take part, in it.

The fear proved groundless.

On the 27th of August there flew over:

> Wing Commander C. R. Samson.
> Flight Lieutenant S. V. Sippe.
> Flight Lieutenant E. Osmond.
> Squadron Commander R. B. Davies.
> Flight Lieutenant C. F. Beevor.
> Squadron Commander E. F. Briggs.
> Flight Lieutenant I. H. W. S. Dalrymple-Clarke.
> Squadron Commander I. T. Courtney.
> Flight Lieutenant H. A. Littleton.
> Flight Lieutenant Lord Edward Grosvenor.

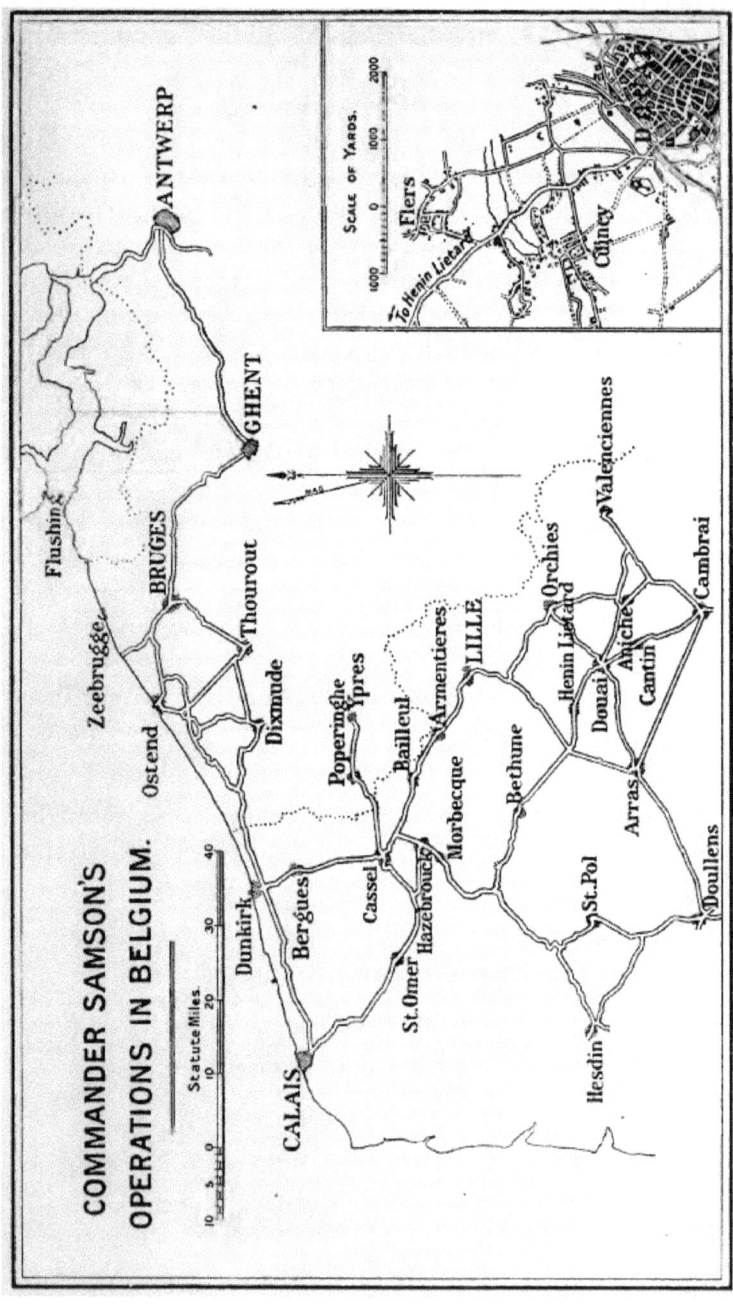

An airship (No. 3) was flown across by Wing Commander N. F. Usborne, with him Flight Lieutenant W. C. Hicks and Flight Lieutenant E. H. Sparling. Squadron Commander R. H. Clark Hall, Captain Barnby of the Royal Marines, and four junior officers of the Royal Naval Volunteer Reserve were attached for special duties. The motor-cars, lorries, and stores were embarked at Sheerness on board H.M.S. *Empress* and s.s. *Rawcliffe*. The machines that were flown over were a various assemblage—three B.E. biplanes, two Sopwith biplanes, two Blériot monoplanes, one Henri Farman biplane, one Bristol biplane, and a converted Short seaplane fitted with a land undercarriage in place of the floats. Warrant Officer J. G. Brownridge, R.N., was in charge of the repair and upkeep of the aeroplanes. In these early days there were no distinguishing marks on aeroplanes; it was arranged that every machine should fly a Union Jack lashed to one of its struts, but this was not done.

The whole force arrived in safety, with only one or two minor mishaps. Wing Commander Samson was fired at by rifles as he was coming down, and after landing was stalked by a couple of British marines, who had come to Belgium to shoot Germans and were aching to get to work.

The force remained at Ostend for three days only. There was no artillery except the guns of the ships lying off the port, and the Marine Brigade had only about half a dozen machine-guns. The defence of Ostend against a German attack in force would have been more than difficult. The aeroplanes carried out reconnaissance flights daily over the area between Bruges, Ghent, and Ypres, and, on the suggestion of General Aston, who commanded the Marine Brigade, Wing Commander Samson made a motor-car reconnaissance as far as Thourout and Bruges, in two cars, one of them fitted with a Maxim gun. Air Commodore Samson says:

> At Bruges we were received with great enthusiasm, the streets being crowded with people. The popular delusion, which we did not contradict, was that we were the advance party of a large British Army. The Civil Guard hastily donned their uniform on our arrival, and turned out briskly, with weapons and valour. They used, we found out later, to be quick-change artists, from uniform to plain clothes, and *vice versa*, according to the circumstances. Having gained some information in the town, we returned to Ostend. The whole party enjoyed themselves

immensely, although some of the more bloodthirsty members were disappointed at not getting a fight. This trip made us consider the question of motorcar operations, and ideas were discussed for armouring the cars.

On the 30th of August orders came that the Marine Brigade and the aeroplane squadron should return at once to England. It was a depressed party that loaded up the stores and transport on board H.M.S. *Empress* and the attendant collier. The aeroplanes flew by way of Dunkirk, where there was a slight haze and they landed. Lord Edward Grosvenor made a faulty landing, and crashed his Blériot beyond all hopes of repair. This accident, which would have been treated as insignificant if it had occurred on the way out, proved important enough to delay the aeroplanes for three days at Dunkirk.

During this time General Bidon, who commanded the French troops at Dunkirk, and Mr. Sarel, the British vice-consul, made urgent representations to the British Foreign Office, pleading that the squadron should be permitted, for military and diplomatic reasons, to co-operate with the French. Meantime, two of the aeroplanes carried out a reconnaissance towards Lille and Douai. On the 1st of September a telegram came from the Admiralty ordering that the squadron should remain at Dunkirk, to operate against Zeppelins and enemy aeroplanes, and to carry out reconnaissances as required by the French general. The policy that was now adopted was subsequently explained at greater length in an Admiralty telegram to the French Ministry of Marine:

> The Admiralty considers it extremely important to deny the use of territory within a hundred miles of Dunkirk to German Zeppelins, and to attack by aeroplanes all airships found replenishing there. With your permission the Admiralty wish to take all necessary measures to maintain aerial command of this region. The Admiralty proposes therefore to place thirty or forty naval aeroplanes at Dunkirk or other convenient coast points. In order that these may have a good radius of action they must be able to establish temporary bases forty to fifty miles inland. The Admiralty desires to reinforce officer commanding aeroplanes with fifty to sixty armed motorcars and two hundred to three hundred men. This small force will operate in conformity with the wishes of the French military authorities, but we hope it may be accorded a free initiative. The immunity of Ports-

mouth, Chatham, and London from dangerous aerial attack is clearly involved.

So, this little naval force began at once to operate from Dunkirk, carrying out reconnaissances by aeroplane, and using motor-cars for raids on the flank of the German communications. It gave assistance to the French and put heart into the much-tried civil population of Belgium. Most of the work at first was done with motor-cars, for the aeroplanes were few in number.

On the 4th of September Wing Commander Samson, having started out with two cars, one of them fitted with a Maxim gun, heard at Cassel by telephone that six German officers in a motor-car had just passed through Bailleul on their way to Cassel. The steep hill down from Cassel to the plain beneath offered him an excellent point of vantage to lie in wait for them, but he was unwilling to take it, for a fight close to the town would have given the Germans an excuse for pretending that they had been attacked by civilians, and for shooting some of the inhabitants.

So, he went out to meet them, and engaged them at a range of five hundred yards on the Cassel-Bailleul road. Two of the Germans were wounded, and their car made off to Bailleul. Wing Commander Samson lay in wait for them for almost two hours, in the hope that they would return reinforced to continue the engagement. During this time an old French captain of *gendarmes*, about sixty-five years of age, with a long-barrelled pistol, arrived in a limousine, accompanied by his wife. He had raised a little army of ten *gendarmes*, who came up soon after, armed with carbines. *Madame* and the limousine then retired from the battlefield, while the gallant captain disposed his army behind the hedge to await the return of the enemy.

But the enemy did not return; a message from the Bailleul post-office told how they had halted only three minutes in Bailleul, and how they and all the other German military cars in Bailleul had gone back post-haste to Lille, leaving behind them a quantity of wine which they had collected from the residents. Air Commodore Samson says:

> We had a tremendous reception from the inhabitants of Cassel, who had enjoyed a splendid view of our little engagement from their commanding position on the hill-top. I was pleased that they had seen Germans running away, as it would remove from their minds that 1870 feeling which there is little doubt the Germans still produced in the minds of civilian Frenchmen.

This fight gave us a prestige in the villages greater than its result called for. Probably the six German officers reported that they had run up against tremendous odds.

In the course of the next few weeks there were many such adventures. On the 5th of September, the eve of the Battle of the Marne, General Bidon reported that the Germans, who had occupied Lille in force, were about to leave, and that he intended to send some infantry, supported by a squadron of cavalry at Bailleul, to capture the transport wagons which were likely to be left behind. He asked for some motorcars to escort the infantry back from Lille. Wing Commander Samson, having borrowed from the French two machine-guns (he had only one of his own) and four French artillerymen, started off early on the morning of the. 6th of September, with four motor-cars (three of them armed with machineguns), six officers, ten of his own men, and the four Frenchmen.

An aeroplane, flown by Flight Lieutenant Dalrymple-Clarke, was detailed to escort them, with instructions to fly well ahead and to come down low and fire a Very light if any of the enemy were sighted. In the outskirts of Lille, the party learned that the Germans, two thousand infantry and eighty cavalry, had left Lille that morning, so they went on into the big square where the Prefecture stands. The square was packed with people. The rest shall be told in Air Commodore Samson's own words:

> We got through the crowd, and took the cars into the courtyard, lining them up abreast facing the square. The *gendarmes* at my request kept the roadway in front of the building clear of the populace, so that we were afforded a clear exit in case we had a fight, although I did not much look forward to one with this seething crowd of civilians in the way. Practically the whole of Lille appeared to be here; they were most enthusiastic, cheering, singing, and shouting out, *Vive l'Angleterre!*
> I did everything I could to impress the people with our discipline and military behaviour, placing four of my men as sentries in a line behind the railings, and one man standing by each machine-gun. Our sentries stood like Guardsmen, and even when beautiful French girls came on the scene, and sponged their faces and brushed the dust off their clothes, they stood like lumps of granite.
> Leaving Davies in charge of the party, I went inside to see the

prefect. He was pleased to see us, and said that our arrival had reassured the town to a most extraordinary extent, demonstrating to the people that they were not entirely at the mercy of the enemy. He then told me of the brutal treatment he had received at the hands of the Germans, showing the marks made on his throat by the fingers of a German lieutenant who had nearly throttled him.

They had gone so far as to lead him out to hang him from a balcony, and he said he had only been saved from this terrible fate by the coolness of his secretary, who told the German that the Prefect du Nord was one of the chief officials in France, and that his murder was a serious matter, not lightly to be undertaken. The *prefect* gave me the German officer's name, and said, "If ever you come across him, do not let him go". I promised I would not. The *prefect* then went on to say that the Germans had been quite worried over the fight at Cassel, and they had got the idea into their heads that there was a large force of English round about Cassel.

Two German officers had been wounded in the fight, one seriously and the other only slightly. There were, he said, about fifty French and some few English wounded in the town; they had been left there by the Germans, and if I signed a proclamation to say I had taken the town they could be evacuated to Dunkirk, otherwise the town would be held responsible. I therefore made out and signed the following Proclamation:

To the Authorities of the City of Lille,
I have this day occupied Lille with an armed English and French Force.

C. R. Samson,
Commander, R.N.
Officer in Command of English Force at Dunkirk.

I added the latter sentence in order to impress upon the Germans that there was a large force at Dunkirk. This proclamation the *prefect* ordered to be immediately printed and posted all over the town. I remained at the Hôtel de Ville until late in the afternoon, and as by then it was found out that the Germans had not left any transports behind, and that there was no chance of any French troops being sent to Lille, I reluctantly decided that I ought to return to Dunkirk. We had an ovation on our return journey through the streets, and our cars were full of flowers, chocolate, cigarettes, &c.; the dense crowds cheered themselves hoarse, and one felt rather as I imagined a Roman general used to feel on being given a Triumph. The only mishap was when an excitable individual threw a bottle of beer at me which smashed the screen and gave me a severe blow on the jaw; I fancy he must have had German sympathies.

On our return to Dunkirk the French general, Bidon, was most complimentary concerning our expedition, which he considered had been of great value.

The fight at Cassel had inspired the people of the district with a plenary belief in the powers of the little English force. A few days later, while Commander Samson was on a reconnaissance near Armentières, he was stopped by an excited civilian in a motorcar who offered to conduct him to a place where he might kill some Germans. The Germans, it appeared, were from two to three thousand in number, with two batteries of artillery, and were going from Lille to Douai. Air Commodore Samson says:

Personally, I thought about two thousand Germans rather a tough proposition for four Englishmen and one unreliable old Maxim, and I regretted that we could not carry out the slaughter he desired. He was very crestfallen, and said, "But I will come too".

The motorcar work was daily gaining in importance; what was needed was a stronger force and armoured cars. Two of the cars were fitted with improvised armour made of boiler-plate at the *Forges et Chantiers de France*, the big shipbuilding firm of Dunkirk, and application was made to the home authorities for a larger force of marines and specially designed armoured cars. The First Lord of the Admiralty (Mr. Winston Churchill) and the Director of the Air Department (Captain Murray Sueter) were quick to support any enterprise that showed life and promise; on the 8th of September there arrived a reinforcement of 250 marines under Major Armstrong, most of them reservists and pensioners, but stout men when it came to a fight.

Further, Wing Commander Samson got into touch with Captain Goldsmith, of the General Headquarters Intelligence Department, and, by his efforts, was put in control of the *gendarmes* in the villages of the zone where he was operating. The aeroplanes daily watched the movements of German troops along the roads, and the motorcars, assisted sometimes by the infantry, carried out sweeps and drives, to surround parties of German horsemen or cyclists. There were some rights. On the 13th of September there was a brush with some German cavalry patrols, on the Albert road, just outside the town of Doullens. Air Commodore Samson says:

> We got out of the cars and opened fire with rifles at about five hundred yards range. We hit five of them. Three were killed, and one was picked up severely wounded. We took him to a hospital in Doullens, where he died without recovering consciousness. It rather made me feel a brute seeing this poor fellow dying, and war seemed a beastly business. He was a rather half-starved looking fellow, and looked as if he had been on short rations for a long time. It was rather a repugnant job searching him whilst he was passing away from this life, but it had to be done. Goldsmith, who could read German, found from his papers that he belonged to the First Squadron of the 26th Dragoons, Wurtemberg. He had a little child's atlas with which to find his way about the country, and the map of France was about three inches square, with only the names of half a dozen towns on it.

The Naval Air Service now looked about for an advanced inland base, with an aerodrome, for their aeroplane and motor-car reconnaissances. They found one at the village of Morbecque, about three miles south of Hazebrouck, and just north of the forest of Nieppe. There, on the 19th of September, they established the headquarters of the unit. Most of the officers and men were housed in an old *château* by the favour of Madame la Baronne de la Grange, who had shown a fine example to her villagers by remaining on duty, and had so impressed the Germans that they left the village untouched. Two aeroplanes and six armoured cars and lorries were the equipment of headquarters, and what in the navy is called the lower deck personnel numbered 187 marines and 31 naval ratings.

Most of the work continued to be done by the motorcars. Some of the lorries were armoured with boiler-plate by the shipbuilding firm at Dunkirk, and new armoured cars began to arrive in driblets from England. A cyclist force was raised from the marines, and a number of French boys who knew the country well were embodied in a boy scout unit. The main idea of these preparations was to organise attacks on the German lines of communication in the zone of country between Lille and Valenciennes. The troops for this purpose were to consist of a brigade of French territorial infantry with a squadron of Algerian cavalry, popularly known as '*Goumiers*', and a battery of the famous '*Soixante-quinze*' field guns.

The Royal Naval Air Service were to operate, with as big a force of armoured cars as possible, under the French general in command. On the 22nd of September the French troops occupied Douai. The cars made a reconnaissance to Aniche, between Douai and Valenciennes, and there had a sharp engagement in the streets with German cavalry. Two days later they had a stiff fight at Orchies, where a French territorial regiment, detached to guard the route between Lille and Douai, was being heavily attacked by two German battalions. The cars helped to extricate the French troops and covered their retirement to Douai. But the German forces in this northern territory were being reinforced strongly, and reconnaissance by road became difficult.

When Wing Commander Samson, on the day after the fight at Aniche, was required to make a reconnaissance to Cantin, a village three or four miles to the south of Douai along the Cambrai road, he started off in a Talbot touring car with Sub-Lieutenant Lord Annesley and Lieutenant F. R. Samson. They had two rifles, ten rounds of ammunition, and three automatic pistols. He says:

> It appeared perfectly evident, that between us and Cantin there were not only the German guns, but plenty of German infantry. I must confess that the three of us did not at all relish the idea of ambling into the whole German Army and the local von Kluck in a touring-car, but the job had to be carried out to keep up our good name and the reputation of the R.N.A.S.

The Germans were in force, as he expected, and after a brisk engagement he returned to Douai. The Douai operations, which were to have been an attack on the German lines of communication, now became a defence of Douai against the Germans. By the 29th of September Douai was virtually in a state of siege, and it became a question whether the French troops could be extricated. On the afternoon of the 1st of October, the end came. By that time the Germans had got into the town and were firing at the Hotel de Ville from the housetops. Air Commodore Samson says:

> A shouting mob of cyclists and infantry rushed into the courtyard of the Hôtel de Ville, yelling out that we were surrounded, and the Germans had taken the Pont d'Esquerchin. I went to General Plantey and said that the only thing to do was to recap-

ture the bridge and drive the Germans away from that sector. He agreed, and said that if I would lead the way with my cars he would follow with what of the troops he could get to fight. There was no doubt that if we did not do something a wholesale surrender was certain. I strongly objected to being mixed up in that. I felt certain that if we could only start a fight the morale would improve and that we would have every chance of extricating the whole force from its predicament.

I led out our cars therefore from the Hôtel de Ville, and forcing our way through crowds of infantry and civilians we reached a corner where I found about four hundred infantry. I implored, and swore, and ordered them to follow us against the enemy, but only one came, jumping on to the step of the last car. From this corner a straight street four hundred yards long led to a bridge over the canal, which bridge was held by the Germans. As we went along this road I certainly thought that here was the end of our little party, and I felt very guilty at bringing Armstrong, Coode, and the other fine fellows to death for no purpose except to keep up the Pride of the Service.

The fact that the infantry would not come on after us made us very fierce, and I am certain, speaking for myself, that this feeling of anger made us far braver than we had felt at first. I took the cars to the head of the bridge and then halted them, and we opened fire along the roadways which ran on both sides of the canal and along the road ahead of us. I ordered the marines out of the cars on to the roadway, and told them to keep up a hot fire on the Germans who were on the opposite bank. Going myself with one marine on to the bridge I saw some Huns on board two barges which were alongside the far bank, and emptied my magazine at them.

I can remember to this day the sound one of their bullets made as it hit the girder alongside my face. We were so excited that I am afraid our fire was very wild, but it made up for lack of accuracy by its volume, our three machine-guns firing like mad. We kept up this game for about five minutes, when I saw the Germans clearing off in all directions. I ordered, "Cease fire", and ordered all on board the cars. I then led the cars at full speed along the main Henin-Lietard road, intending to get to the position we had held in the morning, as from there we could cover the retreat of the French and command the approaches to the Pont d'Esquerchin. . . . I knew that in front of us there was a double trench across the road, and which entailed cars stopping and reversing to get through in the gap left between the two trenches. Just short of this obstacle was a side road leading to Beaumont.

I determined, if we met the enemy at the trench, to hold the corner at the side road as long as we could, hoping that the Infantry would follow on. This side road would be the line of approach of the cavalry division reported close to Beaumont. On arriving at the corner, we encountered a very heavy fire coming from the trench and the high ground close to it. It would have been useless to have attempted to go on against that volume of fire, so we stopped at the corner, where we got some shelter from a cottage, and opened fire with the machine-guns from the two armoured cars, whilst the rest of us lay down on the road and kept up a hot fire with rifles.

We held out at the corner for nearly fifteen minutes until the Germans opened fire with field guns from Le Polygone; the situation then got too hot, as shrapnel was bursting all round us, and the cottage was quickly demolished by high explosives. I therefore gave the order to retire, and we jumped on board the cars and went along the Cuincy-Esquerchin road. After we had put a mile between us and the corner I halted to see how we had fared.

Our casualties now consisted of eight men wounded. All the cars had many bullet marks, but no serious damage had been done to them, except one of the armoured cars had a bullet through its radiator, causing it to lose practically all its water. We only had about 200 rounds of ammunition left, and were running pretty short of petrol, otherwise all was well with us...

... I considered that we had done everything we could to open a line of retreat for the infantry, and that we had held out at the corner as long as was possible.

As it happened we had cleared the way for the French, as the general got 2,500 infantry out of the town across the Pont d'Esquerchin and keeping close to the canal bank he had got them well clear of the Huns without firing a shot, whilst we were fighting them at the corner. I am afraid that a good number remained in the town and were captured. General Plantey was kind enough to write to say that if it had not been for the

English cars who had opened the door he could not have extricated his force.

Just short of Beaumont I came across the cavalry division. I went up to the general, who was a fine martial figure surrounded by an escort of *cuirassiers* with steel breast-plates. After I had told him what had happened, I said that there was every probability of the Douai Force having surrendered, but there was a chance of them having got out whilst we were holding the cross-roads. He was complimentary about our performance and said we had done all we could. He recommended that I should return to Morbecque and report to General Aston. He said that he was not pushing on any farther, but was going to retire to Beaumont.

I therefore went through Beaumont to Béthune and back to Morbecque, where we were received as if we had risen from the dead. Briggs told me that they had fully expected never to see us again. I went to bed after telephoning to General Paris, who had relieved General Aston in command of the Marines. General Paris sent the following report to the Admiralty:

> Commander Samson and all ranks appear to have behaved very gallantly in difficult circumstances, and I consider his action was perfectly correct.

These motorcar operations were no part of the war in the air. But they were carried out by the Royal Naval Air Service, and they illustrate the immense diversity of business which was undertaken by that service during the course of the war. Off the coast of Cornwall or over the rivers of West Africa, in raids on German cities or in expeditions to assist beleaguered Allies, the Naval Air Service were incessantly active on the fringe of things. They were sailors and adventurers by tradition; they adapted themselves to circumstance, and made the best of what they found. Their courage put new heart into desperate men, and their humanity (the greatest tradition of the British navy) added lustre to their courage.

The half-witted pedantry of the German doctrine and practice of war, which uses brutality as a protective mask for cowardice, was far from them. It was against that doctrine and practice, as against an alien enemy, that they fought; and only those who have been guilty of inhuman practices have ever had cause to complain of their cruelty.

Beyond the usual reconnaissances not very much work was done in the air from headquarters. The available aeroplanes were few, and there were many calls on them. Nominally the Dunkirk force was to consist of three squadrons of twelve machines each, but in these early days two or three machines were often the most that a squadron could muster. On the 3rd of September Squadron Commander E. L. Gerrard arrived at Ostend with three additional machines intended to operate from Antwerp against airship sheds in Germany. These machines remained at Ostend, pegged down under the lee of the sand dunes, while Squadron Commander Gerrard went by road to Antwerp to find an aerodrome and to arrange for the proposed raid.

On the 12th of September a violent squall came up from the west and caught the machines, uprooting or breaking the stakes to which they were secured. The machines turned cartwheels along the sands and were totally wrecked. The party returned to Dunkirk to refit, and as the attack on the Zeppelin sheds in Germany was reckoned to be of the first importance, Wing Commander Samson, who was ordered to take charge of the flight, had to give up three of the best machines he had.

It was believed at that time that Antwerp would not fall. When the British Army was moved north from the Aisne to Ypres, the original idea of the Allied strategy was resuscitated. That idea had been to take the offensive in Belgium and to repel the German advance or to make a flank attack on it. But the German blow had been too heavy and too quick for this plan to develop, and in the effort to save Paris the British Army had been driven far southwards into France.

Paris was saved at the Marne, and now that the Germans had entrenched themselves in a corner of France it was hoped that an attack upon their communications would compel them to retreat. Again, the Germans were beforehand. When things came to a standstill on the Aisne, they concentrated a large force in Belgium to make a push for the Channel ports. The British naval division, arriving at Antwerp on the 5th of October, could do no more than delay the fall of Antwerp by a few days.

The Seventh Division of the British Army, under Sir Henry Rawlinson, which was disembarked at Ostend and Zeebrugge on the 6th of October, found that its task was not an assault on the German flank but the defence of the Channel ports from a furious German assault.

Nevertheless, the Naval Air Service carried on. Two attacks were made on the airship sheds at Düsseldorf and Cologne. The earlier of these was made on the 22nd of September by four aeroplanes, two for each place. There was a thick mist extending from the River Roer to some miles east of the Rhine, and only Flight Lieutenant Collet succeeded in finding his objective. He glided down at Düsseldorf from a height of 6,000 feet, the last 1,500 feet through the mist, and came in sight of the shed when he was a quarter of a mile from it at a height of 400 feet. One of his bombs fell short; the others probably hit the shed, but failed to explode. Germans ran in all directions. All four machines were back in Antwerp by one o'clock in the afternoon.

The second and more successful attack was made on the 8th of October, during the evacuation of Antwerp. Antwerp was being bombarded, the panic-stricken retreat of the population had begun, but the Naval Air Service stuck to its aerodrome, and carried out the first notable air-raid of the war. On the 7th of October the machines at Antwerp had been taken out of their shed and planted in the middle of the aerodrome, to avoid damage by splinters if the shed should be hit by a shell. On the forenoon of the 8th the weather was misty, so Squadron Commander Spenser Grey and Flight Lieutenant Marix spent the time in tuning up their Sopwith Tabloid machines.

In the afternoon there was no improvement in the weather, but if an attack was to be made from Antwerp it was important to start, for the Germans were about to enter the city. Flight Lieutenant Marix, starting at 1.30 p.m., flew to Düsseldorf, dived at the shed, and let go his bombs at a height of 600 feet. The destruction was complete. The roof fell in within thirty seconds and flames rose to a height of 500 feet, showing that an inflated Zeppelin must have been inside. The aeroplane was damaged by a heavy rifle- and shell-fire, but Lieutenant Marix managed to get back to within twenty miles of Antwerp, and to return to the city by the aid of a bicycle which he borrowed from a peasant.

Squadron Commander Spenser Grey, starting at 1.20 p.m., flew to Cologne, where he found a thick mist and failed to locate the airship sheds. He dropped his bombs on the main railway station in the middle of the town, and got back to Antwerp at 4.45 p.m. At six o'clock the general evacuation of Antwerp was ordered, and the officers of the Naval Air Service succeeded in reaching Ostend by noon on the following day. The transport and stores had preceded them. Since the 3rd of October Wing Commander Samson's force had been employed in assisting the naval division at Antwerp.

Some seventy motor omnibuses, taken off the streets of the cities of England, and driven by their civilian drivers, who made up in cheerfulness and skill for what they lacked in military science, had been employed to carry the stores of the naval division, and were escorted by the armoured cars. Their stay in Antwerp was brief. When once the Germans had succeeded in bringing their big guns within range the end was certain. Air Commodore Samson says:

> I used to find the streets of Antwerp, a most depressing sight, thronged as they were with Belgians; beautifully dressed ladies were apparently carrying on their usual life, shopping and promenading as if the siege was a minor affair.

The people of a great commercial city are slow to realise the facts of war. When the realisation comes it comes with panic swiftness. The crowd of refugees which hurried by all roads out of Antwerp during the night of the 9th of October bound for anywhere, and fleeing from the destroyers of Louvain, was one of the most disheartening spectacles of the war. There were some bright spots in the prevailing darkness. One of these was General Sir Henry Rawlinson, of the Seventh Division, who took over the command at Ostend. Air Commodore Samson says:

> I came into contact continuously with him for the next month, and I never saw him downhearted once, even in the worst periods at Ypres. I never left his presence without feeling that we were bound to win: he was worth an Army Corps by himself.

The English nurses, who had two omnibus loads of wounded, are another luminous memory of that awful night.

> They were a splendid advertisement for the English race; absolutely unperturbed, calm and competent, amidst the surrounding mob of panic-stricken people. They impressed me more than I can say. Their one job was to get their wounded charges safe to Ostend, and that they would do it was evident to the most casual observer.

The evacuation of Antwerp put an end to all plans for a British offensive in Belgium. Ostend was crowded with refugees, and the streets were full of distressing scenes. The harbour railway station was a seething mass of humanity attempting to get on board the few steamers that went to England. The British forces, and with them the Royal Naval Air Service, retreated by stages. Aerodromes were occupied successively at Thourout, Ypres, and, on the 15th of October, Poperinghe. On this same date Zeebrugge and Ostend fell into the hands of the

Germans. Air Commodore Samson says:

> During the last three weeks, we had been always on the go, without a home, without any idea where we were going to next, without food sometimes, without adequate transport, and yet we had kept going because all ranks had pulled their pound and a bit over.

Thus, ended the Belgian adventure of the Naval Air Service. It had been good while it lasted. If a force of five thousand skilled and fit men, with armoured cars and aeroplanes, had been available for these operations, the German communications might have been seriously disordered. Some critics condemn all such adventures as 'side-shows'. They may be right; but it is always to be remembered that the national character is seen at its best in solitary adventures of this kind, and that the British Empire, from the first, was built up by side-shows—many of them unauthorised by the government. The experience of this war, and of former wars, proves only that these enterprises lose a great part of their value if they are timidly designed or half-heartedly executed.

To condemn them out and out is to prefer the German plan of empire, which depends wholly on central initiative and central control, to the sporadic energy of the British Empire, which can never be killed by a blow aimed at the centre, for its life is in every part. Military theory, based as it is chiefly on the great campaigns of continental conquerors, has so impressed some of its British students that they forget their own nature, renounce their pride, and cheapen their dearest possessions.

The overseas work of the Naval Air Service during the closing months of 1914, from the Battle of Ypres onwards, can be briefly stated. It consisted of help given to the British Army, reconnaissances and attacks carried out along the occupied coast of Belgium, and two great air-raids.

During the Battle of Ypres one naval aeroplane was working for the First Army Corps. Reconnaissances were carried out daily by the few available machines. Squadron Commander Davies on three occasions attacked German machines in the air; they escaped by planing down to behind their own lines. Flight Lieutenant Collet, whose aeroplane had been wrecked, flew as observer to Squadron Commander Davies, and reported the positions of six new German batteries. Flight Lieutenant Pierse, in an old inefficient machine which climbed badly, made many flights along the coast, and was wounded by shrapnel in the air over Antwerp.

Meantime, on the 31st of October, a seaplane base was established at Dunkirk in the works of the shipbuilding company, which occupied a part of the harbour. Under Squadron Commander J. W. Seddon, the seaplanes did some good work; they located enemy guns, dropped heavy bombs on Bruges railway station, co-operated with the ships' guns in the bombardment of the coast, kept a look-out for German submarines, and reported on the enemy defences.

This base at Dunkirk remained an active centre for our seaplane and aeroplane work throughout the war, and did much to defeat the German plans. The possession of the coast of Flanders had a twofold value for the Germans; it served to safeguard the right flank of their invading army and it provided them with a base both for their submarine campaign and for occasional attacks on the naval forces which held the Dover Straits.

There can be no doubt that it was part of their plan to take permanent possession of the Belgian coast. It is not easy to understand why, before the war, when Zeebrugge and Ostend were made into fortified harbours, a clause was inserted in the contractors' orders that the mole at Zeebrugge should be fit to carry hundred-ton guns and to withstand heavy gun recoil; also, that the Zeebrugge and Ostend locks and basins should be capable of accommodating a flotilla of torpedo-boats.

These things were not done in the interests of England, nor had the Belgian Government any reason to fear naval aggression from the west. The plans which had this beginning were developed and completed during the first two years of the German occupation. Bruges, which was joined by canals both to Zeebrugge and Ostend, became the naval headquarters of the German forces, the base for submarines and torpedo-craft, and the centre for construction and repair. Everything was organised on a solid basis, as if to endure; yet at some time during the third year of the war the enemy must have begun to feel doubtful whether he could keep his hold on the Belgian coast.

About thirty miles along the coast from Ostend, and forty or more miles from Zeebrugge, lay the port of Dunkirk, occupied in strength by the navies of France and Great Britain, and by the Royal Naval Air Service. Dunkirk was a thorn in the side of the Germans. The docks and harbours at Bruges, Zeebrugge, and Ostend were incessantly bombed from the air. Ships and works were seriously damaged, but the effect on the morale of the German forces was even more considerable. Repeated alarms, which sent all hands to take shelter in dug-outs, interfered with the work of every day. In the main basin at Bruges, and alongside the Zeebrugge mole, shelters, jutting out over the water, were provided for submarines and destroyers.

The respect felt by the Germans for the menace of Dunkirk is perhaps best witnessed by the fierce nightly attacks from the air which they made on the town during the later period of the war. Admiral Sir Reginald Bacon, who commanded the Dover Patrol from April 1915 until the end of 1917, speaks of these as 'the martyrdom of Dunkirk'. (*The Dover Patrol* by J. J. Bennett, the Royal Navy, the English Channel and the Zeebrugge Raid during the First World War by an eyewitness is also published by Leonaur.)

A great many of the houses in the town were levelled with the ground. Yet the inhabitants, knowing that they were maintaining a force which gave as good as it got, went about their daily business cheerful and unperturbed. They were rewarded in the end. When, after the armistice, the last German submarine came through the lock-gates at Zeebrugge, with her crew fallen in on the fore superstructure, her captain called for three cheers,—'As that's the last you'll see of Flanders.' The cheers were given very heartily—an involuntary tribute to the four years' work of the naval services at Dunkirk.

All these things were yet to come when the third of the naval aeroplane raids into enemy territory was made on the 21st of November 1914. This, the successful attack on the Zeppelin sheds at Friedrichshafen, Lake Constance, was planned and executed to perfection. Lieutenant Pemberton Billing, of the Royal Naval Volunteer Reserve, left England on the 21st of October under Admiralty instructions. He arrived at Belfort on the 24th and, by the courtesy of the French general in command, obtained permission to use the aerodrome within the fortifications and its large dirigible shed as the starting-point for a raid.

German spies were believed to be at work in Belfort, so arrangements were made for the machines to be brought into the place by road transport at night, and for their pilots to be boarded and lodged, during the whole of their stay, in the dirigible shed. Having completed these preliminaries, Lieutenant Billing carried out discreet inquiries which enabled him to draw up a chart of the proposed route, a complete plan of the Zeppelin factory, and a draft of instructions for the proposed raid.

Meantime the French had themselves been meditating a raid on Friedrichshafen, and the Governor of Belfort had received some valuable reports on the factory and the prevailing weather conditions. After some discussion it was decided that as Zeppelins were intended to assist in the destruction of the British fleet, the Royal Naval Air Service should be privileged to pay the first visit, but that this privilege should lapse if the visit were not paid within thirty days.

In the season of late autumn, when the barometer is high and the air calm, the whole of the Swiss plateau and the Rhine valley bordering it is often plunged in a thick mist which reaches to a height of about 3,000 feet. Above this sea of mist the air is clear and the flight of an aeroplane safe and easy.

The course chosen from Belfort to Lake Constance, a distance of about 125 miles, was bent, like an elbow at an obtuse angle, round the northern border of Switzerland, so that Swiss neutrality should not be violated. It lay over country much of which is wooded and sparsely inhabited—first from Belfort to Mülhausen, thence over the Black Forest and some groups of wooded peaks to a point north of Schaffhausen. Here the prescribed course was to bend southwards, between the two arms of Lake Constance which stretch to the north-west, and when once the lake was reached the objective would be full in view.

On the 28th of October Lieutenant Pemberton Billing returned to England to collect men and machines. A squadron of four Avros, with 80 horsepower Gnome engines, had already been formed at Manchester under Squadron Commander P. Shepherd. The four pilots were:

Squadron Commander E. F. Briggs.
Flight Commander J. T. Babington.
Flight Lieutenant S. V. Sippe.
Flight Sub-Lieutenant R. P. Cannon.

There were eleven air mechanics. The machines and stores were shipped at Southampton for Le Havre and arrived in Belfort by night on the 13th of November. When he reached Belfort, Squadron Commander Shepherd fell ill; moreover, the weather was bad, with a falling barometer and a strong easterly wind.

At last, on Saturday, the 21st of November, conditions improved and the raid took place. At half-past nine in the morning the four machines were lined up on the western side of the aerodrome to undergo engine tests and bomb-release tests. They were then dispatched, at intervals of five minutes, Squadron Commander Briggs, on machine 873, being followed by Flight Commander Babington on machine 875, and Flight Lieutenant Sippe on machine 874. Sub-Lieutenant Cannon's machine failed to rise and broke its tail skid. The other three

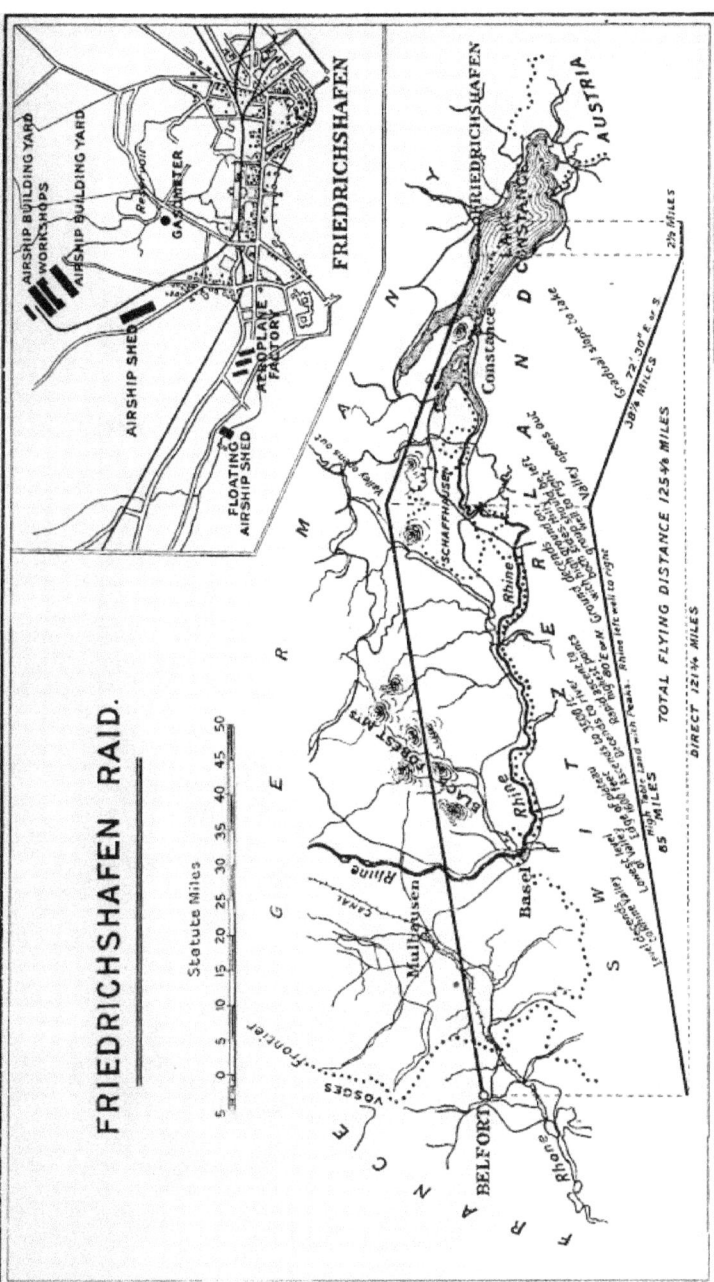

reached Friedrichshafen about noon, almost together, and wrought havoc on the Zeppelin works. Squadron Commander Briggs was brought down by machine-gun fire, which riddled his petrol tank. The other two returned in safety.

Two accounts of this raid shall be quoted, one from the air, the other from the ground. Here is Flight Lieutenant Sippe's log:

Attack on Friedrichshafen, 21st November 1914.

'9.55 a.m. Left Belfort. Shaped course for Basle, following Nos. 873 and 875.

10.25 a.m. Arrived Basle, passed to north, observed No. 873 going away to south, overtook No. 875. No. 873 several miles to starboard. Followed Rhine at height of about 5,000 feet, keeping to north.

11 a.m. Above clouds in Rhine Valley. No. 873 passed across and took up position ahead and about a mile to port. Continued to Schaffhausen, when suddenly lost sight of 873. No. 875 about two miles astern and about same height.

11.30 a.m. Arrived extreme end of lake and came down to within 10 feet of water. Continued at this height over lake, passing Constance at a very low altitude, as considered less likelihood of being seen. Crossed lake and hugged north shore until five miles from objective. Started climb and reached 1,200 feet. Observed twelve or fourteen shrapnels bursting slightly north of Friedrichshafen. Presumed these were directed against No. 873.

11.55 a.m. When half a mile from sheds put machine into dive, and came down to 700 feet. Observed men lined up to right of shed, number estimated 300–500. Dropped one bomb in enclosure to put gunners off aim, and, when in correct position, two into works and shed. The fourth bomb failed to release. During this time very heavy fire, mitrailleuse and rifle, was being kept up, and shells were being very rapidly fired. Dived and flew north until out of range of guns, then turned back to waterside shed to try and release fourth bomb. Bomb would not release; was fired on by two machine guns (probably mitrailleuse), dived down to surface of lake and made good my escape.

1.50 p.m. Arrived Belfort.'

The other account was given by a Swiss engineer who saw the raid from an hotel near the Zeppelin sheds. He counted nine bombs which fell in an area of 700 square yards round the works and sheds, and he said the earth and debris were thrown up to a height of 25 feet. Each machine had four twenty-pound bombs; one of Flight Lieutenant Sippe's bombs, as has been seen, failed to release. That leaves two bombs of the twelve to be accounted for; these fell on the sheds themselves, one greatly damaging a Zeppelin, the other destroying the gas-works, which exploded and sent up gigantic flames in the sky. The bombs made the town tremble; the military officers lost their heads and gave contradictory orders to the troops.

The *mitrailleuse* section, however, kept cool, and fired from 200 to 250 shots before Squadron Commander Briggs was brought down. The three British biplanes crossed, recrossed, and circled at such a speed over Friedrichshafen that many onlookers thought there were six of them. Squadron Commander Briggs was attacked and injured after landing; when captured by the military he was nearly fainting, and was transported to the large Weingarten hospital at Friedrichshafen, where he was tended with every care. In fact, the local officers regarded him with admiration, much as the British public regarded Captain von Müller of the *Emden*. (*The Kaiser's Raider!* by Hellmuth von Mücke, two accounts of the S. M. S. *Emden* during the First World War by one of its officers is also published by Leonaur.)

The damage done was severe, and now that the horse was stolen the German authorities took every care to lock the stable door. A great network construction was built above the sheds. The Bavarian regiments and the night sentinels were doubled; the number of *mitrailleuses* and anti-aircraft guns was much increased. Five powerful searchlights were installed on the hills around the town and were kept at work all night. Two additional gun-boats were stationed in front of the floating shed.

At eight o'clock every evening all the lights of the town were put out. Every civilian was compelled to carry a passport, and no foreigners were allowed to approach. The Zeppelin sheds were not attacked again, but all the men and all the material required for these additional defences were kept out of the war by the four hours' adventure of three British pilots. So true it is that the best defence is attack.

The pilots deserve all praise for their admirable navigation, and the machines must not be forgotten. There have since been many longer and greater raids, but this flight of 250 miles, into gun-fire, across enemy country, in the frail little Avro with its humble horsepower, can compare as an achievement with the best of them, and some part of the credit must be spared for those who planned it and for those who tended and prepared the machines. The men on the ground, or in the engine-room, or in the racing stable, who have no part in the excitement and renown of action, are the invisible creators of victory.

Shortly after the raid the Swiss Government complained that the British aviators had flown over Swiss territory, and had thereby violated Swiss neutrality. Flight Lieutenant Sippe's log, which has been quoted above, certainly gives some ground for this contention. The British Foreign Office, in their reply, said that instructions had been given to the British aviators not to fly over Swiss territory, that it was not their intention to do so, and that it had been the belief of the Foreign Office that they had not done so. The British Government assured the Swiss Government that if Swiss neutrality had been violated it had been by inadvertence, and expressed their great regret that any British aeroplanes should have flown over any part of Swiss territory.

At the same time the British Government were careful to point out that the International Congress of 1910 had failed to come to any agreement as to the recognition of territory in the air, and that Great Britain's desire to respect the wishes of the Swiss Government should not be taken as an admission that:

> Great Britain is necessarily bound in all cases to respect a doctrine which, however it may be viewed by herself, is not accepted and may not be acted upon by other Powers.

This point of law has since been settled. The International Air Convention of 1921, which has been signed by the Allied Powers, sets forth in its first article that:

> Every Power has complete and exclusive sovereignty over the air space above its territory.

The fourth raid into enemy territory, this time by seaplanes, was carried out on Christmas Day of 1914. How deeply the threat of the Zeppelins had impressed the public imagination and the minds of those who were responsible for the Royal Naval Air Service may be seen by this—that all four naval raids were directed against Zeppelin sheds. This fourth raid, though it did not succeed in destroying any German airship, achieved some useful observation, and had the incidental advantage that it brought the navy into conflict with Zeppelins, and diminished the portentous respect in which they had been held. Two naval officers, famous by their achievements in the war—Commodore R. J. B. Keyes and Commodore R.Y.Tyrwhitt—were in command of the supporting force.

Two light cruisers, with eight destroyers of the Third Flotilla, sailed from Harwich for the Bight of Heligoland at 5.0 a.m. on Thursday, the 24th of December, escorting the three seaplane-carriers, each with three seaplanes aboard. The air was clear and the sea calm, but it was bitterly cold. The *Arethusa*, preceded by a screen of four destroyers, led the way; she was followed, at intervals of one and a half cables, or 300 yards, by the *Engadine* and *Riviera*. A mile behind, with a similar screen of four destroyers, came the *Undaunted*, followed by the *Empress*. Two destroyers and ten submarines, under the command of Commodore Keyes, co-operated with this force, to fend off the attacks of hostile ships and to pick up the aviators on their return.

The purpose of the raid was to destroy the airship sheds at Cuxhaven, but the Admiralty were eager to get such information as might be obtainable without detriment to this purpose, and the seaplanes were instructed to report, if possible, on the numbers and classes of ships inside the basin at Wilhelmshaven, or anchored in the Schillig Roads (that is, the estuary of Wilhelmshaven), or in the mouth of the Elbe. The little fleet made straight for the Bight and reached a position some twelve miles north of Heligoland by 6.0 a.m. on Christmas morning. No time was lost in getting the machines out; seven of the nine got away soon after 7.0 a.m., the other two could not get off the water, and were hoisted in again. Then the supporting force cruised for some hours off Heligoland to await the return of the machines.

At a very early hour in the morning it had become evident from the agitated condition of the German wireless that the presence of the squadron had been discovered, but they were not attacked by enemy ships of war. A ship was seen approaching from between Heligoland and the mainland, but she turned back before she could be identified. At 7.35 a.m. a Zeppelin was seen about ten miles distant, coming from the direction of Heligoland, and at 7.55 a hostile seaplane from the same direction. The seaplane attacked the squadron and dropped four bombs, which were not bad shots, but failed to hit. The squadron replied with anti-aircraft guns, maxims, and rifles.

When the Zeppelin was within 11,000 yards, fire was opened on her with 6-inch guns and shrapnel shell at extreme elevation. The *Undaunted* burst several shells fairly close to her; she retreated to Heligoland and was not seen again. Soon after ten o'clock three of the British raiding seaplanes, having returned from the raid, were sighted and recovered, but the cruisers continued to await the return of the remaining four. A second Zeppelin and several hostile seaplanes now approached from the southward; all dropped bombs without success. The British seaplanes, it was known, carried fuel sufficient only for a three-hours' flight; when they had been gone for four and a half hours it was evident that they were not likely to be in the air, so the cruiser and destroyer squadron, after searching the waters of the Frisian coast, reluctantly shaped its course for home.

Commodore Tyrwhitt, in his report of the encounter with the German aircraft, remarks that both Zeppelins practised the same method of attack, namely, to get behind the line of ships and to drop their bombs on the fore and aft line. Their speed was great, but they seemed to suffer from one disability which made them clumsy to handle.

> It was repeatedly noted, that the Zeppelins, when altering course, invariably "wore", and did not appear to be able to turn head to wind. This made them ridiculously easy to avoid in spite of their speed, which was surprising.

That is to say, the Zeppelins did not tack. Perhaps it was their policy to maintain rapid movement, so as not to present a stationary target. To alter their course in the eye of the wind they fell off from the wind and, after presenting their stern to it, came up on the other side.

> The seaplane attacks were of a much more active nature, but they do not appear to have discovered the art of hitting.

German seaplanes, when they approached end on, were very like British seaplanes, so the order was given to wait for a bomb to be dropped before opening fire. This order caused 'considerable merriment' among the ships' companies. Commodore Tyrwhitt says:

> I am quite convinced that, given ordinary sea-room, our ships have nothing to fear from seaplanes and Zeppelins.

For eight hours, in perfect weather, the British squadron occupied German waters just off the principal German naval ports. The Germans knew the composition of the British force, and as visibility was extraordinarily good they must have known also that there were no supports; but their navy made no attempt to interfere with the British ships.

Three of the four missing pilots returned, and were picked up by submarine E11, close to Norderney Gat. They were there attacked by a hostile airship; the submarine, as soon as it had taken the pilots on board, was forced to dive, and the machines were abandoned. The missing pilot, Flight Commander F. E. T. Hewlett, had engine failure, and came down on the sea near a Dutch trawler; he was picked up and detained for a time in Holland. The Cuxhaven sheds were not located, but the German naval ports were pretty thoroughly surveyed, and a good deal of damage was done by bomb-dropping.

Seaplane No. 136, piloted by Flight Commander C. F. Kilner, with Lieutenant Erskine Childers as observer, flew over the Schillig Roads, and reported, lying at anchor there, seven battleships of the *Deutschland* and *Braunschweig* classes, three battle cruisers, apparently the *Seydlitz*, *Moltke*, and *Von der Tann*, one four-funnelled cruiser, probably the *Roon*, two old light cruisers of the *Frauenlob* and *Bremen* classes, ten destroyers, one large two-funnelled merchantman or liner, and three ships which appeared to be colliers. Anti-aircraft guns, firing shrapnel, were used against the seaplane and very nearly scored a direct hit. On issuing from the Roads, the officers in the seaplane saw a large number of ships in the northern part of the fairway of the Weser, and two destroyers east of Wangeroog. As a result of this reconnaissance a part of the German fleet was moved from Cuxhaven to various places farther up the Kiel canal.

The day before the Cuxhaven raid the Germans made their first raid over England, and dropped their first bomb on English soil. The air raids over England during the war were many and serious; they were an important and characteristic part of the German plan of campaign, and their story must be told separately. They began with a curious timid little adventure. On the 21st of December a German aeroplane made its appearance above Dover; it dropped a bomb which was aimed, no doubt, at some part of the harbour, but fell harmlessly in the sea. The aeroplane then went home. Three days later, on the 24th, a single aeroplane again dropped a bomb, this time on English soil near Dover. This was the prelude to a formidable series of air raids, which, however, were not made in strength till well on in the following year.

The close of the year 1914, and of the first five months of the war, saw the German assault on the European commonwealth held, though not vanquished. If the German plans had succeeded, the war would have been over before the coming of the new year. The failure of these plans was inevitably a longer business. The best-informed judges, from Lord Kitchener downwards, recognised that this was not a War which could be ended at a blow. A great nation does not so readily give up the dreams on which it has been fed for the better part of a hundred years. The German people had been educated for the war, taught to regard the war as their brightest hope, to concentrate their imagination on what it might do for them, and to devote their energies to carrying it through.

The movement of so great a mass of opinion and zeal, when once it has begun, is not soon reversed. Germany settled down to the business of winning the war. The Germans had had some partial successes, in the destruction of a Russian Army at Tannenberg, and of a British squadron at Coronel. They began to realise the immensity of their task, but they still believed that they could perform it, and that if they could not beat down the opposing forces, they could wear them down.

Month by month, as the war continued, it spread, and involved nation after nation. In the first summer Japan came in, and in the first autumn, Turkey. As the number of Germany's enemies increased, so did the tale of Great Britain's responsibilities. British troops, during the course of the war, fought upon every front, against every one of the Powers allied to Germany; British help in men, or money or material, was given to every one of Germany's enemies.

Already in August 1914 British naval and military forces were operating in Togoland, in the Cameroons, and at Dar-es-Salaam in German East Africa. By November Basra, in the Persian Gulf, was occupied, and the Mesopotamian campaign had begun. In addition to all these new burdens, the anxieties of administration in many countries, and especially in Egypt, which owed allegiance to the *Sultan*, were increased tenfold by the war. Those who had pleased themselves with the fancy that Great Britain is an island were rudely undeceived.

Aircraft had proved their utility, or rather their necessity, in the campaign on the western front; they were not less needed in all these distant theatres. In uncivilized or thinly peopled countries a single squadron of aeroplanes may save the work of whole battalions of infantry, the great problem of the first year of the war was a problem of manufacture and training, the problem, indeed, of the creation of values. With the instruments that we had at the outbreak of war we had done all that we could, and more than all that we had promised; but what we had achieved, at the best, was something very like a deadlock.

The war, if it was to be won, could only be won in the workshop and the training-school. These places are not much in the public eye; but it was in these places that the nation prepared itself for the decisive struggle. The New Army, and an air force that ultimately numbered not hundreds but tens of thousands, emerged from the discipline of preparation. The process took time; months and even years passed before its results were apparent. But some account of it must be given at this point in the story if the events of the later years of the war in the air are to be made intelligible or credible.

The greatest creation of all, the temper of the new force, was not so much a creation as a discovery. Good machines and trained men, however great their number, are not enough to win a war. War is a social affair, and wars are won by well-knit societies. The community of habits and ideas which unites civilized mankind is too loose a bond for this purpose; it has too much in it of mere love of comfort and ease and diversion. Patriotism will go farther, but for the making of a first-class fighting force patriotism is not enough. A narrower and tighter loyalty and a closer companionship are needed, as every regiment knows, before men will cheerfully go to meet the ultimate realities of war. They must live together and work together and think together.

Their society must be governed by a high and exacting code, imposed by consent, as the creed of all. The creation, or the tended growth, of such a society, that is to say, of the new air force, was one of the miracles of the war. The recruits of the air were young, some of them no more than boys. Their training lasted only a few months. They put their home life behind them, or kept it only as a fortifying memory, and threw themselves with fervour and abandon into the work to be done. Pride in their squadron became a part of their religion.

The demands made upon them, which, it might reasonably have been believed, were greater than human nature can endure, were taken by them as a matter of course; they fulfilled them, and went beyond. They were not a melancholy company; they had something of the lightness of the element in which they moved. Indeed, it would be difficult to find, in the world's history, any body of fighters who, for sheer gaiety and zest, could hold a candle to them. They have opened up a new vista for their country and for mankind. Their story, if it could ever be fully and truly written, is the Epic of Youth.

CHAPTER 8

The Expansion of the Air Force

When the war broke out, the Royal Flying Corps, as has been told, took the field with all its available forces. The four squadrons which were ready for service went abroad at once. In their desire to rise to their great opportunity the officers appointed to command in France made something like a clean sweep, taking abroad with them almost all the efficient pilots, and almost all the serviceable machines. There were at Farnborough at that time a small group of officers belonging to the newly formed Indian Flying Corps, and another small group training as a nucleus for a South African Aviation Corps. All these were swept into the net.

Captains H. L. Reilly and D. Le G. Pitcher, of the Indian Flying Corps, were at once made flying officers of No. 4 Squadron; three others, that is to say, Captain S. D. Massy (an early pioneer, who had flown with the Air Battalion during 1911, and was *commandant* of the Indian Central Flying School at Sitapur), Captain C. G. Hoare, and Lieutenant C. L. N. Newall, were posted to squadrons forming at home. Three officers of the South African Aviation Corps, namely, Lieutenants K. R. Van der Spuy, E. C. Emmett, and G. S. Creed, were at once incorporated in Nos. 2, 3, and 5 Squadrons respectively. Two others, Captain G. P. Wallace and Lieutenant B. H. Turner, joined No. 4 Squadron in the field early in September. Later on, both groups of officers were used for operations in distant theatres.

When in November 1914 the Turks were preparing to attack the Suez Canal, a flight, consisting of Captain Massy, Captain Reilly, and Lieutenant S. P. Cockerell, with three Maurice Farman machines, left England to give to the forces in Egypt the indispensable aerial support. This small flight was the beginning of the Middle East Brigade, which, under the command of Major-General W. G. H. S almond, played so great a part in the campaigns of Mesopotamia and Palestine.

Again, when in November 1914 the Union Government of South Africa undertook to invade German South-West Africa, the officers of the South African Aviation Corps were recalled from their squadrons in France to provide the needed air force. When that campaign was ended, these officers returned to England to form No. 26 Squadron of the Royal Flying Corps, which was immediately dispatched to East Africa, and cooperated with the forces under the command of General Smuts. (*General Smuts' Campaign in East Africa: Military Operations Against German Forces, February 1916-January 1917* by J. H.V. Crowe is also published by Leonaur.)

This rapid summary may serve to show how Farnborough, at the outbreak of war, was a generating centre for the air forces of the British Empire, and how, until the Germans were held in France, all other purposes had to be postponed.

Official returns show that with the four squadrons there went to France 105 officers, 755 other ranks, 63 aeroplanes, and 95 mechanical transport vehicles. At home there remained 41 officers, 116 aeroplanes, and 23 mechanical transport vehicles. But these latter figures are misleading. All the experienced officers at home were fully employed on necessary work, and the hundred and sixteen aeroplanes were impressive only by their number. About twenty of them, more or less old-fashioned, were in use at the Central Flying School for purposes of training; the rest were worn out or broken, and were fit only for the scrap-heap.

By the time that the war was a month old, the efficiency of the machines which had gone abroad was threatened by the progress of events at the front. The B.E. 2, which was generally reckoned the best of these machines, had been designed for the purposes of reconnaissance; it had a fair degree of stability, and gave the observer a clear view around him and beneath him. So long as it was not interfered with in the air it was an admirable machine for the reconnoitring of enemy dispositions and movements.

But the process of interference had begun. During the months of October and November fighting in the air became fairly frequent. This fighting had been foreseen, but only as a speculative possibility. Major-General Seely, speaking on the Air Estimates for 1919-20, told the House of Commons that he had witnessed the first air combat in France, one of those referred to in Sir John French's first dispatch, and that Sir David Henderson had said to him:

This is the beginning of a fight which will ultimately end in great battles in the air, in which hundreds, and possibly thousands, of men may be engaged at heights varying from 10,000 to 20,000 feet.

A call for fighting machines soon followed these early combats. On the 4th of September 1914 General Henderson wired home:

There are no aeroplanes with the Royal Flying Corps really suitable for carrying machine-guns; grenades and bombs are therefore at present most suitable. If suitable aeroplanes are available, machines-guns are better undoubtedly. Request you to endeavour to supply efficient fighting machines as soon as possible.

A day or two earlier a request had been sent home for nine aeroplanes to replace losses, and for a complete new set of reserve aeroplanes for the Aircraft Park.

War is the only adequate training for war, and it was the necessities of the war which revealed the needs of the Flying Corps, and gradually, by hard-won experience, determined the best types of aeroplane and the best kinds of armament. The enemy, driving with all his might for speedy victory, allowed no holiday for research and manufacture. What hope was there that the handful of officers in charge of the few centres of military aeronautics in England would be able to meet the growing needs of the campaign in France?

The outbreak of war found this country practically without an aeroplane engine industry. The few British firms who understood anything about aeroplane manufacture had in time of peace received only small experimental orders, and so were not organised for rapid production. The situation might well be called desperate. How could trained pilots, and machines fit to hold their own in the air, be produced in sufficient numbers to secure for us not the mastery of the air—that was too distant a goal—but the power to keep the air, and to give much-needed assistance to the British Army in France?

No one knows what he can do until he tries. If the situation was desperate, it was also familiar. The English temper is at its best in desperate situations. The little old army held the pass in France and Flanders against enormous odds, and so procured time for the building up of the New Army, the instrument of victory. The Royal Flying Corps, a small body of highly trained men, kept the air in France, alongside of the splendid French air service, while a new and greater air force was brought to birth at home. The creation of this new force was of a piece with that wonder of the war—the creation of the New Army. In some ways it was the most difficult part of that great achievement. The new infantry battalions were made largely by the imitation of a magnificent model and the repetition of methods proved by many past successes.

The men who brought the Flying Corps to an unexpected strength had to explore untried ways; the problems presented to them were complicated and novel; they had no safe models to copy, and no ancient tradition to follow. They had to cope patiently and resolutely with the most recent of sciences, and, more than that, they had to procure and train a body of men who should transform the timid and gradual science into a confident and rapid art. The engine is the heart of an aeroplane, but the pilot is its soul. They succeeded so well that at the opening of the Battles of the Somme, on the 1st of July 1916, the Royal Flying Corps held the mastery of the air, that is to say, they held a predominant position in the air, and were able to impose their will upon the enemy.

At the date of the armistice, the 11th of November 1918, the united Royal Air Force was incomparably the strongest air force in the world. Most of the pilots and observers who were flying at that time are now scattered in civil employ, but they will never forget the pride of their old allegiance nor the perils and raptures of their old life in the air.

It is the business of this history to tell of their doings. But before recording the appearance at the front of squadron after squadron, it is essential to tell something of the making of these squadrons. The whole elaborate system which was the basis of the Royal Air Force, the production of machines and armament and the training of men, was devised and put in action during the first year of the war. It was elastic in character, and was capable of great expansion, but its main outlines were never changed, even when the Royal Flying Corps and the Royal Naval Air Service, after a divorce of four years, were reunited in 1918. Englishmen are much in the habit of decrying their own achievements. This they do, not from modesty, but from a kind of inverted pride.

Even a fair measure of success seems to them a little thing when it is compared with their own estimate of their abilities. Before the war the German power of organisation was tediously praised in England, and our own incapacity for organisation was tediously censured.

There is truth in the contrast; the Germans love organisation and pattern in human society, both for their own sake and for the rest and support that they give to the individual. The British hate elaborate organisation, and are willing to accept it only when it is seen to be necessary for achieving a highly desired end. With the Germans, the individual is the servant of the society; with us, the society is the servant of the individual, and is judged by its success, not only in promoting his material welfare, but in enhancing his opportunities and giving free play to his character. We do not readily organise ourselves except under the spur of immediate necessity. But those of us who are honest and frank will never again say that we cannot organise ourselves. The making of our air force was a masterpiece of organisation. The men who achieved it have earned a place in the memory of their country.

When military aviation had outgrown its early pupilage to the Royal Engineers it came under the immediate control of the War Office. It was dealt with at first by the small committee, under Brigadier-General Henderson, which had prepared the plans for the formation of the Flying Corps, and which was continued in being after the Flying Corps was formed. In November 1912 Captain E. L. Ellington, of the Royal Artillery, succeeded Major MacInnes as secretary to this committee; in June 1913 the committee was dissolved, and its work was taken over by a newly formed section of the Military Training Directorate, with Captain Ellington in charge.

A little later, on the 1st of September 1913, a Military Aeronautics Directorate was established in the War Office, and at once took charge of the military air service. It was independent of the four great departments of the War Office, and the Director-General of Military Aeronautics dealt in person with the Secretary of State for War. There were three sections or branches (officially called subdivisions) of the directorate. The first of these was responsible for general policy, administration, and training. The second was responsible for equipment—the provision and inspection of material. The third had charge of contracts.

It was a new departure to place a contracts branch under the control of a military director-general, but aviation is a highly technical business, and the arranging of contracts for aircraft and air engines could not be profitably separated from the other aspects of the work. In immediate touch with the directorate, and completing the original organisation of military aeronautics, there were the Central Flying School at Upavon, and the Military Wing of the Royal Flying Corps with its eight authorised squadrons, the Royal Aircraft Factory, and the Aeronautical Inspection Department.

In July 1914 Brigadier-General Sir David Henderson was Director-General of Military Aeronautics; Captain Godfrey Paine, R.N., was Commandant of the Central Flying School; and Lieutenant-Colonel F. H. Sykes was the Officer Commanding the Military Wing. When the war broke out Sir David Henderson was appointed to command the Royal Flying Corps in the field, with Lieutenant-Colonel F. H. Sykes as his Chief of Staff.

Thus, at a time when rapid development was essential if we were to hold the air, the two most important officers, who had nursed the Flying Corps from its infancy, were called away to more urgent service. General Henderson still held his directorship of military aviation. If he thought the war likely to be short, he was not alone in that belief. Major Burke's squadron, when they left their quarters at Montrose, fastened up the doors of their rooms with sealing-wax and tape, and affixed written instructions that nothing was to be disturbed during their absence. Meantime, the duties of the directorate and of the home command of the Flying Corps had to be carried on, at high pressure, in the face of enormous difficulties.

The practical work of the directorate was undertaken by the little group of staff officers who were familiar with it, and especially by Major W. S. Brancker, who, on the outbreak of war, was appointed an Assistant Director of Military Aeronautics, and soon after became Deputy Director. The command of the Military Wing at Farnborough was given to Major Hugh Montague Trenchard, and the Royal Flying Corps had found its destined Chief. Charles Lamb somewhere remarks:

We should be modest for a modest man, as he is for himself.

But this is no personal question. What is said of General Trenchard is said of the Flying Corps. The power which Nature made his own, and which attends him like his shadow, is the power given him by his singleness of purpose and his faith in the men whom he commands. He has never called on them to do anything that he would not do himself, if he were not very unfortunately condemned, as he once told the pilots of a squadron, to go about in a Rolls-Royce car and to sit in a comfortable chair. He has never thought any deed of sacrifice and devotion too great for their powers. His faith in them was justified. Speaking, in 1918, to a squadron of the Independent Force, newly brought to the neighbourhood of Nancy for the bombing of the munition factories of Germany, he reminded them that if sending them all at once across the lines, never to return, would shorten the war by a week, it would be his duty to send them.

The pilots listened to him with pride. He had their confidence, as they had his. 'Don't cramp the pilots into never talking,' is one of his advices to commanders, and the system whereby the pilots and observers, returning dazed and exhausted from a raid or a fight in the air, were brought to the office of the aerodrome and encouraged by sympathetic questions to tell what they had seen and done, was a system which grew up at once under his command.

His intuitive understanding of the men who served under him, his quickness in learning the lessons of experience, and his resourcefulness and daring in immediately applying these lessons for the bettering of the Flying Corps, have been worth many brigades to his country. His name will occur often in this record, but here, at his first entry, he must be introduced to the reader.

He was born in 1873, the son of Captain Montague Trenchard, of the King's Own Yorkshire Light Infantry. He was educated privately, and after several failures in examination entered the army by way of the militia, receiving his commission as a second lieutenant in the Royal Scots Fusiliers. After some years in India he served in the South African War, at first with the Imperial Yeomanry Bushman Corps, and later with the Canadian Scouts. During the operations west of Pretoria, in the autumn of 1900, he was dangerously wounded, but served again, during the concluding years of the war, with the mounted infantry in the Transvaal, the Orange River Colony, and the Cape Colony. There followed a period of distinguished service in Nigeria, and then he was at home for a time.

In February 1912, three months before the Royal Flying Corps came into being, he applied for employment with the mounted branch of the Colonial Defence Forces, in Australia, or New Zealand, or South Africa. In May he applied for employment with the Macedonian Gendarmerie. These applications were noted for consideration at the War Office; in the meantime his mind turned to the newly-formed Flying Corps. Mr. T. O. M. Sopwith tells the story of how he learned to fly.

> Major Trenchard (as he was then) arrived at my School at Brooklands one morning in August 1912. He told me that the

War Office had given him ten days in which to learn to fly and pass his tests for an aviator's certificate, adding that if he could not pass by that date he would be over age. It was no easy performance to undertake, but Major Trenchard tackled it with a wonderful spirit. He was out at dawn every morning, and only too keen to do anything to expedite tuition. He passed in about one week from first going into the air as a passenger. He was a model pupil from whom many younger men should have taken a lead.

On the 13th of August 1912 he took his certificate, flying a Farman machine. Then he went to the Central Flying School, where he took the necessary courses and passed the necessary examination. On the 1st of October he was appointed instructor on the staff of the school. These were arduous times; an efficient British air force was yet to make, and the political horizon was even more threatening than it was a year later. He continued at this work till the 23rd of September 1913, when he was appointed assistant commandant to Captain Godfrey Paine, a post which he held up to the outbreak of war. By that time a very large proportion of the officers of the Flying Corps had passed through his hands. His policy was the policy of Thorough. He played his part in producing the efficiency of the original Flying Corps.

On the 7th of August 1914 he was appointed Officer Commanding the Royal Flying Corps (Military Wing), with the temporary rank of lieutenant-colonel. The headquarters, the aircraft park, and the four squadrons left for France at once. Mr. G. B. Cockburn at that time was at Farnborough, where, from April onwards, he had held an appointment in the Aeronautical Inspection Department. He has kindly contributed a note:

> The squadrons hurried off to the front, and in a short time there remained practically nothing in the way of machines or pilots in the country. Colonel Trenchard took charge to create something out of nothing. His presence at Farnborough had a most enlivening effect on everyone who came in touch with him, and as I had to pass through to him all the machines issued in those days, it was my good fortune to have very close observation of those methods which have led to his great success.
>
> In his attempt to create something out of nothing he had the whole-hearted support and help of the small but admirably efficient

aeronautical department of the War Office, directed for the time by Colonel Brancker. One great strength of military aviation in its early days was that it attracted into its service, by natural magnetism, men of an adventurous disposition. The dangers of the Flying Corps, rather than the good pay that it offered, brought to it recruits strong in all the virtues of the pioneer. No one who covets a life of routine, with defined duties and limited liabilities, ever yet took up with aviation as a profession. The men who explored and took possession of the air in the twentieth century are the inheritors of the men who explored and took possession of America in the sixteenth century.

It is one of our chief title-deeds as a nation that adventurers are very numerous among us. We were not the first to show the way, in either case, but because we are a breeding-ground of adventurers we are richer than other nations in the required type of character, and we soon outgo them. When the war came there was a long list of officers and men who were seeking admission to the Flying Corps—the best of them as good as could be found in the world. The very staff of the directorate at the War Office had the same quality. They were men of spirit and initiative, not easily to be bound by red tape. A short account of Colonel Brancker, who was Colonel Trenchard's main support, will illustrate this special good fortune of the Flying Corps.

Major-General Sir William Sefton Brancker, as he now is, began his soldiering in the Royal Artillery. He saw much active service in the South African War, and thereafter was chosen for staff service in India. His opportunity came in the winter of 1910. In that year the British and Colonial Aeroplane Company, in order to demonstrate the new art to the General Staff in India, sent out to Calcutta an expedition consisting of a manager, the French pilot Monsieur H. Jullerot, two British mechanics, and three Bristol box-kites fitted with 50 horse-power Gnome engines.

Captain Brancker, as Quartermaster-General of the Presidency Brigade, was responsible for the disembarkation of the party. What he had already heard of flying had excited his keen interest; he attached himself firmly to the expedition, and was permitted to fly, unofficially, in the character of observer. The first aeroplane was erected on the Calcutta racecourse, and flew in the presence of a huge crowd of spectators.

There were cavalry manoeuvres that year in the Deccan, and General Rimington, who was organising them, set aside a part of his manoeuvre grant to enable Captain Brancker to bring an aeroplane and take part in them. The aeroplane arrived at Aurangabad early in January 1911, and was hastily erected under a tree by the two mechanics, assisted by six willing and jocular privates of the Dublin Fusiliers. It was ready forty-eight hours after detrainment, just in the nick of time.

The first flight was made by M. Jullerot and Captain Brancker, the day before the manoeuvres began, in the presence of twelve generals, one of whom was Sir Douglas Haig, at that time Chief of the Staff in India, and a numerous company of staff officers. Next morning the aeroplane was attached to the northern force at Aurangabad, whose task was to drive back the rear-guard of a southern force retreating towards Jalna. Captain Brancker and M. Jullerot made a flight of about twenty-seven miles at a height of 1,100 feet, and the hostile rear-guard was accurately located. A full report was in the hands of the commander of the northern force in less than an hour and a half from the time of his demand for information.

Subsequent flights were less successful; indeed, the next morning the aeroplane crashed from a height of a hundred feet; the two aviators escaped with a few scratches, but the machine was reduced to matchwood. Nevertheless, the first thorough performance by a military aeroplane of a really practical military mission deeply impressed General Sir O'Moore Creagh, the then commander-in-chief, and, had it not been for lack of money, he would have started a flying organisation in India a year before the Flying Corps in England came into being.

Not long after his return to England, Major Brancker was employed at the War Office under General Henderson. As soon as the opportunity presented itself, he learned to fly. He took the short course at the Central Flying School and was appointed to the Royal Flying Corps Reserve. In October 1913 he succeeded Captain Ellington on the staff of the Military Aeronautics Directorate. He continued to fly. The first really stable aeroplane, the B.E. 2 c, was produced in June 1914; and Major Brancker, who describes himself as 'a very moderate pilot', flew the first of the type from Farnborough to Upavon, without the use of his hands except to throttle back the engine before alighting; during the flight he wrote a full reconnaissance report.

These then, Lieutenant-Colonel Trenchard and Lieutenant-Colonel Brancker, were the two officers on whom fell the chief burden of responsibility at home for the maintenance and increase of the Flying Corps. Others gave invaluable help; but these were the prime movers. The maintenance of the squadrons in the field, that is, the replacing of wastage in pilots and machines, was all that was originally expected of them by the command of the Royal Flying Corps in France. When, just after the outbreak of war, Lord Kitchener took control of the War Office, the creation of new squadrons at once became a question of the first importance. Lord Kitchener has many titles to the gratitude of his country, none of them stronger than this, that he recognised the immensity of the war. The day after the four squadrons took their departure for France he sent for Lieutenant-Colonel Brancker in the War Office, explained to him his policy for the creation of the New Army, and told him that a large number of new squadrons would be required to equip that army.

The position was serious. Farnborough was now the only station occupied by the Royal Flying Corps; it had an assemblage of half-trained and inefficient pilots, and a collection of inferior aeroplanes, discarded as useless by the squadrons which had gone overseas. The Central Flying School itself had been heavily depleted. There was a grave shortage of mechanics. But the officers in charge were not to be disheartened; and they had one advantage, without which the most complete material preparation would have been of no avail—they had the nation behind them.

The invasion of Belgium by German troops during the first few weeks of war, and the ordered cruelties inflicted by those troops on a helpless population, set England on fire; never since the old war with Spain had the fervour of national indignation reached so white a heat. Except the unfit and the eccentric, it might almost be said, there were no civilians left; the nation made the war its own, and miracles of recruiting and training became the order of every day.

The Directorate of Military Aeronautics took the bull by the horns; without Treasury sanction, on their own initiative, they began to enlist civilian mechanics at the rates authorized for the Army Service Corps, up to 10s. a day. In a very few days they had got together eleven hundred good men, trained mechanics, who eventually became the main support of the squadrons which were created during the next two years. They also enlisted some civilian pilots. It was their intention to grade these pilots as non-commissioned officers, but the Admiralty meantime decided to give commissions to all pilots recruited from the civil population, which decision forced the hand of the military. Thus, in the first few days of the war, the question of the rank of pilots was settled at a blow, and it was not until much later in the war that non-commissioned officers were again employed as pilots.

A definite scheme for the steady recruitment of expert mechanics, so many a month, at peace rates of pay, was then laid down by the directorate. Naturally, at the beginning, large numbers could not be absorbed, and as there was no system of control to allot recruits to the work for which they were specially suited, very many of the best mechanics in the country, inspired by patriotism, enlisted in the ranks of the infantry, and were lost to the technical service for ever.

These men would have been of inestimable value for the expansion of the Flying Corps, but no system of classification existed, to meet the needs of a nation in arms. The New Army engulfed men of all professions and all crafts; never, perhaps, in the world's history was there an army richer in diversity of skill. If special services were required from a bacteriologist, or a conjurer, an appeal to the rank and file of the New Army was seldom made in vain. Trained mechanics were glad to forgo all the advantages of their training, and, in their country's cause, to handle a rifle and a bayonet.

The procuring of a sufficient number of expert men for the sheds was only one part of the business of the directorate. They had also to procure and train a large number of pilots, and to arrange for the supply of a very large number of aeroplanes and engines. Until the machine is there, to be tended and flown, there is nothing for pilot or mechanic to do, so the question of the machines naturally came first. As soon as the four squadrons of the expeditionary force had left England, Colonel Brancker conferred with Captain Sueter, the Director of the Air Department in the Admiralty. It was agreed between them provisionally that all aeroplanes available in the British Isles should at once be allotted to the War Office, and all seaplanes to the Admiralty.

It was further agreed that all engines of 100 horse-power and less, together with the 120 horse-power Beardmore engine, should be allotted to the War Office, and that engines of higher horse-power, together with a certain number, for training purposes, of lower-powered engines, should be allotted to the Admiralty. Both services recognised the urgent need for a water-cooled engine of high power, and the two directors combined to persuade Messrs. Rolls-Royce to produce a 250-horsepower water-cooled engine. The experts of the Royal Aircraft Factory gave all possible help; they lent the drawings prepared for the high-powered engine designed by the factory, and so became sponsors for the famous Rolls-Royce engines of the later days of the war. The output of the Rolls-Royce works, in accordance with the agreement, was placed at the disposal of the Admiralty.

This immediate co-operation between the two great services did the work of the old Air Committee, which had quietly faded away. The War Committee could not take its place; it was a large body of Ministers, too numerous to agree on special decisions, and not expert enough to deal with the complicated problems of aviation. The understanding between the two services seemed to augur well for the future.

The available contractors and types of engine having been allotted, it became necessary to decide what orders should be placed. In this matter the initiative rested with the directorate. Very little experience was available as a guide to what the expeditionary force might require in the future. Every order placed was practically a gamble, and every new type of aircraft and engine gave the staff twofold cause for anxiety. Would the new machine prove reliable when the trade produced it, and, if it proved reliable, would it then fulfil the rapidly changing requirements of the war? The quickest way to produce aeroplanes in quantity would have been to choose a few of the best types, and to standardise these for production in bulk at all the available factories. To do this would have been a fatal mistake.

The art of military aviation was changing and growing rapidly; any hard and fast system would have proved a huge barrier to progress, making it impossible to take advantage of the lessons taught every week by experience in the field. At a later stage of the war the Germans standardized their excellent Mercedes engine. This gave them an immediate advantage, but, as knowledge increased and construction improved, what had been an advantage became a brake upon their progress.

Even the lessons of experience were not always easy to read. An aeroplane and its engine are judged by the pilot who uses them. Everyone who knows the Royal Flying Corps knows how sensitive to rumour and how contagious opinion is among pilots. This is only natural; a pilot trusts his life to his machine, and his machine, if he is to fly and fight confidently, must be, like Caesar's wife, above suspicion. To distrust the machine is to suffer a kind of paralysis in the air. The breath of unfavourable rumour easily takes away the character of a machine, and makes it, in effect, valueless. A pilot has one life, and has to take many risks; this is the only risk that he will not take gladly.

It follows that the opinion of pilots concerning their machines is peculiarly liable to error. They talk to one another, and an ill report spreads like wildfire. When the Sopwith Tabloid was first produced, it was unfavourably reported on by those who flew it, and at once fell into disrepute throughout the squadrons. The fact is that the pilots of that time were not good enough for the machine; if they had stuck to it, and learnt its ways, they would soon have sworn by it as, later on in the war, they swore by the Sopwith Camel. A similar ill repute attached itself, like an invisible label, to the De Havilland machine called the D.H. 2. This machine, when it made its first appearance at the front, was nicknamed 'The Spinning Incinerator'.

Like many other machines which are quick to respond to control, the D.H. 2 very easily fell into a spin, and in one accident of this kind it had caught fire. In February 1916, when the Fokker menace was at its height, No. 24 Squadron—the first British squadron of single-seater fighting scouts—arrived in France. It was equipped with D.H. 2's, and the pilots of the Fokkers had no reason to think the D.H. 2 an inferior machine. The historian of No. 24 Squadron says:

'A certain amount of trouble was caused at first through the ease with which these machines used to "spin"—a manoeuvre not at that time understood—and several casualties resulted. Lieutenant Cowan did much to inspire confidence by the facility with which he handled his machine. He was the first pilot really to "stunt" this machine, and gradually the squadron gained complete assurance.'

Nerves are tense in war, and a mishap at the front usually led to an immediate demand for new material or a new policy from those at home who supplied the expeditionary force. Major-General Sir Sefton Brancker, in his notes on the early part of the war, mentions three of these quick demands. When the aeroplane piloted by Lieutenant Waterfall was brought down by infantry fire in Belgium, this first mishap of the kind led to an immediate demand for armoured aeroplanes. The demand was not fulfilled until 1918, and then only in a special type of machine, designed for low flying.

Again, the alarm of the 1st of September 1914, when the machines of the Flying Corps, being unable to fly by night, ran the risk of capture by German cavalry, led to a demand for folding aeroplanes suitable for towing along the road. This demand was never met. Lastly, the rapid movement of the retreat caused a report to be sent home that the canvas sheds on wooden frameworks, called Bessoneaux hangars, were useless. With the coming of trench warfare more stable conditions prevailed, and Bessoneaux hangars housed the Royal Flying Corps in great comfort throughout the war.

Incidents like these serve to show how great was the responsibility which rested on the home command. Fortunately, the home command were cool and farsighted. Colonel Trenchard was the last man in the world to subordinate life to mechanism; and Colonel Brancker knew how to fly without fidgeting with the controls.

The resources to hand were not many. A certain small number of aeroplanes, in July 1914, were actually on order, and were being manufactured in slow and uncertain fashion. These belonged to several types. The earlier variants of the B.E. 2 machine were of government design. Of proprietary designs, on order or in process of delivery, the most important at that time were the British Sopwith and Avro machines, and the French Maurice Farmans, Henri Farmans, and Blériots, which were erected in England from parts supplied by France. Certain new types—the F.E. 2 (a pusher biplane), the R.E. 5 (a tractor two-seater bombing machine), the S.E. 2 (a single-seater tractor scout), the Vickers fighter, the Bristol scout, and several others—were hardly past the experimental stage. Some were in process of design; others were represented by a few experimental machines.

In the matter of engines, the factory was engaged in designing its own, and a few British proprietary designs had been tried, but without sufficient success to warrant an order. In fact, the Royal Flying Corps had to depend entirely on French engines, that is to say, on the 70 horse-power Renault and the 80 horse-power Gnome. Large purchases of these engines were made during the week before the declaration of war; indeed, the whole of the funds available were spent twice over in anticipation of further credits.

When the war came, Avros, Farmans, and Blériots were ordered to the full capacity of the factories that produced them. Vickers fighters were also ordered in numbers, though the latest model of the machine was untried, and though there was no certainty that the necessary 100 horse-power Monosoupape-Gnome engine could be obtained, or that when obtained it would run reliably. On the advice of the superintendent of the Royal Aircraft Factory it was decided to choose B.E. 2 c for production in bulk rather than the earlier variants of the same type. This involved some little delay, for the drawings were not complete, but the superiority of the machine in construction, performance, and stability was judged to be worth the delay.

Some firms which had never before touched aviation took large orders for this machine; the earliest to lend their services were the Daimler Company and Weir Brothers of Glasgow. For fighting purposes, the F.E. 2, a two-seater pusher, which gave a clear field of fire forward, was chosen, and the drawings were pushed on at top speed.

Smaller orders were placed among private firms for untried types of single-seater fighters, especially the Bristol scout and the Martinsyde scout. Messrs. Armstrong Whitworth, on receiving orders for B.E. 2 c's, undertook to produce an equally efficient and more easily manufactured aeroplane, and received permission to do so. Thus, before any definite policy could be laid down, and while experience gained in the field was still very small, the production of a large number of aircraft and air engines had been set on foot in England. Until the orders placed should begin to bear fruit, the Farman pusher machines, which could mount a machine-gun with a clear field of fire in front, were the only suitable fighting machines.

The enlisting and training of pilots, in numbers sufficient for the creation of new squadrons when the wastage in the field had been made good, was a matter of pressing concern. The only expert military pilots available as instructors were those employed at the Central Flying School. These were reinforced, first by certain civilian pilots who at once offered their services, and then, about the end of September, by the return from France of Major Longcroft and some other military pilots who in response to urgent requests were spared from the expeditionary force.

A reserve aeroplane squadron was at once formed at Farnborough, and a large training scheme was initiated. The aerodromes at Netheravon, Gosport, Montrose, and Dover (this last still in process of making) were empty. Montrose, being far from London and from France, was handed over to the army; the others were made into training stations. Brooklands and Hounslow were taken over, and, during September, Shoreham and Joyce Green. New aerodromes were established at Norwich, Castle Bromwich, Beaulieu, Catterick, and Northolt. Each of these, it was decided, should be occupied by a reserve squadron, which, besides the regular work of training pilots, should prepare to throw off an active service squadron. The policy of distributing the new training stations all over England was decided on for several reasons.

The congestion and delay inevitable at a few crowded centres would be avoided. The complete arrest of training by bad weather in one place would be insured against. The scattered aerodromes would be useful halting-places for new machines delivered by air; and, not least important, the New Army, training in various parts of England, would see something of aviation and would gain some knowledge of its uses. The chief disadvantage of the system was temporary; the available talent in instructors was scattered, so that a larger number of instructors was required.

In all these arrangements Lord Kitchener took a keen and detailed interest. He saw Colonel Brancker almost every day. He insisted on the creation of new units as a matter of the first importance. He investigated the possibilities of long-range bombing offensives against Germany, and continually urged the development of aircraft with a fuel endurance and a carrying capacity sufficient for a raid upon Essen. For this purpose, he knew that trained and disciplined flights would be required, and he gave orders that formation flying was to be taught and practised at once. He did not fully understand the crippling effect of the shortage of pilots and the inefficiency of the available aircraft. Soon after the outbreak of war he said to Colonel Trenchard:

'Trenchard, when I come down to Farnborough I want to see machines flying in formation.'

'But that is impossible,' said Colonel Trenchard. 'The machines are all of different types and different performances; we cannot fly in formation.'

'Trenchard, when I come down to Farnborough I want to see machines flying in formation.'

'But, Sir, it cannot be done.'

'Trenchard, when I come down to Farnborough, you will have four machines paraded for me, to fly in formation.'

Lord Kitchener's foresight was unerring, and his will was strong, but the facts were too stubborn even for him. It proved impossible to fly our machines in formation until about a year later. The first formation flying seen over England during the war occurred on the 23rd of February 1915, when H.M.S. *Hearty* reported seven German aeroplanes flying very high over the Maplin Lightship, just off the coast of Essex.

The value of Lord Kitchener's support was immense. In the early months of 1915 an order of battle for the New Army was produced, showing its organisation in corps and divisions. Colonel Brancker, when he saw this order, reckoned that at the rate of one artillery reconnaissance squadron for each division, and two or three fighting and reconnaissance squadrons for each corps, at least fifty service squadrons would be required. This, while the system of training was not yet in full working order, and while the output of engines and aeroplanes was still so small, seemed a very ambitious programme. But the squadrons were needed, so a minute to that effect was circulated among the departments concerned, who promptly added to it their remarks and comments, all critical and sceptical.

At last the paper reached the Secretary of State for War, who, without an hour's delay, sent it straight back by hand to the Deputy Director of Military Aeronautics, bearing an inscription scribbled at the foot—'Double this. K.' These two words, initialled, swept away all conservative and financial obstruction; from that time forward the main difficulty was to prevent the development of the squadrons from running so far ahead of the output of material as to weaken the whole structure. The hundred squadrons took a long time to make; but before the war ended a still more generous programme, with provision for more than two hundred squadrons in the field, was in process of fulfilment.

No account can be given here of all the difficulties, problems, and mishaps which had to be faced, not only at Farnborough or in the War Office, but at the stations all over the country, in the building up of the squadrons. The building went on, and those who did their work on it—the civilian and mechanic volunteers, the novices who learned their business only to teach it again to others, the men of special knowledge, trained engineers, experts in wireless telegraphy, photography, and gunnery, who by their work on the ground contributed to the efficiency of the work to be done in the air—have a living monument in the existence of the Royal Air Force.

The material which lay ready to their hands was little in quantity, but some of it was very good, and served well to set a standard. British aviation was a small and late development compared with the achievement of the French; but the skill and science of the Royal Aircraft Factory, and of the best of the private firms, had already given it a name for safety, quality, and performance, and the zeal and character of its new recruits assured its continued increase and multiplied its merits. What was needed now was a plan for the building.

Bricks and mortar, however good, and labour, however willing, are of no effect until they are disposed by the skill of the architect. It was the happiness of the Royal Flying Corps that that skill was not lacking. Those who designed the work to be executed in human material were worthy of their opportunity. It is not always so. There were many military misadventures in our history which give point to the criticism of the famous French cook, who, when he saw the beef and chickens of England, wept to think of the uses to which that magnificent material would be put by the resolute monotony of British cooking.

Long before the new squadrons were ready a plan had been made for using them, and controlling them, to the best advantage. The command of the Flying Corps were very quick to learn and apply the lessons of experience. These lessons, though not very many, were very important. By the end of October 1914, all the squadrons of the Royal Flying Corps in the field were settled down in the area of the British Army, which held a line running from Givenchy to Zonnebeke. The duties of the Flying Corps had thus become local in character, so that knowledge of the particular piece of country over which they did their work now became very important for pilots and observers.

To enable the several army corps and divisions to obtain full value from the services of the Flying Corps it was necessary that the squadrons should be put into touch directly with the corps commanders. A central command cannot judge the necessities of the case as those on the spot can judge it; and much time is lost in sending messages to and fro. Corps commanders were already calling for squadrons to be put at their disposal for observation and photography. A scheme was worked out whereby squadrons were arranged in groups of from two to four squadrons, each group being called a wing. The scheme was accepted by the command of the expeditionary force, and came into operation in November 1914.

Already the new arrangement had been anticipated in practice. During the Battles of Ypres in 1914, it had been found necessary to detach squadrons, instead of flights, to co-operate with the several army corps; and these squadrons, instead of returning at night to the central landing-place at the Flying Corps headquarters, as they did during the battles of the Marne and the Aisne, remained permanently with the army corps which they were helping. The new scheme regularized and extended this practice.

The creation of wings involved some transfers and promotions. The First Wing, intended to operate with the Indian Corps and the Fourth Army Corps, consisted of Squadrons Nos. 2 and 3; the command was given to Lieutenant-Colonel H. M. Trenchard, who came to St.-Omer on the 18th of November. The Second Wing, intended to operate with the Second and Third Army Corps, consisted of Squadrons Nos. 5 and 6, and was commanded by Lieutenant-Colonel C. J. Burke.

No. 4 Squadron and the wireless unit (afterwards No. 9 Squadron) were kept under the direct control of the Royal Flying Corps headquarters. Shortly before the Battle of Neuve-Chapelle the Third Wing was formed under Lieutenant-Colonel H. R. M. Brooke-Popham, and No. 9 Squadron was dispersed amongst the other squadrons. What had been the Military Wing at Farnborough was now decentralized into two separate commands—the Administrative Wing and the Fourth Wing—each controlled directly by the War Office.

The Administrative Wing, with headquarters at Farnborough, consisting of Nos. 1 and 2 Reserve Aeroplane Squadrons, the Depot, the Aircraft Park, and the Record Office, was placed under the command of Lieutenant-Colonel E. B. Ashmore, who was transferred from the staff of the General Officer Commanding the Home Forces. The Fourth Wing, with headquarters at Netheravon, was placed under the command of Lieutenant-Colonel J. F. A. Higgins, who had commanded No. 5 Squadron in France, and had been wounded, on the 30th of October, in the air above Bailleul. This wing consisted of Nos. 1 and 7 Squadrons, preparing for service in France.

The institution of wings was a great step in advance, and made it easy to provide for later additions to the strength of the Flying Corps. When the newly-formed squadrons began to appear in number, they were formed into wings, and the wings themselves, in the winter of 1915-16, were combined in pairs to form brigades. The brigade became a self-sufficient unit, to work with an army; it was commanded by a brigadier-general, and comprised, besides the two aeroplane wings, a third wing for kite balloons, an aircraft park, and everything necessary for a complete aerial force.

Further, when fighting in the air became all-important, whole wings were made up of fighting squadrons, and these wings were symmetrically paired with other wings made up of squadrons designed for artillery co-operation, close reconnaissance, and photography. The wing which carried out long reconnaissances and offensive patrols, bombing the enemy, attacking him in the air, and, in effect, protecting the machines which did their observation work above the lines, was called the army wing, and worked for army headquarters. The wing which observed and photographed for the corps command, reporting on the character of the enemy defences, the movement of troops, and, above all, the effects of our artillery fire, was called the corps wing, and worked for corps headquarters.

This powerful organisation of the later years of the war was achieved by a natural and easy expansion of the system of wings. In the early days of the war machines of various types were included in one squadron; then uniform squadrons of various types were included in one wing; at last, wings of various types were included in one brigade. The Flying Corps grew and increased in close correspondence with the army to which it lent essential aid. The institution of wings was a formal recognition of the necessity of its services. This recognition had taken some little time to achieve. Military aviation was a wholly new thing, quite unfamiliar to many an old soldier. There was a certain shyness at first between the army and the Flying Corps. The command of the army did not always ask for help from the air, and the command of the Flying Corps did not always offer it. When the squadrons got into touch with the corps commands, and did work for the artillery and the infantry, their value was proved beyond a doubt.

The commanding officer of a wing was given the rank of lieutenant-colonel. To assist him he had an adjutant and an equipment officer. The introduction of equipment officers into the Royal Flying Corps involved a new departure. Up to this time the rule had been that all officers in the Flying Corps, whether employed on the ground or in the air, must learn to fly. But to apply this rule, in time of war, to officers whose duties would never take them off the ground, and who would have to learn at schools already more than fully occupied with training pilots, seemed a waste of energy. There were, for instance, many trained engineers, in civil life, who were eminently capable of supervising the mechanical equipment, but who did not want to learn to fly, and could be made into indifferent pilots only at a great expense of time and labour, and at not a little risk.

At first the equipment officer was concerned only with stores, but soon the same grading was given to specialist officers concerned with wireless telegraphy, photography, or machine-guns. At a later time in the war some senior officers, skilled in the handling of men, learned to fly, and were at once given the command of squadrons. A man with a talent for command, who can teach and maintain discipline, encourage his subordinates, and organise the work to be done, will have a good squadron, and is free from those insidious temptations which so easily beset commanding officers who have earned distinction as pilots.

Yet the instinct of the Royal Air Force is strong—that a commanding officer should know the air, if he is to control aircraft. The right solution, no doubt, is that he should be able to fly well, and should be careful not to fly too much. A born commander who cannot fly is likely to have a better squadron than a born flyer who cannot command.

Technical matters, that is to say, all matters of design and equipment, were controlled by the War Office. This cast a great responsibility on the War Office, and might have worked unhappily, if the authorities at home had concentrated their attention on mechanical improvements without sufficient regard to the men who had to use them. But the two officers who, in the beginning, were chiefly responsible for development at home subsequently held commands in the field, so that theory was not divorced from practice. Colonel Trenchard was the first officer in the Royal Flying Corps to command a wing, and Colonel Brancker, at a later time, from August to December, 1915, was given the command of the Third Wing in France.

The whole development and expansion of the Royal Flying Corps in France was carried on while the conditions were altering every month, at high pressure, in rivalry with the Germans. It was a race to obtain machines of the greatest possible speed consistent with reliability. But no machine is reliable when it is first turned out. Only experience can prove a mechanism, discover its faults, and teach the right method of handling it. This experience had to be gained in war. The conditions of success were never at a stay. As soon as a machine was tried and proved, and the faults of its engine corrected, so that it became comparatively reliable, a faster German machine appeared. This had a depressing effect on the pilot, who, though he had been well satisfied with his own machine, could find no words too bad for it when a German machine left him standing in the air.

After a time a new British machine would appear, and in its turn would outgo the German. In the meantime, the important thing was to maintain the spirit of the pilot. It was the wisdom of General Trenchard to know that our success depended upon this. In his own words, he sacrificed everything to morale. To think only of dangers and drawbacks, to make much of the points in which the Germans had attained a fleeting superiority, to lay stress on the imperfections of our own equipment—all this, he knew, was to invite defeat.

Just before the Battles of the Somme, in 1916, a lively agitation of these matters was carried on by the newspaper press in England. Major Maurice Baring, in his published diary, has recorded that the results of this agitation were—not the hastening of one bolt, turnbuckle, or split-pin (for the factories were fully at work), but a real danger of the spread of alarm and despondency among the younger members of the Flying Corps in France.

More than any other man, General Trenchard averted this danger.

He put confidence into the pilots. He knew that if their hearts were not light they would do worse than die; and he fostered in them, by sympathy, the feelings which make for life and are life. Inferiority in engines and machines could be remedied in time, inferiority in resolution and confidence would have been irremediable.

Among the points which were early brought home by the experience of the war to those who had control of the production of machines, one or two deserve special mention. The absolute necessity for an efficient fighting aeroplane was realised, it has been seen, within a month. The enormous value of artillery observation and the immense superiority of wireless telegraphy over all earlier and more rudimentary kinds of signalling were soon demonstrated, and the call for machines fitted with wireless became insistent.

Some of the pilots and some of the equipment of the wireless section which existed before mobilisation had been used to bring the squadrons of the expeditionary force up to war strength. The section, though much emaciated, was not allowed to lapse; it was attached to No. 4 Squadron, and went out with it to France. The pilots of this section, Lieutenants Lewis, James, and Winfield Smith, worked with the squadron, but spent most of their time in making ready the wireless telegraphy equipment which, when once the retreat was ended and ground stations were established on a fixed front, came into effective use.

Again, the very rapid development of an efficient German anti-aircraft service, and the equally rapid improvement in range and accuracy of anti-aircraft guns, changed the conditions of reconnaissance. In the almost pastoral simplicity of the first days of the war, four thousand feet was held to be a sufficient height for immunity from the effect of fire from the ground. Before long four times that height gave no such immunity. Machines, therefore, had to be built to climb quickly, and had to be given a higher 'ceiling', as it is called; that is, they had to be able to maintain level flight in a more rarefied medium. But observation with the human eye from a height of several miles is almost useless for the detective work of military reconnaissance.

So, it came about that the improvement of the enemy's anti-aircraft artillery gave a direct impulse to the improvement of our aerial photography. A photograph, taken in a good light and enlarged, reveals many things invisible to the naked eye; a series of photographs reveals those changes in the appearance of the earth's surface which result from the digging of new trenches or gun-positions and the making of new ammunition-dumps.

Improvements in mechanical science, to be of any use in war, depend on the skill and practice of those who use them. General Trenchard never forgot this. He thought first of the pilot, and then of the gadgets, he once said:

The good gun-mounting is the mounting that the pilot can work.

This was a thing essential to remember at a time when the pilot got the best part of his training in the war itself. If he could not work the gun-mounting, the gun-mounting would probably survive him. To study the tastes and preferences of pilots, even when these tastes were prejudices, was the only way to efficiency. At the beginning of 1916 General Trenchard made it a rule to supply one experimental machine, without standardized mountings, to every squadron of the Royal Flying Corps, so that the pilots might put their own ideas to the test of practice. They had had but little opportunity to test their own ideas in the course of their training at the Central Flying School or the other training stations. The great practical School of Research for pilots was the war.

During the first winter of the war, the training given at the Central Flying School and the other training stations was still very elementary in character. The main part of the pupil's business was to learn to fly with safety, and when he could do this he was passed out to the squadrons. Such a training would have been terribly inadequate a year or two later, when no one could hope to fly long without fighting.

At the training station in Shawbury, during the winter of 1917-18, Lieutenant W. L. S. Keith-Jopp, who, after losing a hand in the war, continued to be a capable pilot, was in the habit of teaching his pupils all the acrobatics of the air, and would urge them on with the motto—'Stunt, or die.' Those who could not or would not learn to side-slip, to loop, to imitate a fall out of control, and to perform a dozen other gymnastic feats in the air had little prospect of a long flying career in France.

But the first winter of the war was innocent of all these fighting manoeuvres. Group Captain J. G. Hearson, who made acquaintance with the Central Flying School at that time, has kindly contributed some notes on the system then in vogue. The Central Flying School, he says, was the Mecca of all who wished to learn to fly. For serviceable machines, competent instructors, and the material and knowledge necessary to turn out a finished pilot, it was believed to be better than any other training centre. Some of the instructors had seen active service in France, and all were veterans in aviation. Of the pupils a certain number were regular officers, army or navy, but the majority were civilians of promise. The ambition of all was the same, to get into the air as quickly as possible, and to qualify for the coveted wings, which, once obtained, assured their wearer of immediate service, either in France, or with a naval unit. There were lectures on engines, aeroplanes, wireless telegraphy, meteorology, tactics, and organisation.

Flying was taught in four flights of service machines, two of them being made up of various types of the B.E. machines, while the other two consisted of Henri Farmans and Avros. The pupil was first taken up as a passenger, and the method of using the controls was demonstrated to him. He was then allowed to attempt flight for himself, either on a machine fitted with dual controls, or with the watchful instructor on the pounce to save him from dangerous mistakes. If he prospered well, the great day soon came, which, however carefully it may have been prepared for, is always a thrilling experience and a searching test of self-reliance, the day of the first solo flight, sometimes ending in a too violent or too timid landing— that is, in a crash or a pancake.

The training was almost wholly directed to producing airworthiness in the pupil. The various activities which had developed at the front, such as artillery observation, fighting, and bombing, had no counterpart as yet in the training establishment. Most of the pupils were eager to fly and to get to France; they endured workshop instruction as a necessary evil. Most of the instructors were unable to answer the questions of a pupil interested in the science of aviation.

They knew, and taught, that when a machine is steeply banked the rudder and the elevator appear to exchange functions, so that the rudder directs the machine up or down and the elevator turns it to this side or that, but they could not always explain the reason of this mystery. Nor could they explain why in a fog or cloud the compass of an aeroplane is suddenly possessed of a devil, and begins to spin around. But although they were not all well versed in technical knowledge and theory, they were all fit to teach the most important lesson—the lesson of confidence, resource, and initiative.

There was no special school for the systematic training of observers until the spring of 1918, when the school of aeronautics at Bath was "formed with that purpose in view. During the greater part of the war the instruction given to observers in the schools at home was occasional and desultory. From 1916 onwards a certain number were sent to Brooklands to learn wireless telegraphy, and a certain number to the machine gun school at Hythe to learn aerial gunnery. This school had been formed at Dover in September 1915, and two months later had been moved to Hythe, where firing from the air could be more freely and safely practised. In the earlier part of the war the observer's duties were usually undertaken by officers or non-commissioned officers who volunteered for the business.

When they joined the Flying Corps they already had some considerable acquaintance with the things to be observed—the disposition and appearance of the mobile forces and earthworks of a modern army—but their experience of observation from the air had to be gained over the enemy lines. It has always been the tendency of our air forces to make more of the pilot than of the observer. When battles in the air became frequent, this tendency was strengthened. The pilot is the captain of the craft. If he is killed, the craft cannot keep the air. But if more depends on the pilot, it is equally true to say that a higher degree of cold-drawn courage is demanded from the observer.

He suffers with the pilot for all the pilot's mistakes. For hours together, he has nothing to do but to sit still and keep his eyes open. He has not the relief that activity and the sense of control give to strained nerves. He is often an older man than the pilot, and better able to recognise danger. There is no more splendid record of service in the war than the record of the best observers. The two embroidered wings of the pilot's badge are the mark of a gallant profession, and are worn by novices and veterans alike; the single wing of the observer's badge was the mark of service done over the fire of enemy guns.

It has already been told how a large scheme for the expansion of the Royal Flying Corps was set on foot at home by Lord Kitchener, Colonel Trenchard, and Colonel Brancker. In November 1914 Colonel Trenchard was given the command of the First Wing. In August 1 91 5 he succeeded General Henderson in the command of the Royal Flying Corps in France. General Henderson had held this command during the whole of the first year of the war. Under his guidance the new, small, tentative air force, which he had done so much to create and foster, took its part in a great European war, and rapidly gained recognition for itself from the other branches of the service.

When he relinquished his command in the field, General Henderson continued until October 1917 to be General Officer Commanding the Royal Flying Corps, and Director-General of Military Aeronautics. Soon after that, when the Air Ministry was formed, he was given a seat on the Air Council, which he resigned in March 1918. At the close of the war he took over the control of the International Red Cross organisation at Geneva, where he did good work until his death in August 1921. He was a white man, a good friend, and an honourable enemy, high-spirited and sensitive—too sensitive to be happy among those compromises and makeshifts which are usual in the world of politics. The first chief of the Royal Flying Corps was a loyal and simple soldier.

Men take their turn and pass, but their work lives after them. The story of the Royal Flying Corps during the war is a continuous story of growth. Better, faster, and more numerous machines; more powerful, more trustworthy, and more numerous engines; better trained, more skilful, and more numerous pilots—the increase went on, when once the initial difficulties were vanquished, by leaps and bounds. The growth in power and bulk is striking enough, but the vitality of the new force is even better seen in the growing diversity of its purposes, and of the tasks which it was called on to perform.

Reconnaissance, or observation, can never be superseded; knowledge comes before power; and the air is first of all a place to see from. It is also a place to strike from, but, speaking historically, offensive action in the air, on any large scale, began, as had been anticipated, in the effort of the conflicting forces to deprive each other of the opportunity and means of vision. As the British expeditionary force grew, more squadrons of reconnaissance machines were required to serve the armies, their principal duties being to observe for the artillery and to photograph enemy positions. While they could perform these duties, they were content, but before very long they could not perform them.

The change in the situation is well summarised in a letter written on the 31st of July 1915 by Colonel Brooke-Popham to Colonel Ashmore, who commanded the Administrative Wing in England. Colonel Brooke-Popham says:

> The German aeroplanes are becoming far more active, and are making a regular habit of attacking our machines when on reconnaissance, and we are having to fight for all our information. We are now having fights by pairs of machines, as well as individual duels. It will probably be necessary to send machines by pairs or even by flights on all reconnaissances. The General

Officer Commanding, therefore, wants you to practise flying by pairs of machines in keeping station. Simple manoeuvres might also be carried out.

That this forecast was correct is shown by a letter sent in March 1916 from General Headquarters to the War Office.

Under existing conditions, it is essential to provide protection in the form of patrols for machines employed on artillery work. Information can no longer be obtained by despatching single machines on reconnaissance duties. The information has to be fought for, and it is necessary for reconnaissances to consist of at least five machines flying in formtion.

Fighting in the air had by 1916 become a regular incident of reconnaissance work. But when once fighting machines were produced, it was obvious that their use would not be restricted to attacks on enemy aircraft. Bombing raids on enemy positions became a regular duty of the Flying Corps. A machine built to take a heavy load of bombs is clumsy and slow in manoeuvre, not well able to repel the attack of light fighting scouts. To borrow a phrase from the pilots, it is cold meat in the air. Hence bombing raids were carried out chiefly at night, and night flying, on machines designed for the purpose, became another special duty of the Flying Corps.

These raids were what may be called short-distance raids, aimed at the aerodromes, munition stores, and communications of the German forces on the western front. They were followed, later, by long-distance raids, carried out by the Independent Air Force of 1918 against those centres in Germany which were sources of supply for the German Army.

In his dispatch of January 1919, on the work of the Independent Air Force, General Trenchard reviews and summarises what had been his policy from the beginning. It was necessary, he says, to equip the British expeditionary force on the western front with sufficient aircraft to hold and beat the German aerial forces on the western front; the bombing of Germany was a luxury till this had been accomplished, but once this had been accomplished, it became a necessity.

A good general idea of the growth of the Flying Corps can be obtained from a study of the programmes put up in 1915 to Sir John French, and in later years to Sir Douglas Haig, by the command of the Flying Corps in the field. These programmes are consistent and progressive; they look ahead, and attempt to provide the Flying Corps, in good time, with the means of meeting the demands certain to be made on it. On the 21st of August 1915, some two or three days after he had taken over the command in the field, Colonel Trenchard wrote to the Chief of the General Staff at General Headquarters. In this letter he speaks of the number of hostile aeroplanes seen on the Second Army front, and asks for another squadron to be sent out from home by the middle of September.

> I think a guide for the future should be at least one squadron to each corps, one squadron to each army headquarters, and one for General Headquarters.

> The corps squadrons were needed for artillery work and photography; the others to carry out reconnaissances for the three armies and for General Headquarters. On this basis he asks for three more squadrons as soon as possible.

> In addition I would ask that a squadron per army be sent out when formed, for special work such as bomb raids.

His plea for a good supply of antiaircraft guns illustrates a difference which persisted throughout the war between British and German usages. The British corps machines were incessantly at work over the enemy. The German corps machines were more prudent. Their constant practice was to carry out their observation of artillery fire and their photographic work obliquely, from a position in the air low down over their own lines, so that they were protected by their own guns, and could be attacked from the air only at very great risk.

But the German anti-aircraft guns had already succeeded in hitting some of our aeroplanes when they were flying more than three miles inside our own lines, at a height of six thousand feet. If we had guns as good as this, says Colonel Trenchard, and in sufficient number, we could attack the German machines and could protect our own machines when they are at work above the enemy lines. Hostile aeroplanes are easier to see from the ground than from the air, and the bursts of our anti-aircraft shell would serve to show our aircraft the whereabouts of enemy machines.

At this time there were three British armies on the western front. When news came in September that a Fourth Army was about to be formed, General Trenchard at once asked for a fourth wing, to consist of headquarters and three squadrons.

These demands were all fulfilled as soon as the uncertainty of deliveries permitted. In March 1916, some three and a half months before the beginning of the battles of the Somme, General Trenchard took another step forward. The work to be done by the Royal Flying Corps had outgrown its strength. Each of the British armies on the front had allotted to it at this time one brigade of the Royal Flying Corps, consisting of two aeroplane wings, namely, a corps wing and an army wing, and two kite balloon sections.

But in practice it had been found necessary to use the squadrons of the corps wing to help the army wing in patrol work, army reconnaissance, and bombing, so that corps commanders were often deprived of the essential services of the Flying Corps in artillery work and photography. General Trenchard's proposals, accepted and forwarded by the Chief of the General Staff, were based on the assumption that thirty-two squadrons would be in France by the middle of April. Sixteen of these, it was recommended, should be allotted, one to every corps of the four armies, for corps work; twelve to the four armies, at the rate of three squadrons to each army, for army work; and four squadrons to General Headquarters.

Ever since the formation of the Royal Flying Corps a squadron had consisted of twelve machines, that is, three flights of four machines each. It was now recommended and agreed that this number should be raised to eighteen, that is, three flights of six machines each, and that the establishment of pilots should be raised from twelve to twenty for each squadron. It was further agreed that the raising of all squadrons to the higher establishment should take precedence over the formation of new squadrons.

On the 15th of June 1916, a fortnight before the battles of the Somme opened, the Commander-in-Chief, Sir Douglas Haig, wrote to the War Office, submitting further proposals for the expansion of the Royal Flying Corps. By the spring of 1917, he says, the British Army in France will consist of five armies of four corps each. For these a total of fifty-six squadrons will be required, each squadron to consist of eighteen machines.

> I fully realise that my demand for this large number of squadrons involves the provision of a very large number of pilots and observers. The importance of this service, however, is so great that I consider it essential that the necessary personnel should be found even at the expense of a reduction in other directions.
>
> The increased establishment of the squadrons will involve, he adds,

a corresponding increase in the parks and depots; and in addition to all this, a total of sixty kite-balloon sections will eventually be required. This programme of requirements, he concludes, does not allow for long-distance bombing raids on a large scale. An addition of ten more squadrons is recommended for this purpose. Such raids are good and useful if the time and place are carefully chosen in connexion with the needs of the campaign. Otherwise they may do harm; and they are always attended by considerable risk of losses.

During the three months of the Battles of the Somme the Royal Flying Corps maintained a clear measure of superiority over the enemy in the air. At the close of those battles, on the 30th of September 1916, Sir Douglas Haig informed the War Office that the enemy had been making extraordinary efforts to increase the number and develop the speed and power of his fighting machines, and within the last few days had brought into action a considerable number of fighting aeroplanes which were faster, handier, and capable of attaining a greater height than any of the British machines, with the exception of three squadrons composed of Nieuports, F.E.'s, and Sopwiths.

To meet this situation, he asked for more and better fighting aeroplanes, and promised a further statement, to be based on the estimate of the General Officer Commanding the Royal Flying Corps. Fighting in the air continued to increase, and on the 16th of November Sir Douglas Haig asked for twenty additional fighting squadrons.

> Aerial battles on a large scale have practically superseded individual combats, with the result that, in order to get information and to allow artillery machines to carry on their work, it is becoming more and more necessary for the fighting squadrons to be in strength in the air the whole day.

The new types of machine asked for did not arrive until the spring of the following year, and they could not be used to advantage on their arrival, for the pilots had first to learn to handle them. Accordingly, as early as April 1917, General Trenchard wrote to the Director-General of Military Aeronautics, outlining the requirements of the Royal Flying Corps for the winter of 1917 and the spring of 1918.

> I anticipate that the Germans will produce a machine as much better than their present Albatross scout as the Albatross scout is better than the Fokker.

The great need was still single-seater fighters, and he urges that all available energy should be concentrated on these.

These programmes have been quoted, not so much to show how fighting in the air became, in 1916, the most important activity of the Royal Flying Corps, as to illustrate the initiative and foresight of the command. Experience at the front of our own successes and failures, and of the successes and failures of the Germans, suggested the needs of the future; the provision to be made, so that we might be able to meet those needs, was thought out beforehand, and was carefully and completely stated for the information of the authorities at home.

Disappointment was inevitable; there were hitches and delays in design and manufacture; conditions changed and machines improved at such a rate that a programme became an antique almost before it could be completely fulfilled. The growing pains of the Royal Flying Corps were severe, for the growth was fast; but it grew under quick supervision, and was shaped by the lessons of the war. The Flying Corps would take no denial; when the carrying out of a programme was long delayed, they looked yet farther ahead, and planned a still larger establishment.

On the 20th of November 1917 Sir Douglas Haig wrote to the Secretary of the War Office. In this letter he points out that when the programme submitted in 1916 shall be completed, some eighteen months to two years will have elapsed from the date when it was first accepted.

> I consider it expedient, therefore, even at the risk of dislocating existing arrangements, to submit a further programme to cover the requirements of the British armies in France up to the summer of 1919, in so far as these can be foreseen at present.

The approved establishment of the Royal Flying Corps in France, at the time when Sir Douglas Haig wrote, was eighty-six squadrons, ten of which were long-distance bombing squadrons. His new demand was for a hundred and seventy-nine squadrons, that is to say, a hundred and thirteen for the British armies in France and Italy, and sixty-six long-distance bombing squadrons for use against Germany. Further, he asks that the establishment of the fighting squadrons shall be raised to twenty-four machines. Formation tactics have developed; a squadron commonly goes into a fight with three flights of six machines each, working in echelon; to maintain this strength when some machines are temporarily out of action the squadron must number twenty-four machines.

The Army Council approved of all these demands, and suggested further additions, so that the programme, when it left their hands, provided for a total of two hundred and forty squadrons, all told. The coming of the armistice interrupted the fulfilment of these large plans, and saved the world from a carnival of destruction.

The expansion of the air force was a long process. The large plans which were made within a few days of the outbreak of war took years to achieve. In the early part of the war the first duty of those who were in charge at home was to supply needed reinforcements, both pilots and machines, to the original squadrons in the field. This was a small matter in comparison with the efforts of later years, but it was very difficult. Pilots were hard to come by at short notice.

The first demand from France for reinforcements was telegraphed from Amiens on the 18th of August 1914, and asked that Captain H. C. Jackson of the Bedfordshire Regiment and Captain E. W. Furse of the Royal Artillery should be sent to France to replace casualties. These were Staff College students who were nominated for attachment to the Royal Flying Corps on mobilisation.

A few days later, on the 22nd of August, a request came for any spare aeroplanes and for pilots to fly them over. Five machines were scraped together, which were all that were available, namely, an R.E. 1, a B.E. 8, two B.E. 2's, and a Blériot. Five pilots were found to fly them, including Second Lieutenant C. Gordon Bell and Second-Lieutenant B. C. Hucks. On the 9th of September, in response to a request for fighting machines, 'C' Flight of No. 4 Squadron, consisting of Maurice Farman Shorthorn aeroplanes fitted with machine-guns, was sent to France. These machines took part in many aerial combats, but without much success, for they were slower than the enemy machines, and their guns very often jammed at critical moments. In the telegram offering these machines the following sentences occur:

> Lord Kitchener wishes to give you all replacements possible, but at the same time wishes to continue organising squadrons at home for use with reinforcements (that is to say, with the divisions of the New Army). Please say if you like flights of R.E. 5's and Maurice Farmans, but if they go other pilots must be sent home to keep things going here.

If only instructors could be obtained, pilots could be turned out more rapidly than machines. Moreover, pilots, unlike machines, could not be obtained from foreign nations. In the event a small but steady stream of qualified pilots came from the Central Flying School and the supplementary training stations for the reinforcement of the original squadrons.

For the supply of machines during the earlier period of our preparation we were chiefly dependent on the French. They were ready, and we were not. Their magnificent aviation held the air while we prepared ourselves for our task. They had many factories in good working order, so that they were able to supply us with machines and spare parts in large numbers. During the last four months of 1914, from the end of August to the end of December, the Royal Flying Corps received twenty-four machines from home, fitted with French engines, and twenty-six from France. These last were chiefly Blériots and Henri Farmans.

In October General Henderson posted Captain James Valentine of the Royal Flying Corps to Paris, to organise a department for the supply of machines, engines, spares and stores, and to report on the performances of all new machines. In December the Admiralty followed suit and posted Lieutenant Farnol Thurstan to Paris to fulfil similar duties on behalf of the Royal Naval Air Service. The French Government were courteous and willing, but a certain amount of bargaining was inevitable, for if we wanted their aircraft, they wanted our raw material, especially steel, and our Lewis guns. The arrangements were entrusted to a series of conferences, and subsequently to a joint commission.

In spite of difficulties the supply went forward. It was not until 1916 that we began to be independent of the French factories. In the four months August to November 1915 the total value of the orders which were placed in France for aeroplanes, engines, spare parts, and other accessories, was not much short of twelve million *francs*. It was this help from our Allies that enabled us to make progress during the first year of the war. By the 31st of May 1915 five hundred and thirty aeroplanes had been taken into the service and about three hundred had been struck off as lost or worn out. On the same date orders for two thousand two hundred and sixty aeroplanes were in progress.

The story of the expansion of the Royal Flying Corps for military uses is simple and clear, as its main purpose was simple and clear. Its business was to furnish the army with eyes, to observe all enemy operations, and especially the operations of enemy artillery. Its later uses grew out of this, as the branches grow out of the stem of a tree. From the aerodromes which were ranged all along the British front in France our machines crossed the lines every day, to give help to the General Staff, to give help to the gunners and the infantry, to carry destruction to the enemy. The Flying Corps tried to keep pace with the growth of the army which needed its help.

Its own growth was continuous; the problems which presented themselves to those who superintended that growth were problems of supply, adjustment, and efficiency. The need was certain; the only question was how the need might be best and quickest supplied. A good aeroplane, flown by a skilled pilot, could always find work of the first importance waiting for it on the western front.

The story of the development and expansion of the Royal Naval Air Service is a different kind of story. As the first business of the Royal Flying Corps was to help the army, so the first business of the Royal Naval Air Service was to help the navy. But this business of helping the navy was a much more difficult and complicated business than the other. To help the army from fixed aerodromes behind the line of battle was a dangerous and gallant affair, but it was not difficult. In the ease of its solution the military problem was child's play compared with the naval problem. How was the navy to be helped?

As early as 1912 a policy for the employment of the Naval Wing of the Royal Flying Corps was laid before the Board of Admiralty by Captain Murray Sueter. In this statement the duties of naval aircraft were laid down; the two first to be mentioned were:

(1) Distance reconnaissance work with the fleet at sea. (2) Reconnaissance work off the enemy coast, working from detached cruisers or special aeroplane ships.

The policy is clear and sound; but a world of ingenuity and toil was involved in those two short phrases—'with the fleet at sea', and 'working from detached cruisers'. Aircraft must work from a base; when they had to work with the army on land all that was needed was to set up some huts in certain meadows in France. For aerial work with the fleet at sea the necessary preparations were much more expensive and elaborate. Seagoing vessels had to be constructed or adapted to carry seaplanes or aeroplanes and to serve as a floating and travelling aerodrome.

The seaplane itself, in the early days of the war, was very far from perfect efficiency. It could not rise from a troubled sea, nor alight on it, without disaster. Accidents to seaplanes were so numerous, in these early days, that senior naval officers were prejudiced against the seaplane, and, for the most part, had no great faith in the value of the help that was offered by the Royal Naval Air Service.

The Commander-in-Chief of the Grand Fleet well knew the value to the fleet of aerial observation, but the means were not to hand. The airship experiment had broken down. Such airships as were available in the early part of the war had not the necessary power and range. To build a vessel which should be able to carry seaplanes or aeroplanes for work with the fleet was not a simple matter. Such a vessel would be an encumbrance unless it could keep station with the Grand Fleet or with the Battle Cruiser Squadron, that is, unless it could steam up to thirty knots for a period of many hours together.

Further, a stationary ship at sea is exposed to attack by submarines, so that it was desirable, if not necessary, that the flying machines should be able to take the air and return to their base without stopping the ship. This consideration led, at a later period of the war, to the use by the navy of aeroplanes flown from specially constructed decks. But this was a matter of time and experiment. As early as December 1911 Commander Samson had succeeded in flying off the deck of H.M.S. *Africa*, and when the war broke out the *Hermes*, which had formerly served as headquarters for the Royal Naval Air Service, was fitted with a launching-deck for aeroplanes.

The *Hermes* was sunk in the third month of the war; thereafter the *Ark Royal*, the *Campania*, the *Vindex*, the *Manxman*, the *Furious*, the *Pegasus*, and the *Nairana* were each of them successively fitted with a launching-deck. But launching proved easier than alighting. It may seem to be a simple thing for an aeroplane to overtake a ship that is being driven into the wind, and to alight quietly on its afterdeck. But immediately behind such a ship there is always a strong up-current of air. This upcurrent—the bump that the albatross sits on—is what makes the difficulty and danger of the attempt. An aeroplane which resists it by diving through it will almost certainly crash on the deck beyond.

The business of landing an aeroplane on the ship from which it had been launched was not accomplished until the 2nd of August 1917, when Flight Commander E. H. Dunning succeeded, at Scapa Flow, in landing a Sopwith Pup on the forecastle deck of the *Furious*, while she was under way. Five days later, when he was repeating this performance, his machine rolled over into the sea, and he was drowned. His work was not lost; the *Furious* was fitted thereafter with a special landing-deck aft, and it was by naval aeroplanes flown from the deck of the *Furious* that one of the large Zeppelin sheds at Tondern was destroyed on the 19th of July 1918.

The next ships in the succession were the *Vindictive*, the *Argus* (which was the first ship to be fitted with a flush deck), the *Eagle*, and the new *Hermes*, which last two ships were unfinished at the time of the armistice.

In this matter of aerial work for the navy the whole period of the war was a period of experiment rather than achievement. The conditions of experiment were hard enough, when all the shipyards and factories of the country were working at full pressure in the effort to make good our heavy losses in merchant shipping. Yet experiment continued, and progress was made. Three new forms of aircraft deserve special mention. The kite balloon, the small improvised airship called the submarine scout, and last, though not least, the flying boat, were all invented or brought into use by the Naval Air Service during the course of the war.

For stationary aerial observation the means employed in England, before the war, were the captive spherical balloon and the man-lifting kite. Many successful experiments with the man-lifting kite, or groups of kites, had been carried out, especially by Major B. F. S. Baden-Powell, during the closing years of the nineteenth century. But both the balloon and the kite had serious faults. The kite cannot be efficiently operated in a wind of less than twenty miles an hour, and the spherical balloon cannot be operated in a wind of more than twenty miles an hour. The balloon except in the lightest of breezes, and the kite at all times, give a very unsteady platform for observation, so that field-glasses are difficult to use.

The merits of both kite and balloon were combined and the faults of both were remedied in the kite balloon. The attachment of a kite to the upper hemisphere of an ordinary spherical balloon, on the cable side, to prevent the balloon from rotating in a wind, had been proposed by a private inventor as early as 1885, but nothing came of it. The kite balloon which was used in the war was invented in 1894 by Major von Parseval, the German airship designer, and Captain von Sigsfeld.

This balloon is sausage shaped; the cable is attached to the forward portion; the rear end carries an air-rudder, and is weighted down by the car, or basket. Extending outwards at right angles on both sides of the rear portion of the balloon is a wind-sail which does the office of a kite and assists in preventing the rudder end of the balloon from being too much depressed by the weight of the car.

The balloon is divided into two segments; the forward segment is filled with gas, the rear segment is kept full of air through a circular entrance attached, facing the wind, to the under surface of the balloon. But the steadying of the balloon is mainly achieved by the air-rudder, which is another inflated sausage, curved round the underside of the rear end of the balloon, and automatically filled with air through a valve at its forward end. The kite balloon is the ugliest thing that man has ever seen when he looks up at the sky, but it serves its purpose.

Before the war, kite balloons, often called '*Drachen*' balloons, had been a German secret. The French and Belgians had obtained drawings of them, and at the outbreak of war had some few ready for use. Moreover, the French were at work on their '*Cacquot*' balloon, an improvement on the '*Drachen*' in that it made use of a new and more convenient stabilizing, device. Where the '*Drachen*' had used a long and clumsy string of parachute streamers attached to the tail, the '*Cacquot*' achieved the same result by means of stabilizing fins attached to the balloon itself.

In October 1914 Wing Commander Maitland was sent to Belgium in command of a captive balloon detachment, to carry out aerial spotting for the guns of monitors working off the coast between Nieuport and Coxyde. His two balloons, which were spherical, proved to be useless in a strong wind. In January 1915 he made acquaintance with a '*Drachen*' balloon which the Belgians were using in the neighbourhood of Alveringheim. He was allowed to inspect this balloon and to take measurements and photographs. In January and February, he sent home reasoned reports to the Air Department of the Admiralty, urging that kite-balloon sections should be formed in the British air service. He also sent Flight Commander J. D. Mackworth to Chalais-Meudon, the French kite-balloon centre, and in the second and fuller of his reports he embodied the technical information which had been gathered from the French.

These reports were acted on at once. Wing Commander Maitland was recalled from Belgium, and a centre was established at Roehampton, to train kite-balloon sections for active service. In March 1915 two kite balloons, an old type of winch, and a length of cable were received from the French, who also lent competent instructors and a generous supply of accessories.

Just at this time General Birdwood, who had been sent by Lord Kitchener to the Dardanelles to report on the possibilities of a landing, and Admiral de Robeck, who was in command of the naval forces there, telegraphed to the War Office and the Admiralty that a man-lifting kite or a captive balloon would be of great use to the navy for spotting long-range fire and detecting concealed batteries.

The Admiralty at once appropriated a tramp steamer, S.S. *Manica*, which was lying at Manchester, fitted her with a rough and ready apparatus, and on the 27th of March dispatched her with a kite-balloon section under Flight Commander J. D. Mackworth to the Dardanelles. This was the first kite balloon used by us in the war, and, it is believed, the first kite-balloon ship fitted out by any navy. The observation work done from the *Manica* was good and useful, especially during the earlier phase of the operations, and the difficulties encountered suggested many improvements in the balloon and in the ship. Orders were given for six balloon ships to be fitted out.

Admiral Beatty, in August 1915, recommended that the work of aerial observation for the fleet should be done by kite balloons, towed by vessels accompanying the Battle Cruiser Squadron, and some trials were made which demonstrated the value of this suggestion. But here again very elaborate experiments were necessary before authorising any large programme of construction, and in the meantime production on a considerable scale had become difficult, for the kite balloon, which was first manufactured in this country to the order of the navy, was already in great demand by the army for use on the western front.

As early as April 1915 the Army Council had asked the Admiralty to supply kite balloons for aerial observation with the expeditionary force in France, and by August of that year five kite-balloon sections had gone overseas and were doing invaluable work on the western front. At this point the kite-balloon sections working with the army were taken over by the War Office, but the Admiralty continued to provide the necessary material and equipment. Great Britain was involved in the greatest land war she had ever known, and the navy, with all the wealth of its inventive resources, stood by to help the army.

The two other forms of aircraft which were invented or adapted by the navy for the needs of the war, that is to say, the submarine scout airship and the flying boat, must here be mentioned and their origin described; but their great achievement belongs to the later period of the war, when the defeat of the German submarine campaign had become a matter of life or death for the British Commonwealth.

The small airship called the 'S.S.', or Submarine Scout, was an invention of the first year of the war. On the 28th of February 1915

Admiral Fisher sent for Commander E. A. D. Masterman and Wing Commander N. F. Usborne, and told them that he wanted some small, fairly fast airships to operate against the German submarines, and that he wanted them at once. There was no time for experiment or the elaboration of new designs; speed in production was essential, and speed could not be attained except by the adaptation of existing types and the use of standard parts. The navy is seen at its best when it has to rise to an unforeseen occasion; within three weeks the first of the now famous S.S.'s was ready for service.

For the design of this airship it is as difficult to apportion credit among the small band of naval officers who had a hand in it as it is to divide the praise for the first flying machine between the brotherhood of the Wrights. The idea seems to have been struck out during a conversation in the mess at Farnborough at which there were present the late Wing Commander N. F. Usborne, Flight Lieutenant T. R. Cave-Browne-Cave, and Mr. F. M. Green of the Royal Aircraft Factory. In the result the body, or fuselage, of a B.E. 2 c aeroplane was slung on to the envelope of a Willows airship, and the job was done.

The success of this airship was as great as its design was simple. It fairly fulfilled the main requirements—to remain aloft for eight hours in all ordinary kinds of weather, with a speed of from forty to fifty miles an hour, and carrying a load which should include a wireless telegraphy installation for the purposes of report and a hundred and sixty pounds' weight of bombs for more immediate use.

The first twenty-five of these ships to be produced were fitted with the 70 horse-power Renault engine. Variations and improvements of the design followed in steady succession, providing greater endurance, and more comfortable cars for the crew. One of these variants, the C. 1 or coastal type, used an Astra-Torres envelope and a car made from two Avro fuselages with the tails cut off; a later and larger design, the N.S. 1, or North Sea type, in use at the end of the war, had an endurance, on occasion, of from two to three days.

Airship work against submarines, an authority on the subject has remarked, partakes of the nature of research work. An airship is comparatively slow in manoeuvring, and is an instrument of knowledge rather than of power. For swift assault on submarines, once they are located, the seaplane is better; but the seaplane was not seaworthy. The need for some kind of aircraft which should be able to search the North Sea far and wide for submarines, and, having found them, should be able to destroy them without calling for the assistance of surface craft, was met by the development of the flying boat.

There was a flying boat in use by the navy before the war—the small pusher Sopwith Bat boat. It had a stepped hull, like a racing motor-boat, about twenty feet long and four feet in the beam. This was the only flying boat used by the Naval Air Service when the war began; when it ended they were flying the *Felixstowe Fury*, a giant boat triplane which, with its load, weighed fifteen tons, was driven by five 360 horse-power engines, and carried four guns in addition to a supply of heavy bombs. The development of this type of aircraft for the purposes of the war must be credited chiefly to the late Lieutenant-Colonel John Cyril Porte, who had been an officer of the Royal Navy and a pioneer of aviation.

As early as 1909, when he was a naval lieutenant, he had experimented with a glider on Portsdown Hill, near Portsmouth. Two years later he was invalided out of the service, and devoted his enforced leisure to aviation. He learned to fly at Rheims, on a Deperdussin monoplane, and in 1912 was appointed technical director and designer of the British Deperdussin Company. The first British-built monoplane of this type, with a 100 horsepower Anzani engine, was of his design, and was flown by him at the Military Aeroplane Trials on Salisbury Plain in 1912.

After the trials he flew to Hendon, a distance of eighty-two miles, in one hour and five minutes. During the following summer he spent some time experimenting with a waterplane at Osea Island in Essex. When the British Deperdussin Company was broken up he went to America, and joined Mr. Glenn Curtiss at Hammondsport, New York, in the task of designing a flying boat to cross the Atlantic. Then the war came; on the day it was declared he sailed for England, re-entered the navy, and was at once made a squadron commander of the Royal Naval Air Service.

For a time, he was in command of the newly-formed naval air station at Hendon, where he trained pilots for the service; then, in September 1915, he was given the command of the Felixstowe Naval Air Station. This was his opportunity, and he did not let it slip. The Curtiss flying boats which were procured from America were of inferior workmanship and had many faults. He patiently went to work to improve and perfect them. One who worked with him says:

'There would probably not have been any big British flying boats, but for the vision, persistence, and energy, in the face of disbelief and discouragement, of Colonel J. C. Porte, C.M.G., who designed and built at Felixstowe Air Station the experimental machine of each type of British flying boat successfully used in the service. His boats were very large, the types used in the war weighing from four and a half to six and a half tons, and carried sufficient petrol for work far out from land, and big enough bombs to damage or destroy a submarine otherwise than by a direct hit. . . . The boats were very seaworthy, and no lives were lost in operations from England owing to unseaworthiness.'

The technical problems to be faced were very difficult; and powerful flying boats were not in action till the spring of 1917. But this was in the nick of time to meet the great German submarine effort. During the following year—the crucial year of the naval war—forty flying boats were put into commission; they sighted in all sixty-eight enemy submarines, and they bombed forty-four, some of which it was subsequently proved that they had sunk.

Through all his strenuous work for the navy, Colonel Porte had to do battle with ill health; he retired in 1919, and in October of that year died suddenly at Brighton, in the thirty-sixth year of his age. The shortest possible list of those who saved the country in its hour of need would have to include his name.

Another purely naval use of aircraft, on which, during the war, much effort was spent, was their use for the carrying and launching of torpedoes. The torpedo has long been one of the chief weapons of naval warfare; it is commonly carried by surface or submarine craft to the place where it can be launched against the enemy. If it could be carried and launched by rapid aircraft, its value would be enormously increased, and the torpedo-carrying aeroplane or seaplane would outrival the submarine as a weapon of offence against enemy shipping. This was very early recognised by those who were concerned in developing naval aircraft.

The first experiments are said to have been made in 1911 by an Italian, Captain Guidoni, who made use of a Farman machine, and released from it a torpedo weighing 352 pounds. In the same year the little group of naval officers who were superintending the construction of the *Mayfly* at Barrow-in-Furness had many discussions on the subject. One of them, Lieutenant Hyde-Thomson, subsequently drafted a paper on torpedo aircraft, with some rough sketches; in 1913 a design was got out at the Admiralty, and in the same year Mr. Sopwith constructed two sample machines.

From this time onward, the hope of using the torpedo, launched from the air, against ships which are sheltered and protected from naval attack, was never long absent from the minds of those who directed the activities of the Royal Naval Air Service. It was this hope, more than anything else, which inspired the production of larger seaplanes and higher powered engines. At the naval review of July 1914, a Short seaplane of 160 horse-power had been fitted, in a temporary fashion, to carry a 14-inch torpedo weighing 810 pounds. With the same end in view, after the war broke out, the principal manufacturers of motorcars were encouraged to develop air engines of high power, especially the Sunbeam engine of 225 horse-power, and the Rolls-Royce engine, which played so distinguished a part in the war.

When H.M.S. *Engadine* was fitted out as a carrier in the first month of the war, it was expressly stated by the Admiralty that her business was to carry torpedo seaplanes to the scene of action. Later on, at Gallipoli, seaplanes shipped in the *Ben my Chree* succeeded in flying across the Isthmus of Bulair and in torpedoing a merchant ship on the shore of the Sea of Marmara, an ammunition ship at Ak Bashi Liman, and a steam tug in the Straits.

All this seemed full of promise. The modern torpedo is a very efficient weapon, and the problem of designing an aeroplane or seaplane to carry it was a problem requiring adaptation rather than new invention. Yet the development of torpedo aircraft during the war was, in the words of an official memorandum, 'astonishingly slow.' After the Gallipoli exploits nothing of importance in this kind was achieved during the years that followed, until the very end of the war.

The causes of this disappointment were many. In the first place the seaplane, which seems almost as if it had been designed to carry a torpedo suspended between its floats, was itself a disappointment. It proved to be a fair-weather craft. Seaplanes were used, early in the war, to carry out reconnaissances in the neighbourhood of the Ems river; of those launched for this work more than half had their floats broken up, and sank before they could rise from the water. Moreover, in addition to this main objection, there were other obstacles to the development of torpedo-carrying aircraft. The chief of these were what are officially described as 'operational difficulties'.

On the high seas, it must be remembered, and in other easily accessible waters, there were no enemy ships to be attacked. To use torpedoes against warships in their harbours or sheltered waters, specially designed aircraft must first make long and difficult flights. In the meantime, while the war was young, there was a distressing shortage of aircraft for other and more immediate purposes nearer home. The ships assigned as carriers for aircraft had to be employed at times in mine-seeking and other necessary operations. The machines themselves were much in demand for the purposes of reconnaissance.

Experiment continued at Calshot; practice attacks were carried out with machines from Felixstowe, and convinced the naval authorities of the value of torpedo aircraft; a successful torpedo aeroplane, called the *Cuckoo*, was designed in 1916 by Messrs. Sopwith, and was produced in the following year by Messrs. Blackburn; finally, in 1917, the Commander-in-Chief of the Grand Fleet asked for two hundred torpedo aeroplanes to be provided for the fleet at the earliest possible date. The bulk of these machines had to be made by inexperienced firms, so that the first squadron of torpedo aeroplanes for the fleet was not completed till October 1918, when it embarked in H.M.S. *Argus*.

There had been earlier schemes for a torpedo seaplane school at Felixstowe and at Scapa in the Orkneys; but now, in the summer of 1918, a torpedo aeroplane school was established at East Fortune, and the 1918 programme arranged also for another torpedo aeroplane school and a torpedo aeroplane experimental squadron, both at Gosport.

In any future war there can be no doubt that torpedo aircraft will prove to be a weapon of enormous power. As Lieutenant Hyde-Thomson remarks in a paper which he prepared in 1915, they will be a menace to the largest battleship afloat. They have double the speed of a destroyer, and a large measure of that suddenness of attack which is the virtue of a submarine and the dread of its victims. The technical difficulties connected with the release and aiming of the torpedo have been met and conquered, so that these craft, though they played no considerable part in the war, were brought by the pressure of war, which quickens all things, to the stage of practical efficiency.

Some minor causes of the delay in the development of torpedo aircraft may perhaps be found. Those who pinned their faith to the Dreadnought as the mainstay of naval power were not likely to be eager to improve a weapon which, more than any other, seemed likely to make the Dreadnought belie its name. Moreover, the burden of a torpedo was never very popular with pilots. A torpedo can be used only against its preordained target; it gives no protection to the aircraft that carries it, and its great weight makes the machine slower in manoeuvre and more vulnerable.

This objection was well stated by a German pilot who was taken prisoner in June 1917. The Germans, in the early part of that year, formed at Zeebrugge a flight of torpedo seaplanes, which had this advantage over our torpedo aircraft, that suitable targets were not lacking. These seaplanes sank three of our merchant ships in the vicinity of Margate and the Downs. Two of the seaplanes were shot down on the morning of the 11th of June 1917 by the armed yacht *Diana*. In the report of the examination of the German pilots it is told that both the prisoners seemed to deprecate this mode of flying, and to glory chiefly in their own single-seaters, which were smaller, swifter, and without encumbrance. One of them said:

> Once you are given a two-seater, the authorities start loading you up with cameras, machine-guns, bombs, and wireless, and now, to crown all, they actually hang a torpedo on your machine!

The new types of naval aircraft which were invented or developed during the course of the war have now been briefly described. When a critical account shall hereafter be rendered of the doings of the years 1914 to 1918, regarded as an incident in the ever-lengthening history of human warfare upon earth, these new departures in the use of naval aircraft will probably be recognised as the chief contribution to sea-power made by the late war. Their importance is enormous, but their place in the actual history of the earlier years of the war is comparatively small.

The weapons of the Royal Naval Air Service, so far as purely naval uses were concerned, were in a rudimentary state at the outbreak of war. A fighting service, suddenly engaged in a great war, must use the weapons it has; it cannot spend more than a margin of its time and thought on problematic improvements. The Naval Air Service, when the war began, had good machines and good pilots. The army had endeavoured, before the war, to establish, on behalf of the nation, a centralised control of aeronautical manufacture, and the benefits of that policy, when the war came, have already been described.

The navy, following its traditional plan, and working on freer lines, had done all it could to encourage private effort, and so had greatly stimulated aeronautical invention and progress. There was nothing inconsistent in the two policies; they were stronger together than either could have been alone. When the great effort was called for, the only thing that could be done at once was to multiply the best existing types of machine, and to attempt, with the means available, to perform such tasks as might present themselves.

Before the war the principal firms employed by the Admiralty in the manufacture of flying machines were: for seaplanes, Messrs. Short Brothers at Eastchurch, Messrs. Sopwith at Kingston-on-Thames, and Messrs. J. Samuel White & Co. at Cowes, who had produced the Wight seaplane; for aeroplanes, Messrs. Short and Messrs. Sopwith as before, the British and Colonial Aeroplane Company at Bristol, and Messrs. A. V. Roe & Co. at Manchester. Orders as large as they could handle were placed with all these firms on the outbreak of war. Further, a very large order for B.E. 2 c machines was placed with various firms, who were to construct them by the aid of Government plans and specifications; and Messrs. Vickers received orders for their gun-carrying two-seater pusher aeroplane known as the Vickers fighter.

The navy naturally paid more attention than the army to fighting in the air. They were committed to the defence of the coast and the beating off of hostile air-raids. In France, where the guns were going all day, the first need was for reconnaissance machines; the navy, who were farther from the enemy, had set their hearts on machines that should do more than observe—machines that could fly far and hit hard. They diligently fostered the efforts of the leading motor-car companies, especially the Sunbeam and Rolls-Royce, and so were instrumental in the production of very efficient engines of high horse-power. In the second year of the war the Admiralty proposed a competition among aeroplane-makers for a large bombing machine and a fast fighting aeroplane.

In the result the Short machine for bombing, fitted with a 250 horse-power Rolls-Royce engine, was produced. Later on, the single-seater Sopwith Pup and the two-seater Sopwith 1½ Strutter set the fashion in fighting machines, and did good work with the army at the battles of the Somme. The fact is that in the early part of the war the best of the existing types of aeroplane were more useful, as things stood, to the army than to the navy, and when this was recognised a great part of the work of the Royal Naval Air Service took the form of help given to the British Army.

When in August 1915 Mr. Maurice Baring was sent to Rome on business connected with aircraft, he records how he had speech with General Morris, who was in charge of Italian aviation. General Morris said:

What I am going to say to you will be absolutely unintelligible and unthinkable to you as Englishmen, but I regret to say that here, in Italy, it is a fact that there exists a certain want of harmony—a certain occasional, shall I say, friction?—between the military and naval branches of our flying service.

Mr. Baring was amused by this speech, but he kept a grave countenance, and murmured, 'Impossible.'

Both the Royal Flying Corps and the Royal Naval Air Service were eager to serve their country. Their rivalry was creditable to them. When they were called on to co-operate, their relations were friendly and helpful. But the pressing need for more and more aeroplanes on the western front dominated the situation. The Admiralty were many times asked by the military authorities to hand over to the Royal Flying Corps large numbers of machines and engines which were on order for the Royal Naval Air Service. To the best of their ability they fulfilled these requests, but the zealous members of a patriotic service would be more or less than human if they felt no regret on being deprived of the control of their own material.

When the Royal Flying Corps was formed, in the spring of 1912, it was intended that either wing should be available to help the other. But before the war broke out the two had almost ceased to co-operate. The methods and subjects of instruction were distinct. The discipline and training of the one wing were wholly military, of the other wholly naval; and this severance had been officially recognised, just before the war, by the transformation of the Naval Wing into the Royal Naval Air Service. In truth, while reconnaissance continued to be, what it was at the beginning of the war, almost the sole duty of aircraft, effective co-operation between the two services was difficult or impossible. Most of the naval air pilots knew little of the business of military reconnaissance; nor could the military observer be expected to recognise and identify enemy shipping.

The demand for squadrons to assist the land campaign seemed likely to be greater than the supply, and on the 24th of August 1914 the Government had approved the formation of two Royal Naval Air Service squadrons, to be trained for military duties. The Admiralty took action at once, and these two squadrons were formed, one at Fort Grange, the other at Eastchurch, during the early days of October. They were only a few days old when news came that the army chiefs did not approve of the plan.

Writing on the 17th of October 1914 Sir John French said that the efficiency of the Flying Corps for military purposes was principally due to its organisation and training, he added:

> It is therefore most desirable that any reinforcements should be organised, trained, and equipped in exactly the same manner as the squadrons now in the field. Owing to the complete divergence between methods and equipment of the naval and military air services, I do not consider that units of the Royal Naval Air Service would be suitable as reinforcements to this force.

Lieutenant-Colonel Brancker, in a minute on this letter, dated the 22nd of October, suggested that the army should undertake all aerial work with the expeditionary force abroad and with the mobile forces at home, while the navy should undertake the aerial work for all fixed defences at home. A few weeks later the Army Council, replying to the offer of the Admiralty, suggested that the best way for the Admiralty to help would be by handing over to the War Office the aeroplanes which were being provided to the order of the Admiralty, so that the additional military squadron might be the earlier completed. Lastly, on the 2nd of December, Lieutenant-Colonel Brancker addressed an urgent appeal to the Air Department of the Admiralty. The squadrons with the British forces in the field, he said, were very seriously short of aeroplanes.

There was also a shortage of flying officers, especially for the training of pilots at home. He suggested that the entire output of the Avro factory, and all the Vickers fighters, should be placed at the disposal of the War Office; that four Maurice Farmans under construction in Paris for the Admiralty should be delivered direct to the headquarters of the Royal Flying Corps in France; and that any number up to twenty good pilots, and the same number of wireless operators, should be lent by the Admiralty to the War Office.

The Admiralty replied at once that they were willing to hand over to the Army Council twelve Vickers fighters and six Maurice Farman machines, and that they were preparing a squadron of eight Avro machines and four Sopwith scouts under Squadron Commander Longmore, to proceed overseas about the middle of January, and to work under the orders of the officer commanding the Military Wing. On the 1st of January 1915 the War Office, after consulting Sir David Henderson, refused this offer of a naval squadron. Lieutenant-Colonel Brancker wrote:

'It has been decided to send no further new aeroplane squadrons to join the Expeditionary Force until the winter is over; the bad weather renders aerial reconnaissance difficult, and we find that owing to the impossibility of protecting the machine from deterioration it will be better to keep our new units at home until conditions improve.'

In the event about a hundred machines, and as many more American Curtiss machines, built and building, were turned over by the Admiralty to the War Office during the first year of the war, but no further suggestion for the use of naval squadrons on the western front was made until March 1916; and it was not until October of that year that the first complete naval squadron got to work as a self-contained unit under military command.

Service men will understand better than civilians the difficulties of a mixed service. Each of the great services has always been willing to help the other so long as it is allowed to preserve its own traditions intact. Their quarrels are lovers' quarrels, springing from a jealous maintenance of separate individualities. Moreover, the war, during its early course, was regarded by most civilians and most service men as likely to be a short war.

The attention of soldiers late in 1914 was concentrated on the decision that was expected in the following spring. Lord Kitchener's famous prediction of a three years' war was regarded as a wise insurance against foolish over-confidence, but was not believed. The officers responsible for the Flying Corps in France were concerned chiefly for the maintenance of that admirable little force in full efficiency. They suffered continually from a shortage of aeroplanes, and although their casualties had been far lighter than anyone had anticipated, they had every reason to fear a shortage of flying officers. Their first demand was not for new squadrons, but for a reserve of pilots and machines, to keep the existing squadrons in working trim. It was only by degrees that the portentous dimensions of the war began to be perceived—a war which, just before it ended, was employing ninety-nine squadrons of British aeroplanes on the western front alone.

The discovery, or rather the practical development, of new uses for aircraft in war quickened the demand for additional squadrons and made it easier for the two branches of the air service to co-operate. As the war progressed aerial fighting and bomb-dropping became more and more important. These were new arts, and required no special naval or military training; they belonged to the air. When the Fokker fighting monoplane appeared in strength on the western front in the early months of 1916, the losses of the Royal Flying Corps in reconnaissance and artillery observation became very heavy.

It was then that the Admiralty were again appealed to for help, and four Nieuport scouts, with pilots and mechanics, were dispatched from Eastchurch, arriving at the aerodrome of No. 6 Squadron, at Abeele, between Cassel and Poperinghe, on the 29th of March 1916. Before this time the pilots of the Royal Flying Corps in the Ypres salient had had only the barest acquaintance with the pilots of the Naval Air Service at Dunkirk. Some of the earlier Flying Corps pilots had met those of the other service at the Central Flying School; some of the later pilots had had occasion to land at Dunkirk and had been filled with admiration and envy when they were shown the machines and equipment belonging to the Naval Air Service.

Sometimes a naval pilot, flying a little south of his usual beat, would come across a military pilot in the air, and the two would make some token of recognition. But the four naval Nieuport scouts of March 1916 sent to the salient to help to meet the attacks of German fighting scouts were the first naval detachment to co-operate with the Royal Flying Corps in the field under military command.

The experiment, though it lasted only for eighteen days, was a success. The naval officers and ratings were treated royally, as guests, and there was complete harmony between the two services. The little Nieuport scouts brought reassurance to the lonely artillery pilots on the front, and had a happy effect on the German fighting pilots, who were led to suspect the presence of a whole new squadron of Nieuports. On the 16th of April No. 29 Fighting Squadron of the Royal Flying Corps, which had been delayed by accidents, arrived at Abeele, and the naval machines returned to Dunkirk.

This experiment showed the way and encouraged fuller measures. During the battles of the Somme, which began on the 1st of July 1916, the Royal Flying Corps maintained a resolute and continuous offensive over the enemy lines. They suffered very heavy casualties, at a time when training and construction at home, which were in process of development, were unable to make good all the losses.

Then the Admiralty, on the urgent appeal of the Army Council, agreed to detach from the Dunkirk command a complete squadron of eighteen fighting aeroplanes, under Squadron Commander G. M. Bromet, for temporary duty with the army. The squadron consisted of six two-seater Sopwiths, six single-seater Sopwiths, and six Nieuport scouts. They arrived at Vert Galand aerodrome, which is situated eleven miles north of Amiens on the Amiens-Doullens road, on the 16th of October 1916.

After three weeks spent in machine-gun practice and flights to learn the country, the first full day's work was done on the 9th of November. There were many combats, and three enemy machines were driven down in a damaged condition. This squadron continued to operate with the army in France.

By the beginning of 1917 there were in France, working wholly with the army, thirty-eight Royal Flying Corps squadrons; that is to say, nineteen artillery squadrons and nineteen fighting squadrons; and the one fighting squadron belonging to the Royal Naval Air Service. It was anticipated that the Germans, who had appointed a single officer, General von Hoeppner, to take charge of all their military aircraft, and had produced several improved types of machine, would make a great effort in the spring of 1917 to recapture the air. To meet this effort more fighting squadrons were needed. The machinery at home for the reinforcement of the Royal Flying Corps was working at high pressure, and could not at once supply the need.

So, an appeal was once more addressed to the Admiralty, who agreed to provide four more fighting squadrons to be used on the western front. These squadrons made a punctual appearance, and during the earlier half of 1917 did magnificent work in helping to maintain the British supremacy in the air. Naval Squadron No. 3, for instance, under Squadron Commander R. H. Mulock, was at work on the western front from the beginning of February to the middle of June. During this time, it accounted for eighty enemy aircraft with a loss of only nine machines missing, and provided highly respected escorts for photographic reconnaissances and bomb raids. From July 1917 onwards the naval squadrons, having bridged the gap, were gradually replaced by squadrons of the Royal Flying Corps, and were returned to Dunkirk.

The loan of these squadrons naturally diminished the force available for aerial operations under naval control, but the spirit in which the help was given is well expressed in a letter of Wing Captain C. L. Lambe, who was in command of the naval air forces at Dover and Dunkirk. Writing in August 1917 he points out the serious effects on the force under his command of the wastage of pilots, but concludes:

> I would remark, however, that the loan of these squadrons to the Royal Flying Corps must have been of the greatest value to the Empire, since the official record issued by the Royal Flying Corps states that up to August 3rd, 1917, a hundred

and twenty-one enemy machines have been destroyed by naval squadrons, and two hundred and forty have been driven down out of control.

When help was needed by the army, it was generously given by the navy, but the difficulties which inevitably present themselves when the attempt is made to secure the smooth and efficient collaboration of two separate forces cannot be solved by generous feeling. Most men are willing to help their country, but a country's revenue cannot be raised by free gift. Without justice and certainty there can be no efficiency, and for justice and certainty law and regulation are required. The chief administrative problem of the war in the air had its origin in the need for a large measure of co-operation between the military and naval air forces.

The repeated attempts to solve this problem, the problem of unity of control, by the establishment of successive Air Boards, and the achieved solution of it by the amalgamation in 1918 of the two services under the control of an Air Ministry—these events took almost as long as the war to happen; indeed, the story of them might truly be called the Constitutional History of the War in the Air. That story cannot be told here; it shall be told at a later point, in connexion with the foundation of the Royal Air Force. The method of government of the Royal Flying Corps has already been described; all that can fitly be attempted here is a brief account of the government of the Royal Naval Air Service, and the earlier vicissitudes of that government.

The union of the two wings of the Royal Flying Corps, that is to say, of the original Naval and Military Wings, was a one-sided and imperfect union, because the Royal Flying Corps, in its inception, was under the control of the War Office. The naval officers who joined the Naval Wing remained under the control of the Admiralty, and before the war the Admiralty had established an Air Department, with Captain Murray Sueter as its Director, to be responsible for the development of naval aeronautics. But the Director was less happily situated than his military counterpart, the Director-General of Military Aeronautics at the War Office, who, it will be remembered, dealt at first hand with the Secretary of State for War. The Naval Director of the Air Department had less power and less independence.

From the time of Mr. Samuel Pepys, throughout the eighteenth century, and down to the year 1832, the navy had been administered by the office of the Lord High Admiral, assisted by a Navy Board, which was composed, for the most part, of civilian members of Parliament. In 1832 the Navy Board was abolished, and the modern Board of Admiralty was created to control the navy. The business of this Board was divided up among its various members. Finance fell to the Parliamentary Secretary; works, buildings, contracts, and dockyard business were the portion of the Civil Lords; while all kinds of service business, that is to say, preparation for war, distribution of the fleet, training, equipment, and the like, were assigned to one or other of the Sea Lords.

When the Air Department was formed to take charge of the Naval Wing of the Royal Flying Corps, its Director was not only generally responsible to the Board of Admiralty, he was responsible to each of the Sea Lords in matters connected with that Sea Lord's department. This divided responsibility, which, by old custom, works well enough in a body with established traditions, like the navy, was not a good scheme for controlling the unprecedented duties, or for encouraging the unexampled activities, of an air force.

When the Naval Wing of the Royal Flying Corps was first established, in 1912, H.M.S. *Hermes*, under the command of Captain G. W. Vivian, was commissioned as its headquarters. During the following year naval air stations came into being at the Isle of Grain, at Calshot, Felixstowe, Yarmouth, and Cromarty, and in December 1913 the duties of the captain of the *Hermes* were taken over by Captain F. R. Scarlett, who was given the newly created post of Inspecting Captain of Aircraft, with headquarters at the Central Air Office, Sheerness. At the time of the outbreak of war the Royal Naval Air Service was administered by the Admiralty, and consisted of the Air Department at Whitehall, the Central Air Office at Sheerness, the Royal Naval Flying School at Eastchurch, the various naval air stations, and such aircraft as were available for naval purposes.

The Sheerness office was under the Nore command, and the Inspecting Captain of Aircraft, who took his instructions from the Director of the Air Department, was also responsible to the Commander-in-Chief of the Home Fleets in all matters relating to aircraft operations with the main fleet.

The coming of the war soon multiplied air stations as well as aircraft; inland stations were established at Hendon, Chingford, Wormwood Scrubs, and Roehampton; squadrons were dispatched abroad, and seaplane ships were commissioned; so that efficient control by the Nore command was no longer possible. In February 1915 the Admiralty decided that the whole of the Royal Naval Air Service should be forthwith placed under the orders of the Director of the Air Department, who was to be solely responsible to the Board of Admiralty. The Central Air Office was abolished, and Captain Scarlett was appointed to the staff of the Air Department to carry out inspection duties.

When this decision took effect in Admiralty Weekly Orders, certain points of difficulty were at once raised by the Commander-in-Chief of the Nore.

> Is the personnel of the air stations to be subject to local Port Orders? I can hardly imagine that their Lordships intend otherwise. There are 77 officers and 530 men, including 94 naval ratings, in the three air establishments at present in my command (Eastchurch, Grain, and Kingsnorth), and it is understood that these numbers will shortly be increased by the personnel of three additional air stations (Clacton, Westgate, and Maidstone).'

Further, he asked whether the Commander-in-Chief was to remain the controlling authority with regard to punishments; and he added:

> I strongly urge the re-establishment of some Central Air Authority in the port under my command with whom I can deal on defence and other important matters without reference to the individual air stations, which may often be commanded by officers of small naval experience to whom the naval aspect of the situation may not especially appeal.

It was felt in the air service that owing to the technical nature of the work the question of punishments should not be relegated to anyone outside the air service. The Commander-in-Chief of the Nore had invoked the King's Regulations, so the question was referred to the naval law branch of the Admiralty, which, in April 1915, replied that:

> The discipline of the air service is governed entirely by the King's Regulations, which provide that the powers conferred upon commanding officers by the Naval Discipline Act shall be subject to the approval of a Flag officer whose flag is flying or the Senior Naval Officer.... As a matter of fact the Director of the Air Department has no disciplinary power under the Naval Discipline Act, and the reference of warrants to him would neither be in accordance with the King's Regulations nor the Naval Discipline Act.

This verdict threw the organisation of the Royal Naval Air Service once more into the melting-pot. The question of discipline was at the root of the whole matter. The navy were not willing to hand over the control of discipline to a body which, though it was called the Royal Naval Air Service, was much looser in discipline than the Royal Navy. The causes of this comparative laxity are easily intelligible. When the war came, the need for new pilots was pressing; the training accommodation at the Central Flying School and at Eastchurch was wholly inadequate; so, the Admiralty had at once made arrangements for entering officers direct from civilian life, and for training them at civilian schools of aviation, such as the schools at Brooklands, Hendon, and Eastbourne.

The important thing at the outbreak of war was to get officers who could fly a machine, and to get them quickly. Of professional training in naval knowledge and naval discipline there was perforce little. The spirit of adventure brought many youths at a very early age into the Naval Air Service; some of them were entered as commissioned officers, and were paid fourteen shillings a day at an age at which the regular sea service officer was being paid one shilling and ninepence a day, less threepence for the naval instructor. It is not to be wondered at that the high spirits of some of these untrained youths, and their festive behaviour, exposed them to the criticism of older officers who cared for the high traditions of the navy.

The expansion of the Naval Air Service was too rapid to admit of that slow maturing process which makes a good sailor. When, at the end of May 1915, Mr. Winston Churchill vacated his appointment as First Lord of the Admiralty, he remarked on the rapid expansion of the service during his period of office.

> At the beginning of hostilities there were under a hundred officers and six hundred men. Most of these were transferred from the navy proper, a small percentage only being civilians. At present there are over fifteen hundred officers and eleven thousand men. . . . We had at the beginning of the war a total of sixty-four aeroplanes and seaplanes. This of course represents a very minute proportion of our present numbers, of which all that I can publicly say is that they total more than one thousand.

During the first winter of the war a short course in gunnery was arranged for young officers at the naval gunnery school at Whale Island, Portsmouth, where they were instructed also in drill, discipline, and the handling of men. This was a beginning, but it was not enough. The pioneers of the Naval Air Service had had an uphill task; they had worked untiringly in the cause of naval aeronautics, to achieve progress in the new art, and to get recognition for it from the Sea Lords. The recognition, when it came at last, was overwhelming.

The navy claimed the Royal Naval Air Service as its own, and absorbed it into itself. The immediate motive for this was disciplinary, but the thing was a compliment, none the less, to the work of the air service. In the summer of 1915 the German submarine menace in the Channel became serious, and the officer in command of the Dover Patrol, who was responsible for the Straits, knew that for the work to be done from his bases at Dover and Dunkirk aircraft were essential.

In July the whole question was brought before the Board of Admiralty, and regulations for the reorganisation of the Royal Naval Air Service were approved, to take effect on the 1st of August. These regulations are explicit and clear.

> The Royal Naval Air Service (so they begin) is to be regarded in all respects as an integral part of the Royal Navy, and in future the various air stations will be under the general orders of the Commander-in-Chief or Senior Naval Officers in whose district they are situated. The Commander-in-Chief or Senior Naval Officer will visit the stations within his command or district from time to time, or depute a suitable officer to visit them on his behalf, to ensure that the discipline of the station is maintained. . . . Copies of reports on operations are to be forwarded direct to the Admiralty. It will be the duty of the Director of the Air Department to visit the various air stations from time to time . . . with a view to ensuring that the technical training of the personnel is being carried out as laid down by their Lordships, and that the station is efficiently organised and equipped in respect to works and materiel.

These are the main provisions of the new orders. The grouping of the air stations (which by this time were more than fifty in number) under the various commands was given in detail. The detachments stationed at Dunkirk and elsewhere in France and Belgium were put, for disciplinary purposes, under the orders of the Rear-Admiral, Dover. The inland stations at Hendon, Chingford, Wormwood Scrubs, and Roehampton were put immediately under the Admiralty. Sweeping changes followed in appointments.

The post of Director of the Air Department was abolished, and Commodore Murray Sueter was placed in charge of the construction section of the remodelled department. An officer of flag rank, Rear-Admiral C. L. Vaughan-Lee, was given the newly created post of Director of Air Services. A senior Naval Air Service officer, Wing Commander C. L. Lambe, R.N., who had been captain of the *Hermes*, was appointed to command the air patrols at Dover and Dunkirk, under the orders of Vice-Admiral R. H. Bacon. Other changes which followed were so numerous that in effect a new service was formed. When the Air Department was reorganised in the spring of 1916, it was divided into two sections—Administration and Construction.

Each of these sections included a considerable diversity of business, which was classified, and placed under the separate control of eight responsible officers. Of these eight only two—Squadron Commander Clark Hall, who was responsible for aeroplane and seaplane design, and Squadron Commander W. Briggs, who was responsible for engines—were officers of the original Royal Naval Air Service. Most of the newly appointed administrative officers had no previous knowledge of aircraft or aircraft operations; what they were chosen for was their power of organisation, their strict sense of discipline, their untiring energy, and their pride in the ancient service to which they belonged. The senior naval officer who was inexperienced in the air was promoted over the heads of the pioneers of naval aviation who were junior in the navy.

There is no unmixed good on earth. The debate between discipline and progress can never be settled dogmatically one way or the other. Those who have to lead men into battle are agreed that without discipline progress is useless. A crowd of undrilled men of science could not stand the push of a platoon of common soldiers. On the other hand, it is all-important that the higher command in war shall be susceptible to science, and it has been maintained, not without evidence, that the life of discipline and loyalty which procures promotion in a public service does not usually increase susceptibility to science.

The immediate practical advantages which were aimed at by the reorganisers of the Naval Air Service were attained. In place of the old scattered training stations a central training depot was set up at Cranwell in Lincolnshire, and a complete system for the instruction and graduation of pupils was instituted. A designs department was set up at Whitehall; the airship service was taken in hand and developed for anti-submarine patrol work. What may be called the most important unit of the Royal Naval Air Service was created by the amalgamation under Wing Commander Lambe of the squadrons which had their bases at Dunkirk and Dover. This unit, later in the war, became the famous Fifth Group, under the same command. The arrangements made at the time of change continued in force up to the time of the union of the military and naval air services, and progress was continuous.

In January 1916 the Admiralty approved that the overseas establishment of the Royal Naval Air Service should have three wings, each wing to have two squadrons, and each squadron two flights, with six machines to a flight. One of these wings was based at Dunkirk; for the others two new aerodromes were established, in the spring of 1916, at Coudekerque and Petite Synthe, and were occupied, the first by No. 5 Wing, under Squadron Commander Spenser Grey, the other by No. 4 Wing, under Wing Commander C. L. Courtney, R.N. No. 5 Wing was specially trained for the work of long-distance bombing.

From the very beginning the Naval Air Service had set their heart on the fitting out of big bombing raids against distant German centres—Essen, or Berlin. It was a grief to them, when the war ended, that Berlin had suffered no damage from the air. The success of their early raids on Düsseldorf and Friedrichshafen naturally strengthened their desire to carry out more destructive raids over more important centres. In this way, they believed, they could best help the army. This idea inspired some of the documents drawn up by Mr. Winston Churchill while he was First Lord of the Admiralty.

When in February 1916 Rear-Admiral Vaughan-Lee submitted to the Admiralty his scheme for the employment of the reorganised Royal Naval Air Service the same idea dominated his advices. His report concludes:

> I consider that we should develop long-distance offensive work as much as possible.

The preference shown by the navy, in their orders from the makers, for powerful bomb-carrying machines tells the same story. When the navy set about carrying out this policy by the formation of a special force, called No. 3 Wing, at Luxeuil, for the express purpose of making long-distance raids over German munition centres, the army, which was preparing its great effort on the Somme front, and which needed more and yet more machines for the immediate purposes of the campaign, protested against the use of British aircraft for what seemed to them a luxury in comparison with their own dire needs. So, the Luxeuil Wing was, for the time, broken up; but the idea took shape again later when the Independent Force came into being.

The sound doctrine on this matter is laid down in General Trenchard's reports, which shall be given hereafter. Yet it may be admitted, without prejudice to that doctrine, that if bombing raids had been possible over Essen and Berlin their effect would have been very great. The Germans spent not a little effort on their raids over London, and hoped for the weakening or shattering of the British war temper as a consequence of those raids. Their belief in Rightfulness was a belief in fright. They judged others by themselves. No people on earth, it may readily be admitted, can maintain the efficiency of its war activities under the regular intensive bombing of its centres of population; but the Germans, during the greater part of the war, knew nothing of this fierce trial, and their trust in their army would have been terribly weakened if that army had proved to be no sure shield for the quiet and security of civil life.

Such differences as arose between the British naval and military authorities concerning the use of aircraft in the war were, for the reasons that have been given, not easily avoidable. They were ultimately composed by the union of the military and naval air forces under a single control, and the emergence of a new air force.

Wars have for many centuries been conducted on land and on sea. A third and larger theatre has now been found for them. The air flows over both land and sea; more than either land or sea it is the place of vision, and of speed and freedom of movement. What we of this generation are witnessing is a process whereby the air shall come into its own. It will become the great highway for the traffic of peace; and in war, which cannot be abolished while man has interests that are dearer to him than his own comfort and safety, the forces of the air will be, not a late-found timid auxiliary to the forces of the land and of the sea, but their overseer and their director.

ALSO FROM LEONAUR
AVAILABLE IN SOFTCOVER OR HARDCOVER WITH DUST JACKET

THE FALL OF THE MOGHUL EMPIRE OF HINDUSTAN *by H. G. Keene*—By the beginning of the nineteenth century, as British and Indian armies under Lake and Wellesley dominated the scene, a little over half a century of conflict brought the Moghul Empire to its knees.

LADY SALE'S AFGHANISTAN *by Florentia Sale*—An Indomitable Victorian Lady's Account of the Retreat from Kabul During the First Afghan War.

THE CAMPAIGN OF MAGENTA AND SOLFERINO 1859 *by Harold Carmichael Wylly*—The Decisive Conflict for the Unification of Italy.

FRENCH'S CAVALRY CAMPAIGN *by J. G. Maydon*—A Special Correspondent's View of British Army Mounted Troops During the Boer War.

CAVALRY AT WATERLOO *by Sir Evelyn Wood*—British Mounted Troops During the Campaign of 1815.

THE SUBALTERN *by George Robert Gleig*—The Experiences of an Officer of the 85th Light Infantry During the Peninsular War.

NAPOLEON AT BAY, 1814 *by F. Loraine Petre*—The Campaigns to the Fall of the First Empire.

NAPOLEON AND THE CAMPAIGN OF 1806 *by Colonel Vachée*—The Napoleonic Method of Organisation and Command to the Battles of Jena & Auerstädt.

THE COMPLETE ADVENTURES IN THE CONNAUGHT RANGERS *by William Grattan*—The 88th Regiment during the Napoleonic Wars by a Serving Officer.

BUGLER AND OFFICER OF THE RIFLES *by William Green & Harry Smith*—With the 95th (Rifles) during the Peninsular & Waterloo Campaigns of the Napoleonic Wars.

NAPOLEONIC WAR STORIES *by Sir Arthur Quiller-Couch*—Tales of soldiers, spies, battles & sieges from the Peninsular & Waterloo campaigns.

CAPTAIN OF THE 95TH (RIFLES) *by Jonathan Leach*—An officer of Wellington's sharpshooters during the Peninsular, South of France and Waterloo campaigns of the Napoleonic wars.

RIFLEMAN COSTELLO *by Edward Costello*—The adventures of a soldier of the 95th (Rifles) in the Peninsular & Waterloo Campaigns of the Napoleonic wars.

AVAILABLE ONLINE AT www.leonaur.com
AND FROM ALL GOOD BOOK STORES

ALSO FROM LEONAUR
AVAILABLE IN SOFTCOVER OR HARDCOVER WITH DUST JACKET

WINGED WARFARE *by William A. Bishop*—The Experiences of a Canadian 'Ace' of the R.F.C. During the First World War.

THE STORY OF THE LAFAYETTE ESCADRILLE *by George Thenault*—A famous fighter squadron in the First World War by its commander..

R.F.C.H.Q. *by Maurice Baring*—The command & organisation of the British Air Force during the First World War in Europe.

SIXTY SQUADRON R.A.F. *by A. J. L. Scott*—On the Western Front During the First World War.

THE STRUGGLE IN THE AIR *by Charles C. Turner*—The Air War Over Europe During the First World War.

WITH THE FLYING SQUADRON *by H. Rosher*—Letters of a Pilot of the Royal Naval Air Service During the First World War.

OVER THE WEST FRONT *by "Spin" & "Contact"* —Two Accounts of British Pilots During the First World War in Europe, Short Flights With the Cloud Cavalry by "Spin" and Cavalry of the Clouds by "Contact".

SKYFIGHTERS OF FRANCE *by Henry Farré*—An account of the French War in the Air during the First World War.

THE HIGH ACES *by Laurence la Tourette Driggs*—French, American, British, Italian & Belgian pilots of the First World War 1914-18.

PLANE TALES OF THE SKIES *by Wilfred Theodore Blake*—The experiences of pilots over the Western Front during the Great War.

IN THE CLOUDS ABOVE BAGHDAD *by J. E. Tennant*—Recollections of the R. F. C. in Mesopotamia during the First World War against the Turks.

THE SPIDER WEB *by P. I. X. (Theodore Douglas Hallam)*—Royal Navy Air Service Flying Boat Operations During the First World War by a Flight Commander

EAGLES OVER THE TRENCHES *by James R. McConnell & William B. Perry*—Two First Hand Accounts of the American Escadrille at War in the Air During World War 1-Flying For France: With the American Escadrille at Verdun and Our Pilots in the Air

KNIGHTS OF THE AIR *by Bennett A. Molter*—An American Pilot's View of the Aerial War of the French Squadrons During the First World War.

AVAILABLE ONLINE AT www.leonaur.com
AND FROM ALL GOOD BOOK STORES

www.ingramcontent.com/pod-product-compliance
Lightning Source LLC
Chambersburg PA
CBHW031612160426
43196CB00006B/100